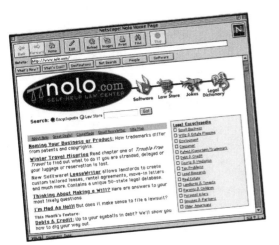

1ST EDITION

The Complete IEP Guide

How to Advocate for Your Special Ed Child

BY ATTORNEY LAWRENCE M. SIEGEL

Your Responsibility When Using a Self-Help Law Book

We've done our best to give you useful and accurate information in this book. But laws and procedures change frequently and are subject to differing interpretations. If you want legal advice backed by a guarantee, see a lawyer. If you use this book, it's your responsibility to make sure that the facts and general advice contained in it are applicable to your situation.

Keeping Up to Date

To keep its books up to date, nolo.com issues new printings and new editions periodically. New printings reflect minor legal changes and technical corrections. New editions contain major legal changes, major text additions or major reorganizations. To find out if a later printing or edition of any Nolo book is available, call nolo.com at 510-549-1976 or check our website at www.nolo.com.

To stay current, follow the "Update" service at our website at www.nolo.com. In another effort to help you use Nolo's latest materials, we offer a 35% discount off the purchase of the new edition your Nolo book when you turn in the cover of an earlier edition. (See the "Special Upgrade Offer" in the back of the book.)

This book was last revised in: **June 1999.**

First Edition	
Second Printing	JUNE 1999
Editor	MARCIA STEWART
Illustrations	MARI STEIN
Book Design	TERRI HEARSH
Cover Design	TONI IHARA
Index	JANE MEYERHOFER
Proofreading	ROBERT WELLS
Printing	BERTELSMANN INDUSTRY SERVICES, INC.

Siegel, Lawrence M., 1946-
   The complete IEP guide: how to advocate for your special ed.
child / by Lawrence Siegel.
          p.   cm.
   Includes index.
   ISBN 0-87337-408-8
   1. Special education--Law and legislation--United States--Popular
works.   2. Dispute resolution (Law)--United States--Popular works.
3. Special education--Parent participation--United States--Popular
works.   I. Title.
   KF4209.3.Z9S57   1998
   371.9'0973--dc21

                                                          98-23481
                                                          CIP

Dedication

To the memory of Becky Luftig, my first client, and a remarkable young woman for whom "disability" was an attitude and nothing more

To my parents, and

To my wife Gail, for that first day on the Wheeler steps, and ever since, her joyous smile.

Acknowledgments

My appreciation to the entire Nolo Press staff which, to a person, has always been professional and friendly and never seemed to feel those two concepts were incompatible.

Special thanks to Marcia Stewart for her superb editing, her patience as we worked through and wrote about the complexities of the IEP process, and her clear goal of making the IEP process friendly to and useful for families of children with disabilities.

Several other Nolo staff deserve special thanks:

Jake Warner, for his enthusiasm about the project

Robin Leonard, for her extensive editing and excellent work developing the list of resources for families of children with disabilities

Stanley Jacobsen, for his helpful research assistance

Terri Hearsh, for her terrific design work

Toni Ihara, for her delightful cover (and patience)

Michele Crim, Jennifer Spoerri, Jennifer Macko and Kelly Rosaaen, for their kindness and marketing/pr expertise

Erin Douglass, for putting together clearly written cover copy and being a pleasure to work with, and

Karen Turk, for her editorial assistance, especially on forms and checklists.

Thanks also to my colleagues and friends on the California Advisory Commission on Special Education.

Table of Contents

10 Preparing for the IEP Meeting

11 Attending the IEP Meeting

12 Resolving IEP Disputes Through Due Process

13 Filing a Complaint for a Legal Violation

Appendices

Index

1

Introduction to Special Education

Some years ago, a parent came to my office to discuss the difficulties her teenager was having in school. The parent was a kind and thoughtful person, but looked overwhelmed. Her child had learning disabilities and increasing emotional problems, and the pain of the child was etched on the face of the parent. Her child was falling further behind, losing the confidence she once had, and missing the academic skills and emotional strength she would need for adulthood.

My client sat quietly for some time and then asked in a whisper, "What in the world can I do for my daughter?"

Whether you and your child are entering special education for the first time or the tenth time, you have probably asked the same question. You have a dozen concerns and a hundred fears. You don't know where to begin. The problems seem insurmountable. There are more than 5,000,000 children with disabilities in the U.S., and at some point their parents have felt the same as my client did—and you probably have, too.

Fortunately, Congress enacted a law called the Individuals with Disabilities Education Act, or IDEA, to assess children with disabilities and provide special education programs and services to help them succeed in school. Before IDEA was enacted in 1975, public schools frequently ignored children with disabilities or shunted them off to inferior or distant programs. IDEA represents a long-overdue recognition that individuals with disabilities have the right to access public institutions, be served appropriately and be treated with dignity and respect.

The detail and reach of IDEA are remarkable—no other law in this nation provides such clear and unique legal protection for children. Everything you do to help your child secure an appropriate education is connected to, and determined by, the legal requirements of IDEA.

A. Special Education: An Introduction

"Special education" is the broad term used to describe the educational system for children with disabilities. The term is used in this book to describe that portion of your child's school system which provides special services and programs for children with disabilities. There are three fundamental questions to consider as you begin the special education process:

- Where is your child now?
- Where do you want your child to be?
- What do you need to get your child there?

IDEA entitles your child to an "appropriate" education which meets his unique needs. You'll likely have a good sense of what is meant by an appropriate education as you read this book. Broadly speaking, an appropriate education involves the following educational components:

- The specific program or class (called "placement") for your child. Placement is more than just a classroom; it also includes characteristics such as location, class size, teacher experience and peer make-up.
- The specific services (called related services) provided your child, as well as the amount and frequency of those services and who provides them.
- Other educational components, such as curricula and teaching methods.

Special education centers around a process for evaluating your child and the development and provision of an *individualized education program*, or IEP. The acronym IEP refers to several inter-related things:

- the meeting where the school district determines whether or not your child is eligible for special education (called the IEP eligibility meeting)
- the yearly meeting where you and school representatives develop your child's educational plan (called the IEP program meeting), and

- the actual detailed written description of your child's educational program.

Special education then is essentially about the "what," the "where" and the "how" of your child's educational program as developed through the IEP process.

"Disability" Is a Loaded Term

Webster's *New World Dictionary* defines disability as an illness, injury or physical handicap which "restricts" or causes "limitations" and "disadvantages." Advocates in special education and disability rights understandably object to the term disabled, preferring the term child with disabilities—this is the term we use throughout this book.

More importantly, all human beings come into this world with a variety of qualities and characteristics. Having special education needs does not mean that your child should be treated as "different" or denied the care and respect that all children deserve. Human beings are complex and a determination of who is able and "disabled" is an effort in futility. Franklin Roosevelt was president four times and could not walk. Stephen Hawking is severely disabled and understands the universe like few on this earth.

It is not a cliché to say that we all have some kind of disability, even as we realize that the difference in degree between one or another disability can be significant and life-altering. Defining terms should not be judgmental terms. I have many colleagues who are deaf. They are, to be sure, without hearing, but to consider them ineffective or incapable would be ludicrous. They cannot hear, but communicate in a beautiful, complex and effective way. In a meeting of deaf people, it is my halting sign language which is ineffective and disabling to me.

B. Special Education Basics

Special education laws give children with disabilities and their parents important rights not available to children in regular education and their parents. These include the right to:

- have the child assessed
- secure information about the child
- attend an IEP meeting
- develop a written IEP plan, and
- resolve disputes with the school district through an impartial administrative and legal process.

While the specifics of any one child's special education needs may vary—one child may need placement in a private school while another needs a one-to-one aide for full-time participation in a regular class (called mainstreaming)—mastering the IEP process is central to securing an appropriate education for your child. But equally important, the IEP process is entirely individual. The program developed by you and the school district must fit your child, not the other way around. What works for other students is irrelevant if it won't work for your child. IDEA was written in a way so as not to tell you or the school district specifically how your child will be educated. Rather, IDEA provides rules to govern the process, so the IEP decides what is appropriate for your child.

C. Being Your Child's Advocate

Advocating for your child is easy. You want the best for her. Still, there will be bumps along the way. The IEP process is maze-like, involving a good deal of technical information, intimidating professionals and confusing choices. For some families, it goes smoothly, with no disagreements; for others, it is a terrible encounter in which you and your school district cannot even agree on the time of day. For most people, the experience is somewhere in between.

Don't fall into the trap of thinking that teachers, school administrators and experts know everything and that you know nothing. Right now, you may not have all the information you need and you don't know where to look for it. But the law states that you and your school district are equal decisionmakers, and, further, that the school district must provide you with a good deal of information along the way.

You do not need to be a special education expert or a lawyer to be an effective advocate for your child. The general strategies for helping a child in the IEP process are not complex and can be easily mastered. The cliché that knowledge is power is absolutely true in the IEP process.

D. Using This Book

The purpose of this book is to help parents effectively proceed on their own through the IEP process, whether it's the first time or the fifth time. The book is for parents whose child has a mild or severe learning disability, has emotional difficulties, is deaf or blind or has other physical conditions, or has a multitude of disabilities. In other words, it's for every parent of a child with disabilities.

Specifically, this book can help you:
- develop an understanding of special education law
- understand eligibility rules and the role of assessments
- gather current and develop new information and material about your child— become an expert about your child
- determine your child's specific goals and educational needs
- gather current and develop new information and material about various school programs, as well as options outside the school district
- prepare for the IEP meeting
- attend the IEP meeting and develop your child's IEP plan, and
- resolve disputes with the school district.

Mastering these tasks requires you to be generally organized (but not fanatically so), willing to ask questions and make use of resources that are widely available. The suggestions and helpful forms in this book will help you get—and stay— organized throughout the IEP process. Because organization is half the struggle, this book focuses with equal vigor on what the law means and how to organize yourself around the law.

Detailed Appendices provide invaluable information, including:
- copies of key federal special education statutes and regulations
- addresses and Web sites of federal and state special education agencies
- addresses and Web sites of 125 national and state advocacy, parent and disability organizations
- a bibliography of other helpful books, and
- two dozen tear-out forms, letters and checklists to help you through every stage of the IEP process.

Some of the material will be very familiar to parents who have been through many IEPs—for example, you may already know too well the list of characters and the basic legal requirements. Still, we recommend that you review each chapter, even the ones with which you are familiar. We may have new insights or angles on old problems. Of course, you can skip material clearly not relevant—for example, if your child is already in special education, you don't need to prepare for an eligibility meeting.

If you are new to special education, very little in this book will be familiar to you. We suggest that you first take a quick look at the chapter titles and table of contents to become familiar with key ideas and how they relate to each other before you start reading. As you read, check the index and jump among chapters if it makes sense. Highlight points you want to remember and note in the margin the page numbers of related topics in other chapters.

The special education process has a discernible beginning and end. In general, it takes a year. There are similarities and differences between the first IEP year and subsequent years. For example, each year you will gather information and prepare for the yearly IEP program meeting, at which time you and the school district will determine placement and related services. But the first year always includes assessing your child and determining whether she is eligible for special education. In subsequent years, your child may or may not be assessed. Eligibility is rarely addressed after the first year, unless you or the school district feels a change is justified—for example, if your child no longer needs special education or may qualify under a different eligibility category.

There is a certain chicken-or-egg quality to some of the chapters. For example, the chapter on assessments comes before the chapter on eligibility. You will soon learn that your child must be assessed before determined to be eligible, but you need to know how a child becomes eligible before you arrange an assessment. Which chapter do you read first? It really doesn't matter, as long as you read both.

Scope of This Book and IDEA

IDEA provides rights and procedures for children between the ages of three and 22. There is as well a procedure for children under three, but this book's fundamental focus is on children between three and 22. There are also certain IDEA issues which involve very complex and detailed procedures which are only briefly discussed in this book, such as transition services to help children over age 14 prepare for a job or college, including independent living skills. This book does not address issues regarding discipline of special education students, including suspension and expulsion. This issue is complex; you should contact an attorney or at least a support group (see Appendix 3) regarding discipline issues.

E. Icons Used Throughout

The icons listed below appear throughout this book to help you along.

Books or organizations that give more information about the issue or topic discussed in the text.

Related topics covered in this book.

Slow down and consider potential problems.

You may be able to skip some material that doesn't apply to your situation.

A practical tip or good idea.

A tear-out copy of the form discussed in the text is in the Appendix.

 State law may vary on this issue.

F. Getting Help From Others

Throughout this book, we recommend that other parents, local groups and regional or national organizations can be of great help as you wend your way through special education. The amount of information these folks have can be amazing. Other parents and parent groups can be your best resource and certainly a source of support to help you through hard times. Others who have been through the process before can help you to avoid making mistakes or undertaking unnecessary tasks. Most importantly, they can be a source of real encouragement. Chapter 15 provides further thoughts on making use of your local special education community.

Note: Reference is made throughout this book to parents, but the term is used to include foster parents and legal guardians. ■

2

Overview of the IEP and Special Education Law

As mentioned in Chapter 1, a federal law, the Individuals with Disabilities Education Act, or IDEA, furnishes a formal process for assessing children with disabilities and providing specialized programs and services to help them succeed in school. Special education is unique because of the central role parents play in determining their child's educational program. Under IDEA, the program and services your child needs (the "what" and "where") will be determined through the individualized education program or IEP process. The term IEP is used to describe both a meeting about and a written description of your child's program. Your ability to understand and master the IEP process is central to your child's educational experience. Indeed, the IEP is the centerpiece of IDEA.

This chapter discusses IDEA, its specific mandates and how they apply to your child. It provides an overview of your child's legal rights to special education and the IEP process, so you can effectively advocate for your child.

As you read this chapter, keep in mind the following:

- Don't let the word "law" throw you. The actual language of IDEA, and more importantly its underlying purpose, can be easily mastered. The legal concepts in IDEA are logical and sensible.
- Developing a broad understanding of the law will help you when you review later chapters on eligibility, assessments, IEPs and other key matters.
- The actual language of IDEA appears infrequently in the body of the book. While we provide plain English descriptions of special education law, you can find the actual law as passed by Congress in Appendix 1. IDEA is found in the United States Code at 20 U.S.C. §1400 and following. Key sections of IDEA's regulations (these are in the Code of Federal Regulations at C.F.R. §§300.1-756) are also in Appendix 1. IDEA regulations are frequently referred to in this book because they include greater detail than the statutes.

A. Basic Legal Concepts of IDEA

The key legal concepts under IDEA are discussed below. They will provide you with a broad overview of IDEA's requirements.

1. Eligibility Under IDEA

Every school district has the specific legal duty to identify, locate and evaluate children with disabilities (20 U.S.C. §1412(a)(3)). Once a child is identified and located, the school district must find him eligible for special education through an evaluation and IEP process before specific programs and services can be provided.

IDEA defines "children with disabilities" as individuals between the ages of three and 22 with one or more of the following conditions (20 U.S.C. §1401(3)(26); 34 C.F.R. §300.7):

- mental retardation
- hearing impairment (including deafness)
- speech or language impairment
- visual impairment (including blindness)
- serious emotional disturbance
- orthopedic impairment
- autism
- traumatic brain injury
- specific learning disability, or
- other health impairment.

For your child to qualify for special education under IDEA, it is not enough that he has one of these disabilities. In addition, there must be evidence that your child's disability adversely affects his educational performance.

Your child has a right to an initial evaluation or assessment, with subsequent evaluations at least every three years. If you are not satisfied with the initial evaluation or you feel your child's disability or special education needs have changed, your child is entitled to more frequent assessments if you so request, and even outside or independent assessments (20 U.S.C. §1414; 34 C.F.R. §§300.530-543).

 Eligibility for special education services is discussed in detail in Chapters 6 and 7. The very specific rules regarding the initial and subsequent assessments are described in Chapter 6.

2. Nature of the Education

Under IDEA, your child is entitled to the following fundamental educational rights (20 U.S.C. §1401(8)(25)):

- **Free appropriate public education (FAPE).** Your child is entitled to an *appropriate* education at no cost to you.
- **Special education.** You child is entitled to an education *specially designed* to meet his or her *unique* needs.

IDEA fundamentally requires that the educational program should fit your child, not the other way around.

 Chapter 5 discusses how to develop a blueprint of your child's program and service needs.

For example, it is not appropriate for a school district to place a deaf child in a class for developmentally disabled children or a learning disabled child in a class of emotionally disturbed students. These would not be individually tailored IEPs. The classroom setting, teaching and services provided would not be appropriate for the deaf or learning disabled child. "Appropriateness" is the standard for evaluating all IEP components—the goals, services and placement.

Appropriate, Not Necessarily the Very Best

The law does not require that your school district provide the very best or the optimum or the maximum education, but an appropriate education. "Appropriate" is an elusive, but tremendously important concept. It is used throughout IDEA and frequently in the IEP process. For one child, appropriate may mean a regular class with minor support services, while even a hospital placement might be appropriate for another.

Keep in mind that "appropriate" will become more concrete for you and your child as you go through this book and develop a clear sense of the kind of program your child needs.

---

3. Individualized Education Program (IEP)

As noted, the IEP is the centerpiece of IDEA. It is discussed in detail in Section B of this chapter.

4. Educational Placement or Program

Your child's educational placement or program, along with related services (discussed in Section 5), should take center stage in the IEP process. These two items are subject to important IDEA law.

a. Least Restrictive Environment

At the core of IDEA is the requirement that children with disabilities be placed in the "least restrictive environment," or LRE. Congress expressed a clear preference for LRE or what is commonly referred to as "mainstreaming."

IDEA describes LRE as follows:

A child with disabilities will not be removed from a regular classroom unless he cannot achieve satisfactorily even with the use of supplementary aides and services (20 U.S.C. §1412(a)(5); 34 C.F.R. §300.550).

LRE also requires that a child be educated *as close to home as possible and in the class she would attend if non-disabled* (20 U.S.C. §1412(a)(5); 34 C.F.R. §§300.550-552).

Finally IDEA now also requires that the IEP team provide an "explanation of the extent, if any" to which the child will not participate with non-disabled children in the regular classroom and in other school activities (20 U.S.C. §1414(d)(1)(B)(iv)).

Even from the moment of passage in 1975, IDEA has caused confusion about the LRE mandate. First, LRE is really a characterization of a placement or program, not necessarily a specific place—even though, again, IDEA prefers a regular classroom. Second, the LRE placement for a child is primarily the location of the program, but should also involve the programmatic components—for example, the size of the class, the kinds of children and the type of school. LRE then is like "appropriate," a somewhat slippery and changeable term.

Always keep in mind, though, that the educational placement or program, including the location and kind of program your child needs, is a fundamental right under IDEA.

b. Range of Placements

While IDEA expresses a preference for regular education, it recognizes that some children with disabilities should not be in a regular class. Individual need determines the appropriateness of a placement. If regular classroom placement is not appropriate, IDEA requires that the school district provide a range of alternative placements, including the following:

- regular classes for part of the school day
- special classes in regular schools—for example, a special class for children with learning disabilities

- special public or private schools for children with significant difficulties, such as a school for emotionally troubled students
- residential programs
- home instruction, and
- hospital and institutional placement.

It is important to remember that LRE or the placement part of IDEA can be easily misunderstood. While IDEA prefers mainstreaming, it recognizes that a non-regular classroom or placement may be LRE for a specific child. For example, a small non-regular classroom on a small campus may be fundamentally LRE for a child with significant fears who is a runaway threat, while a regular classroom would certainly not be LRE given this child's unique needs.

LRE and General Curriculum

In its most recent (1997) reauthorization of IDEA, Congress used for the first time the concept of "general curriculum" (20 U.S.C. §1414(d)(1)(A)(I)). IDEA now requires that if your child is not mainstreamed, he have access to the general curriculum taught in the regular classroom. IDEA further requires that the IEP specifically address this issue (34 C.F.R. §300.347 (a)(1)(i), (2)(ii), (3)(ii)). IDEA isn't clear as to whether teaching the general curriculum is the same as or in lieu of LRE. But it is a separate concept from LRE and does not change the law's requirement that a child be educated in the LRE. As school districts respond to new IDEA language on general curriculum, we'll have a better sense of what this means to children in special education.

5. Support or Related Services

The second center stage item under IDEA is support or related services. IDEA requires schools to provide related services for two reasons:

- in order for your child to benefit from special education, and
- to insure that your child has the chance to "achieve satisfactorily" in a regular classroom (the LRE, discussed in Section 4, above).

Under IDEA, related services include the following (20 U.S.C. §1401(22) and §1414(d)(1)(A)(iii); 34 C.F.R. §300.22):

- speech-language pathology and audiology services
- psychological services
- physical and occupational therapy
- recreation, including therapeutic recreation
- social work services
- counseling services, including rehabilitation counseling
- orientation and mobility services
- medical services for diagnostic and evaluation purposes
- sign language or oral interpreter
- psychotherapy
- one-to-one instructional aide
- transportation
- art therapy
- technological devices, such as FM/AM systems or special computers, and
- nursing care.

This is not an exhaustive list. Because everything under IDEA is driven by a child's individual needs, the IEP team has the authority to provide any service which your child needs, including one not listed specifically under IDEA.

6. Transition Services

IDEA requires that the IEP team consider, for a child who is 14 or older, her vocational and advanced-placement needs and courses, and any involvement with noneducational agencies that provide vocational and other support services for individuals with disabilities (20 U.S.C. §1414(d)(1) (A)(vii); 34 C.F.R. §300.347(b)).

7. Due Process

In law, "due process" generally refers to the right to a fair process for determining individual rights and responsibilities. Under IDEA, and as used in this book, due process means your child's right to be evaluated, be provided an FAPE, be educated in the LRE, have an IEP and be given notice of any changes in the IEP.

Due process also refers to your specific right to take any dispute you have with your child's school district—whether a disagreement about an assessment, eligibility or any part of the IEP, including the specific placement and related services—to a neutral third party to help you resolve your dispute. These rights are unique; children not in special education do not have these rights (20 U.S.C. §1415; 34 C.F.R. §§300.500-517).

When you have a disagreement, you can go to mediation and a due process or "fair hearing." Mediation is the process where you and the school district meet with a neutral third party who helps you come to an agreement. The mediator has the power of persuasion, but no authority to impose a decision on you.

If you cannot reach an agreement in mediation (or prefer to skip mediation altogether), you can request a fair hearing, in which you and the school district present written and oral testimony about the disputed issues before a neutral administrative judge, who will decide who is right and issue an order imposing a decision. If you or the school district disagree with the decision, you can appeal to a federal or state court, all the way to the U.S. Supreme Court. But before you conjure up images of walking up the marble stairs to the highest court in the land, you should know that virtually all disputes with school districts are resolved before a hearing and certainly before you find yourself in a courtroom.

Chapter 12 discusses in detail how to resolve disputes through mediation or a fair hearing.

If you believe that your school has violated a legal rule—for example, by failing to hold an IEP meeting—you would file a complaint (discussed in Chapter 13). The complaint process is quite different from due process. A due process matter involves a factual dispute between you and the school district. A complaint involves a failure by the district to follow the law.

8. Other Key Legal Components

IDEA provides for many rights, including the following additional mandates:

a. Suspensions and Expulsions

IDEA provides specific rights and procedures for children in special education who are suspended or expelled for use or sale of drugs, possession of a weapon or assaultive behavior (20 U.S.C. §1414(k)). These rights and procedures are quite complex and would require a separate book to discuss. If your child is in special education and is subject to some form of disciplinary action, contact a parent support group or a special education attorney to discuss the ramifications of such action and what legal rights your child has.

b. Summer School

IDEA requires your child be provided summer school or "extended school year" if necessary to meet his needs or if, without summer school, his skills will be affected by the pause in program and services.

c. Private School

IDEA gives your child the right to be placed in a nonprofit or private (including parochial) school if your school district cannot provide an appropri-

ate program (34 C.F.R. §§ 300.302, 349, 403, 450-462).

There must be an IEP agreement or due process or court ruling that the private school is appropriate before the school district is required to pay for a private school placement. If you place your child in a private school unilaterally, on your own, your school district is not required to pay.

IDEA does, however, require that the school district still offer special education and related services in a public program to a child in a private school. IDEA further states that the school district can actually provide those special education services at a private (including a parochial) school if it so chooses—with limitations on how much money the district can spend on such special education and services (20 U.S.C. §1412(a)(10)). This part of IDEA is complicated. If your child is in private school in this type of situation, contact a special education attorney or one of the support groups listed in Appendix 3.

d. Special Education in Prison

IDEA requires that children between 18 and 21 with disabilities who are in prison and who were identified and had an IEP prior to incarceration, are also entitled to an FAPE (34 C.F.R. §300.311).

More Information: Individuals with Disabilities Education Act

For a copy of IDEA and key authorizing regulations, see Appendix 1. For more information on IDEA and special education law, contact your local school district, your state department of education or the U.S. Department of Education's Office of Special Education and Rehabilitative Services (OSERS). See Appendix 2 for contact information.

See Chapter 14, Section F, for advice on doing legal research on IDEA.

B. Individualized Education Program

IEP may seem complicated—it is a meeting, a document and the description of your child's entire educational program. While the IEP is discussed in detail in Chapters 10 and 11, here are a few introductory concepts:

- By law, you are an equal partner in the IEP process; as a general rule, no part of the IEP can be implemented without your approval.
- Your child's first time in special education will follow an initial eligibility IEP. Thereafter, IEP meetings will be held yearly, focusing on the specifics of your child's current educational program and what next year's IEP will look like. While the procedures for these two kinds of IEPs (what we call eligibility and program IEPs) are the same, they have some important differences—see Chapters 7, 10 and 11.
- You and the school district must agree to and sign an IEP before your child either initially begins special education or begins a new school year.
- Whenever you or your child's school district wants to change your child's current IEP, the district must schedule a new IEP meeting and develop a new written IEP.
- You are entitled to an IEP meeting whenever you feel one is needed—for example, if you have concerns about your child's progress, there are classroom problems or if the support or related services or the placement are not working.
- The IEP, once signed by you and the school district, is binding; the school district must provide everything included in that IEP.

The written IEP and IEP meeting are discussed in detail in Chapters 9, 10 and 11. Appendix 4 includes a sample IEP form.

This section provides details about the written IEP. Every IEP, in every school district, in every state must include the same information (although forms will vary).

1. Current Educational Status

The IEP must include a description of your child's current status in school in the areas of cognitive skills, linguistic ability, emotional behavior, social skills and behavior and physical ability (20 U.S.C. §1414(d)(1)(A)(i)(I)). Current functioning may be reflected in testing data, grades, reports or anecdotal information, such as teacher observations. IDEA calls this the "present level of educational performance," and this part of the IEP must describe how your child's disability affects her involvement and progress in the general curriculum. Formal testing or assessments of your child will provide a good deal of information.

 Chapters 6 and 8 cover assessments and how to develop useful evidence of your child's educational status and needs.

2. Goals and Objectives

Goals and objectives are the nuts and bolts of your child's daily program as detailed in the IEP, and generally refer to academic, linguistic and other cognitive activities, such as reading or math. IDEA specifically calls these "measurable annual goals, including benchmarks or short-term objectives" related to your child's specific educational needs and involvement in, if appropriate, the general curriculum (20 U.S.C. §1414(d)(1)(A)(ii)).

Example:

Goal: John will increase his reading comprehension.

Objective: John will read a three-paragraph story and answer eight out of ten questions about the story.

While the goals and objectives are usually academic and cognitive in nature, there is no restriction on what goals and objectives may cover or say. They should reflect whatever the IEP team determines is important to your child's education. Goals and objectives can relate to physical education, how your child socializes with peers, even how your child will move about the school.

Whether your child is receiving a "free appropriate public education" (FAPE) may depend on whether the program offered by the school district can help her achieve her goals and objectives. If you and the school district disagree about a specific placement or service, one key issue will be whether your child's goals and objectives can be met without a particular placement or service.

Because writing goals and objectives is so important, we devote all of Chapter 9 to writing them to support the placement and service needs of your child.

3. Instructional Setting or Placement

The IEP must include information about the instructional setting or placement for your child. Section A.4, above, discussed various placement options; here are a few examples of specific IEP placements:

Examples:
- A child with significant physical disabilities or learning disabilities might be placed in a regular classroom with support services.
- A child with significant language and cognitive delays might be placed in a special class.
- A child who is terrified of large spaces and crowds could be placed in a small, protected non-regular school.
- A child with serious emotional difficulties might be placed in a residential program.

4. Related Services

As mentioned in Section A.5, above, related services are developmental, corrective and other supportive services necessary to facilitate your child's placement in a regular class or to allow your child to benefit from special education. These must be specifically included in the IEP.

Once the IEP team determines the appropriate related support services, the team would specify the nature of each service, including:
- when it begins
- the amount (such as all day, once a day, twice a week, once a week, once a month)
- the duration (such as 15, 30, 45 or 60 minutes per session)
- the ratio of pupils to related service providers, and
- the qualifications of the service provider.

5. Other Required IEP Components

As part of the 1997 reauthorization of IDEA (20 U.S.C. §1414(d)(3)(B)(i)-(v)), the IEP must include specific statements regarding:
- how your child's disability affects her involvement and progress in general curriculum found in the regular classroom
- how your child's need to be involved in general curriculum will be met
- how special education and related services will help your child advance toward attaining annual goals, be involved in general curriculum, extracurricular and nonacademic activities and participate with children with and without disabilities
- how parents will be regularly informed of their child's progress
- how your child will participate in any district or statewide assessment of student achievement as used for the general education population, and whether he needs any modifications or accommodations in order to take the district or statewide assessment

- how your child's transition services will be provided, and
- how your child's need for assistive technology will be met.

For blind and visually impaired students, the IEP team must provide for instruction in Braille and the use of Braille, unless the IEP determines that Braille is not appropriate (U.S.C. §1414(d)(3)(B)(iii).

In addition, IDEA requires that the IEP team "consider" the following:

- strategies, including positive behavioral interventions, to address the needs of children with behavior difficulties (U.S.C. §1414(d)(3)(B)(i))
- the language needs of children with limited English proficiency (U.S.C. §1414(d)(3)(B)(ii)), and
- the communication needs of deaf and hard of hearing children, including opportunities for direct communication with peers and staff and instruction in the child's language and communication mode (U.S.C. §1414(d)(3)(B)(iv)).

Because these items are fairly new to IDEA, your school district may still be in the process of determining how to deal with these at the IEP meeting. For more details, contact your school district, state department of education (Appendix 2) or a disability group (Appendix 3). Also, see Appendix 4, for a sample IEP which includes new language and sections as the result of the reauthorization of IDEA in 1997.

6. Optional Components

The IEP may include other components, such as specific teaching methods or class subjects, or anything else the IEP team agrees should be included (20 U.S.C. §1414(d)(1)(A)).

Examples:

- An autistic child may be instructed in a method called Lovaas.

- A deaf child may be taught in American Sign Language.

C. State Special Education Laws

IDEA is a federal law, binding on all states. The federal government provides financial assistance to the states to implement IDEA; in exchange, states must have laws which implement IDEA.

State laws generally parallel IDEA and often use identical language. State law can provide children with more, but not fewer, protections than IDEA does. IDEA is always your starting point, but you should check to see what your state law says about special education—it may provide more rights.

Each state educational agency has responsibility for making sure local school districts comply with the federal law. The federal government allocates between three and four billion dollars a year to the states for special education. The pressure on states to provide special education funding is significant, particularly given competing interests for education dollars. Moreover, while Congress promised when IDEA was passed to provide approximately 40% of the cost to states, it has actually provided only about 8%, creating significant shortfalls for states and the local school districts. The funding process varies from state to state, but it is often complex. While you may want to learn as much as possible as to how your state funds special education, it is most important that you remember this general rule: Money (and how it gets from Washington to your state to your district to your child) should not determine what is in your child's IEP.

More Information: State Special Education Laws

State special education laws (statutes) are normally found in the education code of each state, and state departments of education will often have their own regulations implementing the law.

Appendix 2 includes addresses, phone numbers and Web sites of state departments of education. We highly recommend you get a copy of your state laws from your state department of education (many are online) and any publications explaining your legal rights. Ask about the state special education advisory commission—IDEA requires that each state have one, composed of educators and parents.

Because laws and policies change, it is important to keep up to date, especially if you are involved in a dispute with your school. For more information on legal research, see Chapter 14.

D. You, Your School District and the IEP Process

Most, if not all, of your dealings will be with your local public school district which has the legal responsibility for your child's IEP, and is bound by both federal and state law. Sometimes, however, special education programs are the responsibility of a larger educational unit, such as a county office of education. This is often the case when a school district is small or there are not enough children to establish a specific special education class.

The term used to describe the appropriate local educational agency can vary from state to state. Always start with the school district in which you reside. It has the ultimate responsibility for your child, even if there is a larger, area-wide agency involved. We use the term local school district to refer to whatever educational unit is involved.

1. Key Players in the IEP Process

The key participants in the IEP process are:
- you (the child's parents)
- your child (if appropriate)
- your child's teacher (potentially the best or worst ally you have in the IEP process), whether a regular teacher or a special education teacher
- a school administrator with responsibility for special education—a site principal or special education administrator
- specialists, such as a school psychologist, speech or occupational therapist, communications specialist or physical education specialist, and
- anyone else you or the school wants to attend, such as your child's physician, your lawyer, the school's assessor or an outside independent assessor you selected.

Chapter 10 covers the IEP participants in detail, including who has the critical roles, who has authority and who should attend the IEP meetings. Chapter 10 also covers how to prepare yourself and your IEP participants for the IEP meeting.

2. The Realities of Schools and Special Education

School districts and their special education administrators are as varied as parents. Their programs, services and personalities will vary as will their budgets. All of these factors influence the kind of programs school districts offer and how they deal with children and parents. Depending on the population breakdown in the district, there may be many special education programs or only a few. Philosophical differences may have an impact on programs and services. Some administrators believe very firmly that most, if not all, children with disabilities should be mainstreamed or in regular education. Some administrators believe with equal vigor that special programs are important and children with disabilities, more often than not, belong in special classes.

Finding out what programs are in your district and what personalities and philosophies abound, is important. Ask around. Talk to your child's teacher and other parents; go to a PTA meeting. Many school districts have community advisory committees for special education; the parents involved in that group can be invaluable resources and will likely know the specific programs and approaches in your school district.

Chapter 8 provides detailed advice on how to explore available school programs. Chapter 15 discusses parent groups.

More Information: Special Education and Local Schools

Your school district is required by IDEA to provide you with a copy of federal and state statutes and regulations and any relevant policies. Be sure to request this information, along with the school's IEP form. Most school districts have some kind of parent guide, as do most states. Contact your school district for a copy.

E. Some Overriding IEP Principles

In any endeavor, the details—particularly technical matters and legal language—can be overwhelming: IEP, due process, least restrictive environment, goals and objectives, related services. What do these words really mean and how do you use them to help your child?

As you go through this book and the IEP process, you will become more familiar and comfortable with IEP terms. Particularly in the early stages of your planning, keep your focus on the following key factors.

1. Your Child's Needs Dictate What Is in an IEP

IDEA uses the term "unique" in describing your child's needs. As we've emphasized in this chapter, the IEP must fit the child, not the other way around. Practically speaking, this means that if your child needs a small class (fewer than ten children), a teacher with specific skills and a variety of support services, then your local school district is required to provide these. Always ask whether a particular goal, service, placement or other IEP component is providing your child with a free appropriate public education as required by law, and is serving her unique needs.

2. Factors Determining Individual Need

Your child's age, disability and specific needs—academic, social, linguistic, emotional, cognitive and physical—are key elements in determining his IEP. Of course, other factors may come into play, including necessary educational strategies, methodologies and curricula. You and your school district may disagree when it comes to what is meant by unique needs.

Keeping Current on Special Education Law and 1999 IDEA Regulations

While the general requirements of IDEA are permanent, Congress can make changes in the detail of the law. In 1997, Congress added new rights and rules to IDEA. This book includes all of those new and important changes as reflected in IDEA statutes that became effective in July, 1998. (Appendix 1 includes a copy of these statutes.) New IDEA regulations implementing these statutes were subsequently developed and became effective in May, 1999, after publication of this book. Appendix 1, which includes key sections of IDEA regulations, does not cover the May 1999 revisions. These changes involve the following areas:

- charter schools
- additions to the list of eligible "disabilities," including ADD/ADHD
- participation of special education children in statewide assessments
- related services, such as orientation and mobility services
- special education students who are incarcerated
- requirements regarding migrant and homeless children
- procedures for children who are removed from school because of inappropriate behavior
- assistive technology devices
- the use of mediation to resolve disputes
- special education children's access to the general curriculum, and
- special factors that the IEP team must consider for children who have limited English proficiency, who are deaf, hard of hearing or visually impaired, or whose behavior impedes learning.

We recommend that you see the new IDEA regulations for a full description of the changes that became effective in May, 1999. You can find the most current regulations online at www.access.gpo.gov/nara/cfr. Look at Title 34 of the Code of Federal Regulations, Part 300. You can also get a copy of current IDEA regulations from the U.S. Department of Education, Office of Special Education, or your state department of education. See Appendix 2 for addresses and phone numbers of federal and state departments of education. Also, be sure to contact your local school district if you have questions as to how the new regulations will affect your child. Finally, check "Legal Resources for Parents of a Special Education Child" Appendix 3 for information on the latest IDEA regulations.

IDEA, like many laws, is always in a state of change. As new (and old) issues come to the forefront and are addressed in courts or through new legislation, IDEA is reinterpreted and given new meaning. Chapter 14, Section F.3, on legal research, discusses how court decisions change the original law.

3. Specific Classroom and Instructional Services

Your child's needs must translate into specific support or related services and a specific class or program. All the discussion in the world about unique needs will be meaningless, if you and the IEP team don't eventually discuss services and placement.

4. Broad Discretion in Determining the IEP

It is human nature to want specificity. At some level, we may have liked Congress to have said exactly what should be part of a special education program, exactly what should go into the IEP. But in passing IDEA, Congress knew it could not say specifically what should be in an IEP for child #1 or #999 or #99,999. There are too many variables and too many individual considerations.

That is why IDEA does not say that a child with learning disabilities will be placed in a particular program with particular services. Instead, the unique needs of each child must determine what specific program and services are required. Thus, the IEP team has broad discretion. This flexibility is good for you, but also requires hard work and preparation on your part.

Section 504 of the Rehabilitation Act of 1973

Separate from any rights under IDEA, your child may also qualify for special services under the Rehabilitation act of 1973 (29 U.S.C. § 794), more commonly known as Section 504. This is essentially an access law that prohibits a school district from denying your child access to an educational program or educational facilities. For more information on Section 504, see Chapter 7, Section F.2.

3

Entering Special Education: Tips for All Parents

If your child has had a disability since birth or from a young age—perhaps he is in a wheelchair and needs support to access a regular classroom, is developmentally disabled, has difficulty writing or has a hearing loss or reduced vision—entering special education is a moment you've anticipated for a while.

If you've just recently realized that your child is having difficulty in school—it may be a simple problem with reading or math or a profound problem involving cognitive functioning or emotional difficulties—entering special education may be something you've never considered before. Perhaps a teacher, pediatrician, neighbor or friend has pointed something out to you. The recognition may come as surprise or even a shock. What does this mean for your child's immediate educational experience? What does it mean for the future? Will your child now be labeled—as learning disabled, visually impaired, emotionally disturbed?

The process you are about to embark on can be hard and frustrating. There may be times when the school makes life very tough, or your child's difficulties seem unchanged or even worse. At times, the problems may seem insurmountable. There may be a teacher shortage or insufficient school funds or awful program options. For all your preparation, you may feel like you're getting nowhere. We know how difficult and frustrating the IEP process can be.

There may be times you ask yourself: Why did this happen to our family? But if you plan, organize and persevere, if you take small, daily steps (rather than try to solve the problem in one major act), you will help your child. You may not make the school experience perfect, or even always tolerable, but your child will benefit from your efforts.

While you or your child's teacher may discover the difficulty, your school district has a clear legal responsibility under IDEA to ensure that all children with special education needs within the district are identified, located and evaluated, regardless of the severity of their disability. Normally this means (or should mean) that your child's teacher or the school principal, or perhaps the school psychologist, will contact you, indicate the areas of initial concern and perhaps suggest a meeting to discuss these concerns. They will then likely recommend an assessment by a specialist in your child's disability. An assessment of your child is the first major step toward special education eligibility and the development of an IEP. Chapter 6 discusses assessments in detail.

Parents of Children Between Three and Five Years Old

If your child is between ages three and five and not yet enrolled in school, contact the local school district. Your child may nonetheless be entitled to services under IDEA. To be eligible your child must be experiencing developmental delays in physical, cognitive, communication, social or emotional, or adaptive development (20 U.S.C. §1401(3)(B)(i)). If your child is found eligible, the IDEA rules and IEP procedures outlined in this book will apply to your child.

While your school district has the responsibility to start the process, don't wait for the school to contact you if you have concerns. If you suspect that your child has special education needs and you haven't heard from the school district, get in touch with them.

If your child has already been found eligible for special education or you have had experience with the IEP process, you can skip Section A. Even if you have been through the IEP process, however, be sure to read the discussion on securing your child's complete records in Section B. Many intelligent and determined parents who have been through numerous IEPs have not taken one of the most important, first steps—securing their child's complete school records.

A. Getting Started

What's the first thing you do when you believe your child is eligible for special education? There's no number to look up in the phone book; you don't go on the Internet. This section provides some suggestions on what is often the hardest step—the first one.

1. Recognizing Your Child's Special Needs

It is very common for parents to realize their child has unique needs and simply not know what to do. It may be that your child's problems can be isolated and addressed very specifically, or the problems may be more serious. But don't assume the worst; let the information you gather determine how serious the matter is and your best course of action.

Start by focusing on your child's specific difficulties. Think back and look for incidents of any of the following:

- academic problems in reading, spelling or math
- delays in developmental areas, such as language or fine motor skills
- difficulties processing or retaining information, such as understanding simple instructions or problems with short- or long-term memory
- social or emotional problems
- trouble sleeping, eating or getting along with the family
- sustained difficulties in paying attention or staying focused
- inappropriate or hyperactive behavior, or
- delays in physical milestones or other physiological difficulties, such as hearing loss, sight problems, difficulties with mobility or handwriting problems.

Don't get bogged down in things such as testing, special classes or eligibility. Just write down what you can remember about your child's past behavior or what you've observed recently. Try to think clearly, focusing on specific behavior patterns. You may feel some emotional upheaval or fear. You may worry that you have done something wrong. These feelings are normal. Almost everyone who has had a child in special education has felt exactly as you do right now.

Because your child is currently having difficulty in school, it does not mean that he will be in special education or even qualify for special education. There may be interim steps or non-special education solutions for your child. Those steps are discussed below, in Section A.3.

At this stage, you may also want to contact the school principal to request information about special education.

A sample letter requesting information on special education is below; a tear-out copy is in Appendix 5.

Get into the habit of writing. You can request information about special education by calling the school principal, who is likely to either provide you the information or refer you to the district's special education administrator. Better yet, make your request in writing. A letter is more formal, is not as easily forgotten as a phone call and is a record of your contact with your school district. In this book, you will be frequently reminded of the importance of putting things in writing. Chapter 4, Section A, for example, discusses the importance of keeping an IEP journal and sending confirming letters to follow up on conversations or meetings.

Once you've written down your observations and contacted the school about special education programs, you still have much information gathering to do. Nevertheless, you may feel you want to start the special education process at once—that is, to have your child assessed. If you want to know more about assessments first, read Chapter 6.

Request for Information on Special Education

Date: February 20, 19xx

To: Ronald Pearl, Principal

Mesa Verde Elementary School

123 San Pablo Ave.

San Francisco, CA 94110

Re: Amber Jones, student in 2nd Grade class of Cynthia Rodriquez

I am writing to you because my child is experiencing difficulties in school. I understand there is a special process for evaluating a child and then determining eligibility for special education programs and services. Please send me all written information about that process. Would you also send me information about how I can contact other parents and local support groups involved in special education.

Thank you very much for your kind assistance. I look forward to talking with you further about special education.

Sincerely,

Mary Jones

Mary Jones

243 Ocean Ave.

San Francisco, CA 94110

Phones: 555-1234 (home); 555-2678 (work)

2. Making a Formal Request to Start the Special Education Process

At any time you can and should formally request that the process of special education evaluation begin. To start:

- call your school and ask for the name and phone number of the special education administrator
- call the special education administrator and ask about the eligibility-assessment process in the district, and
- follow up your phone call with a written request.

A sample letter making a formal request to start the special education process and conduct an assessment is below; a tear-out copy is in Appendix 5. You will see other sample letters in this chapter which make slightly different requests. You can combine the different purposes for each letter into one request letter.

3. Taking Interim Steps

Whether you plan to continue with information gathering or begin the formal assessment process, here are a few suggestions on how to proceed.

a. Talk to Your Child's Teacher

Find out what your child's teacher thinks is going on and recommends as a possible solution. Here are a few specific questions to ask:

- What are the teacher's observations? What are the most outstanding and obvious problems and how serious are they? Is it a problem with math or reading, or broader cognitive issues (processing information or memory lags)? Are there social or emotional manifestations?
- Does she think that some adjustments in the classroom might work, such as extra help from the teacher, after school tutoring or measures to address behavioral problems?
- What recommendations might be useful at home? Does she think that you need to spend more time on homework, walking your child through certain subject matters?
- Has she consulted any other school staff, and if so what are their observations, conclusions and recommendations?
- Does she believe the difficulties are serious and require more formal, special education involvement? If so, what are the next steps?

If you and the school agree to go ahead with interim, non-special education steps, be sure to monitor them so you can determine whether or not they are working. Chapter 8, Section B, provides suggestions about monitoring your child's progress.

b. Talk to Your Child's Pediatrician

Your child may have an organic or medical problem. While your pediatrician may not be an expert in special education, she can discuss your child's developmental stage, other health-related matters that will affect the educational experience, and cognitive, physical, linguistic and emotional factors that might impact on special education eligibility and possible educational solutions.

c. Talk with Other Parents

The local PTA should have information on parents with special education children, and most school districts have advisory committees of parents with children in special education. Call the school principal to find out about these.

Chapter 15 explains how to find or start a parents' group. Appendix 3 has information on various national special education support groups.

Request to Begin Special Education Process and Assessment

Date: _February 20, 19xx_

To: _Ronald Pearl, Principal_

Mesa Verde Elementary School

123 San Pablo Ave.

San Francisco, CA 94110

Re: _Amber Jones, student in 2nd Grade class of Cynthia Rodriquez_

I am writing you because my child is experiencing difficulties in school. _As I mentioned to you over the phone this morning, she is way behind in reading [or include whatever specific difficulties your child is exhibiting]._

I am formally requesting that the school's special education process begin at once, including initial assessment for eligibility. I understand that you will send me an assessment plan which explains what tests may be given to my child. Because I realize the assessment can take some time, I would appreciate receiving the assessment plan within ten days. Would you let me know when the assessment will be scheduled, once you receive my approval for the assessment?

I would also appreciate any other information regarding the assessment process, how eligibility is determined and the general IEP process.

Thank you very much for your kind assistance. I look forward to working with you and your staff.

Sincerely,

Mary Jones

Mary Jones

243 Ocean Ave.

San Francisco, CA 94110

Phones: 555-1234 (home); 555-2678 (work)

d. Check Books and Articles on Special Education

Look for written materials on special education and your child's area of difficulty. A wealth of information is available online.

Appendix 3 has information on special education materials and organizations, both general and disability-specific.

B. Obtaining Your Child's School Records

As a part of information-gathering, it's important to find out what is in your child's school file, what it means and what effect it will have on the IEP process. This information is crucial as you assess the seriousness of your child's difficulties and the possible need for special education. If your child is found eligible for special education, reviewing the school file will help you determine the services and programs that may be appropriate.

Whether you are new at this or have been through many IEPs, whether you anticipate a major change in your child's educational program or no change at all and whether it is questionable that you even want your child in special education, it is important to secure copies of your child's school file on a yearly basis. New and important items may be added by your school district each year.

While the contents of your child's file may vary, it is likely you will find:

- report cards and other progress reports
- medical data (immunization records, health reports)
- attendance records
- disciplinary reports
- testing data
- assessment and other testing material
- teacher comments and other observations, and

- pictures of your child (it's fun to see the kindergarten picture, the second grade picture with the missing teeth and so on).

1. Your Right to Access Your Child's School File

You have a legal right to inspect and review any education records relating to your child. If your child is already in the special education system, you have this right under IDEA (20 U.S.C. §1415(b)(1); 34 C.F.R. §§ 300.501, 560-562). The rules in this section refer to children already in the special education system.

If your child has not yet been found eligible for special education, you still have a legal right to her file under the Family Educational Rights and Privacy Act (FERPA) (20 U.S.C. §1232 (g)). State law may also provide a right to your child's file, separate from IDEA or FERPA rights. State law can vary, however, and you may want to find out the specifics—such as how requests are made and how long the school has to provide you the file. Call your state department of education or your school district for information regarding the rules and law on securing files for a child who has not yet been found eligible for special education.

2. How to Get Copies of Your Child's File

When seeking a copy of your child's school file, make a written request and ask for *everything*. The written request should go to the administrator in your school district who is responsible for special education. That may be the school principal or a person in your district's central office. The site principal can refer you to the appropriate person.

A sample letter requesting your child's school file is below; a tear-out copy is in Appendix 5.

IDEA requires that your child's school fulfill your request without unnecessary delay and before any IEP meeting. In no case can the school take more than 45 days to send you the file, although it can and should take less time (34 C.F.R. §300.562(a)). (The Family Educational Rights and Privacy Act also requires provision of the files within 45 days of your request.)

If you have any problem getting a copy of your child's school file in a timely manner, you can then:

- Call and write the appropriate administrator, indicating that the law requires provision of the records without "unnecessary delay."
- If the principal or administrator does not respond to your request, contact the school district superintendent and your state department of education. Failure to provide you with your child's records is a violation of the law. Chapter 13 covers procedures for addressing violations of the law by your district.

Your state special education law may provide a shorter deadline for schools to provide copies of your child's record than the 45-day limit provided by IDEA. California schools, for example, must provide copies of the record within five days of a parent's request. Get a copy of your state's special education laws from your department of education early on so you know your rights, and can cite the law when you request your child's file.

3. Cost of Getting Files

The school may charge a fee for making copies of your child's records, as long as the fee "does not effectively prevent you from exercising your right to inspect and review those records" (34 C.F.R. §300.566). This means that you cannot be charged an excessively high fee or *any fee*, if you can show you cannot afford it. In addition, the school cannot charge a fee for searching and retrieving records.

If your child is not in special education, any fee for records would possibly violate the Rehabilitation Act of 1973 (29 U.S.C. §794) and the federal Freedom of Information Act. At least one court (*Tallman v. Cheboygan Area School*, 454 N.W. 2d 171 (Mich. Ct. App. 1990)) has said that charging a fee for search and retrieval would violate the Freedom of Information Act.

While some districts can be very uncooperative about providing free copies of your child's file,

Request for Child's School File

Date: _March 3, 19xx_

To: _Ronald Pearl, Principal_

Mesa Verde Elementary School

123 San Pablo Ave.

San Francisco, CA 94110

Re: _Amber Jones, student in 2nd Grade class of Cynthia Rodriquez_

I would like a copy of my child's file, including all tests, reports, assessments, grades, notes by teachers or other staff members, memoranda, photographs—in short, *everything* in my child's school file. I understand I have a right to these files under _IDEA, specifically 20 U.S.C. §1415(b)(1) and 34 C.F.R. §300.562 [or the Family Educational Rights and Privacy Act (FERPA) (20 U.S.C. §1232 (g)) if your child has not yet been found eligible for special education]._

I would greatly appreciate having these files within the next five days. I would be happy to pick them up. I will call you to confirm the details of getting copies.

Thank you for your kind assistance.

Sincerely,

Mary Jones

Mary Jones

243 Ocean Ave.

San Francisco, CA 94110

Phones: 555-1234 (home); 555-2678 (work)

others provide them as a matter of course. If your district charges you an excessive fee for searching and retrieving the file or charges you when you can't afford to pay a fee, write a letter to your administrator.

Request for Reduction or Waiver of Fee Charged for Child's School File

Date: March 20, 19xx

To: Ronald Pearl, Principal
   Mesa Verde Elementary School
   123 San Pablo Ave.
   San Francisco, CA 94110

Re: Amber Jones, student in 2nd Grade class of Cynthia Rodriquez

On March 3, 19xx, I requested copies of everything in my child's school file. Your secretary called me on March 19, 19xx, and stated that there would be a fee for the copies [or a too high fee or a fee for searching and retrieving]. IDEA (34 C.F.R. § 300.566) specifically states that you cannot charge a fee if it prevents me from exercising my right to inspect and review my child's file. I am on a fixed income and I cannot afford the fee you are charging.

[or: IDEA prohibits you from charging such a high fee. A fee of 15¢ a copy seems fair, not $1 a copy]

[or: IDEA specifically prohibits you charging a fee for searching and retrieving the files]

Therefore I would appreciate it if you would send me copies, at no cost, at once. Thank you for your kind attention to this matter.

Mary Jones
Mary Jones
243 Ocean Ave.
San Francisco, CA 94110
Phones: 555-1234 (home); 555-2678 (work)

Go for the Copies

IDEA allows you to inspect and review your child's school file as well as receive copies (34 C.F.R. §300.562). These are two different rights. We recommend that you go to the school and inspect and review, but in any case you always want to secure actual copies.

4. What to Look for in Your Child's School File

Items that you are likely to find in your child's file are listed at the beginning of this section. As you review those documents, look for any information about your child's performance and needs, as well as the opinions of his teacher and other professionals.

 Chapter 4 discusses in greater detail how to organize your child's records.

5. Amending Your Child's File

You have the right to request that any false, inaccurate or misleading information, or information that violates the privacy or other rights of your child be amended, or removed from your child's school file (34 C.F.R. §300.567). You also have the right to an explanation of the records (34 C.F.R. §300.562(b)(1)).

If the school refuses to amend or remove the information, you have the right to a due process hearing on the issue.

 Chapter 12 discusses due process hearings.

 A sample request to amend the child's school file is below; a tear-out copy is in Appendix 5.

Request to Amend Child's School File

Date: _April 1, 19xx_

To: _Ronald Pearl, Principal_

Mesa Verde Elementary School

123 San Pablo Ave.

San Francisco, CA 94110

Re: _Amber Jones, student in 2nd Grade class of Cynthia Rodriquez_

I recently reviewed a copy of my child's file and would like to have a portion of the file amended, specifically:

The assessment/memorandum from the school psychologist, Ms. Taylor, stating my

child had severe emotional problems is inaccurate and inappropriate because

Ms. Taylor did no testing and only briefly observed my child. This is insufficient for the

conclusion she reached.

IDEA provides that I have the right to request that all information that is "inaccurate or misleading, or violates the privacy of [my] child" be amended (34 C.F.R. §300.567). I feel that this is just such a case and, therefore, request that you immediately rectify the situation.

Please notify me in writing as soon as possible of your decision regarding this matter. Thank you.

Sincerely,

Mary Jones

Mary Jones

243 Ocean Ave.

San Francisco, CA 94110

Phones: 555-1234 (home); 555-2678 (work)

4

Getting Organized

Whether you are entering special education for the first time or preparing for your child's tenth IEP, you will be dealing with many issues and tasks and vast amounts of written material. This chapter provides important suggestions on how to organize information you'll need throughout the IEP process. It also discusses how to most effectively plan your IEP year.

Gathering information, getting organized and developing a sense of how your child's program should look are interrelated. If you haven't yet read Chapter 3, be sure to review Section B on securing your child's school file before proceeding. And when you get to Chapter 5 on developing an IEP blueprint for your child's ideal program and services, you will use much of the information from this chapter.

Use the Forms in This Book

Nearly two dozen sample forms, checklists and letters appear throughout this book, with tear-out copies in Appendix 5. You can simply photocopy (make as many copies as necessary) and insert the relevant forms into your IEP binder—either as a separate section or folded into one of the major sections we list below. The IEP Blueprint (discussed in Chapter 5) is one key document you should include as a separate section in your binder. Another is the IEP Material Organizer form (discussed in Chapter 10) which you'll use to highlight key information in your binder and easily access your materials during the IEP meeting. These and other forms have spaces for far more information than you'll be ready to provide right now. That's okay. You're just starting. It's perfectly fine to leave many of the form sections blank. You can fill them in later, when you have more information—both as you read this book and go through the IEP process.

A. Start an IEP Binder

Many parents have found using three-ring binders with clearly labeled sections to be an invaluable organizing tool. A binder allows you to keep everything in one convenient location—from report cards to IEP forms.

Include every item of value in your IEP binder. What's an item of value? Anything containing substantive information about your child or procedural information concerning how and when things happen in the IEP process. While certain items can probably go into a file drawer labeled "not relevant," if you have any doubt add them to your binder.

Listed below are some of the most important materials for your binder. Make as many sections as necessary to help you easily locate the information you'll need throughout the IEP process.

1. Your Child's File and Relevant School Materials

Your child's school records will play a key role at the IEP meeting, in developing the IEP itself and possibly at any due process mediation or hearing. As emphasized in Chapter 3, Section B, secure copies of *everything* in your child's school file, including report cards, attendance and disciplinary records, assessments and testing data and teacher comments. Review the documents carefully and put important items in your binder.

You can put everything in one large section of your binder labeled "school records," or you can divide the material into several sections. You'll probably have an easier time locating the information if it's broken down into separate binder sections.

In addition to your child's file, include other relevant school materials in your binder, such as:

- samples of your child's work
- notes from your child's teacher and other staff members
- correspondence to and from the school

- past IEPs
- your notes and information on available programs and services, including qualifications of particular teachers or service providers within the school district (Chapter 8 discusses how to develop information on available school options), and
- forms and informational materials sent to you by the school district, such as the school's IEP form and copies of key statutes and regulations on special education. (As mentioned earlier, the school is required by IDEA to provide you with a copy of federal and state statutes and regulations.)

It's never too early to secure a copy of your school's IEP. If you're new to the IEP process, be sure to get a copy of the local form (this varies from district to district) and any school guidelines on the IEP process. Keep the form and related materials in your binder so you can become familiar with the IEP items.

Binder Versus File Drawer

As your child progresses in school, your binder could get very large. Consider developing a new one each year. You can keep a file drawer or box of dated material—for example, "1996 assessment," or "1998 report cards." Include in your binder only information that is relevant to the current IEP year.

---

2. Your Child's Health and Medical Records

Your child's school file will probably include some medical information such as the results of hearing or vision tests done at school. Be sure your binder includes these as well as medical records and important letters from your child's pediatrician and other health professionals.

3. Independent Assessments

As explained in Chapter 8, an independent assessment or evaluation of your children may be the most important document supporting what you want for your child. It's obviously important to keep a copy of all independent assessments in your binder.

4. Information on Programs and Services Outside the School District

If you're exploring private programs or service options for your child, such as a specialized school for children with learning disabilities, be sure to include details in your binder, such as suggestions made by other parents, school brochures and notes of your conversations and visits. (Chapter 8 explains how to develop information on programs and services outside of your school district.)

5. Special Education Contacts

This is a list of the names, mailing addresses, phone and fax numbers and e-mail addresses of people you will deal with on a regular basis, such as your child's teacher, the district's special education administrator, your child's physician, the school nurse, staff members who provide related services, parents or parent groups and the like.

Keep this list of contacts in a prominent place in front of your binder. Also, keep a copy with you, should you need to phone or write any of your contacts when you're away from home.

A sample Special Education Contacts form is below; a tear-out copy is in Appendix 5. Make as many copies as you need.

Special Education Contacts

Name, Address, Phone & Fax Numbers, and E-Mail Address

School Staff

School: Lewis Elementary, 123 Rose St., Chicago, 60611; 555-1234 (main phone); 555-5678 (fax)

David Werner, Principal, 555-9876, DWE@aol.com

Charlene Hanson, District Special Ed. Administrator, 4444 Main, Chicago, 60611, 555-4201 (phone), 555-7451 (fax); chsed @dusd.edu

Thayer Walker, Carrie's teacher, 567 Elm Ave., Chicago, 60611 (home), 555-0111 (classroom), 555-0114 (home)

Dr. Judy Goffy, school psychologist, 555-4333 (phone), 555-7455 (fax), drjg@aol.com

Outside Professionals

Dr. Hugh Maloney, independent assessor, 780 Spruce Lane, Chicago, 60612, 555-5169 (phone), 555-5170 (fax), drhm @compuserv.com

Martha Brown, tutor, 2229 Franklin, Chicago, 60612, 555-1490

Other Parents

Kevin Jones (child in Carrie's class), 7 Plainview Dr., Chicago, 60614, 555-5115, kj@aol.com

Melaney Harper, District Community Advisory Chair, 764 Rockly, Chicago, 60610, 555-7777 (phone); 555-9299 (fax)

Support Groups

Chicago Learning Disabilities Association (contact: Mark Kelso), 775 Kelly Rd., Chicago, 60610, 555-6226 (phone), 555-7890 (fax), chldas@aol.com

State Department of Education

Special Ed. Office (contact: Dr. Hillary Casper), State Department of Education, 88 Capitol Row, Springfield, 61614, 217-555-8888 (phone), 217-555-9999 (fax), ilsped@worldnet.att.net

Other

Dr. Joan Landman, Carrie's pediatrician, 32 Ashford Rd., Chicago, 60611, 555-2222 (phone), 555-0987 (fax)

Illinois Special Ed. Advocates (Steve Miller, Esq.), 642 Miller Dr., Chicago, 60611, 555-4511(phone), 555-8709 (fax), spedatt@netcom.com

6. IEP Journal

The importance of keeping a record of all conversations, visits and information-gathering activities, whether on the phone or in person, cannot be over-emphasized. In particular, you want to note the following in an IEP journal:

- the date and time of the conversation or meeting
- the names and positions of all people who participated in the discussion, such as your child's teacher, other school staff, the special education administrator, your pediatrician or another parent, and
- what was said by whom (this is *really* important).

You'll want to fill in your IEP journal just as soon as possible after a conversation or meeting has ended. The longer you wait, the more likely you will forget certain details or confuse dates, times and statements or promises made. Don't be shy about taking notes when you meet or talk with someone. To establish written verification of what you've been told, you'll want to send a confirming letter soon after your conversation. Confirming letters are covered in the following section.

A sample IEP Journal page is below; a tear-out copy is in Appendix 5. Make several copies and keep a few with you—for example, if you make phone calls from work.

Use the Class Visitation Checklist in Chapter 8, Section C, to keep detailed notes on visits to school programs.

IEP Journal

Date: 11/3/99   **Time:** 4:30 ~~a.m.~~/p.m.

Action: ☒ Phone Call 201-555-0105   ☐ Meeting _____

☐ Other: _____

Person(s) Contacted: Dr. P. Brin (Sp. Ed. Administrator)

Notes: I explained that Steve is having problems in reading, comp. and spelling, plus some social difficulties.

I said Steve needs an aide.

Dr. B: "We can't do that now; wait until the IEP."

I said we need IEP at once.

Dr. B: "We just had one; can't schedule another for at least two months."

IEP Journal

Date: 11/5/99   **Time:** 2:10 ~~a.m.~~/p.m.

Action: ☐ Phone Call _____   ☒ Meeting Washington School

☐ Other: _____

Person(s) Contacted: Met w/ T. Walker (teacher)

Notes: T. Walker said, "Steve will need at least two hours/per day of a 1:1 aide next year."

I asked if he needs an aide now.

T. Walker: "Probably."

7. Confirming Letters

Confirming what someone has said to you establishes verification of that conversation. A confirming letter can provide useful evidence—of what was said, by whom and when—for an IEP meeting or even a due process hearing.

To be sure the school district receives confirming letters, send them certified mail, return receipt requested.

Example:

Your son needs a good deal of one-to-one help. You believe that a qualified aide should sit with him to work on reading, math and spelling at least half of the school day. Your child's teacher tells you during a classroom visit that he agrees that your son needs one-to-one help for much of the day. In addition, the special education administrator admits to you that the current amount of aide time your son is receiving is not enough. You note both of these conversations in your IEP Journal and send the administrator a confirming letter. Later, at the IEP meeting, the administrator balks at providing your son with more aide time. Your confirming letter will be quite helpful in establishing that both your son's teacher and the school administrator told you your son needs more aide time.

Sample Confirming Letter

Date: May 14, 20xx

To: Salvador Hale, Special Education
Administrator
Coconut County School District
1003 South Dogwood Drive
Oshkosh, WI 50000
Re: Rodney Brown,
4th grader at Woodrow Wilson School

I appreciated the chance to speak with you yesterday regarding Rodney's current problems with reading comprehension. I agree with your comment that he will need at least half of the day with a one-on-one aide. I look forward to our IEP meeting next week and resolving Rodney's current difficulties in school.

Sincerely,

Martin Brown

Martin Brown
145 Splitleaf Lane
Oshkosh, WI 50000
Phones: 555-4545 (home); 555-2500 (work)

8. Calendars

Section B, below, describes the typical tasks and events during the yearly IEP process, and Section D explains how to keep track of these tasks and events on a monthly calendar. To stay organized, keep a copy of your calendar in your binder.

B. The Yearly IEP Cycle

Part of successful organizing is having a clear sense of when things happen in the IEP cycle. Once your child is assessed and found eligible for special education, the yearly IEP process will involve the same three broad considerations:

- Review—how are things currently going?
- Reassess—what additional information is needed?
- Rebuild—will the program be the same next year or does it need changing?

These three considerations, as well as the general rules below, will help you understand the yearly IEP cycle.

1. Know the Legal Requirements

IDEA requires that an IEP be in place before your child begins the school year (34 C.F.R. §300.342).

2. Give Yourself Enough Time

Know your deadlines. If you are preparing for your first IEP meeting or IEP eligibility meeting, or you anticipate a significant change in your child's current IEP program, then give yourself several months to get a copy of the school file, to meet with school staff and other professionals and prepare for the meeting.

3. Finish Before Summer

To make sure that all special education issues are resolved before the school year begins, you will want a spring IEP meeting. This will give you time to resolve any disputes before the next school year starts. Because school personnel are usually gone during the summer, plan for the IEP meeting in May—or better yet April—in case there is a dispute which would require due process resolution—mediation or a hearing.

4. Request Your Meeting During the Winter

To insure that your child's IEP meeting takes place in the spring, put the school district on notice by submitting a written request in February or March stating that you want the annual IEP meeting in April or May.

5. Begin Planning in the Fall

You'll need to be well-prepared for the spring IEP meeting. Don't start collecting information a few weeks or even a month or two in advance. You'll need much more time than that. Start in the fall or early winter of the preceding year. Section C, below, provides more planning information.

Keep in touch with your child's teacher. It's crucial to monitor your child's progress throughout the school year: Talk regularly with your child's teacher, and spend time in the classroom, if at all possible. By keeping in touch with the school, you'll be able to assess how your child's reading, writing and other goals are being met. This will also give you the opportunity to identify problems early on that might require an immediate IEP. Chapter 8, Section B, provides advice on keeping tabs on your child's progress.

6. The Cycle Isn't Set in Stone

Let's say you've just discovered that your child's problems in school make her a candidate for special education. It's October. You didn't participate in the IEP cycle the previous year because it wasn't an issue. You'd prefer not to wait until the spring to have an IEP meeting to develop a plan for the following year, as your child would lose a year of school. Or, you went through the IEP cycle the previous year, but the current program is not working. It's November, and you don't want to wait until spring for a new program. What do you do?

Speak up. Don't wait until spring to raise issues that need immediate attention. Start gathering information, and request an assessment and IEP meeting ASAP. The IEP cycle is an ideal.

When you want an immediate IEP meeting, request one.

⚠️ **Don't perpetuate mid-year IEP meetings.** Many students' IEP meetings take place in December or January. While you can request an IEP meeting at any time, and should when there is an immediate concern, it is not generally a good idea to have your yearly IEPs after school starts. Otherwise, you'll be making decisions after your child is already in a program. The easiest way to get back on schedule is to indicate at the mid-year IEP meeting that you want another one at the end of the school year, preferably in April or May. Follow-up your request with a confirming letter.

C. Sample Year in the Life of Your Child's IEP

Let us assume you are planning for the school year that begins in the fall of 2000. Ideally, by starting your preparation a year ahead of time, in the fall of 1999, you will have enough time without rushing or facing last minute problems.

The sections below follow the general IEP yearly calendar and are intended to give you an introduction to the IEP year. Specific tasks are listed in each section, but the details are in Chapters 5-11.

1. Information Gathering: Fall 1999 (September-December)

No matter how many times you have been through the special education process, the fall months are generally a good time to gather information and develop a sense of what your child's program should be. The specific tasks include the following:

- Talk to teachers, school staff and other parents (Chapter 3, Section A.3).
- Request copies of your child's school records (Chapter 3, Section B).
- Request an assessment of your child as appropriate (Chapter 6).
- Begin drafting your child's blueprint (Chapter 5).
- Schedule visits to your child's class or other programs you think might be viable (Chapter 8, Section C).
- Gather other information such as letters from your pediatrician and your child's tutor (Chapter 8, Section F).

2. Assessment: Winter 2000 (January-February)

After the first few months of school, the key issues for your child should begin to crystallize for you. You will know that your child needs to be in special education, or, if already eligible for special education, what programmatic components make sense. Now is the time to assess what information you have or need to make a strong case for eligibility or the "what" and "where" of your child's program. Steps to take include the following:

- Assess the current information in your child's record and decide whether it supports your IEP goals for your child.
- Monitor the progress your child is making under the current program.
- Complete additional assessments, if you need more supporting information (discussed in Chapters 6 and 8). Depending on who will be doing any additional assessments and their calendars, you may need to plan for those assessments earlier in the year.
- Continue developing your child's IEP blueprint (Chapter 5).

3. IEP Preparation and IEP Meeting: Spring 2000 (March-May)

Spring is the time you focus on working toward getting an IEP program in place for your child. This may be the most labor-intensive time of the whole cycle. Tasks include the following:

- Finalize your child's IEP blueprint of program and service needs (Chapter 5).
- Draft your goals and objectives for your child's IEP program (Chapter 9).
- Prepare for the IEP meeting and invite participants who will speak on your child's behalf (Chapter 10).
- Attend the IEP meeting (Chapter 11).

4. Dispute Resolution: Spring-Summer 2000 (June-August)

If you did not reach an agreement with the school administrators on your child's IEP program, then you can, as discussed earlier, go to due process

(mediation or a hearing). It is important that due process is completed before the beginning of the new year. See Chapter 12.

5. School Begins: Fall 2000 (September)

You've been through your first (or another) IEP cycle. You'll want to monitor your child's progress in school and see if the IEP program is working. Remember, if it's not, you can request another IEP meeting and try to come up with some changes that make sense.

D. Keep a Monthly Calendar

We cannot overemphasize the importance of writing down details of IEP tasks, such as drafting goals and objectives, and events, such as assessments, school visits and the IEP meeting.

Write down all details on a monthly calendar (your own or the form we provide here), including dates on which:

- you were told things would happen—for example, "Scott's school file should be mailed today"
- you need to schedule a meeting—for example, "Request IEP meeting no later than today"
- you need to call or meet with someone such as a teacher, pediatrician or another parent, or
- you need to start or complete a particular task, such as develop an IEP blueprint.

A sample Monthly IEP Calendar is below; a tear-out copy is in Appendix 5. Make 12 copies of this for each month of the year.

Monthly IEP Calendar

Month and Year: ___Oct '99___

1	2	3 Call Dr. Brin (Request visits)	4	5 Follow-up assessment request if not received	6	7
8	9 Meet w/ Janice re: her son's experiences	10	11	12 Call Dr. Pearl re: recomm. on auditory problem	13	14
15	16	17 Call at 4 p.m. T. Walker to discuss Steve's sign. reading problem	18	19 Send school written request for assessment	20	21
22	23 Call J. Brown of parent group	24	25 4:15 meet w/ T. Walker	26	27	28
29	30	31 Begin Steve's IEP blueprint				

5

Developing Your Child's IEP Blueprint

At some point in the IEP process, you'll need to describe in detail what you believe your child's educational program should look like, including the placement and support services your child needs. We call the specifics of this program a blueprint. Despite the fancy name, a blueprint is just a list of items or components that make up the "what" and "where" of your child's program.

The importance of creating this blueprint cannot be overstated. In order for your child to have an appropriate education, you must be able to state what you want.

There are a few other reasons for creating a blueprint:

- It forces you to be specific. For example, stating that your child needs help in reading is not as effective as saying your child needs a one-on-one reading specialist one hour per day, four days per week.

- By being specific, you'll know exactly what documentation you will need to support your request at the IEP meeting. Continuing with the example, if your blueprint includes a one-on-one reading specialist one hour per day, four days per week, it will be imperative that information from your child's school record or a person at the IEP meeting supports that position.

- IDEA requires that the program fit the child, not the other way around. There is a natural tendency to assume that what is offered is appropriate. A blueprint helps you determine what may be missing from the program suggested by the school.

- The blueprint serves as a standard against which you can evaluate your child's existing program and options currently available to you.

- The blueprint provides you with a continual reference point as you talk with others about your child's needs and move toward and prepare for the IEP meeting.

In essence, the blueprint represents your ideal IEP program. It is your starting point—a sort of "druthers" test. That is, if you had your druthers, if you could be the special education administrator for your school district for one day, this is the IEP program you would design for your child.

You may think it's too early to draft a blueprint. Perhaps your child was just assessed and found eligible for special education, but hasn't been in special education yet. Or maybe your child has been in special education for some time, but is scheduled for a new assessment in another month. It's possible a new special education administrator will take over in the spring, with promises of new program options about which you know little. In any of these situations, you may think you don't know enough. In truth, there's always more information you can gather. But you have to start sometime and now is as good as any. Don't worry if your blueprint is skeletal at first; it's for your use only.

Even the parents newest to special education usually have some intuitive sense of what their child needs. Take a moment to think about it. By the time you finish this chapter, you'll have the beginnings of a useful blueprint, not just vague notions of what your child needs. And as you go through other chapters, and follow suggestions on how to gather information on your child's needs, you'll be able to fully develop a blueprint.

A. Begin at the End: Define Your Child's Needs

It's the first day of school in the upcoming school year. Close your eyes and picture what your child's classroom will look like. Is there a tutor? A sign language interpreter? No more than ten kids in the room? Is it a regular classroom? A special education class in a neighboring school district? A special private school? Don't hold yourself back. Here's an analogy. Imagine that you are remodeling your home. You're in charge of the architectural plan. The IEP, like the plan, is a picture of the finished product.

Sit down with a pad of paper and pen or in front of your computer and write out the ideal program and services for your child. Remember that your blueprint is your wish list for your ideal IEP. Don't dwell on the fact that you fought over the IEP last year or you're expecting a fight again. Don't draft your blueprint with the school district's program if you think it's wrong or not enough for your child.

B. Preparing an IEP Blueprint

This section covers the seven key components of a blueprint. Always keep in mind that these are the items you want included in your child's IEP. And while the blueprint does not precisely parallel the IEP form, it can be used in conjunction with it. (Chapter 11, Section C, explains how.)

Some components are quite general, such as ideal classroom setting; others are very specific, such as a particular class. Some of these seven components are not relevant to your child's situation and may be ignored. You may not have enough information to complete each section now; naturally, as you know more, you should fill in your blueprint.

A sample IEP Blueprint is below; Appendix 5 includes a tear-out copy. Be sure to put your blueprint draft into your binder, along with supporting information and documents. (See Chapter 4.)

1. Classroom Setting and Peer Needs

In this section, specify the type of classroom you'd like your child in, including the kinds of peers she should be with. Specific items to identify (when relevant) include:

- regular versus special education class
- partially or fully mainstreamed
- type of special education class (for example, for learning disabled)
- number of children in the classroom
- ages and cognitive ranges of children in class
- kinds of students (similar or dissimilar disabling conditions) and what behaviors might or might not be appropriate for your child—for example, a child with attention deficit disorder may need a classroom where other children do not act out, and
- language similarities—for example, a deaf child may need a class of children who use the same sign language.

2. Teacher and Staff Needs

Use this section to identify your desires concerning teachers and other classroom staff, such as:

- number of teachers and aides
- teacher-pupil ratio—for example, your child may require a ratio of no more than four students to one teacher
- experience, training and expertise of the teacher—many special education classes are set up for children with specific disabilities; if your child has communicative disabilities or emotional problems, a class with a teacher for the learning disabled may not be appropriate, and
- training and expertise of aides.

IEP Blueprint

The IEP Blueprint represents the ideal IEP for your child. Use it as a guide to make and record the educational desires you have for your child.

Areas of the IEP	Preferred Situation for Your Child
1. Classroom Setting and Peer Needs— issues to consider:	
☐ regular versus special education class	
☐ partially or fully mainstreamed	
☐ type of special education class	
☒ number of children in the classroom	A class of no more than 10 students
☒ ages and cognitive ranges of children in class	Age range 9-10; same cognitive range as Mark
☒ kinds of students and what behaviors might or might not be appropriate for your child, and	No behaviorally troubled students No mixed "disability" class
☐ language similarities.	
2. Teacher and Staff Needs— issues to consider:	
☒ number of teachers and aides	1 teacher; 1 full-time aide or (2 half-time aides)
☒ teacher-pupil ratio	10:1 pupil-teacher ratio
☒ experience, training and expertise of the teacher, and	Teacher with specific learning disability training, experience, credentials
☒ training and expertise of aides.	Aide: previous experience working with L-D students
3. Curricula and Teaching Methodology— be specific. If you don't know what you *do* want, specify what you *don't* want.	Slingerland method Large print material Teaching strategies which include significant repetition

Areas of the IEP	Ideal Situation for Your Child
4. Related Services—issues to consider:	
☒ specific needed services	1:1 aide two hours per day
☒ type of services	Speech and lang. therapy three times/week, 40 min. per session, 1:1
☒ frequency of services, and	
☒ length of services.	30 minutes of psych. counseling once a week with psychologist experienced with children with learning disabilities and emotional overlay
5. Identified Programs—specify known programs in known schools you think would work for your child.	Special day class (5th grade) for learning disabled at Washington School (Ms. Flanagan)
6. Goals and Objectives—goals are long range in nature, while objectives are more short term.	Improve reading fluency and comprehension: Read three-paragraph story with 80% comprehension; complete reading within 10 minutes.
	Improve peer relationships: Initiate five positive peer interactions/week.
7. Classroom Environment and Other Features—issues to consider:	
☒ distance from home	No more than five miles and less than 30-minute bus ride to neighborhood school.
☐ transition plans for mainstreaming	
☐ vocational needs	
☒ extracurricular and social needs, and	Involvement in afterschool recreation and lunch-time sports activities
☒ environmental needs.	Small school (no more than 250 students); quiet classroom; protective environment (school procedures to ensure students do not wander); acoustically treated classroom

3. Curricula and Teaching Methodology

In this section, you'll want to identify the curricula and teaching method or methods you feel are appropriate for your child. You may have no idea right now. As you gather information, however, you will begin to learn about the various teaching methods, materials, strategies and curricula used with children with disabilities.

Be as specific as possible. If you don't know what you *do* want, specify what you *don't* want. For example an autistic child will require very different curricula and teaching methods than a child with a learning disability. A child in a regular classroom may require only a minor adjustment to the regular classroom curriculum.

4. Related Services

Include in your blueprint a list of specific needed services, both type and amount of services (such as number of times per week and length of time per session).

 Chapters 2 and 8 provide details on related services, such as speech therapy, aide support, physical therapy, transportation and psychological services.

5. Identified Programs

In Section 1 of the blueprint, you may have stated whether you want your child in a regular classroom or special education classroom. If there's a known program in a known school you think would work best for your child, be it in a regular classroom or a special education classroom, public or private, identify that now, or as soon as you know.

6. Goals and Objectives

As discussed in Chapter 2, goals are long range in nature, while objectives are more short term.

Examples of goals include:

- improve reading comprehension or other academic skills, such as math, spelling or writing
- improve social skills
- resolve a serious emotional difficulty which impedes school work
- improve fine or large motor skills
- develop greater language and speech skills
- develop independent living skills, or
- improve auditory or visual memory.

Objectives may tie in specifically to the goals identified just above. For example, if your goal is to improve your child's reading skills, then a specific objective may be to improve reading comprehension from the 3rd to the 4th grade level or to master specific speech sounds.

 Chapter 9 discusses how to prepare goals and objectives.

7. Classroom Environment and Other Features

Use your blueprint to identify any other features of the program you want for your child, such as:

- distance from home
- transition plans for mainstreaming
- vocational needs
- extracurricular and social needs, and
- environmental needs—protective environment, small class, small campus, acoustically treated classroom or the like.

C. Other Sources of Information for the Blueprint

Developing your blueprint is an important part of gathering information and developing a sense of what your child needs. As you learn more about your child's needs from professionals and others, and find out what services and programs are available, add to or change the information on your blueprint.

People you trust and who know your child—such as other parents, your pediatrician, the classroom teacher or a tutor—are excellent sources of information for your blueprint. Pose your question like this: "Terry is having some problems with reading (math, cognitive growth, language development, social issues, emotional conflicts, mobility, fine or gross motor activities or whatever) and I'm wondering if I should look for a new program (or different related services). Do you have any suggestions of who I might talk to or what programs or services I might consider?"

Chapter 8 contains important information about gathering information, visiting school programs and developing supportive material, such as an independent assessment; this information will help you work on your blueprint.

D. What's Next?

If you are new to special education, the next step is to learn about the assessment and eligibility processes—how your child is evaluated for special education and how he becomes eligible for special education. Review Chapters 6 and 7 carefully.

If you are not new to special education, the next step may vary. Your child may need an assessment before the IEP meeting. If your child does not need an immediate assessment, read Chapter 8 before reviewing the IEP chapters. ■

6

Assessments

Assessments are relevant for children both new to special education and who have been through the IEP process before. For first-timers, an assessment provides information so the IEP team can determine whether or not a child is eligible for special education by evaluating the child's current ability levels and potential areas of need (20 U.S.C. §1414(a)(1); 34 C.F.R. §§300.320, 527, 531-535). This kind of assessment is called the initial assessment.

For children previously found eligible, re-evaluation assessments take place at least once every three years (more often if the parent or child's teacher requests) to review ability levels and potential areas of need (20 U.S.C. §1414(a)(2); 34 C.F.R. §§300.321, 536).

In either situation, a good assessment report also makes recommendations as to needed programs and services for your child.

 If you are new to special education, you will quickly learn that assessments and eligibility are closely related. Should you read the assessments chapter before Chapter 7 on eligibility, or vice-versa? While it ultimately doesn't matter as long as you read both, you might better understand eligibility if you read this chapter on assessments first.

The specific contents of the assessment report will be central to what's in your blueprint and a key factor in decisions made at an IEP meeting about your child's program and services. Ideally, the assessment report will support what you want included in the IEP. For example, if you feel your child needs placement in a specific special education program, and the assessment report addresses that issue and makes a specific recommendation, your chances of securing that placement are increased.

This chapter covers assessments done by local public school districts. You have the right to have your child assessed by someone outside of the school district, often referred to as a private or independent assessment. As discussed in Chapter 8, such independent assessments are of value when you disagree with the school district's assessment or feel that an independent assessor will provide an evaluation supportive of your child's blueprint.

A. When Assessments Are First Done

An assessment must be completed before your child's eligibility for special education is determined and an initial IEP program developed. Eligibility decisions are first made at an IEP meeting. As discussed in Chapter 7, Section E, program decisions may be made at the same time or in a separate IEP meeting.

While you can wait for the school district to initiate the initial assessment process, you don't want to unnecessarily delay. If you haven't heard from the school, make a formal request for an assessment.

A sample Request to Begin Special Education Process and Assessment is found in Chapter 3, Section A.2; a tear-out copy is in Appendix 5.

General Steps in Assessment Process

The following are the general steps involved in the assessment process:

1. Your child is identified by the school as possibly needing special education or you request an assessment. (See Chapter 3.)

2. The school presents you with an assessment plan listing all testing to be done on your child in order to determine eligibility for special education, or to assess your child's current status if already in special education.

3. You approve the assessment plan and recommend other tests or evaluation tools be added.

4. You meet with the assessor to discuss specific concerns and your own evaluation of your child's problems, based on your personal observations, physician reports and the like.

5. Your child is assessed by the school.

6. You receive a copy of the school's assessment.

7. You schedule independent assessments if necessary. (See Chapter 8.)

8. You attend the IEP eligibility meeting.

IDEA does not require that your school district submit an assessment plan to you and complete the assessment within a specific time. Nevertheless, the school must complete the assessment within a reasonable time after receiving your request or your consent to an initial assessment.

States may have their own timelines. For example, California requires that an assessment plan be provided within 15 days of your request for an assessment. California law further requires that an IEP program be developed within 50 days from the receipt of the parent's request for the assessment. Contact your state department of education to see if your state laws include more specific timelines than IDEA.

This chapter is about assessments, not eligibility or the IEP meeting. But all three are closely related. As you go through the initial assessment process, bear in mind that IDEA requires that the school hold an IEP program meeting within 30 days of the determination that a child is eligible for special education. Eligibility and joint eligibility/program meetings are covered in Chapter 7; IEP meetings are discussed in Chapters 10 and 11.

B. Assessment Components

Assessments almost always include objective tests leading to numerical conclusions about a child. Depending on your child's disability, many tests are available—including ones to evaluate general intelligence, reading comprehension, psychological states, social development and physical abilities. You may have already heard of some of them, such as the Wechsler Test, Kaufman Assessment and Draw-a-Person. For each test given, the assessment report should include an explanation of the test and the test's results.

An assessment need not be made up of only formal tests. It can also include supportive material that provides information or recommendations about your child's educational status, such as:

- a general description of your child
- teacher and parent reports
- full-scale evaluations by experts specializing in your child's disability
- letters from a family doctor or counselor
- daily or weekly school reports or diaries, and
- other evidence of school performance, including work samples.

Finally, the assessment report should contain a conclusion as to special education eligibility and specific recommendations about strategies, curricula, interventions, related services and programs needed for your child. The best assessment recommends everything in your blueprint.

Legal Requirements for Assessments

Under IDEA (20 U.S.C. §1414(a)(6)(B); 34 C.F.R. §300.532), initial or subsequent assessment material must:

- include a variety of assessment tests or tools and strategies to gather information about your child
- not be racially or culturally discriminatory
- be given in your child's native language or communication mode (such as sign language if your child is deaf or hard of hearing)
- be valid in determining your child's status—that is, the right test, given your child's suspected areas of disability
- be given by trained and knowledgeable personnel in accordance with the instructions provided by the producer of the tests
- not be used to only determine intelligence
- if your child has impaired speaking or sensory skills, accurately reflect your child's aptitude or achievement level and not your child's specific impairment
- assess your child in "all areas of suspected disability" including health, vision, hearing, social and emotional status, general intelligence, academic performance, communicative status, motor abilities, behavior and cognitive, physical and developmental abilities, and
- provide relevant information that will help determine your child's educational needs.

In addition, IDEA requires that the assessment process include a review of other material on your child, such as information you provide (a doctor's letter or a statement of your observations), current classroom assessments and observations (objective tests or subjective teacher reports) and observations by other professionals (20 U.S.C. §1414(c)(1,2,4); 34 C.F.R. §300.533).

C. Assessment Plans

Before the school district begins the formal assessment process—either an initial assessment or a re-evaluation assessment—it must send you a written assessment plan and receive your written approval (20 U.S.C. §1414(a)(1)(C); 34 C.F.R. §300.505).

The assessment plan must include:

- specifically-named tests
- a section where you can request additional tests or other methods of evaluation, and
- a place for you to provide your written approval.

1. Evaluating the Assessment Tests

In almost all cases, a person in your school district knowledgeable about special education will determine which tests are to be given to your child. There's a very good chance that this person will also administer the assessments or supervise whoever does the assessments. How will you know if the proposed tests are appropriate for your child?

The best source of information is people familiar with special education testing in general and the specific tests in particular. Likely candidates include the person who developed the assessment plan, your child's teacher, other parents and your pediatrician. Other possibilities include independent special education assessors you've worked with or school special education personnel you trust. You may also want to talk to organizations that represent the specific disability of your child, such as the Council for Exceptional Children or a state association for learning disabilities.

Chapter 8 discusses independent assessments. Appendix 3 provides a list of advocacy, parent and disability organizations you might consider contacting for information on different types of assessments. Appendix 3 also references nearly a half-dozen books on testing and assessments.

Here's what you want to find out:
- the appropriateness of the proposed tests
- what the tests generally measure, such as general cognitive skills or language abilities
- whether the tests' results are usually numeric scores or more descriptive statements about your child's performance or both
- whether the tests' results will provide a basis for specific recommendations about classroom strategies, teaching methods and services and programs for your child
- how the tests are administered—for example, are they timed
- the assessor and his specific expertise, training and experience in doing this kind of assessment, and
- how the results are evaluated—for example, will your child score in a certain percentile ("Mary is in the 88th percentile," meaning she scored better than 87% of the children taking the test) or will your child be given a different result ("Mary scored at the second grade level").

2. Adding to the Assessment Plan

If you are not content with the assessment plan submitted to you, you have every right to ask for changes. IDEA specifically states that the assessment process include evaluations and information provided by the parents (34 C.F.R. §300.533(a)(1)(i)). You can request that specific tests be administered to your child. In addition, you can request that certain information be used to evaluate your child and included as part of the assessment report, such as a formal interview with you, a review of your child's school work, a teacher's observations or a pediatrician's report. Be as specific as possible in your request. For example, if your child has limited fine motor skills and problems with handwriting, ask that the assessor analyze his handwriting samples.

 How do you know what "other information" makes sense to include in the assessment plan? By this time, you have probably gathered information about your child—secured his school file and talked to his teacher, other parents or experts—and have some sense of the key issues. Be sure to take a look at your blueprint, no matter how incomplete it may be. See Chapter 5.

Be aware that many special education assessors are not comfortable evaluating testing and other data that don't produce a numerical result. The assessment plan you receive may consist primarily of standardized tests. The school district may object if you ask for an evaluation of subjective reports or anecdotal observations. Nevertheless, you have the right to insist that this information be included in your child's assessment. Subjective reports and anecdotal observations are very important, will speak for themselves and may be key in coming up with the ultimate IEP program.

If the assessor refuses to make the changes to the assessment plan you request, send a letter to the school district's special education administrator. Explain that you are exercising your right under IDEA, 34 C.F.R. §300.533(a)(1)(i), requesting that additional materials be added to your child's assessment plan and that the assessor refused. Describe exactly what you want included and the reasons the assessor gave you for the refusal. As always, keep a copy of your correspondence.

3. Approving or Rejecting the Assessment Plan

Ultimately, you must sign the assessment plan, indicating whether you accept or reject it. Signing the assessment plan need not be an all or nothing proposition. You can:
- accept the plan
- accept the plan on condition, or
- reject the plan.

a. Accepting the Plan

If you accept the plan as submitted to you, mark the appropriate box—most assessment plans have approval and disapproval boxes—sign and date it and return it to the school district. If there is no acceptance box, write "plan accepted," sign and date it and return it. Be sure to make a photocopy of the assessment plan and add it to your IEP binder.

b. Accepting the Plan on Condition

There are two possible reasons you might accept the plan with a condition. The first is that you accept the tests proposed, but you want additional tests administered or additional information considered. In this situation, try to get the assessor to agree informally or ask for help from the school district. (See Section C.2, above.)

The other reason is that you don't want certain proposed tests administered to your child—perhaps you believe they aren't reliable or that they test for a problem that your child doesn't have. Whatever the reason, indicate your partial acceptance of the plan on the form as follows:

> I approve only of the following tests:
> Wrat, Kaufman
>
> Date: March 1, 19xx
>
> Signature: *Jan Stevens*

c. Rejecting the Plan

You have every right to reject the assessment plan and force the assessor or school district to work with you to find an acceptable plan. Your reasons for rejecting will fall into one or more of the following situations:

- the assessor insists on administering tests you feel are not appropriate
- the assessor won't administer the additional tests you've requested or include the

materials you want as part of the evaluation, or

- you reject the assessor based on his qualifications or expertise.

Evaluating the Assessor

Under IDEA, any assessment of your child must be "administered by trained and knowledgeable personnel in accordance with any instructions provided by the producer of the tests" (34 C.F.R. §300.532(c)(ii)). How can you judge the qualifications of the assessor?

- Ask the special education administrator for the credentials of the assessor. If the administrator refuses, assert your right to know under IDEA.
- Ask other parents and your child's teacher.
- If you are working with an independent assessor (see Chapter 8), ask her if she knows the school's assessor.
- If possible, meet with the assessor prior to the testing. (See Section D, below.)

To reject the assessment plan, check off the disapproval box, sign and date the form and return it to the school district. If there is no box, write "assessment plan rejected," sign and date the form and return it. Keep a copy.

If the assessment plan is not clear or does not give you enough room, you should attach a letter to the assessment plan. A sample letter is below. Use this as a model and adjust it depending on your specific situation.

Sample Letter Rejecting Assessment Plan

Date: December 14, 19xx

To: Carolyn Ames, Administrator, Special Education
Central Valley School District
456 Main Street
Centerville, Michigan 47000

Re: Assessment Plan for Michael Kreeskind

I am in receipt of the November 21, 19xx, assessment plan for my son Michael. I give my permission for you to administer the Vineland, PPVT-III, and Wechsler tests, but not the rest of the ones on your list. I have investigated them and feel they are too unreliable.

In addition, I am formally requesting that the assessment plan reflect the following:

- that the assessor will meet with me and my husband to review Michael's entire history and will include the issues raised during that meeting in the assessment report, and

- that the assessor will evaluate samples of Michael's work and letters from professionals who have observed Michael.

I have one final concern. I have reviewed the credentials of Brett Forrest, the assessor selected by the district to evaluate Michael. I am concerned that Mr. Forrest has no prior experience evaluating children with Michael's disability. Specifically, I do not believe he is trained or knowledgeable about the specific tests to be administered, as required under IDEA, 34 C.F.R. §300.532(c)(ii). Therefore, I do not approve of the assigned assessor, Brett Forrest, and request that an appropriate one be assigned, and that we be provided proof of the assessor's qualifications.

Thank you very much.

Michelle Kreeskind
Michelle Kreeskind
8 Rock Road
Centerville, Michigan 47000
Phones: 555-9876 (home); 555-5450 (work)

After submitting your rejection (partial or complete) of the assessment plan, the assessor or school district will probably attempt to find a plan that meets your approval. If the district feels the assessment should proceed under the plan you've rejected, it has the right to proceed to mediation or a hearing under the due process to force this issue, although this is rarely done. (See Chapter 12.)

D. Meet With the Assessor

After you accept the assessment plan proposed by the school district, the assessor will contact you to begin to schedule the testing of your child. Now is the time to think ahead. In a few months, when you are at the IEP meeting planning your child's IEP program, the school district will pay most attention to the evaluation done by its own assessor. Therefore, you will want to take some time to establish a positive relationship with the assessor before testing begins.

A good relationship is one in which the parties don't come to it with pre-conceived ideas or view each other with hostility. Try to put aside negative comments you've heard about the assessor from other people (or any bad experiences you've had with the assessor in the past). Start with the assumption (or new attitude) that the assessor is there to help your child get an appropriate education. We realize that this may not be as simple as it seems. The assessor may not be easy to talk to or may be put off by parents who demand things as part of the assessment. No matter what attitude the assessor adopts, you should remain rational and pleasant.

Reality Check: The Assessor Works for the School District

While you should assume the assessor wants to develop a good and appropriate educational plan for your child, don't lose sight of the fact that the assessor is an employee of the school district. The assessor probably knows what the school district will offer regarding your child's eligibility for special education or in terms of an IEP program, and the assessor's report may very well reflect the school's position. Some assessors know exactly what a school district can provide, and unfortunately tailor their assessment reports accordingly, rather than prepare a report based on what a child truly needs.

On the other hand, just because the assessor's report doesn't support what you want, it doesn't necessarily follow that the assessor is acting against your child's best interests. Her conclusions may be well reasoned and supported by the data. Be objective. Are her recommendations consistent with or contrary to the data? If you conclude that the assessor is biased against you, request a new one. Remember, you always have the right to an outside or independent assessment (see Chapter 8).

Your job is to educate the assessor about your child. She'll have test results to evaluate and reports to read. But she doesn't live with your child or stand before your child in a classroom. To the extent possible, help the assessor see your child from your perspective, particularly as it relates to the academic programs and services you feel are necessary for your child. Ideally, you want the assessment report completed by the assessor to specifically report what you want for your child as articulated in your blueprint (in Chapter 5).

So how do you go about getting your points across to the assessor? If possible, you want to meet with the assessor before the testing is done.

The law doesn't require an assessor to meet with you, but the law does not prohibit it either. Call up and ask for an appointment. State that you'd appreciate the chance to talk, are not familiar with all the tests, would like to find out how they are used and would just feel a lot better if you could meet for 10-15 minutes. If the assessor cannot meet with you, ask for a brief phone consultation or consider sending a letter expressing your concerns.

Whether you meet in person, talk on the phone or state your concerns in a letter, you'll want to be clear and objective.

Eligibility assessment. Let the assessor know the specific problems your child is having in school, the material you have documenting those problems and why you believe those problems qualify your child for special education.

Example:

"Carl has had a terrible time with reading. He's only in the second grade, but he is way behind. His teacher agrees—I have some notes of my conversation with her from last October. I could provide you with a copy of them if that would help. I'd greatly appreciate your focusing on Carl's reading problem in your assessment."

 Eligibility is covered in greater detail in Chapter 7.

IEP program assessment. If your child is already in special education or is likely to be found eligible, let the assessor know of the IEP program components you believe are important. Here are a few examples.

Examples:

"Billy needs a small class where none of the children exhibit behavioral problems and with classroom strategies and methodology geared for children with his specific learning disability."

"Howard needs the Lovaas method for autistic children. I would like you to evaluate the reports done by his doctor, his teacher and the classroom aide, and address their suggestions in your recommendations section."

Be careful about how specific you get. The assessor may think you're trying to do his job and might not appreciate being told exactly what to include in the assessment report. For example, a straight out, "Please recommend that Mary have a full-time, one-on-one aide" or "Please write that Tom be placed in the learning disability program at Center School" may be met with hostility. You may need to be less direct, such as "The teacher wrote that Mary cannot learn to read without constant one-on-one attention. Please address that need in your report." Remember, your blueprint is a good guide here.

This part of the process is not easy. Don't be disappointed if the assessor doesn't agree fully or even partially with what you are asking for. The best you can do is be clear on what your child's problem is, what you feel your child needs and what materials support your conclusions. The rest is up to the assessor. Ultimately, if the assessor does not address your questions and there is good evidence to support those questions, the value of the school's assessment may be diminished.

E. Reviewing the Assessment Report

After your child is evaluated by the assessor, the assessor will issue his report. Some assessors issue their reports in two stages: a *draft* report and a *final* report. Ask the assessor how and when he plans on issuing his report. Ideally, the assessor will issue a draft report that you can review before he submits his final report prior to the IEP meeting.

Even if the assessor will issue only one version of the report, it is imperative that you see it before the IEP meeting. Under IDEA, the school district must provide you with a copy of the evaluation report and with information documenting eligibility (34 C.F.R. §300.534(a)(2)).

By asking to see the report (preferably a draft of the report), you convey to the school district your intention to carefully review the assessor's work. This will help you keep a sense of control over the assessment process and prepare for the IEP meeting. It also keeps you from wasting valuable time at the IEP meeting reading it there for the first time.

A sample letter requesting the assessment report is below; a tear-out copy is in Appendix 5.

If the assessor does show you a draft of the report and you disagree with anything in it or feel something is missing, talk to the assessor and ask him to make a change or add the missing information. Be prepared to point to material outside the assessment report that supports your point of view. If the assessor refuses, put your request in writing, with a copy to the special education administrator.

If the assessor won't make the changes—or sends you only the final version—what can you do if you disagree with the final assessment report? You can reject it. While you can express your disagreement before the IEP, it might be strategically wise to wait for the meeting and prepare your counter-arguments with the evidence you have, including existing material and your independent assessment (if any).

Remember the point made at the beginning of this chapter: You have the right to have your child assessed by someone outside of the school district, often referred to as a private or independent assessment. As discussed in Chapter 8, such independent assessments are also of value when you disagree with the school district's assessment. The independent assessor can specifically analyze the district's assessment and perhaps point out its shortcomings.

Letter Requesting Assessment Report

Date: _____ November 1, 19xx _____

To: Harvey Smith, Assessment Team

Pine Hills Elementary School

234 Lincoln Road

Boston, MA 02000

Re: Robin Griffin, student in 1st Grade class of Sean Jordan

I appreciate your involvement in my child's assessment and look forward to your report. Would you please:

1. Send me a copy of a draft of your report before you finalize it. As you can imagine, the process can be overwhelming for parents and it would be most helpful to me to see your report because the proposed tests are complicated and I need time to evaluate the results.

2. Send me your final report at least four weeks before the IEP meeting.

Again thank you for your kind assistance.

Sincerely,

Lee Griffin,

Lee Griffin

23 Hillcrest Road

Boston, MA 02000

Phones: 555-4321 (home); 555-9876 (work)

7

Who Is Eligible for Special Education?

Eligibility is the process the school district uses to determine whether or not your child qualifies for special education. This is a two-step process. First, your child is assessed. Then, you meet with school administrators at an IEP meeting where the school actually determines whether or not your child is eligible for special education. This IEP meeting is different from the IEP meeting where your child's annual academic program is developed, although they may be combined (as discussed later in this chapter). To distinguish between the two IEP meetings, we refer to the eligibility IEP meeting as the "eligibility IEP," and an IEP meeting in which the specifics of the program are determined as the "program IEP."

Eligibility, like assessments, IEP meetings and other aspects of the special education process, is bound by the rules of IDEA. And like those other procedures, eligibility is frequently the source of disagreement between parents and a school district.

If your child has already been found eligible for special education, skip ahead to Chapter 8. If your child hasn't yet been found eligible and you haven't read the chapter on assessments, read Chapter 6 before reading this chapter.

Your child may be found eligible for special education for any number of reasons—for example, because she has a learning disability, has sensory or physical impairments or has psychological problems. Sections A and B, below, discuss the key criteria for special education eligibility.

Eligibility Is Not an Annual Event

Your child's eligibility does not have to be re-determined each year. In only three situations might your child's eligibility be redetermined:

- she had dropped out of special education and wants to reenter
- you or the school district proposes a change from one eligibility category to another, or
- there is evidence that your child no longer qualifies for special education.

A. Eligibility Definitions

IDEA provides a list of disabling conditions which qualify a child between the ages of three and 22 for special education. The list includes:

- hearing impairments, including deafness
- speech or language impairments, such as stuttering or other speech production difficulties
- visual impairments, including blindness
- multiple disabilities, such as deaf-blindness
- orthopedic impairments caused by congenital anomalies, such as a club foot
- orthopedic impairments caused by diseases, such as polio
- orthopedic impairments caused by other conditions, such as cerebral palsy
- learning disabilities (see sidebar, below)
- serious emotional disturbance (see sidebar, below)
- autism
- traumatic brain injury
- mental retardation, and
- other health impairments that affect a child's strength, vitality or alertness, such as a heart condition, tuberculosis, rheumatic fever, nephritis, asthma, sickle cell anemia, hemophilia, epilepsy, lead poisoning, leukemia or diabetes.

 The specific legal definition of each of the above disabilities is found in IDEA at 20 U.S.C. §1401(3) and 34 C.F.R. §300.307. See Appendix 1 for a copy of key sections of the statute and authorizing regulations.

Having one of the listed disabilities is not in and of itself enough to qualify a child for special education. IDEA requires that the disability adversely affect a child's performance at school. (See Section B, below.)

Learning Disabilities and Special Education

Of all the IDEA categories, learning disability is the largest and in some ways the most elusive. Under IDEA, learning disability is defined as "a disorder in one or more of the basic psychological processes involved in understanding or in using language, spoken or written, that may manifest itself in an imperfect ability to listen, think, speak, read, write, spell or to do mathematical calculations, including such conditions as perceptual disabilities, brain injury, minimal brain dysfunction, dyslexia and developmental aphasia" (34 C.F.R. §300.7(b)(10)).

Perhaps because the learning disability category applies to so many children, IDEA provides that the IEP team "may determine that a child has a specific learning disability if he does not achieve commensurate with his or her age and ability levels ... and has a severe discrepancy between achievement and intellectual ability in one or more of the following areas: oral expression, listening comprehension, written expression, basic reading skill, reading comprehension, mathematics calculation or mathematics reasoning" (34 C.F.R. §300.541). The problem may be reflected in low reading scores or difficulties in math computation, processing information, converting thought into the written word or thinking sequentially.

A great deal of information about learning disabilities is available through the national Learning Disabilities Association and other excellent organizations. (See Appendix 3.)

Emotional Disturbance and Special Education

Emotional disturbance is given special mention because issues of emotional difficulties, misbehavior and their relationship to learning are complex and often confused. In addition, your child may have a specific disability, such as a learning disability or hearing impairment, which also impacts on his emotional well-being. IDEA considers an emotional disturbance to be a condition which has existed over a long period of time, is significant and has an impact on your child's educational performance (20 U.S.C. §1401(3)(A)(i); 34 C.F.R. §300.7(a)(4)). Conditions that qualify as an emotional disturbance include one or more of the following:

- inability to learn not explained by intellectual, sensory or health factors
- inability to build or maintain satisfactory interpersonal relationships with peers and teachers
- inappropriate types of behavior or feelings under normal circumstances
- general pervasive mood of unhappiness or depression, or
- tendency to develop physical symptoms or fears associated with personal or school problems.

Emotional disturbance must adversely affect your child's educational performance in order to qualify for special education. (See Section B.2, below.)

Attention Deficit Disorder: Is It a Disability?

Attention deficit disorder (ADD) and attention deficit hyperactivity disorder (ADHD) appear on the list of "qualifying" disabilities in IDEA regulations that became effective in May 1999 (after this book went to press). The new regulation is 34 C.F.R. §300.7 (c)(9)(i). See "Keeping Current on Special Education" at the end of Chapter 2 for information on securing copies of the new IDEA regulations. Also, Appendix 3 includes information on ADD and ADHD resources.

B. Making Sense Out of Eligibility Definitions

Remember—for your child to be eligible for special education, her disability must adversely affect her educational performance. There is no quantitative process for determining this. As a general rule, you must establish a link between the disabling condition and your child's educational performance.

1. Disabling Condition

Finding the right condition to prove that your child is disabled and finding data to back up the diagnosis can be heart-wrenching, to say the least. But it's a necessary part of qualifying for special education. Here are some tips on making it do-able.

A Word About Labels

The list of eligibility categories in Section A asks you to define your child as "this" or "that." Labeling is one of the difficult and unpleasant parts of this process. Many people feel that labels are unnecessary, and to some degree they are right. On the other hand, you must have accurate information about your child for her to be found eligible. If you can, focus on the specifics of your child's condition, and not the label. Remember, your goal is to secure an appropriate education for your child; proving that your child qualifies for special education under one of the eligibility categories is part of the process. It's a fine line between acknowledging the label for the purpose of meeting an eligibility category and making sure your child does not become defined by the label. Mary is learning disabled for purposes of knowing what she needs and qualifying for special education. More importantly, Mary is an enthusiastic goalie on her soccer team, refuses to take out the garbage, nurses every injured animal in the neighborhood and is determined to do the best she can. These are the qualities that label her.

- **Take it slowly.** Some of the qualifying conditions, such as emotional disturbance, contain a multilayered definition. Don't try to take it in all at once. By breaking a definition down into parts you understand, you'll find it easier to accept the diagnosis and find evidence that your child meets all the requirements of the definition.
- **You're not a doctor and don't have to become one.** Many of the qualifying conditions use clinical or medical terms. For now, you need a basic understanding of the condition and how it affects a child's educational experience. Ask your pediatrician, the school nurse and the assessor. Contact other parents. A local or national support or advocacy organization will probably have a lot of information as well. (Chapter 15 discusses parent organizations and Appendix 3 lists useful resources.)
- **Focus on key portions of each definition.** Pay attention to words such as "severe" or "significant." These are clues that a minor disability may not qualify your child for special education. If your child doesn't fall under one of the delineated conditions, pay close attention to the catchall category, "other health impairment." If your child has limited strength, vitality or alertness due to a chronic or acute health problem, he may very well qualify under this category.
- **The IEP team has flexibility in finding eligibility.** The list of qualifying disabilities is long, but not exhaustive. If your child exhibits the characteristics of any one of the disability categories, even if she hasn't been formally diagnosed with that condition, she may very well be deemed eligible for special education. In addition, the IEP team has some discretion in determining eligibility. If your child has been diagnosed with a mild condition, it's up to the IEP team to determine if it is serious enough to justify a finding of eligibility.

2. Adverse Affect

For your child to be determined eligible for special education, her disability must have an adverse impact on her educational performance.

Although grades are what a school district usually considers when determining if the disability adversely affects educational performance or achievement, grades don't tell the whole story. IDEA does not say anything about grades. A parent can (and should) argue that a child who receives Cs and Ds but cannot relate to her peers is not benefiting from her education and her disability is directly affecting her educational experience.

If you believe your child qualifies for special education but is getting passing grades, you will need to make the connection between your child's disability and school performance. Factors to consider other than grades include:

- failure to progress—for example, little or no improvement in reading, math or spelling even though the teacher does not fail your child
- difficulties in cognitive areas, such as mastering concepts or memory problems
- discrepancy between performance and ability—for example, the child is developmentally and chronologically age ten, but reading at a six-year-old's level
- evidence of emotional or social difficulties, or
- physical difficulties, such as handwriting or hearing problems.

As pointed out in Section B.1, above, the IEP team has a great deal of discretion in determining eligibility. Measuring the adverse impact of your child's disability on her educational performance may be one area where the team will have to exercise that discretion if your child has passing grades. But you may meet an obstacle: The school district may focus primarily or even exclusively on grades. Nothing is more frustrating than hearing, "We realize Leo is having trouble reading, but he received all Cs, and therefore does not qualify for special education." Remember, IDEA does not define "adversely affects" or refer to grades in the law.

When the School Ends the Discussion

Your school district may argue that your child is not eligible for special education because her grades are passing. An administrator might try to close off the conversation with "We can't do that," "It does not follow our rules," "John is not eligible because his grades are okay" or "Fran cannot have that service because our policy won't allow it." Don't accept this. Ask to see a written copy of the rule or policy.

Then state that you don't think the law says what the administrator is saying. IDEA says nothing about grades—and specifically does not say that a passing grade means a child will not qualify for special education. IDEA uses the term "adversely affects education." It is reasonable to conclude that educational performance involves any number of factors, as described above.

Section C, below, has more information on preparing for the eligibility meeting. Chapter 11, Section B, provides advice on dealing with intimidating comments and other general rules for dealing with school districts.

---

3. Eligibility: What's Not in the Law

Almost as telling as what IDEA requires is what it doesn't. The following information may help you prepare for the eligibility meeting.

a. Requirement of Numeric Proof

IDEA does not require that your child score at a certain level on specific tests to qualify for special education. Numeric information is important, and may prove a key element in determining eligibility, but the mere existence of a test number is not the end of the story.

Some state laws do include specific numeric requirements, particularly for a finding of eligibility as learning disabled. California, for example, requires that your child demonstrate a certain quantifiable gap between his ability and his test results. California also gives the IEP team the discretion to determine eligibility on non-numeric factors, for example student work or parent or teacher observation. Parents outside of California don't always have this additional option. Check with your school district or your state department of education to find out whether there is any state law on eligibility. Appendix 2 includes information on how to contact your state department of education.

b. One Test as Sole Determinant

Eligibility cannot be determined based on the results of one test. IDEA specifically requires that any evaluation to determine eligibility include information provided by the parents of the child (34 C.F.R. §§300.533(a)(1)(i) and 300.535(a)(1)). Furthermore, IDEA requires that the school district draw upon information from a variety of sources, including aptitude and achievement tests, teacher recommendations, the child's physical condition, social or cultural background and adaptive behavior.

c. Eligibility Based on Environment, Cultural or Economic Status

IDEA specifically states that a child cannot be determined eligible for special education solely because of limited English proficiency or environmental, cultural or economic disadvantage (34 C.F.R. §§300.7(b)(10)(ii) and 300.534(b)(1)). These factors may be considered, however, as part of the overall picture.

C. Preparing for the IEP Eligibility Meeting

After your child is assessed, the school district will schedule an IEP meeting to discuss your child's eligibility for special education. Depending on the circumstances of your case, your school district may hold off scheduling the IEP program meeting until after your child is found eligible. But if eligibility seems likely, the school district may be prepared to hold the IEP program meeting immediately after the eligibility meeting; otherwise, it must do so within 30 days of determining that your child is eligible for special education (34 C.F.R. §300.343 (b)).

The strategies for a successful IEP eligibility meeting are the same as for a successful IEP program meeting. In preparing for the IEP eligibility meeting—or the possibility of a joint IEP eligibility and program meeting—review Chapters 10 and 11.

Specific suggestions for preparing for the eligibility meeting include the following:

- **Get a copy of your child's school file.** If you don't already have a copy, see Chapter 3.
- **Get copies of all school assessments.** Assessments are covered in Chapter 6. A sample letter requesting the assessment report is in Chapter 6, Section E.
- **Know the school district's position in advance.** If the assessment report recommends eligibility, call the special education administrator and ask if the district will agree with that recommendation. If the answer is yes, ask if the IEP eligibility meeting will go right into an IEP program meeting. If the assessment report is not clear about eligibility, call the administrator and ask what the district's position is on your child's eligibility. If the assessment recommends against eligibility, be prepared to show why your child is eligible. Here are a few suggestions:

▲ *Review the school file and assessment report.* Cull out test results and other information that supports your child's eligibility.

▲ *Organize all other reports and written material that supports your position on eligibility.* Observations from teachers and teachers' aides are especially important. If possible, ask anyone who has observed your child and agrees he should be in special education to attend the IEP eligibility meeting. If a key person cannot attend, ask for a letter or written observation report.

- **Consider having your child assessed by an independent assessor.** An independent assessor may be necessary if the school district assessment report concludes that your child is not eligible for special education. Even if your child is found eligible, you may disagree with the school's recommendations regarding services and programs—many times these are spelled out in the school district's assessment report.

- **Get organized.** Have all your documentation organized by the eligibility meeting.

Chapter 8 provides tips on how to best organize existing material—and develop new information—to make your case at an IEP eligibility or program meeting. Chapter 8 also discusses how to use an independent assessor.

D. Attending the Eligibility Meeting

Many of the procedures and strategies used at the IEP eligibility meeting are similar to those used at an IEP program meeting. Chapters 10 and 11 explain how to prepare for and attend an IEP meeting. This section highlights some issues of particular relevance to eligibility meetings.

1. Who Should Attend?

Who should attend the eligibility IEP meeting depends a great deal on whether or not you anticipate a debate about eligibility. If your school district appears ready to find your child eligible for special education, then you probably don't need anyone at the meeting other than you and your child's other parent. If the school district does not agree that your child is eligible, or you don't know the district's position, you may want to ask people who can support your position to attend the meeting. Such people might include:

- an independent assessor
- your child's current teacher, and
- other professionals who may know your child.

Having any of these people attend the IEP eligibility meeting may depend on their availability, the strength of their point of view and cost. Sometimes, a letter from your pediatrician or other professional might be just as effective and certainly less expensive than paying your pediatrician to attend in person. As a general rule, do not pay others to attend the IEP eligibility meeting unless you are certain of a disagreement and the need for that participant. In most cases of disagreement, the independent assessor is most effective.

2. Preparing Your Participants

Be sure your participants are prepared to:

- describe who they are, their training and how they know your child
- discuss their conclusions about your child's eligibility for special education and why—observation, long-term knowledge of your child, testing or whatever, and
- contradict any material concluding that your child is not eligible for special education.

3. Submitting Your Eligibility Material

As you prepare for the IEP eligibility meeting and accumulate material (such as an independent assessment) supporting your child's eligibility, you are faced with the question of whether or not to provide the school district with a copy before the meeting. IDEA does not require you to do so, but consider the kind of relationship you want to establish with the school district. Certainly if you ask for the school district's assessment in advance it would only be fair to offer the district a copy of yours. Granted, you will give the school a chance to prepare a rebuttal. On the other hand, if you submit an independent assessment or other material at the IEP meeting, the school may ask to reschedule the meeting in order to review your material. In the long run, your best bet is to treat the school district as you want to be treated. If you have favorable material not in the school district's possession, submit it in advance or at least call the administrator and ask if he wants your information ahead of time.

4. Meeting Procedures

An IEP eligibility meeting generally proceeds as follows:

- general introductions
- review of school material

- review of any material you want to introduce, and
- discussion of whether or not your child qualifies for special education and, if so, on what basis.

 Chapters 10 and 11 discuss how to prepare for IEP meetings in general and write the IEP plan. Remember that IDEA requires the IEP team to carefully consider a variety of information (34 C.F.R. §300.535). As the team considers the information for or against eligibility, be sure to highlight all supportive information, pointing out specific statements.

Learning Disabilities: Special Requirements for Documenting Eligibility

IDEA requires that when an IEP team finds a child eligible for special education based on a learning disability, the team provide a written statement supporting the determination. The statement must include the following:

- basis for making the determination
- relevant behavior noted during observations of the child
- relationship of that behavior and the child's academic functioning
- degree of discrepancy between achievement and ability that cannot be corrected without special education, and
- effects of environmental, economic or cultural conditions on the child.

Each member of the IEP team must state whether the determination of eligibility reflects her own conclusion. If it does not, that member must submit a separate statement presenting her conclusions (34 C.F.R. §300.543). The purpose of this requirement is to ensure that the IEP team does not qualify a child as learning disabled based on the wrong reasons—such as economic disadvantage.

5. Outcome of Meeting

If the school district determines that your child is eligible for special education, then it will prepare for the IEP program meeting—either to happen immediately (see Section E, below) or on another date. If the school district finds that your child is not eligible for special education, see Section F, below.

E. Joint IEP Eligibility/ Program Meeting

IDEA does not prevent the school district from combining the IEP eligibility and program meetings into one. In such a situation, your child would be found eligible for special education, and then the IEP team would shift gears and immediately begin developing the IEP program—goals and objectives, program placement, services and the like. One meeting may save you time and scheduling headaches, but it also requires that you do a lot of up front preparation. If you're not ready to discuss the IEP program at the IEP eligibility meeting, ask for another meeting to give yourself time to prepare.

On the other hand, if you'd like to combine the meetings (assuming your child is found eligible), ask the school district in advance of the IEP eligibility meeting if you can develop the IEP program at that same meeting.

 A sample Request for Joint IEP Eligibility/ Program Meeting is below; a tear-out copy is in Appendix 5.

F. If Your Child Is Not Found Eligible for Special Education

You may attend the IEP eligibility meeting, point out significant information supporting your child's eligibility, argue your point worthy of Clarence Darrow and yet the school district is oblivious to it all. What then? You have two options.

1. Exercise Your Due Process Rights

As explained in Chapter 2, Section A.7, due process is your right to take any dispute you have with your child's district—whether a disagreement about an assessment, eligibility, or any part of the IEP—to a neutral third party to help you resolve your dispute. The two avenues available to you when you disagree are mediation and a hearing. See Chapter 12 for the details of due process.

2. Seek Eligibility Under Section 504 of the Rehabilitation Act

Section 504 of the federal Rehabilitation Act (29 U.S.C. §794) is a law entirely separate from IDEA. It requires all agencies that receive federal financial assistance to provide "access" to individuals with disabilities. Historically, Section 504 has been used to require public agencies to install wheelchair accessible ramps, rest rooms and other features and to provide interpreters at meetings. Section 504 also requires school districts to ensure that children with disabilities are provided access to educational programs and services through interpreters, note takers, readers and the like.

Section 504 requires your school district to have a "504 plan" to provide services to ensure that accessibility. Section 504, like IDEA, has eligibility requirements. You should contact the U.S. Department of Education, Office of Civil Rights (contact information in Appendix 2), your school district, your local community advisory committee or one of the disability groups listed in Appendix 3 for more information about Section 504.

A copy of Section 504 regulations is in Appendix 1.

Request for Joint IEP Eligibility/Program Meeting

Date: ___March 10, 19xx___

To: _Valerie Sheridan_

McKinley Unified School District

1345 South Drive

Topeka, KS 00000

Re: _Carl Ralston, student in 4th Grade, Eisenhower School_

I believe there is sufficient information for us to discuss my child's eligibility for special education and then the specific IEP goals and objectives, services and program. I would appreciate it if you would plan enough time to discuss both those important items at the ___April 14, 19xx___ IEP meeting. I would also like to see any and all reports and other written material that you will be introducing at the IEP meeting, at least two weeks before the meeting.

Thanks in advance for your help. I hope to hear from you soon.

Sincerely,

Albert Ralston

Albert Ralston

78 Elm Drive

Topeka, KS 0000078 Elm Drive

Phones: 555-1111 (home); 555-2222 (work)

8

Exploring Your Options and Making Your Case

The purpose of this chapter is to help you develop material supporting your child's IEP eligibility or program and service needs. By now, you should have a copy of your child's school file and the school district's assessment report. You should also have developed a rudimentary IEP blueprint for you child. In addition, you may have spoken to other parents, your child's teacher and classroom aide, your child's pediatrician and others who have recently observed your child. In other words, you may have a mountain of information available about your child and his educational needs.

The key to a successful IEP meeting is knowing how to develop and use information that supports your position regarding your child's educational needs. Here are some suggestions:

- Be sure you've carefully read your child's school file and the school district's assessment report.

- Keep tabs on your child's current progress in school.
- Investigate what special education programs and services are available—both in and out of the school district—that may be appropriate for your child.
- Review your binder (see Chapter 4) and blueprint (see Chapter 5) to determine what data you have relating to the specific goals you have for your child. Make a chart such as the one shown below to highlight key elements of your child's program. Note where the school district data support your position and where you have gaps—no or little information to back up eligibility or a particular program or service you feel is necessary for your child to receive an appropriate education.

Key Elements for Child's Program

Child: William Smith		
Date: June 1, 19xx		
Desired IEP Components	District Material	District Position
Placement in regular class	4-4-98 Assessment	Agrees, p. 4
1:1 aide for regular class	4-4-98 Assessment	No position
	3-12-98 Bi-Weekly Teacher Report	Teacher agrees
Adaptive Physical Ed.	5-2-98 Adaptive P.E. Assessment	Disagrees (but see comment on p. 5)

- Make a list of possible other materials you might generate to support your position, such as:
  - ▲ an independent assessment
  - ▲ a statement from your child's teacher, or
  - ▲ a statement from your child's pediatrician or other professional.

Chapter 10 provides a system for organizing all material—positive and negative—to best make your case at your child's IEP meeting.

A. Review the School District Information

As you look over your child's school file, assessment report and other school district items, consider several issues.

1. Look for the Obvious and Not So Obvious

Can you find the school district's position by simply reading your child's file and assessment report? Sometimes it's easy—for example, "Martha qualifies for special education as a student with specific learning disabilities," or "Henry needs speech therapy twice a week." Sometimes it's not so clear, such as "Henry has difficulty in producing the 'th' and 's' sounds," but no mention of needed services. Don't be surprised or upset to find more vague statements than definitive ones.

2. Sources of the School District's Data

A school district's position can be found in a variety of material. Most likely it will be in an assessment report. But you may also find the school district's position in a letter, teacher report or memo, your child's report cards or another written item in your child's file. It's possible, too,

that your child's teacher, the school assessor or other district employee has stated the school district's position in a conversation.

If the school district employee's statement supports your position, be sure to send a confirming letter. See Chapter 4, Section A.7.

3. Providers of the School District's Data

Who is saying what in the school district's material is important. They are the district's experts and their opinions will greatly influence the IEP process. Specifically, you'll want to know each person's:

- name and position—for example, a teacher, teacher's aide or assessor
- training and expertise, and
- first-hand experience with your child.

4. Changing a Report or Assessment

If there is something in your child's school file or the assessment report that is harmful to your child (and you feel is inaccurate), find out how amenable the school district is to changing the statement. Start with a phone call; for example:

"Hello Mr. Crandel, I'm Vickie Jones's father. I read your assessment and I appreciate your help in evaluating Vicki's needs. I did want to ask you a question. You say on page 4 that Vickie does not need help with her reading comprehension. Did you see the teacher's report (or anything else that supports your point of view)?"

To make a formal request for a change, see Chapter 3, Section B.5 (changing something in a school file), and Chapter 6, Section E (changing a draft assessment report).

B. Keep Tabs on Your Child's Progress

As you prepare for an IEP eligibility or program meeting, take some time to learn how your child is currently doing in school—regular or special education. If your child is doing poorly in school and you're preparing for an IEP eligibility meeting, you'll want to describe at the IEP meeting exactly how your child is floundering. If you are preparing for an IEP program meeting, be ready to explain why the current program is right for your child or why it needs changing.

Here are a few suggestions for getting current information about your child.

- Ask the teacher, teacher's aide and service provider for periodic reports focusing on key areas of need for your child—reading, behavior, language development, social interaction, spelling, physical mobility and the like.
- Ask the teacher for samples and reports of your child's work.
- Visit your child's class (see Section C, below).
- Set up periodic meetings with your child's teacher. If your child already has an IEP, ask the teacher if and how the current IEP goals and objectives are being met.

Example:

One current IEP objective is that your child read a three-paragraph story and demonstrate 80% comprehension by answering questions. Ask the teacher first, if your child can read a three-paragraph story. Then ask what your child's reading comprehension level is. If it's not up to 80%, where is it—60%? 40%? 20%?

To easily organize this material, you can create a chart which your child's teacher can complete on a regular (such as monthly) basis, updating your child's progress in key areas such as math, reading, behavior and motor development, as well as emotional and psychological issues and self-help skills.

A sample Progress Chart is below; a tear-out copy is in Appendix 5. You can tailor this chart to your child's particular goals and objectives. This form will help you track progress generally and goals and objectives specifically. See Chapter 9 for more details on developing goals and objectives.

C. Explore Available School Programs

To prepare for the IEP program meeting, you will want to gather information about your child's existing program and other possible programs that may be appropriate for your child. Information gathering is crucial.

The possible programs include:

- placement in a regular classroom, perhaps with support services—ask about local options, including your child's neighborhood school
- placement in a program specifically designed for children with learning disabilities, difficulties with communication or other disabling conditions—ask about special day classes at your neighborhood school, nearby schools or other schools in the area, or
- placement in a specialized program, such as a private school or residential program—ask what programs exist where.

1. Ask About Available Programs

Contact your child's teacher, the school assessor, the district special education administrator, other parents, your PTA and local community advisory committee. Ask about programs generally used for children with similar needs.

Don't be surprised if the school administrator (or even the classroom teacher) is reluctant to tell you about programs. You may hear, for example,

Progress Chart

Student: Mary Hamilton

Class: Ms. Frank's 3rd Grade

Date: February 23, 19xx

Key Goals and Objectives	Current Status	Comments
Math	Progressing appropriately? [X] yes [ ] no	On schedule to complete goals and objectives
Reading	Progressing appropriately? [X] yes [ ] no	On schedule to complete goals and objectives. Need to improve reading fluidity.
Writing	Progressing appropriately? [X] yes [ ] no	On schedule to complete goals and objectives.
Spelling	Progressing appropriately? [ ] yes [X] no	Reversals continue to be problem.
Social-Behavioral	Progressing appropriately? [ ] yes [X] no	Still problems with focus; hard time not teasing others.
Language development	Progressing appropriately? [X] yes [ ] no	On schedule, but some problems going from specific to general.
Motor development	Progressing appropriately? [ ] yes [X] no	Small motor problems affecting handwriting.
Other	Progressing appropriately? [ ] yes [X] no	When struggling with spelling and handwriting, seems to feel high level of stress.

"It is way too early to be looking at programs for next year, Mr. and Mrs. Smith. We've just started this year." Or "We don't think it is appropriate to discuss programs until the IEP team meets and goals and objectives are drafted. Then we can talk about programs."

While there is some truth to these assertions, emphasize that you are not looking to change programs or for an IEP decision—you are merely trying to gather information. You might respond, "I appreciate what you are saying, Ms. Casey, but it will be most helpful to me and my child to begin as early as possible to plan ahead. I am not looking to change programs or for a commitment on your part. Is there a problem with me gathering information about programs in the district?"

2. Visit Programs

While a school administrator may provide you with some information about existing programs, she may be reluctant for you to actually visit a program before the IEP meeting. While it may be that the IEP team won't know what program will fit your child until after you have the IEP meeting, nothing in IDEA prevents you from visiting

potential programs before the meeting, provided your requests are reasonable.

If the administrator continues to refuse to let you visit programs, put your concerns in writing.

A sample Program Visitation Request letter is below; a tear-out copy is in Appendix 5.

Obviously, you don't need a school administrator's permission to visit private programs in the area. Simply call and schedule your own appointments.

If the administrator still refuses your request, don't give up. Indicate that you understand her concerns, but feel that you could not possibly make a decision in the IEP about placement without some basic information about the programs being offered. Make it clear that you are more than willing to visit programs again after the IEP meeting.

If you get nowhere, contact the administrator's superior. If that fails, you can file a complaint with your state department of education or other appropriate educational agency as discussed in Chapter 13. It is possible the complaint will not be processed until after the IEP meeting. You'll have to decide whether to postpone the IEP or

Program Visitation Request Letter

Date: _April 6, 19xx_

To: _Mr. John White, Special Education Administrator_

Carlson Unified School District

8709 Fourth Street

Helena, MT 00000

Re: _Elizabeth Moore_

I appreciate the concerns you have and realize you can't know what programs are appropriate for my child until after the IEP meeting. Nonetheless, I think it would be very helpful for me to see existing programs so I can be a more effective member of the IEP team. I do not feel I can make an informed IEP decision without seeing, firsthand, all possible options. I want to assure you that I understand that by giving me the names of existing programs, you are not stating an opinion as to their appropriateness for my child.

I assure you that I will abide by all rules and regulations for parental visits. If those rules and regulations are in writing, please send me a copy.

Thanks in advance for your help. I hope to hear from you soon.

Sincerely,

Arnette Moore

Arnette Moore

87 Mission Road

Helena, MT 00087

Phones: 555-3334 (home); 555-4455 (work)

ask at the IEP meeting to see the programs after the meeting. In that case, you may not be ready to sign the IEP. See Chapter 11, Section E, on signing the IEP.

a. When to Visit Programs

Ideally, you will want to visit programs in the fall of the school year. While it may seem logical to visit right before the IEP meeting, the earlier you see possible program options—including your child's current one—the better.

- The sooner you see a particular program, the sooner you'll have a sense of whether or not it is appropriate for your child.
- If you can't judge the appropriateness of a program, there will be time for others, such as an independent assessor, to take a look and give you their opinion.
- You'll have time to visit a program more than once, and you should, if it's necessary.

b. Visitation Guidelines

The purpose of your visits is to gather information. As you plan your visits, keep in mind these points:

- Ask to visit *all* program options.
- Observe all policies and rules established by the school district, school site administrator and teacher.
- If an independent assessor or other professional will attend the IEP meeting, it is a good idea to have him visit with you. Be sure to inform the school district.
- Do not ask for any personal information about the students, such as names of individual children. A teacher should *not* give you this information. You can (and should) talk with any parents you know who have children in the possible programs.
- Secure as much detail as possible about each program or class. This is basically the same information as your blueprint (Chapter 5):

  ▲ student description (number of students in the program; students' disabilities, age, cognitive range and language range)
  ▲ staff description (details on teachers and aides)
  ▲ teacher-student instruction: teacher-to-class, small group or individual
  ▲ curricula, methodology and other teaching strategies used
  ▲ classroom environment: behavior problems, noise level, number of teachers and teacher aides and how much time teacher aides are in class
  ▲ related services: how many children leave the class to go to another program and how often; how many children receive related services in the class, and
  ▲ any other comments you have on the program.

  Although IDEA does not require that the teacher provide you with this information, you should ask in a pleasant, matter-of-fact way. If the teacher balks, indicate the information you seek is important and noncontroversial, and should be made available.
- Write down your observations and the answers to your questions. You can write as you watch the class and talk to the teacher. If you "interview" the teacher with notebook in hand and pencil poised, however, the teacher may be intimidated. By admitting, "I have a poor memory; do you mind if I take notes while we talk?" you may put the teacher at ease. If not, try to take notes in an unobtrusive way or wait until you're outside and write down what you remember as soon as possible.

A sample Class Visitation Checklist is below; a tear-out copy is in Appendix 5. Be sure to keep copies of this important form in your IEP binder.

Class Visitation Checklist

Date: _9/11/99_ Time: _9:00-10:15_ a.m./p.m.

School: _Jefferson School, Chicago_

Class: _3rd Grade Special Day Class for Learning Disabled (Teacher: Sue Avery)_

Student Description:

Total students: _17_ Gender range: _12 boys; 5 girls_

Age range: _7 - 10 (ten kids are nine or younger; seven ten-year olds)_

Cognitive range: _"Wide range; probably from pre-K through 5th grade skills," says S. Avery (teacher)_

Language/communication range: _Two students with hearing impairment; two other students with delayed communication skills (1st grade level)_

Disability range: _12 students have specific learning disability, three are borderline retarded, one has emotional disturbance and one autistic-like behavior_

Behavioral range: _Five students acting out throughout class, four other students constantly demanding of teacher. Two students sent to principal because of behavior. Rest of class generally cooperative, quiet._

Other observations: _Overall impression was of a class of children with varied needs and behavior, which made it difficult for the teacher to focus on any one group of children for very long._

Staff Description:

Teachers: _Sue Avery has four years' experience working with learning disabled children. She was generally very patient with students (less so with the behaviorally troubled children), but she seemed easily distracted._

Aides: _In class two hours per day; worked with all children, no one child more than few minutes. Seemed mostly to superficially check in with students, but not provide any sustained 1:1 help. Aide has no specific training working with learning disabled children._

Other observations: _Neither teacher nor aide seemed fully comfortable with curriculum, particularly given varied needs of students. Both were very nice to students._

Curricula/Classroom Strategies:

Curricula: "Using Mathematics," (Book 2) for math, teacher-developed materials for spelling and "Project Explore" for science lessons.

Strategies: Teacher/aide when working 1:1 in reading divided words into simple sounds using much repetition; no overall strategy or specific curriculum designed for learning disabled children.

Classroom Environment:

Description: Classroom had tiled floor so sound echoed. Quite loud; no other apparent acoustical treatment to reduce noise; all added to a noisy room. Various work stations and cubicles set up so students can work 1:1 or by themselves. Somewhat effective, but noise was distracting to all students. Classroom situated near playground, so much visual stimulation outside classroom window and noise from outside.

Related Services:

At least four students received their related services in class, one had speech therapy, another had a special aide that worked with her in the corner.

Other Comments:

School site principal (Lee Parsons) is interested in special education, but has no training or expertise in the field. She did express reservations about excessive mainstreaming of children with disabilities into regular classrooms. Visited one mainstreamed class, teacher seemed interested, but expressed concern that the school had not provided any support or training for dealing with special education students in her regular class.

How This Program Relates to IEP Blueprint:

Program does not meet Tara's blueprint:

- Cognitive and behavioral range of students too wide
- Teacher unable to provide individual attention
- Aide not trained for working with L-D kids
- Question about curriculum

D. Find Out About Related Services

Classroom programs are only one component of your child's IEP program. Another is related services, such as occupational, physical or speech therapy, discussed in Chapter 2.

Gathering information about related services will be a little different from gathering information about programs. You'll still want to talk to your child's teacher, the school assessor, the district special education administrator, other parents, your PTA and a local parent group for disabled children to find out about related services for children with similar needs. But the similarities end there.

Service providers, such as a physical therapist, usually work one-on-one with individual children or in small groups. So visiting these specialists in action may not be possible. Instead, when you talk to people about the services available, ask about the background, training and experience of the specialists. Candid conversations with other parents should be most helpful.

Keep detailed notes of your conversations and include them in your IEP binder.

E. Compare Your Blueprint With the Existing Program and Services

Once you have information about your school district's programs and services, you will want to compare what's available to what you believe your child needs. Obviously, if the school provides services you feel will meet your child's needs (the blueprint), the IEP process should be relatively simple. On the other hand, if there is a gap between what your child needs and what is available, you face the task of convincing the IEP team that the school options are inappropriate.

You'll need to detail the shortcomings of the programs and services offered by the school district. Be as specific as possible: Is the problem the frequency or location of a service, the pupil-teacher ratio, the qualifications of the teacher or service provider, the specific work to be done with a service provider, the class make-up, the teacher methodology or curriculum or anything else important?

In short, make a comprehensive side-by-side comparison of your blueprint and what you know about the school's options, and put the details on the bottom of the Class Visitation Checklist.

F. Generate Additional Supporting Information

Once you've reviewed your child's school file, developed your blueprint, reviewed the school assessment, evaluated your child's progress and gathered information about program and service options, you may need further data to support your goals—whether it's your child's eligibility or a particular program or service. This material will be invaluable in preparing for the IEP meeting.

1. Help From School Personnel

Contact any teachers, assessors or service providers who you feel are likely to support your position. You can do this by phone or in person. Explain what programs and services you want for your child (your blueprint), and why you feel they are appropriate. Note any discrepancy between what you want and what you believe the school district has available. Explain why you want what you want for your child and ask for their ideas and opinions.

Ask if the teacher, assessor or service provider would be willing to write a statement supporting what you want for your child or state his position at the IEP meeting.

If the person supports your point of view, but doesn't want to put anything in writing, follow up the conversation with a confirming letter (see Chapter 4, Section A), such as: "Thank you for the chance to chat today. I appreciate your frankness and was glad to hear that you agree that Max needs an aide in order to function effectively in the regular class."

Be aware that a confirming letter can put the teacher in an awkward position. If the teacher says one thing to you (and you confirm it in a letter) and then says another thing at the IEP meeting, the letter may be important proof of what was originally said—but this may lead to some friction between you and the teacher. If the teacher changes tunes at the IEP meeting and will not speak frankly, however, the confirming letter will show another side.

No matter what, be sure to keep notes of what was said, by whom and when with as much detail as possible. This is your record in case the school representative changes his mind later on.

2. Help From People Outside the School

Anyone who knows your child, has some expertise in special education or your child's disability may be of value. This includes your child's doctor, tutor, therapist or other specialist.

Ask each person to write a letter to the IEP team stating:

- how she knows your child
- her specific expertise
- specific comments on your child's condition that relates to the educational experience, and
- her recommendation for your child in terms of program, service or other IEP component.

Example:

"Teresa needs extensive help with small and large motor skills and should work with an occupational and physical therapist at least three times a week."

G. Independent Assessments

An independent assessment of your child may be the most important document supporting what you want for your child. An independent assessment, like the school district's assessment, can be as comprehensive or as narrow as your child's needs dictate. In most cases, an independent assessment will use a variety of tests to evaluate your child's needs.

Chapter 6 discusses assessments in general, and Chapter 11 covers how to present an independent assessment at the IEP meeting.

Under IDEA, you have an absolute right to have an independent assessment of your child. Moreover, your school district is required to provide you with information on where such an assessment may be obtained (34 C.F.R. §300.502(a)).

While IDEA requires that the results of the independent assessment be considered by the school district in any decision regarding your child's education, it does not require that your school district agree with the results. While an independent assessment may include persuasive information, your child's school district can reject the conclusions. (You do have the right to go to due process (mediation session or hearing) to prove the district is wrong. See Chapter 12.)

Independent assessments can be expensive. Under certain circumstances, IDEA requires that the school district pay for your independent assessment with important qualifications. See Section G.7, below, for the details.

1. When to Use an Independent Assessment

You may want an independent assessment because you need more information about your child or, as we noted, because the school district's assessment does not support what you want.

Before you hire an independent assessor, be certain about this. If the district's position is clear—and you disagree with it—an outside assessment may very well be needed.

2. Finding Independent Assessors

Independent assessors generally are either in private practice or affiliated with hospitals, universities or other large institutions. How do you find a qualified independent assessor?

- **Ask parents of children with similar disabilities.** Check with the PTA or your school district's advisory committee of parents with children in special education.
- **Get recommendations from the school.** A trusted teacher, aide, service provider or other school employee may give you the names of independent assessors.
- **Talk to your child's pediatrician.**
- **Call a local hospital, particularly a university medical hospital.** A department which employs experts in your child's disability may be able to do the assessment or refer you to an independent assessor.
- **Contact an organization that specializes in your child's particular disability.** See Appendix 3.
- **Call local private schools for disabled children.** Private schools often work with credible independent assessors.

How Not to Find an Independent Assessor

Assessors are often psychologists. If you look in the phone book, you will see a long list of psychologists. Choosing randomly from the phone book is a poor method for selecting a reputable and knowledgeable assessor.

3. Selecting the Right Assessor

Speak to various independent assessors, and ask the following questions for each person:

- Does the assessor have significant expertise, training and experience in dealing with your child's disability?
- Is the assessor affiliated with a well-respected institution?
- Were you referred by someone who actually worked with the assessor?
- Do you trust the person (or institution) who recommended the assessor?
- Will the assessor give you references?
- Did the assessor's references like the results of the assessor's work and find the assessor easy to work with?
- Is the assessor impartial? (An assessor who has previously done work for your child's school district and been paid by the school district, may not be truly independent.)
- Can the assessor complete the assessment and written report well in advance of the IEP meeting?
- Can the assessor attend the IEP meeting, if necessary?

The answers to these questions, your own sense of the individual and recommendations from others are key factors in making your decision. It is also important that the independent assessor is able to clearly articulate her position and not be afraid to state that position professionally and vigorously.

4. Getting an Independent Assessor on Your Side

The reason you are hiring an independent assessor is to support your goals for your child concerning her educational needs. Be very clear on your plans and perspectives.

Examples:

- You have very specific desires (your blue-print) concerning the related service you believe is best for your child—you know what you want in terms of type, amount and duration of service, type of service provider, and teacher-pupil setting you want. Be sure the assessor makes the recommendations that support the program and services you want for your child: "Given Michelle's need to develop expressive speech, she requires speech therapy four times a week, each session of 50 minutes. She also needs one-to-one work with a qualified speech therapist experienced in working with children who have an expressive language delay."

- You want your son placed in a school for children with emotional disturbances. Ideally, the assessor will write, "Philip requires placement in a program with no more than ten children, a full-time aide, a teacher qualified to work with emotionally troubled children in a class where there are no behavioral problems. The Woodson School in Boston is the only program that can meet Philip's needs."

If the assessor can't or won't name a specific school or program, then make sure she will name the specific components of an appropriate program. Continuing the example above, if the independent assessor won't say Philip needs to be placed in the Woodson School, she should say that he needs placement in a program that has the characteristics of the Woodson School.

It is of course possible that your goals may not be supported by the data. A good assessor will not write something he disagrees with or make a recommendation he does not believe in. A good assessor will tell you when the evidence—the testing data—does not support what you want. This means you want an assessor who will:

- show you a draft assessment report
- consider your concerns about the draft report

- make specific recommendations about your child's educational status and appropriate programs and related services to meet your child's needs, and
- provide written rationale for these recommendations.

5. How an Independent Assessment Proceeds

Most independent assessors will meet with you, review your child's school file, the school district's assessment and other district material. The assessor will then explain to you what testing will be done, secure your approval, do the testing and prepare a report. Depending on your child's characteristics and needs, the assessor may also want to observe her in class.

6. When to Submit the Independent Assessment

Just as you want to review the school district's assessments before the IEP meeting, the school district will likely want to see your independent assessment before the IEP meeting. Of course, the more time the school has to review the independent assessment, the more time the administration will have to find data to counter its conclusions. Does this mean you should delay giving the school district your assessment? While such a strategy has its attractions, the bottom line is that the school district is entitled to the same courtesy that you are.

Holding off on giving the district a copy of your assessment could ultimately prove counter-productive. The district may distrust you and your assessment. The delay may be grounds for postponing the IEP meeting. And your relationship with the district may be affected. Because you will likely be working together for many years, maintain a positive relationship, if possible. If one party will be nasty, unfair or untrustworthy, let it be someone other than you. While there is no hard-and-fast rule here, providing the independent assessment (and other key material) a week before the IEP meeting is appropriate.

7. Cost of an Independent Assessment

Independent assessments can be quite costly, anywhere from several hundred dollars to several thousand dollars.

But you may not have to pay for the assessment. Under IDEA, a parent has the right to an independent educational evaluation of her child (by an assessor of your choosing) at public expense if you disagree with an evaluation obtained by the school district. The school district must pay for that independent assessment unless it exercises its due process rights under IDEA and convinces the hearing officer that the school district evaluation was appropriate (34 C.F.R. §300.502(b)). This part of IDEA is not often used by schools.

While it is rare that a school district proceeds to due process on the issue of paying for an independent assessment, that is not to say that a school district won't pursue due process and won't prevail. The district has to show only that its own evaluation was appropriate, normally demonstrated by evidence that the assessment included the necessary tests, the assessor was properly trained and knowledgeable and your child was evaluated in all areas of suspected disability.

So the real problem for parents is how to get the district to pay for the assessment, particularly since IDEA does not require the school district to pay in advance or provide assurances that it will pay for the independent assessment. If you want the school district to pay, you will probably have to pay the assessor yourself and seek reimbursement from the district.

Here are some ideas on how to get the district to pay.

- Ask the assessor to bill the school district directly. Because the assessor wants to be paid, however, she may not be willing to do this. But there's no harm in asking.
- If the assessor won't bill the district, pay her bill and submit a copy to the district, with a statement that IDEA requires the district to pay unless it pursues due process. Reference the law, too (34 C.F.R. §300.502).
- If the district doesn't go to due process and still won't pay, file a complaint as discussed in Chapter 13. ∎

9

Writing Goals and Objectives

Goals and objectives are the nuts and bolts of your child's education. These are the general academic, cognitive, linguistic, social and vocational aims you have for your child (goals) and the specific work items (objectives) needed to reach those goals. Objectives focus on the precise skill accomplishment for a broader goal. In other words, they are the skills your child must master to reach a stated goal. An IEP program may include one or many objectives for each broad goal.

Examples:

Goal. Tim will improve his reading comprehension.

Objective. Tim will read a four-paragraph story and demonstrate 75% comprehension using objective classroom tests.

Goal. Ellen will improve her peer relationships.

Objective. Ellen will initiate three positive peer interactions per day, per teacher observation.

Goal. Juan will master all third grade math skills.

Objective. Juan will identify sets of ones and tens with 90% accuracy, using appropriate textbook tests.

Goal. Jane will improve her writing skills.

Objective. Jane will write a three-sentence paragraph with subject and predicate sentences, per teacher evaluation.

Goal. Mark will improve short-term auditory memory.

Objective. Mark will be able to listen to a set of ten related items and list them with 75% accuracy.

Goals and objectives are intimately related to your child's IEP program. IDEA requires that an IEP program include a statement of measurable annual goals, including benchmarks or short-term objectives for two reasons (34 C.F.R. §300.347(a)(2)):
- so that the child is involved in and progressing in the general curriculum, and
- to meet the child's other educational needs that result from the child's disability.

Since IDEA requires the school district to provide an appropriate education for your child, the question underlying many IEP decisions is, "Can this child's goals and objectives be met in a specific program or with a particular related service?" The school's ability to meet the goals and objectives may very well determine whether the education provided is an appropriate one.

What Goals and Objectives Are Not

- Goals and objectives are not for students who are in regular education. They are written for special education students—even special education students mainstreamed into regular classes.
- Goals and objectives are not part of a contract between you and the school district—that is, the school is not legally liable if your child does not meet his goals and objectives. Goals and objectives are a way to measure your child's progress.
- Goals and objectives are not your child's instructional plan. They are important aims to be accomplished during the school year.

A. Areas Covered by Goals and Objectives

Goals and objectives can cover a wide variety of skill or need areas. If your child is not having difficulties in certain areas, however, the IEP team typically will not develop goals and objectives in those areas.

The wide range of areas for which goals and objectives may be written include the following:

- academic skills, such as math computation, reading comprehension, spelling and writing
- cognitive skills, such as abstract thinking and memory skills
- emotional and psychological issues, such as overcoming fears or improving self-esteem
- social-behavioral skills, such as relating to peers
- linguistic and communication skills, such as expressing oneself effectively
- self-help and independent living skills, such as using money, dressing or toileting, using transportation
- physical and recreational skills, such as improving fine and large motor skills, and
- vocational skills, such as work skill development.

B. Developing Goals and Objectives

IDEA does not specify how to write goals and objectives, what subjects to cover, how many to include or how to implement or measure them. The details of your child's goals and objectives are up to the IEP team and are included in the IEP program. This flexibility allows you to develop goals and objectives useful for your child with the programs and services you want for your child.

This section describes the typical elements of goals and objectives.

A sample Goals and Objectives form appears later in this chapter. Also, see the section on goals and objectives in the sample IEP in Appendix 4.

1. Child's Present Level of Performance

The IEP program should spell out your child's current level of skill in each particular goal-objective area. For example, with a reading comprehension goal and objective, a child's present level of performance may state, "Beth's current reading comprehension is at the mid-fourth grade level. She enjoys reading, but requires help in maintaining focus."

2. Who Implements Goals and Objectives

Normally, your child's classroom teacher is responsible for implementing your child's goals and objectives, Depending on the goal and objectives, however, an aide or support professional may also be involved. For example:

- A child's language goals-objectives may be the responsibility of a speech therapist.
- Physical education or motor goals, such as handwriting improvement, may be the responsibility of an occupational or physical therapist.
- Emotional goals and objectives may be covered by a school counselor or therapist.

3. Completion Dates for Goals and Objectives

Goals and objectives are normally written for a one-year period, but this is not set in stone. In fact, because objectives are concrete, bite-sized, do-able tasks, by their very nature they may be completed in less than a year.

Example

Lily is in a special day class with no mainstreaming in a regular classroom. Her IEP reading goal and objective has a completion time of one year. Lily's parent feels she can reach her reading goal and objective in a shorter time if she is in a regular classroom. Establishing a shorter period may be crucial in mainstreaming Lily.

4. Measuring Goals and Objectives

There are a number of ways to measure goals and objectives, including objective testing, teacher or other staff observation, assessment of work samples or any other method agreed to by the IEP team. Many IEP goals and objectives include a quantifiable accomplishment level, such as "Mia will read a four-paragraph story with 90% reading comprehension as measured by the Woodcock Reading Mastery Test."

Beware of Setting Your Objectives Too Low

Be careful if an IEP team member from the school district suggests setting your child's objectives fairly low. It may be because the school wants to keep your child in a special day class rather than a regular class, or wants to eliminate a particular support service, such as a one-on-one aide.

IDEA does not require that a goal and objective necessarily be a quantifiable aim—that is, reduced to something measured in numbers. Granted, numbers can be of value, but not everything of value can be reduced to numbers. For example, how does one measure numerically whether a goal and objective was met in areas relating to emotions, psychology, self-help or vocational skills?

Example:

As a part of Sue's IEP program, Sue will explore whether she wants to go to college or begin work right after high school. As goals and objectives, these are stated as follows:

Goal. Sue will explore at least five areas of vocational interest.

Objective. Sue will read about five areas of vocational interest, write a brief explanation of each and visit local examples of each.

The best ways to "measure" Sue's achievement may be teacher observation or Sue's completion of a personal diary.

C. When to Draft Goals and Objectives

While specific goals and objectives are approved at the IEP meeting by their insertion into the IEP program, it makes sense to draft them ahead of time.

In fact, it is not uncommon for school representatives to write goals and objectives in advance. Under IDEA, the school cannot simply present them at the IEP meeting, refuse to discuss other goals and objectives and insist that you accept their goals and objectives. That would violate a basic tenet of IDEA—that the IEP team make all IEP decisions. Still, you should anticipate that the school district might draft goals and objectives in advance. Be prepared for the IEP meeting by asking the school district, in writing, for a copy of any pre-drafted goals and objectives at least two weeks before the IEP meeting.

You, too, should draft goals and objectives in advance of the IEP meeting. You do not have to give a copy to the school district before the IEP meeting, unless you are asked for them, which would be unlikely.

Even if you aren't asked for a copy, you can give your goals and objectives to the school district in advance. Some advocates might argue against doing this because it gives the district time to counter your goals and objectives. Others would disagree with this point of view, because the school administrator might say, "We appreciate your giving us these goals and objectives, but we will need to reschedule the IEP so we can review them."

In general, we think it best to be open and provide the school district information in advance, unless the element of surprise is necessary in your particular situation.

D. Writing Effective Goals and Objectives

Writing goals and objectives for the first or second time may seem as foreign to you as writing a medicine prescription or nuclear physics equation. They aren't. Like much of the IEP process, writing goals and objectives involves information gathering, asking questions and a little practice.

1. Get Your School's IEP Form

Every school district has its own form on which the IEP program is written, and as we've mentioned earlier in this book, you should get a copy and any guidelines that accompany it. As you begin to draft your child's goals and objectives—even if this is her tenth year in special education—refer to the school's current IEP form for guidance.

2. Gather Your Information in One Place

Your dining room table or desk may be overrun with special education papers. If they are not already organized in a binder (as recommended in Chapter 4), take some time to gather them together. Specifically, get the following:
- your child's school file
- all assessment reports
- written reports from professionals, and
- your blueprint.

Start with your blueprint—your desires for your child's education. The goals and objectives should support what's in your blueprint. While the blueprint won't show you how to write

specific goals and objectives, it will help you think about what you ultimately want for your child.

3. Talk to Professionals

Talk with your child's teacher, other support staff, your independent assessor, service providers and others who know your child. They might be willing to suggest specific goals and objectives or at least to review yours.

If this is your child's first IEP, ask the professionals what areas your goals and objectives should cover and how to make them as specific as possible. Be sure to explore with them all the areas that you feel require goals and objectives.

If this is not your child's first IEP, ask professionals the following questions.
- What previous goals and objectives should be retained?
- If previous goals and objectives are carried over, why were they not accomplished before? What can be done to better insure completion this year? Using the Progress Chart in Chapter 8, Section B, will help you monitor goals and objectives throughout the year.
- What new goals and objectives should be developed?

By talking with your child's teacher and other staff members about goals and objectives, you may sense what they feel about your child's placement and services. You may also develop an agreement on goals and objectives in preparation for the IEP meeting.

4. Talk to Other Parents

If you know other special education families, ask to see their IEPs, particularly if their child's needs are similar to your child's. Even if the needs are not the same, other parents may have very valuable information about how to draft goals and objectives; many are probably old pros at writing goals and objectives.

Also, check with the PTA or school district's local advisory committee on special education for written material on goals and objectives, for advice and for the names of any local individuals or organizations that provide help to special education parents. Chapter 15 discusses parent organizations.

Finally, check Appendix 3 for support organizations you can contact for help.

5. List Your Goals and Objectives Areas

Your job is to develop general goals and specific objectives for each skill area that relates directly to your child's needs. We listed eight such areas in Section A, above. Be as precise as possible. For example, don't simply state "academic achievement." Specify reading, writing, math, cognitive, spelling and the rest. Under social-behavioral, you might specify peer goals and objectives as well as self-control goals and objectives.

A sample Goals and Objectives Chart is below; Appendix 5 includes a tear-out copy. This chart is intended to give you a feel for what goals and objectives look like and provide you with language often used for different types of goals and objectives. Also, be sure to see the sample IEP form in Appendix 4.

6. Compare Your Goals and Objectives Areas to Your Child's Education

An ideal goal and objective would make a direct and clear reference to the program and services you desire for your child. In fact, the goals and objectives in our sample form do just this. In the case of Leah, the sample is very descriptive—a "small and protected educational environment" and "in a quiet and safe school environment." While not all goals and objectives are written this way—schools often argue that the goals and objectives area is not the place to mention program or services—IDEA does not prevent such added language, you should argue for it, and at a minimum, include it in your draft goals and objectives.

Goals and Objectives Chart

Skill Area	Annual Goal	Short-Term Objective (or Benchmark)	Present Performance Level	How Progress Measured	Date of Completion
Reading	Ted, in a special day class of no more than 10 students, will improve reading comprehension.	Ted will demonstrate 90% comprehension of three-paragraph stories from the fourth grade reading text.	Ted demonstrates 50% comprehension of a two-paragraph story from the fourth grade reading text.	End-of-chapter questions in the reading text.	June 2000
Math	Bob, in his mainstreamed class, will master fourth grade math skills.	Bob will subtract a one-digit number from a two-digit number, with 90% accuracy.	Bob subtracts a one-digit number from a two-digit number 25% of the time.	Teacher material	June 2000
Emotional and psychological	Leah, in a class of no more than 12 students in a small and protected educational environment, will reduce her outward anger.	Because Leah is adversely affected by acting out behavior of others, she will, in a quiet and safe school environment, develop a better self-awareness of her anger and reduce her angry outbursts from five to two a day.	Leah averages five daily angry outbursts as observed.	Teacher and therapist observation and recording.	June 2000

Skill Area	Annual Goal	Short-Term Objective (or Benchmark)	Present Performance Level	How Progress Measured	Date of Completion
Social-behavioral	Sara will improve her peer relationships.	With the support of her aide and in a class of no more than ten students, Sara will initiate three positive peer interactions per day.	Sara is unable to initiate positive peer interactions.	Teacher-aide observation and recording.	June 2000
Linguistic and communication	Adam, in his tri-weekly, 45 minute, one-to-one speech therapy sessions, will improve articulation.	Adam will produce the s, sh and c sounds.	Adam produces the s, sh and c sounds irregularly.	Speech therapist observation and recording.	June 2000
Self-help and independent living skills (transition services)	Nina will develop independent living skills.	Nina, with the support of her regular classroom peers, will be able to purchase her lunch in the school cafeteria, make change, locate her school bus and take that bus home.	Nina cannot make change and is unable to ask for help in locating her bus.	Teacher and other staff observation and recording.	June 2000

When including references to a specific program or service, be as precise as you can. If you can mention the name of a special school or the detail of the service, so much the better. If you don't have the exact information, then add something that will describe your broad IEP program goals.

The key here is to write the goals and objectives so that an objective person will conclude that your child will need the particular program or service to meet the goals and objectives. Even if the school district doesn't include the language in the final goals and objectives, you can use your draft as a reminder of what you want.

The examples are intended to give you a sense of how goals and objectives can be used to more effectively support your program and service goals. Look at your blueprint, think about the program and service hopes you have for your child, consider her skill areas and then take out a pad of paper and pencil and play around with language to be used for your goals and objectives.

Write a variety of goals and objectives for each skill area, incorporating specific language and reference to the desired program and services. Then write a second set, omitting references to the program and services, but describing the programs and services you want. For example, let us assume you want your child in a regular class-room with a one-to-one aide in order to improve her reading comprehension. The ideal goal would be, "Mary, in Ms. Jones's regular third grade class at Spencer School, will improve her reading comprehension, using her full-time one-to-one aide." The alternative method would be, "With the assistance of her one-to-one aide and by modeling her regular peers, Mary will improve her reading comprehension." If the school district disagrees that Mary should be mainstreamed, suggest implicit, instead of explicit, language, such as "modeling her regular peers."

Ultimately, the IEP team will either agree or disagree on the goals and objectives. Do your best to make the goals and objectives as "blueprint-specific" as possible. ■

10

Preparing for the IEP Meeting

Preparing for the IEP meeting will make you a better advocate for your child, allow you to effectively influence the IEP meeting agenda and reduce your own anxieties. In short, preparation increases your chances of success.

If you are attending your first IEP meeting, it is important to read this entire chapter. If you've done IEPs before, you'll want to at least skim this chapter. There are suggestions that even the most experienced IEP participants may not have considered.

Everything in this book is intended to prepare you for the IEP meeting. If you've skipped any of the following chapters, go back and read them before reading this chapter.

- Chapter 2—Understanding your child's legal rights to special education and obtaining a copy of your school district's IEP form.
- Chapter 3—Gathering and evaluating your child's school records.
- Chapter 4—Organizing assessments, teacher reports and other important information; developing an IEP binder and planning the IEP process.
- Chapter 5—Developing a blueprint of the program and services you want for your child.
- Chapter 6—Preparing for your child's assessment.
- Chapter 8—Developing supportive material from the school and other sources, such as an independent assessor; exploring your options as to programs and related services.
- Chapter 9—Writing goals and objectives.

If you're preparing for an IEP eligibility meeting, be sure to read Chapter 7 for advice.

A. Establish the Location, Date and Time of the IEP Meeting

IDEA sets out rules on the basics of the IEP meeting (34 C.F.R. §§300.343, 300.345):

- It must be held at a time and location convenient for all parties, especially the

parents. The school district cannot simply set a meeting in the morning when you are at work or pick a time without your input.
- It must be held at least once a year.
- It must be long enough to cover all issues.

Do You Need an Interpreter?

The school district must take necessary steps to ensure that you understand the IEP proceedings, including hiring an interpreter if you are deaf or hard of hearing or if your first language is not English. Be sure to let the school district know in advance if you need an interpreter at the IEP meeting.

1. Date of the IEP Meeting

As discussed in Chapter 4, ideally you want your IEP meeting in the spring, preceding the school year for which you are developing the IEP plan. In setting a date, you may have to make several calls to the district administrator and your attendees to make sure all key people can attend. Once you've set the date, give yourself at least a month to prepare for the meeting.

2. Time Budgeted for the IEP Meeting

Although IDEA does not require that the IEP meeting be for a specific length of time, check in advance with the school administrator to find out how much time has been put aside. Two or three hours is common. If the administrator has allotted less time than you think is necessary, explain why you think a longer meeting is needed, particularly if it may eliminate the need for a second meeting. If the administrator insists that the time allotted is enough, put your concerns in writing and send a copy to the superintendent of schools. If you're really concerned, you can file a complaint (see

Chapter 13), but there is no IDEA rule that the IEP be a certain length of time.

Sample Letter Requesting More Time for IEP Meeting

Date: September 28, 19xx

To: Ms. Julia Warner
    Director of Special Education
    Monroe School District
    892 South 4th Street
    Salem, OR 00000

Re: Karen Jamison, student in 1st grade class
    of Drew Bergman

You indicated that we had one hour for my daughter Karen's October 14th IEP meeting. As I mentioned on September 27, I believe we have several issues to discuss and will require at least two hours. It would be a hardship on our family to attend two meetings.

I will be calling you within the next few days to discuss this. I appreciate your understanding in this matter.

Sincerely,

Denise Jamison

Denise Jamison
909 Hanson St.
Salem, OR 00000
Phones: 555-3090 (home); 555-5000 (work)

cc: School Superintendent Phyllis Bander

As discussed in Chapter 7, IDEA requires that an initial IEP meeting be held within 30 days after the school district determines your child is eligible for special education (34 C.F.R. §300.343(b)(2)). If this is your child's first IEP meeting and the administrator insists on a one-hour meeting, mention that if you have to schedule a second one, the meeting might be more than 30 days after the eligibility determination and therefore in violation of IDEA.

B. Establish the IEP Meeting Agenda

Knowing the IEP meeting agenda in advance will help you tremendously. Although IDEA does not require that the district provide you with an agenda, it does require that you be given the opportunity to participate and understand the proceedings (34 C.F.R. §300.345(a)(e)). It would not be unreasonable, therefore, to know what issues will be discussed. Ask the school district special education administrator for an agenda.

Most IEP meetings cover the following:
- child's current status—how he's doing, whether or not previous goals and objectives were fulfilled, what the current assessments state
- specific goals and objectives
- specific support or related services, and
- specific program, including the type, make-up and location of the class.

After you receive a copy of the agenda, check your blueprint. This will tell you what topics *you* feel should be covered at the meeting. If an item important to you is not on the agenda, let the administrator know, preferably in writing.

C. Organize Your Materials

Having access to key material is vitally important in an IEP meeting. You don't want to be fumbling about, looking for that one report or one quote that can really help. We recommend the following specific steps to help you organize the mountain of material you have.

1. Review Your Blueprint and All Written Material

Your starting point is your blueprint. Gather together your blueprint and all written material, such as assessments, previous IEPs, notes and reports from your child's teacher and other staff members, work samples and letters to and from your child's school district. These should all be in your IEP binder, clearly labeled and organized for easy reference.

Review all documents. Plan to bring to the meeting all materials that support your goals for your child—such as a particular methodology, service or program. Also, bring all materials that counter the negative points the school district representatives are likely to raise.

2. Highlight Supportive Material

Go through your binder and highlight or underline all important positive and negative statements. You may want to tab certain key statements for easy reference. How do you know what statements to highlight? Focus on the following.

- Test results, staff observations, reports and other information on your child's current educational status. Highlight descriptive statements, such as "Tom scored at the first grade level on the Brigance Test, Counting Subtest" or "Sheila has difficulty staying focused in class; any activity beyond three-five minutes can be quite taxing for her."
- Recommendations regarding program placement, related services, goals and objectives and methodology. Look for statements such as "Carla would benefit from 30 minutes of speech therapy a week" or "Jim needs to be in a small classroom in which there are minimal disturbances or acting out behavior."
- The consequences of providing or not providing specific placements, services, methodology and other program components —for example, "Teri has significant fears about large groups and open space; placing her in a larger class and big campus will increase those fears and put her at risk for serious emotional difficulties."

As you go through all your IEP-related information, you probably will highlight a lot of what you read, making the task of organizing the material seem overwhelming. To make it manageable, use different colored highlighters or tabs to differentiate the important from the less important statements or items—such as yellow for very important, green for somewhat important and blue for less important. You can also make second copies of all significant items and keep them as a separate section in your IEP binder.

3. Use an IEP Material Organizer Form

Once your material is highlighted, we strongly recommend an additional set of sheets which can further help you put key information together and give you an easy way to access that information. We call it, for want of a more creative term, an IEP Material Organizer form.

A sample IEP Material Organizer is shown below and Appendix 5 includes a blank, tear-out copy. Do one sheet for each major issue.

IEP Material Organizer Form

Use this form to track documents and persons that provide support for or opposition to your goals.

Issue: _____ Related Service: 1:1 Aide

Document or Witness* Name(s):	Binder Location (if applicable)	Helps You	Hurts You	Key Supportive or Oppositional Information	Rebuttal Document or Witness Name(s) (If hurts) (If none, what will you say at meeting?)
Lee Portaro's (District) 3/1/99 assessment	1C		✓	Recomm. #s 3, 6, 8, 10 (p.8)	Brown Assessment
Suzanne Brown 2/4/99 Assessment (Independent)	1B	✓		Narrative (p. 3, ¶s 4, 5). Recomm. #s 1-7, p. 12	Portaro Report: No IEP Agreement on Aide
Weekly Teacher Reports	1F	✓	✓	9/6/98, 10/4/98, 1/17/99 Support 10/14/98, 11/5/98, 2/2/99 Against	
5/2/98 IEP	1A	✓	✓	Narrative (¶s 7, 8) Against Narrative (¶s 2, 5) Support	
Dr. Baker (Pediatrician) 1/22/99 letter	1G	✓		P. 2, Concerns for psychological impact if no aide	Portaro p. 3 (¶2)
Phil Anderson (tutor) 12/6/98 letter	1H	✓		Reports positive results with direct work, 1:1 work	
Karla Jones (District Psychologist)	1M		✓	Sees Steve once/month Reports no adverse psych. impact	Brown, p. 3, ¶s 6, 9
Student Work	1P	✓		Steve on 10/5 assignment writes "Don't understand, who cares."	

* A "witness" is someone (teacher, doctor, assessor, tutor, psychologist) who gives their oral or written opinion regarding your child's needs at the IEP meeting.

An IEP Material Organizer divides your written information, notes and reports into important components, such as related services, keyed to your blueprint. As you can see from the sample form, the IEP Material Organizer form allows you to easily reference specific information—such as an assessment report, pediatrician letter and key statements made by a teacher or other potential witnesses—that support or dispute your blueprint items.

An IEP Material Organizer can be further divided depending on your child's specific needs or issues. For example, for placement you might have class size, peer needs, type of class, location of class and the like. Under the related service of a one-to-one aide, you might add how much time, the qualifications of the aide and how to use the aide. Under a curricula/methodology issue such as the reading program, you might include when the reading work is done or at what pace.

Feel free to use the IEP Material Organizer form to subdivide issues as necessary.

4. Identify Negative Material and Prepare Rebuttals

Keeping in mind your blueprint and goals for your child, what materials hurt your position? Do test results, staff observations or assessor recommendations state the opposite of what you want for your child? Do lines such as "Ben does not need any special education services now" or "Leo should be provided one hour of aide time a week" (you believe he needs one hour per day) or "Nicole cannot function in a regular classroom at this time" (you're in favor of mainstreaming) stare you in the face?

Some negative material is less direct. For example, a test result may not reflect the difficulties your child is actually experiencing. If an assessment concludes that "Sandy is at age level for reading," you might face an uphill climb in convincing the school district she needs additional help. Or, an observation may undermine a placement or service you want. A teacher's statement that "Steven frequently acts out and disrupts classroom activities" may make it very hard for you to have Steven mainstreamed.

Here are some ways to counter negative material:

- Look for anything that directly or indirectly contradicts a troublesome statement or report. For example, an aide's statement "While Steven's behavior is erratic, with help he can control his behavior and focus effectively and quietly on his work" might help you convince the school that Steven can be mainstreamed.
- Look for professional opinions contrary to the school's position. Usually statements in an independent assessment can counter school data.
- Are the qualifications of the person who wrote the unfavorable statement appropriate? If a psychologist completed the school assessment, find out if she has expertise in the specific areas in which she made the negative comments.
- Is the negative statement crystal clear? For example, what exactly does the following observation mean: "While Jane does not need a small class, there is some indication that she has a difficult time in a large school environment...." The reference to a large school environment may indirectly support a small class placement.
- Is the unfavorable statement supported by data, testing results or anecdotal information? If not, be prepared to point that out.

Use the IEP Material Organizer form to identify negative statements and rebuttal information. While you should be prepared to address or rebut a troublesome statement, conclusion or recommendation, this may simply not be possible. As a general rule, don't bring up negative statements unless the school district raises them first.

5. Provide Documents Before the IEP Meeting

In preparation for the IEP meeting, have everything in your binder marked, tabbed, highlighted and referred to in your IEP Material Organizer. Also, make copies of material you want the school district representatives to see at the IEP meeting. This includes anything that supports your blueprint or rebuts negative information. The material can be in any form—a letter, report, independent assessment, teacher's report, work sample or anything else. You may want to make enough copies for everyone attending the meeting to have their own.

Provide the school district with a copy of all material you've generated, such as an independent assessment. Give these to the district a week before the meeting. This way, school representatives can't argue that they need more time to review your material and must postpone the meeting.

As we mentioned before, there may be a reason to surprise the district at the IEP by introducing a particular item for the first time. For example, the item may be highly controversial. As a general rule, however, it is best to play it straight and provide material ahead of time.

D. Draft Your Child's IEP Program

IDEA requires that the IEP program be developed jointly by you and the school district. This does not mean, however, that you cannot—or should not—draft key portions of the IEP program beforehand. This logical step follows the development of your blueprint.

The key portions of the IEP program are:
- goals and objectives
- specific programs and placement
- related services, and
- other components, including curricula, methodology and a description of the placement.

Writing out your IEP program will not only help you learn your material, but it will also force you to think again about how to make your case for the key issues. In doing a draft of the IEP program, you can either fill out a blank school district IEP form—we suggest you get a copy early in the process—or, you can simply have your statements written and ready for discussion at the IEP meeting. As the IEP team proceeds, bring up the specific components you want in the IEP program.

Please keep in mind that your blueprint and IEP Material Organizer form will help you draft an IEP and attend the IEP meeting. Chapter 11, Section D, discusses how the IEP form and blueprint work together and how to include as much of your blueprint as possible on the IEP form.

1. Goals and Objectives

As discussed in Chapter 9, goals and objectives include both broad goals for your child—usually involving reading, math and language skills, social development, behavior issues and other cognitive areas of need—and specific tasks to reach those goals.

2. Specific Programs and Placement

These refer to the exact program and class you want for your child.

Examples:
- Placement in the special day class for learning disabled students at Hawthorne School.
- Placement in a special day class for learning disabled children, no more than 12 students with no disruptive behaviors and a teacher qualified to work with learning disabled students; either SDC at Laurel or Martin Schools are appropriate.
- Placement in Tina's home school, the regular third grade class.

3. Related Services

Related services are developmental, corrective and other supportive services, such as transportation, that your child needs to benefit from special education or to be placed in a regular class.

Examples:
- Jason needs three speech therapy sessions per week, each session for 30 minutes, one-on-one with a qualified speech therapist.
- Maria needs a full-time one-on-one aide in order to be mainstreamed in a regular fifth grade class, the aide to be qualified to assist Maria specifically in the areas of reading comprehension, spelling, fifth grade math and developing positive peer relationships.

4. Other Components

Other components of the IEP program include:
- curricula, including how your child will be involved in and progress in the general curriculum found in the regular classroom, and whether specific related services or special education is needed to assure your child's involvement and progress
- teacher methodology
- transition plans, including vocational needs, and
- extracurricular activities such as after-school clubs, lunchtime activities and sports activities.

Chapter 2, Section B, provides details on programs and placement, related services and other components of your child's IEP.

Child Profile

The school district might balk at a fully drafted IEP program or a blueprint. In the alternative, you might prepare a statement for the IEP meeting that incorporates important information without necessarily triggering school district opposition. Instead of emphasizing goals and objectives and placement and services, emphasize your child and her needs.

Example:

Sally has a learning disability with specific difficulties with auditory memory, spelling and reading comprehension. She has some emotional difficulties because of her learning disability, which appear in the forms of anxiety, fear of other children and concern with safety. She has on a few occasions run off campus. When placed in a large classroom her fears can be increased.

Sally needs a program in which the environment is not overly active, with no behavioral problems; she should not be on a large campus, which might overwhelm her. She needs to be in a classroom of no more than 15 children; she benefits from the Slingerland method and requires instruction in simple, small steps. She needs one-on-one help with reading for at least two hours a day, with such one-on-one work in at least 30-minute, continuous increments.

This child profile combines parts of the blueprint with a description of your child and her needs. It is not unlike a school district's assessment, which normally includes a narrative section, describing your child. Although you will want to draft the child profile for the meeting, do not give it to the school district in advance. Focus on:
- describing your child (quiet, kind, determined, afraid)
- your child's areas of need, including academic, social and environmental, and
- weaving in references to specific service and placement needs.

E. Establish Who Will Attend the IEP Meeting

Under IDEA, a person with knowledge or expertise relevant to your child may attend the IEP meeting. This includes the following people (34 C.F.R. §300.344):

- you and your child's other parent
- your child, if appropriate (see Section 2.b, below)
- a representative of the school district who is qualified to provide or supervise your child's special education
- your child's special education teacher
- your child's regular classroom teacher if your child is in any mainstreamed classes
- a person who can interpret the assessments and their impact on instructional strategies
- at your discretion or the discretion of the school district, other people who have knowledge or expertise regarding your child or her needs, and
- if your child is 14 or older, someone who knows about transitional services.

Representatives From Noneducational Public Agencies

Sometimes, representatives from other public agencies may attend an IEP meeting, particularly if responsibility for certain IEP services is entrusted to an agency other than the school district. In California, for example, mental health services are provided by the county mental health department, and therefore a representative from that agency will often be present. In Vermont, a representative of an agency other than the school district will attend to discuss transition services. If the child has been involved with the juvenile authorities, for example, a probation officer may attend, depending on the laws in your state.

Prior to the IEP meeting, talk with any of these additional folks and find out their reason for attending the meeting, what they will do there (such as report on your child) and any position they have about your child's needs.

---

1. Representing the School District

Knowing who will attend the IEP meeting on behalf of the school district will help you prepare. The school district should inform you in writing, but if you are not told at least two weeks before the meeting, write the district and ask for the following information for each person who will attend:

- name
- reasons for attending
- qualifications and specific title, and
- whether or not he or she knows your child and if so, in what capacity.

Prepare a list of all participants, including what their likely positions will be.

A sample IEP Meeting Participants form is shown below and Appendix 5 includes a blank, tear-out copy.

IEP Meeting Participants

Name	Position/Employer	Purpose for Attending	Point of View
Fred Brown	Third grade teacher, Kentington School District	Gene's teacher	Supports Gene's placement in regular class; does not think Gene needs aide
Diana Hunt	Psychologist, Kentington School District	Did assessment	Recommends placement in special day class
Violet King	Psychologist, Independent assessor	Did independent assessment	Supports regular class and aide
Jane Gough	Speech therapist, Kentington School District	Representative of school district	Agrees with need for speech therapy, but not on amount
Phil Chase	Administrator, Kentington School District	Representative of school district	No stated position

a. Your Child's Teacher

If your child currently is now in a regular class, then his current teacher must attend the IEP meeting (34 C.F.R. §300.344(a)(2)). Your child's teacher is important for obvious reasons—she has the most knowledge about your child's education. The teacher may write reports about your child's progress, help write goals and objectives, be responsible for seeing that they are fulfilled and make recommendations for the next school year.

The teacher is potentially the best or worst ally you have in the IEP process, and often the most convincing team member. The teacher's opinion may carry the most weight and may influence how far your school district will pursue a dispute. If the teacher supports your position, you have a better chance of success. If the teacher does not, the school district may feel it would win any due process dispute and therefore may not accede to your wishes at the IEP meeting.

Making sure the teacher understands your concerns and is prepared to speak frankly about them is crucial, but not always easy to achieve. Teachers work for their school districts; at times, a teacher's professional opinion may conflict with what an administrator believes to be right or feasible given budgetary and other constraints. A teacher who speaks frankly regardless of what a school administrator thinks is invaluable—but not always easy to find. It is therefore vital that you keep in contact with the teacher, ask his opinion and indicate your specific concerns. Be specific, direct, fair and always conscious of the teacher's time.

Chapter 8, Section B, discusses the importance of regular contact with your child's teacher and talking with teachers and other school personnel before the IEP meeting.

b. School Administrator

In most cases, someone representing the school district will attend the IEP meeting. This may be the district special education coordinator, student services director, county or regional office of education administrator or school principal. There are all kinds of administrators, just like there are all kinds of parents. The administrator may be a kind, cooperative and terrific advocate for your child—or may be burned-out, unpleasant and remarkably bureaucratic.

You will be working with the administrator a good deal and will want to know where he stands on your child's IEP. Your inclination might be to ask the administrator in advance of the meeting what his position is regarding the key issues for your child. Is it a good idea to do so? Many a wise administrator will let you know when he agrees with you, but will not let you know in advance if he disagrees. That doesn't mean you can't ask, but it does mean you should consider the pros and cons of asking the administrator's position prior to the IEP meeting.

Pros

- You will find out if the administrator agrees with you.
- If you get an honest answer, you'll know what the administrator thinks and how determined he is for the IEP plan to reflect his position.
- If you disagree with the answer, you may convince him to change his mind, or you will better know how to prepare for the IEP meeting.
- You may learn about options you like.

Cons

- The administrator will learn your goals and be able to counter them if he disagrees.
- You may put the administrator on guard, making it difficult for you to communicate with staff, visit programs and the like.

In general, it is useful to know where people stand in advance and so you may want to ask. If

c. School Psychologist and Other Specialists

Depending on your child's condition and needs, other professionals may be involved in the IEP meeting, such as a school psychologist, speech therapist, occupational therapist, physical therapist, adaptive physical education specialist or resource specialist. They may provide assessment reports and other information regarding your child and are likely to have opinions about goals and objectives, services and placement. Like your child's teacher, these specialists may be great allies or great obstacles.

As with the teacher or administrator, speak with the specialists ahead of time to find out their positions on key issues.

d. Limits on School Representatives

Are there limits to who can attend the meeting? Federal policy states that a school may not invite so many people as to make the IEP intimidating. State laws and policies, too, cover who may attend IEP meetings. California, for example, requires that the IEP meeting be "nonadversarial," and thus having ten district employees may make the IEP meeting very adversarial.

If someone seems inappropriate, notify the school in writing (even if you initially call) of your concern—state why the individual is not qualified to attend or why her attendance is not relevant. If the school insists that the person attend, see Chapter 13 on filing a complaint. And at the IEP meeting, state for the record, without being personal, that you feel so-and-so should not be there. When it's time to sign the IEP plan, reiterate your objection.

A sample letter objecting to a certain person attending the IEP meeting is shown below; a blank tear-out copy is in Appendix 5.

the administrator states his opposition to your goals for your child, consider the following:

- If the administrator indicates he will not support you on a particular item, he may have violated IDEA—that is, made a decision before the IEP meeting. This may be the basis of a formal complaint against the school district (see Chapter 13). We are not suggesting you trap the administrator into making a decision outside of the IEP meeting. But if he does, be aware of your rights.

- If the administrator has not made a decision, you may want to share the materials you have that support your position. You might give the administrator some ideas as to why the district might agree with you. On the other hand, you may help the administrator prepare to rebut you at the IEP meeting. You'll have to judge the chance of making the administrator into an ally versus helping him better prepare to defend against what you want.

Sample IEP Meeting Attendance Objection Letter

Date: _May 15, 19xx_

To: _Dr. Sean Gough_

Hamilton School District

1456 Howard Ave.

Little Rock, AR 00000

From: _Eva Crane_

88 2nd Street

Little Rock, AR 00000

Phones: 555-1998 (home); 555-8876 (work)

Re: _Amy Crane, student in third grade class of Carol Smith_

I understand that _Joan Green, the district's psychologist,_ ,
will be at _Amy's_ IEP meeting. _Joan Green_
knows nothing about _Amy_ and appears to have no knowledge that
might be of use to the IEP team. I am formally requesting that _Ms. Green_
not attend, unless there is some clear reason that makes _Ms. Green's_
attendance appropriate and necessary for the development of _Amy's_
IEP plan. As you know, IEP meetings can be particularly difficult for parents. We are already
anxious about ours and would prefer that you not take action that will heighten our stress
level.

If you insist on _Ms. Green_ attending without any reason, then we
will file a complaint with the state and federal departments of education.

I will call you in a few days to find out your decision on this issue. Thank you for considering
my request.

Sincerely,
Eva Crane

Eva Crane

88 2nd Street

Little Rock, AR 00000

Phones: 555-1998 (home); 555-8876 (work)

One Teacher Too Many

I once represented a child at an IEP meeting where there were a dozen school representatives, including several administrators, the school nurse and Bruce, the "teacher of the day." I asked Bruce if he knew my client, Laura. The answer was no—he had neither met her nor knew anything about her. I asked him why he was there. Without hesitation he said he was there to "represent the teachers of the area." The involvement of someone like Bruce—or anybody else with no knowledge of your child or the relevant educational issues—would violate federal policy and the underlying purpose of the IEP meeting.

2. Representing the Parents

While some of the people representing the school district may support your goals for your child, you may want some or all of the following people to attend the IEP meeting on your behalf:

- you and your spouse
- your child
- others who know your child, such as a relative or close family friend
- independent assessors or other professionals who have worked with your child, and
- an attorney.

As you prepare these people for the IEP meeting, be sure to contact them well in advance to insure their attendance. Give them the date, time, location and likely duration of the meeting. Make sure they understand the key topics that will arise during the IEP meeting, and the issues and solutions they are there to discuss. Let them know the positions of the various school representatives on the key issues, and be sure to show them copies of materials that both support and are contrary to your goals.

Remind your attendees that the IEP meeting is informal and that points of view should be stated in a positive, but firm way. Disagreements can be spirited, but should remain professional and even friendly.

Some of the people you ask to attend—such as an independent assessor, a pediatrician, other specialist or a lawyer might charge you a fee. Understand the cost ahead of time. If you can't afford to have the person stay for the entire meeting, let the school administrator know in advance that you will have someone attending who needs to make a statement and leave. Before the meeting, ask the administrator to set aside a specific time for that person.

Some people you want to attend might not be able to, or you might not be able to afford paying them to attend. In either situation, ask the person to prepare a written statement for you to read at the meeting. Some people's testimony may in fact be better in written rather than live form—for example, someone who is timid or reluctant to strongly state a position in person.

Chapter 8, Section F.2, discusses items to include in a written statement from your child's doctor or other people from outside the school.

a. Parents

While work schedules or living arrangements may make attending the IEP meeting difficult, it is generally best if both parents attend, even if you are divorced or separated. If you have differences of opinion, resolve them before the IEP meeting. If you argue with each other during the IEP meeting, you will most likely damage your credibility and chances of success.

If one of you cannot attend, prepare a strong and emotional statement for the other to read.

Sample Statement to IEP Team

To: Marilyn Haversham's IEP Team

From: Claudine Haversham (Marilyn's mom)

Date: March 1, 199x

I cannot attend the March 15th IEP meeting, but I wanted you to know that I very concerned that Marilyn might be removed from her regular program. She is such a happy child now that she is mainstreamed. As her mother, I see the joy in her eyes when she gets up in the morning to get ready for school. A placement in a more restrictive environment would be devastating to my daughter. I must be frank and tell you that we will vigorously oppose any efforts to remove Marilyn from her current program.

I greatly appreciate your sensitivity to Marilyn's needs and your past assistance in making her educational experience a positive one.

Sincerely,

Claudine Haversham

Claudine Haversham

b. Your Child

IDEA says that the student shall attend the IEP meeting if it is appropriate or if the IEP team is considering transition services for a child who is 14 or older (34 C.F.R. §§300.344(a)(7) and 300.347(b)(i)(ii)). See Chapter 2, Section A.6, for a discussion of transition services.

When is it considered appropriate for a child to attend? If your child can speak about his hopes and needs, he may be a compelling self-advocate. But be careful—if he's unpredictable or unsure of the importance of the meeting, you may not want to risk him giving a "wrong" answer. For example, you want your child to remain in his mainstreamed program. A school district representative says, "Tell me Tommy, do you want to stay in your

class?" You're not going to be happy if Tommy responds, "Nope."

If your child does attend, have him focus on his feelings and hopes. You probably want to avoid referring to the written materials, unless he's older—perhaps a teenager. In that case, you can ask something like, "Carl, the school assessor says you had a hard time in Ms. Shaver's class, particularly with other students. Why do you think that was so?" Be sure you know what his answer will be.

c. Relatives, Friends and Child Care Workers

It is important to limit the number of people who attend the IEP meetings, because meetings can drag on. Therefore, you'd normally not bring a relative, friend or child care worker to the meeting. But if someone can present a view of your child that wouldn't otherwise be told, you might want them to come. For example, if your child's regular babysitter can say how your otherwise shy and reserved child talks for the first 30 minutes after she gets home about how she loves being in a regular class, it may be powerful testimony.

Generally a sibling or peer of your child, particularly a young one, should not attend unless she is the only person who can speak to an issue or has a really powerful presence. Preparing a young attendees will be very important, with focus on the sibling or peer's "feelings" about your child, rather than more formal information.

Bring a Notetaker to the IEP Meeting

Ask a friend or relative to attend the IEP meeting and take notes for you—paying careful attention to who says what regarding important items. A notetaker can be invaluable, particularly if you anticipate a controversial meeting.

d. Independent Assessors and Other Professionals

Because the conclusions reached by any independent assessor who tested your child will probably be instrumental in helping you secure the services and placement you want for your child, it is crucial that she attend the IEP meeting. The assessor must be able to clearly articulate her professional opinion on the key blueprint items, as well as her opinion on all assessment data. She must also be prepared to rebut contradictory information presented by the school district.

Other professionals, such as a pediatrician, private tutor, therapist or psychological counselor, can be important witnesses on your behalf if they know your child and can speak to key issues affecting the IEP plan. Prepare these individuals as you would prepare an independent assessor.

e. An Attorney

If you hire or consult an attorney during the IEP process, that person can attend the IEP meeting. You can also hire a lawyer just for the IEP meeting. (See Chapter 14 for information on working with lawyers.) As a general rule, you would want an attorney at the IEP meeting if your relationship with the school district has badly deteriorated and you anticipate a complicated and difficult IEP meeting.

If you bring an attorney to the IEP meeting, school representatives are likely to be on guard and are less likely to speak frankly. On the other hand, if the school administrators haven't been cooperative and you feel the plan that will emerge from the IEP meeting will be harmful to your child, bringing an attorney shows you mean business. You're much better off not using an attorney—it does change the entire experience—but if you must, then find one who is reasonable and cooperative.

If you plan to have an attorney at the IEP meeting, you should notify the school district reasonably in advance. Except in unusual situations, you will be responsible for paying your attorney with little chance of reimbursement. (See Chapter 14, Section D, for information on when you might be reimbursed for lawyer's expenses.)

F. Final Preparation Concerns

As you finish your IEP preparation, consider these additional recommendations.

1. Taping the IEP Meeting

You (and the school district) have the option of tape recording the meeting. While a tape recording may be the best proof of what was said, it may have an inhibiting effect. People don't always want to "go on record" as having made a particular statement. In addition, tape recordings are not always of great quality; people are not always audible and it's hard to discern what was said and who said it.

If you decide to tape record, bring a good quality recorder. Bring extra tapes and batteries in case an outlet is not accessible. The school district can tape record even if you object—just as you can tape even if school representatives object. If the school district tapes the meeting, you are entitled to a copy of the tape and it becomes part of your child's file—just as the district can ask for a copy of your tape.

We strongly recommend you notify the district in advance of your desire to tape record to avoid problems at the meeting. See "School Resistance to Tape Recording," below.

School Resistance to Tape Recording

The U.S. Department of Education, Office of Special Education Programs, has issued several statements reinforcing the right of parents to tape record IEP meetings. If, once you get to the meeting, the special education administrator says you cannot tape record, ask to reschedule the meeting or state that this affects your ability to function at the IEP meeting, it is against the law and you will file a complaint. (After the meeting, follow up with a letter to the school administrator; see Chapter 13 for advice on filing a complaint.)

2. Reducing Your Anxiety

Since it is a given that you will be nervous at the meeting, don't worry about being anxious. But do give some thought to what you might do before the IEP meeting to relax. It may be taking a walk or jogging, soaking in the bathtub, going out for breakfast or any other activity that helps you. If you need a babysitter or to take time off from work, set it up well in advance, so you're not scrambling the day before the meeting.

By preparing—knowing your material, completing your IEP blueprint, drafting your IEP plan and talking to your IEP participants ahead of time—you will do much to reduce your anxiety.

IEP Preparation List

Things to do before the IEP meeting
- Find out the date, time and location.
- Get a copy of the school's agenda.
- Make own agenda.
- Prepare your IEP Material Organizer.
- Draft IEP plan.
- Find out who is attending on behalf of school district.
- Invite and prepare your own IEP participants.
- Give the school a copy of the following:
  - independent assessments
  - documents such as formal reports and work samples from others
  - names and titles of people attending IEP
  - notice of intent to tape record IEP meeting (if applicable).
- Create meeting reminder list of items you want to be sure to remember:
  - "Make sure we read statements of Dr. Wilson and Rona (babysitter), who can't attend."
  - "Make sure Dr. Ramirez covers Lydia's physical therapy needs."
  - "Remember we don't have to sign all of the IEP—we can object."

11

Attending the IEP Meeting

Your IEP meeting is soon. You'll enter the room, sit down, put your binder on the table, take a deep breath and do just fine. You'll do fine because being nervous is natural, the school administrators probably feel the same way, and most importantly, you are prepared for this meeting. You've developed your child's blueprint and drafted an ideal IEP, supported by various documents. You're familiar with the school's IEP form, policies, programs and services. You know who will attend the meeting and where each person stands on key issues. You have people with you prepared to help you make your case.

Chapter 10 provides valuable advice on preparing for the IEP meeting. Chapter 7 provides tips on preparing for and attending an IEP eligibility meeting.

A. Arriving at the IEP Meeting

IEP meetings can take a lot of time. Therefore, it's very important that you be on time. In fact, you'll want to be at least ten to 15 minutes early so you can get the lay of the land, see the meeting room and perhaps say a few words to the teacher or school administrator. More importantly, being early will give you the chance to talk to your participants and make sure everyone is clear about their roles at the meeting.

1. What to Bring

Bring your IEP binder and the written material you've gathered, including assessments, letters, reports and your IEP Material Organizer form. Make sure you have extra copies of key documents, such as an independent assessment.

2. Get the Notetaker Organized

We recommend in Chapter 10 that you bring someone to take notes, particularly if you anticipate a controversial meeting. Make sure you provide your notetaker with paper and pens (unless they're using a laptop computer). Remind your notetaker to take detailed notes regarding important items, particularly those that relate to your blueprint—who and what was said are especially important. These notes, particularly for items that you and the school district disagree on, will be extremely important should you end up filing for due process (Chapter 12) or making a formal complaint (Chapter 13).

3. Set up the Tape Recorder

If you're planning to tape record the meeting, set up the equipment and check that it's working.

Chapter 10, Section F, emphasizes the importance of notifying the school district in advance of your intent to tape record the IEP meeting, and how to deal with any dispute that arises about taping the meeting.

4. How the Meeting Will Begin

The IEP meeting is typically led by the school administrator responsible for special education programs, although it may be the school site principal, the school district assessor or even, on some occasions, a teacher.

Most IEP meetings begin with the introduction of all participants. School representatives explain their roles at the meeting. You should do the same with your participants. If, for example, a friend will take notes or an outside assessor will explain her report, make that clear.

After introductions, the administrator will probably discuss the agenda, and then explain how the meeting will run and how decisions will be made.

 Obtaining the agenda in advance is discussed in Chapter 10, Section B.

If the agenda is different from what you anticipated, or omits issues you want covered, bring up your concerns at the beginning of the meeting. You have the right to raise any issue you want at the IEP meeting. Also, if the agenda appears too long for the allotted time, explain that you don't think there will be enough time to cover everything and ask that certain items be discussed first. If your request is denied, do your best to keep the meeting moving forward.

While most IEP meetings follow a certain pattern, (discussed in Section D, below), don't be surprised if yours seems to have a life of its own, going in directions you did not anticipate. Just make sure your key issues are covered before the meeting ends.

IEP Meeting Basic Dos and Don'ts

Is there an etiquette to the IEP meeting? There should be. As in any potentially difficult encounter, try to proceed in a positive way.

Dos:
- Do respect other opinions.
- Do try to include all IEP team members in the process.
- Do ask questions in a fair and direct way.
- Do state your position firmly, but fairly.
- Do explore ways of reaching consensus.

Don'ts:
- Don't interrupt.
- Don't accuse.
- Don't make personal attacks.
- Don't raise your voice.
- Don't question another's motives.

You might begin by saying that you appreciate everyone's attending, the time and energy they're giving to your child and their professional dedication. Emphasize that you are determined to discuss all issues in a fair and thorough way, and that you are looking forward to a challenging but ultimately positive meeting in which everyone's point of view is respected.

B. Simple Rules for a Successful IEP Meeting

Several simple rules can help you in the IEP meeting.

1. Know Your Rights

IDEA was created for your child and provides for him:

- free appropriate public education (FAPE) in the
- least restrictive environment (LRE), based on an
- individualized education program (IEP).

Parents are co-equal decisionmakers—just as important as everyone else at the IEP meeting.

Chapter 2 explains your and your child's legal rights under IDEA. Appendix 1 includes the relevant statutes and regulations.

2. Don't Be Intimidated

You have special knowledge of your child's needs. School personnel are not the only experts. If you have documents to support each item you want in the IEP plan, you may be better prepared than school representatives.

At the same time, don't automatically assume that teachers or other school officials are wrong. There are many dedicated teachers and school administrators who want to provide the best education for your child, have expertise in educating children with disabilities and have been through this process numerous times before. This doesn't mean you won't encounter opposing opinions, or

---

How to Deal With Intimidating or Nasty Comments

For many parents, dealing with teachers and school administrators in an IEP meeting can be intimidating. You don't want to (but may) hear:

- *I'm sorry, Mr. Walker, but you're wrong.*
- *I'm sorry, Ms. Richards, the law doesn't say that.*
- *Your assessment report is incorrect.*
- *Our policy precludes that.*
- *Maybe they do that in another school district, but we don't.*
- *I will not agree to that!*
- *That's enough on that subject!*

In most cases, you can ignore these kinds of comments or make a simple response. (Section B.5 discusses how to challenge blanket assertions.) Try to determine whether the comment is anything more than just an impolite or negative remark. If it is unimportant, say your piece and move on.

"I don't appreciate your tone of voice, Ms. Hanson. I have treated you with respect and expect the same from you. Even if we disagree, we can do it in a civil way. More importantly, your statement is not correct (or reasonable or productive or conducive to a positive IEP meeting)."

If the comment seems important, you may need to be more assertive.

"Ms. Hanson, I resent your comment and believe you are undermining this IEP meeting. Please understand, I will do what is necessary to ensure my child receives the program she needs and bring your behavior to the attention of the appropriate individuals."

If you don't feel calm and your voice is shaky, that's okay too. Just don't yell or get overly aggressive. If necessary, you may want to raise the possibility of filing a formal complaint regarding something that seems illegal—such as the district won't allow you to discuss your independent assessment. (Chapter 13 covers complaints.) But don't make a threat without first thinking it through. Do you really have grounds to file a formal complaint? Is there any validity to the school representative's comment? Is it worth alienating the school district and changing the atmosphere of the IEP meeting? In most cases, you can make your point without threatening to file a formal complaint.

someone who is just plain nasty or incorrect. But as a general rule, most of the folks are in special education because they want to help.

3. Focus on Your Child's Needs—Not Cost or Administrative Constraints

IDEA recognizes that each child's needs are unique and therefore each individual program will be different. If you can show that your child needs a specific service, such as a one-to-one aide or two hours of occupational therapy each week, then the law requires it.

If the school district does not have the staff to provide the related service your child needs, such as a speech therapist, then the school should pay for a private therapist.

A child's needs—not cost—should influence an IEP decision. For example, the school administrator cannot refuse to discuss or provide a service or placement because it "costs too much." An administrator may try to get the point across indirectly, by saying something like "If we provide that service for your child, another child will not get services she needs." Don't argue the issue; simply respond with something like this:

> *Mr. Keystone, it is wrong for you to make my child responsible for your budgetary difficulties. I won't be put in the position of making a choice between my child's needs and the needs of other children. The law is clear that we should be discussing an appropriate education for my child, not the cost.*

If you can't reach agreement, and the school district representatives continue to admit that there is an administrative or budget problem, be sure you (or your notetaker) has written this down in case you end up in due process.

This is not to say that cost is never an issue. Let's say you want your child in Program X and the school offers to put your child in Program Y,

which is less costly for the district. You're unable to reach an agreement and decide to resolve the matter through due process. If the district can prove Program Y is appropriate for your child, it will likely prevail at the due process hearing.

Remember—IDEA does not require the best education for your child, but an appropriate one. Don't fight for the ideal program when an appropriate one is available.

 Use the terms appropriate, never the words best or optimum or maximum. If you feel that a program or service offered by the school isn't right, characterize it as inappropriate.

4. Know When to Fight— and When Not To

It is important to realize when you don't have a case. Understanding the IEP process and having a clear step-by-step strategy does not mean that all problems will always be resolved in a manner you think best. You may be fully prepared, do a superb job in the IEP meeting and still not have enough evidence to support your position. Knowing the strength of your case will help you to know when to fight and when to concede.

In addition, fight for the crucial issues and be more flexible on others. For instance, goals and objectives and test protocol may be important, but ultimately, the related services, placement, and methodology are what matter in your child's education. Fighting for 30 minutes over the wording of one goal or objective is probably a waste of time; spending 90 minutes on a major issue like placement is probably worth the time.

5. Ask Questions

In several situations you will want to ask questions: to obtain basic information, to persuade someone of your position or to question a blanket assertion.

a. Obtain Basic Information

During the IEP meeting, many technical terms will be used, such as FAPE, LRE, multi-sensory strategies, Wisc-R, WISC III, due process, mediation, fair hearing, ot/pt, norms, emotional overlay, NPS, integrative mode, peer support systems, syntactic comprehension at least 50% of the time, behavior modification and present levels of performance. If you don't understand something, ask what it means. It's better to ask—even for the tenth time—than to proceed without understanding.

Most important, find out what these terms mean for your child. Knowing that your child scores at the 42 percentile on the Wechsler is useless unless it tells you something about areas of concerns and implications for improvement.

b. Persuade

Asking questions can be an effective way of persuading someone that your position is right and his may be wrong. State your questions positively, such as "Do you [IEP team members] agree with the recommendations on page eight of Dr. Calderon's report?" or "Ms. Porter, do you agree that Amy should be placed in a regular eighth grade class with a one-to-one aide?"

Sometimes you may need to establish agreement on preliminary matters before asking these kinds of big questions.

Example

You want a particular IEP member to agree with you on placement. You realize that you must first establish agreement on the assessment supporting that placement. You first ask, "You read Dr. Harper's report. She states that Carolyn needs, and I am quoting, 'a quiet environment in which there are no behavioral problems or acting out by other students.' Do you agree with Dr. Harper?" The IEP member agrees and you follow up by asking, "Given Dr. Harper's report and our desire that Carolyn be placed in the special day class at the Manning School, do you agree with that placement?"

c. Challenge Blanket Assertions

Nothing is more frustrating for a parent than hearing lines like the following:
- *"Unfortunately, we are not allowed to discuss that issue."*
- *"We don't provide that service."*
- *"That's not our policy."*
- *"Sorry, but you can't do that."*
- *"That's not the law."*

If an assertion seems illegal or illogical, ask why or why not. If the administrator says something vague like, "It's our policy," "It's the law," "It's our best judgment" or "It's the way things are," keep asking why. Request a copy of the law or policy.

If possible, refer to your documentation. For example, the district administrator says that as a general rule, the district doesn't provide more than two hours of a related service per week. An assessment states that your child needs three hours. Point that out and ask how the district's rule complies with IDEA, which requires that the specifics of a service be determined by the IEP team.

The administrator may say something like, "Mrs. Wasserman, that is just the way it is and I won't respond any further to that question." You'll want to follow up with something like, "I'm sorry you won't answer my question; I will ask your superintendent or the school board the question." If the issue is key, you may want to file a complaint as discussed in Chapter 13.

Or the school district will not agree with you on an important IEP component. For example, you feel there is clear support for a specific placement, but the administrator disagrees. Ask her to explain why and to provide you a detailed explanation with references to objective material.

6. Pay Attention to What's Written on the IEP Form

Make sure you know what statements are entered onto the IEP document and voice any objections immediately—whether it's about a particular goal or objective or a general statement made on the narrative page of the IEP form. (Section D.7 discusses the narrative page.)

7. Keep Your Eye on the Clock

Whether the school has allotted two hours or five hours for the IEP meeting, keep track of time. If it's 45 minutes into a 90-minute meeting and the IEP team is still talking in generalities, you should say, "We need to move on to a specific discussion of Cora's goals and objectives, placement and related services."

A good school administrator will keep the meeting on schedule. If she's not doing so, take the lead. Be ready to suggest moving on to the next issue when the discussion on a particular issue has gone on long enough.

8. Don't Limit Your Options to All or Nothing

At some point during the IEP meeting, you may realize that you will not reach agreement on all issues. For example, you feel your child needs at least two sessions of speech therapy a week, 30 minutes per session. The district offers one 30-minute session. You've done your best to persuade them to no avail. What do you do?

The school district cannot present you with a "take-or-leave-it" position—for example, "We've offered speech therapy once a week. You want it twice a week. You can either agree with us and sign the IEP or disagree and go to a hearing." Furthermore, the school district cannot insist that you give up your right to due process—for instance, "We've offered speech therapy once a week and that's all we'll offer. We'd advise you to sign the IEP form and not make waves."

Your best bet is to make sure the IEP document specifically states that you agree that a specific service is needed—or that a particular placement is appropriate—and that your child will receive at least what the school district has offered. Then make sure your opinions are reflected on the parent addendum page.

You can agree to the lesser amount of a service such as speech therapy, and indicate on the IEP form that you believe your child needs two sessions of speech therapy, but will accept the one session so he will have something while you pursue due process. Or you agree on placement and related services, but not certain goals and objectives (or vice versa).

Section F discusses how to prepare and use a parent addendum page which is a very important IEP tool for any disputed items.

9. Don't Be Rushed Into Making a Decision

If you're on the fence about a particular issue, don't be rushed into making a decision. Ask for a break and go outside for a few minutes to think about what the school has offered. If you are concerned that pausing on some issues may mean delay on others, ask for a day or two to make up your mind on a particular issue so that the IEP team can proceed with other items. This may mean a second IEP meeting, unless you eventually agree with the rest of the IEP team on the issue. If an item is that important, however, then a second meeting is worth the time.

C. Getting Familiar With Your School's IEP Form

As suggested several places earlier in this book, get a copy of your school district's IEP form before the IEP meeting. While forms vary, they will almost always have sections on the following:

- present level of educational performance
- goals and objectives (and evaluation procedures)
- related services
- placement/program
- effective dates of the IEP
- attending summer school or an extended school year, and
- a narrative page or pages for recording various important statements, such as comments on assessments, or keeping a running account of the meeting discussion. This important part of the IEP is described in Section D.7.

In addition, IEP forms typically include the following types of information:

- identifying information, such as your child's name, gender, date of birth, grade and the school district where she's enrolled, and parents' names and addresses
- the type of IEP (eligibility or annual review) and date of IEP meeting
- your child's eligibility status and category of disability
- the amount of time in a regular or mainstreamed program, if applicable
- your child's English proficiency, and
- signatures of IEP team members and parents.

The IEP team may include other important information in the IEP, such as a specific curricula or teaching methodology, a specific classroom setting, peer needs or a child profile.

For an example of how a completed IEP form looks, see the sample IEP form in Appendix 4.

The IEP Form and Your IEP Blueprint

The IEP form itself and your blueprint (your list of desired program components) are closely related, but are not identical.

Most of your blueprint items, such as related services and placement, have a corresponding section in the IEP, but in some cases, you may find that the IEP form does not have space for all the details you included on your blueprint. For example, the IEP form will allow you to specify the kind of program or placement—such as a regular class or special day class—but might not provide space for or reference to the detail of the placement—such as peer numbers and make-up, the classroom environment and the school environment. Other blueprint items, such as methodology and curricula, may not have a corresponding section on the IEP form.

As you prepare for the IEP meeting, keep in mind that while the IEP form may not reference all of your blueprint items, IDEA provides that the IEP team can discuss and agree on any element it feels is necessary for your child. These types of details can go on the IEP narrative page (Section D.7) or, if the school disagrees, a parent addendum page (Section F).

D. Writing the IEP Plan

Usually, someone from the school district will write up the IEP plan as the meeting progresses, including filling in specific sections and checking off boxes on the IEP and, very importantly, completing the narrative page.

You should frequently ask to see what has been written, to make sure it accurately reflects what was discussed or agreed upon. You may want to check every 30 minutes or so, with a simple "Excuse me, but can we break for just a few minutes? I want to see what has been written on the IEP so far." If 30-minute breaks seem forced, ask to review the form each time you complete a section. Pay special attention to the narrative page—this will likely be more subjective than other parts of the IEP.

How does the IEP team make an actual decision on IEP components? Do you vote? IDEA establishes no set method for reaching agreement. The school administrator may not even raise the question of how agreement is reached. You can request voting, but in most IEP meetings, the team tries to reach consensus through discussion. No matter how the administrator proceeds, make sure your objections are heard and no one assumes consensus when there isn't any.

How items are recorded on the IEP plan is equally important. From the beginning to the end of the IEP meeting, you want to be sure that the IEP's narrative page, goals and objectives, placement and related services reflect, as much as possible, your point of view.

The Importance of a Parent Addendum Page

As mentioned throughout Section D, we strongly recommend you attach to the IEP a statement of your point of view, particularly on disputed items. Section F explains the parent addendum.

1. Child's Current Educational Status

If your child is presently enrolled in school, the IEP team will review your child's current IEP's goals and objectives, program and related services. Your child's current status may be reflected in testing data, grades, and teacher reports or observations. If this is an eligibility IEP meeting, the team will review assessment data; it will do the same every three years when your child is re-assessed. Discussion of your child's current status

may be broad or specific. It may occur at the beginning of the IEP meeting or as you review specific items, such as goals and objectives, for the upcoming year.

Watch what you—or anyone else—says about your child's current situation. For example, if you are concerned about the current program, you won't want the IEP narrative page to state that "Sam's placement has been highly successful this past year." If such a statement is made and entered onto the IEP document—perhaps on the narrative page—be sure to object, with something like "I'm sorry but I don't think that statement is accurate and I certainly cannot agree with it. It should not be on the IEP as reflecting our consensus."

2. Assessments

A school district representative (most likely the assessor) will either read or summarize the school district's assessment. If the assessor starts reading the report, ask her to synthesize the salient points, rather than spend precious time reading the assessment verbatim. You especially don't need it read if you reviewed a copy before the meeting, as suggested in Chapters 6 and 10.

This may be the time to use your IEP Material Organizer (see Chapter 10) to point to other documents—such as previous IEP plans, an independent assessment, other reports, teacher notes and the like—to support or contradict the school assessment.

If you haven't already introduced the independent assessment, you will do so once the district has finished presenting its assessment. You or your assessor should provide a synopsis of the report, focusing on:

- the assessor's credentials
- the reason for the assessment
- the tests used
- the key conclusions regarding the testing, and
- the specific recommendations made.

Be sure to highlight the test results and recommendations not covered in the school assessment. This is also the time to introduce any other supporting material, including letters, work samples and other professional opinions.

On most IEP forms, reference is made to the assessments on the narrative page. The IEP plan might specify the sections, results or statements in the assessments on which you all agree. Even if there is only one statement in the assessment you all agree on, be sure it's on the IEP document if it is essential to your child's needs. If the person drafting the IEP plan includes something from an assessment with which you disagree, make sure your objections are noted.

Sometimes, the assessments are attached. This can work in your favor. Attaching the assessment might imply agreement with it—either the school district's or an independent assessment—and incorporation of it into the IEP.

If an assessment is not attached, or it is clear that there is not agreement on the assessment, the narrative page should specify what parts of the assessments are included or excluded.

Examples
- The IEP team agrees with Sections 1, 2, 4, 6 and 8 of the school assessment and Sections 3, 5, 9, 10 and 12 of the independent assessment and incorporates them into the IEP.
- The IEP team disagrees with the rest of both assessments and does not incorporate them into the IEP.

You can use the parent addendum page to voice your disagreement. (See Section F.)

3. Goals and Objectives

If this is not your child's first IEP, the IEP team will next review the previous year's goals and objectives. This discussion is likely to lead to one of four different outcomes:

- You and the school district agree that the goals and objectives were met.
- You and the school district agree that certain goals and objectives were met, but others were not. You may also agree that an objective was met, but not the larger goal. For example, if John met the objective of successfully adding two-digit numbers 75% of the time, it does not necessarily mean that John achieved the larger goal of doing third grade math or that John understood the process.
- You and the school district agree that the goals and objectives were not met.
- You and the school district disagree on whether the goals and objectives were met.

Although you won't be working on placement and services during this part of the meeting, keep in mind the link. If your child met the goals and objectives, perhaps it means her placement is correct and should continue. Or maybe it means she is ready to be mainstreamed. If she didn't meet the goals and objectives, she may need a smaller class. Or maybe the placement is fine, but she needs more tutoring (a related service).

Once you finish reviewing the previous goals and objectives—or if this is your child's first time in special education—it's time to write goals and objectives for the coming year. Chapter 9 covers drafting them in advance. It's possible the school representatives did so as well.

Remember, your goal is to have an IEP team agree on goals and objectives that support the placement and related services you want for your child.

What if you disagree with each other's goals and objectives?

- Do your best to convince school members of the IEP team that your goals and objectives are consistent with the recommendations made by others, such as assessor, the classroom teacher or your child's aide.
- Ask school members what they specifically disagree with in your goals and objectives.

- If you can't agree on all goals and objectives, try to reach consensus on some—better half a loaf than no loaf.
- If attempts to compromise fail, suggest dropping all pre-drafted goals and objectives and coming up with something new.

If you and the school representatives disagree about past or future goals and objectives, be sure the IEP document clearly states that. At the very least, record your concerns on your parent addendum. (See Section F.)

4. Transition Services

If your child is 14 or older, the IEP team must discuss transition services regarding her course of study, including advanced courses and vocational classes.

Specifically, the IEP team should consider strategies to assist your child in assessing, securing information about and taking steps regarding vocational, employment, independent living and post-high school educational plans. Investigating transition services can include many different possible processes, including looking at potential jobs, learning how to function in the community, accessing other agencies that will provide support for adults with disabilities and researching college opportunities.

5. Related Services

The discussions regarding related services (and placement—next section) are likely to generate the most debate. You and the school district may have very different notions of the type and amount of related services that are appropriate for your child.

Under IDEA, related services are considered to be developmental, corrective and other support-ive services, including transportation, needed for a disabled child to benefit from special education. They are also those services needed for your child to be educated in a regular classroom. Remember, the burden is on the school district to show why your child cannot achieve satisfactorily in a regular classroom with the use of some related services.

Independent assessors and others supporting your position should be prepared to state their opinions in detail—for example, "Given Gavin's severe difficulties in articulation, he needs a minimum of three 30-minute sessions each week, one-to-one with a speech therapist with a lot of experience in articulation work." If someone is not there to make this statement, be prepared to point to written materials that support the particular related service.

The related services section of the IEP docu-ment requires more detail than any other. It's not enough to say "Gavin will receive speech therapy." The IEP team must specify how often (such as three sessions per week), how long (such as 30-minute sessions), the ratio of pupils to related service provider (such as one-to-one) and the qualifications of the service provider.

The more vague the description, the more flexibility the school district has. Speech therapy two to three times a week is very different from speech therapy three times per week. Try to avoid terminology such as "or," "about," "to be determined" or "as needed." When in doubt be specific; it's that simple.

Most IEP documents have a specific section for related services. Your agreement on related services can be recorded there or on the narrative page.

Related services cannot be denied your child because of budgetary or administrative constraints. See Section B.3, above.

Some Related Services May Be the Responsibility of Other Agencies

As explained in Chapter 10, Section E, in some states, some related services, such as mental health services, are the responsibility of a non-educational public agency. Still, these services should be discussed at the IEP meeting, and it's the responsibility of the school district to make sure representatives of those other agencies attend the meeting. Those noneducational agencies have the same responsibilities as the school district and therefore the same role to play at the meeting regarding the services they must provide.

6. Placement or Program

Placement or program is both the kind of class (such as a regular class, special day class or residential placement) and the specific location of the program (such as a regular fifth grade class at Abraham Lincoln School). Placement or program is sometimes referred to on the IEP form as the instructional setting, and is central to a successful IEP and effective educational experience. IDEA requires that your child's school district offer a continuum of placement options (34 C.F.R. §300.551). Placement or program is most often some kind of public program, but IDEA requires placement in a private school if there is no appropriate public option. Placement or program is generally the last item discussed at the IEP meeting.

As explained in Chapter 2, IDEA requires that your child be educated in the "least restrictive environment." This means that to the maximum extent appropriate, children with disabilities are to be educated with children who are nondisabled. Special classes, separate schooling or other removal of children with disabilities from a regular class should happen only if the nature or severity of the disability is such that education in a regular class with the use of supplementary aids and services cannot be achieved satisfactorily.

Despite the least restrictive environment guideline, there is no absolute rule that your child be mainstreamed or not be mainstreamed. IDEA prefers a mainstreamed placement, but many courts have ruled that a child's individual needs determine the appropriateness of a placement.

If you don't want your child mainstreamed, point out that although the law favors regular classroom placement, individual need is still the most significant determinant of placement. Stress that courts have clearly stated that there is no prohibition to placing a child in a non-regular class, and in fact if a child needs such a placement, it is by definition the least restrictive environment. (See *Geis v. Board of Education,* 774 F.2d 575 (3d Cir. 1985) and *Stockton By Stockton v. Barbour County Bd. of Educ.,* (4th Cir. 1997) 25 IDELR 1076.)

If you want your child mainstreamed you should emphasize the appropriateness of the education and your child's basic right to the least restrictive environment. You should also emphasize your child's right to be as close to home as possible, and educated in the school the child would attend if not disabled. Ultimately, the burden is on the school district to prove why your child should be removed from a regular classroom.

School representatives may be prepared to discuss a specific program in a named school or may have in mind the kind of class, such as a special day class, but want to leave the specific location up to the school administration. If the school representatives suggest this latter option, object. The IEP team should decide the kind of class (such as a special day class for language-delayed children) and specific location (such as a regular class at King School).

More likely, you and the school administrator will know before the meeting where each other stands on placement. Still, an open-minded IEP team should fully discuss your child's placement needs. The school administrator will probably state that the IEP team has reviewed your child's record, agreed on goals and objectives and resolved related services, and that a particular placement is called for—such as, "We recommend placement in the special day class at Johnson School."

If you disagree with the administrator's conclusion, state your preference and refer to supportive materials—particularly items that are very persuasive about placement. Then ask (or have your independent assessor ask) pointed questions, such as:

> *Ms. Parton, you said Betsy should be placed at Johnson School in the special day class. We believe Betsy should be placed in the regular class at Thompson School with a one-to-one aide. The assessment by Dr. Jones is specific about that and Betsy's current teacher agrees. Can you explain why you disagree?*

If the school administrator is not persuaded or does not adequately answer your question, be direct and frank:

> *With all due respect, I think your answer is vague and does not address the specifics in Dr. Jones's report and your own teacher's comment about Betsy's readiness for a regular classroom. I feel very strongly about this, and we will go to due process on the issue of placement if we have to. I also think that with the documentation and the law on mainstreaming, we will be successful in due process. I really feel to have to go in that direction is a bad use of school resources and will only make the ultimate move that much more expensive for you. I just don't understand—given the evidence—why you want to put me and my wife, your district personnel, and, most importantly, our child through that.*

7. Narrative Page

The narrative page is the place to record information that can't be included by way of a checkbox or for which there isn't enough space to write the details. The narrative page can include information on any other topic covered by the IEP document, or on a topic that would otherwise be omitted. Here some examples of narrative page statements.

Examples
- The IEP team agrees that the school district and outside assessments are complete and appropriate and are incorporated into the IEP.
- The IEP team incorporates the child profile provided by Steven's parents into the IEP.
- The IEP team agrees that Melissa needs a school environment in which there are no behavioral problems.
- The IEP team agrees that Henry is beginning to show signs of emotional distress; the classroom teacher will report on a weekly basis to the family about any signs of such distress. The district psychologist will observe Henry in class. The IEP team agrees to meet in three months to review this matter and to discuss the possible need for more formal assessment or the need for additional related services.
- The IEP team agrees with the recommendations made by Dr. Jones on page 4 of her report.
- Ms. Brown, Steve's teacher, is concerned about Steve's lack of focus.
- The IEP team agrees with recommendations 1, 2, 5, 7 and 9 made by Dr. Jones on page 4 of her report.
- Carolyn's parents expressed concern about class size.

Sometimes, the person recording the IEP document may write something for which there is no clear agreement or where there is, in fact, disagreement between parent and school personnel. Make sure the narrative is changed to reflect your disagreement or to indicate that the statement reflects only the point of view of the school personnel. Basically, you don't want the narrative to imply agreement when there is none.

Include a Child Profile in the IEP Plan

In Chapter 10, Section D, we suggested that you create a child profile to give school officials a perspective on your child beyond numbers and test results. The school administrator may question whether law or policy allows something like a child profile to be included in the IEP document. Since IDEA does not prohibit it, nothing prevents the IEP team from discussing and including a child profile.

Emphasize that your statement about your child will help the school staff implement the goals and objectives, and for that reason it should be included in the IEP document. If the school administrator disagrees, ask specifically what is objectionable. Try to convince the team of the importance of the profile. If the administrator continues to refuse, use the parent addendum to include it.

E. Signing the IEP Document

At the end of the IEP meeting, the school administrator will ask you to sign the IEP document. School officials will be signing the form as well. You don't have to sign the IEP document on the spot. You may want to take it home and return it in 24 hours. This will give you time to think about issues you are not sure you agree or disagree with. It also gives you time to record your disagreements coherently on a parent addendum (discussed in Section F).

Of course, if you are 100% in agreement with the school representatives on all issues and don't need time to mull over issues, then go ahead and sign. Read the document carefully, however, to make sure the statements and information are correct and reflect the IEP team's intentions. Also, make sure that everything on your agenda was covered and that all important issues have been resolved.

If you do take the IEP document home, be sure that all other participants have signed off on all the agreed-to items. Either they will have already signed or you can indicate the other IEP team members can sign if they are in agreement.

Every IEP form has a signature page with a variety of checkboxes, including:

- a box to indicate you attended
- a box to indicate that you were provided your legal rights
- a box to indicate your approval of the IEP document
- a box to indicate your disapproval.

There may also be boxes to indicate partial approval, and whether or not you want to initiate due process.

Take care in checking the appropriate boxes. If you don't approve of the IEP document, don't check that box. If you partially agree, check the partial agreement box or, if no partial agreement box, check the approval box—*but* carefully and clearly write next to it: "Approval in part only; see parent addendum." (Section F discusses the parent addendum.)

It is absolutely key to state your position clearly on the IEP. There are no legally required phrases to use—plain and direct English will do fine.

1. Full Agreement

Congratulations! Check the correct box and sign the form.

2. Nearly Full Agreement

It's possible that you agree on all important items concerning related services, curricula-methodology and program or placement, but you disagree on some secondary issues, such as goals and objectives or statements in an assessment. In this situation, you have two choices:

- You can check the box to indicate your approval and sign your name. This might make sense if the issues on which you disagree are minor and you want to foster a good relationship with the school district.
- You can check the box to indicate partial approval, list the items you dispute (on the signature page if there's room or on the parent addendum) and sign your name.

Sample

> Date: April 24, 19xx
>
> Signature: *Lucinda Crenshaw*
>
> I agree with all of the IEP except for:
>
> - items 3, 4 and 6 on the district's assessment
> - goals and objectives numbers 2 and 5.

You Don't Have to Accept "All or Nothing"

Remember—the school district cannot present you with an "all or nothing" choice. For example: "We're offering two sessions of occupational therapy. Either agree with the two sessions or there will be no occupational therapy for your child." You can agree to the two sessions without giving up your right to seek more. See Sections B.8 and F for examples.

3. Partial Agreement

In this situation, you agree on some, but not all, of the big issues (related services, curricula-methodology and program or placement). You can check the box to indicate partial approval, state that your disagreements are on the parent addendum, spell out your disagreements on the parent addendum and sign your name.

Sample

> Date: April 24, 19xx
>
> Signature: *Lucinda Crenshaw*
>
> I agree with all of the IEP except for those items listed on the parent addendum page, designated as "Attachment A" and attached to the IEP.

 See Chapter 12 if you want to go to due process to resolve the disagreement.

4. Nearly Total Disagreement

In this case, you don't agree on any of the major items concerning related services, curricula-methodology and program or placement, but do agree on certain goals and objectives, parts of the assessment and other minor items. Again, you can check the box to indicate partial approval, state that your disagreements are on the parent addendum, spell out your disagreements on the parent addendum (see Section F, below) and sign your name.

 See Chapter 12 if you want to go to due process to resolve the disagreement.

5. Total Disagreement

Although it's rare, in some instances the parents disagree with everything on the IEP form. If so, sign your name after checking only the box acknowledging that you attended the meeting and the disapproval box. You could also refer to the parent addendum page.

At this stage, your options are informal negotiations, mediation or a fair hearing.

See the Chapter 12 discussion of due process, including the discussion on your child's status when there is no IEP agreement.

F. Parent Addendum Page

As you go through the IEP meeting, when you disagree with the school personnel and cannot reach a compromise, indicate your position. Make sure you or your notetaker keeps a list of all issues you dispute on a separate piece of paper.

A parent addendum page is the place you record your point of view concerning any issue on which there is no—or only limited—agreement. There is no IDEA requirement for an addendum page, and your district's IEP form is not likely to have one. There is no formality to the addendum page—a blank piece of paper will do.

You will most likely complete the addendum page at or near the end of the meeting. The content of the addendum page is vastly more important than its format. Your statement should:
- relate specifically to issues concerning your child's education—don't use the addendum to state general complaints
- be in plain English, and
- state specifically your point of view on all key items of dispute.

As shown in Section E.3, state on the signature page that you disagree with part of the IEP document and refer to the attached addendum page for the detail of the disagreement.

If you school's IEP form includes an addendum page, use it; otherwise, mark "Attachment A" at the top of a blank piece of paper and write something like the following:

> Parent Addendum Page of Carol and Steven Stack
> IEP for Beatrice Stack
> March 12, 19xx

You have an absolute right to state your position, but if, for some reason, the school district does not allow you to attach an addendum, indicate on the signature page that you do not agree with everything in the IEP document, that you want to attach an addendum but that the school administration would not let you. Then file a complaint. (See Chapter 13.)

Example Addendum Statements

- The district does not agree with recommendations of Dr. Jones's independent assessment, but has refused to state why. We believe that her assessment is valid and should be fully incorporated into the IEP as representing useful and valid information about Tonya.
- We do not agree with recommendations 3, 6, 9 and 14 of Dr. Lee's assessment of January 21, 19xx. We do agree with the rest of her report.
- We believe the independent assessment by Dr. Okuru is valid, provides important information about Jane and should be incorporated into the IEP. The school has indicated disagreement with Dr. Okuru's report, but has not specifically stated why.
- The IEP team agrees with sections 3, 7, 8 and 9 of the school's report and all of Dr. Friedman's assessment, but the school will not put this agreement into the IEP. We believe those agreed-to sections should be incorporated into the IEP.

- Dr. Pentan of the school district stated that we have no right to include a child profile in the IEP. IDEA does not say that and if the IEP team agrees, the profile can be part of the IEP. We believe the profile provides valid and important information regarding Fernando.
- While the teacher reported that Stanley increased his reading comprehension (this relates to goal #4 on page 2), we have observed at home, over a long period of time, his reading comprehension seems substantially below the test results.
- We don't agree that Sandy's goals and objectives were met because the evaluation of the goals and objectives was inaccurate.
- The district offered speech therapy one time a week, 20 minutes per session. Moira needs three, 40-minute sessions per week, each session to be one-to-one with a licensed speech therapist. This is supported by the May 2, 19xx, report of Dr. Shawn Waters. We accept the one session and give permission for that to begin, but this acceptance is not to be construed as agreement about the amount of the related services, only agreement as to the need.
- The IEP agrees that Nick be placed in the regular fifth grade class at Kennedy School. We agree with placement in the regular fifth grade class at Kennedy School, but we believe Nick needs an aide to meet his needs and allow him to achieve satisfactorily in that regular class.
- We believe that the regular seventh grade class at Roosevelt School is the only appropriate placement for Tony. We believe placement in the special day class at Roosevelt as offered by the school district is inappropriate. We agree to placement in the regular classroom at Roosevelt for three periods a day, although such agreement is not to be construed as agreement on partial mainstreaming. We will proceed to due process on the issue of full-time mainstreaming in the regular seventh grade class at Roosevelt.

IDEA Notice Requirements and Private School Placements

If you plan to remove your child to a private program, you must notify the school district of your intent either:

- at the most recent IEP meeting you attended prior to removing your child from public school, or
- at least ten business days before the actual removal

(20 U.S.C. §1412 (a) (10) (C).

If you don't provide this notice, and then pursue due process to seek reimbursement for your child's placement in a private school, that reimbursement may be denied or reduced.

12

Resolving IEP Disputes Through Due Process

The purpose of this book is to help you successfully develop an IEP plan for your child, therefore making this chapter irrelevant. But the nature of the IEP process is such that disagreements arise, and some cannot be resolved informally.

Under IDEA, you have the right to resolve these disputes with your school district through "due process" (20 U.S.C. §1415; 34 C.F.R. §§300.500-517). There are two possible due process avenues available to you when you disagree: mediation and a hearing.

In mediation, you and representatives of the school district meet with a neutral third party who helps you reach a compromise. The mediator has the power of persuasion, but no authority to impose a decision on you.

If you cannot reach an agreement in mediation or if you'd prefer to skip mediation altogether, you can request due process or a "fair hearing," where you and school district personnel present written evidence and have witnesses testify about the disputed issues before a neutral third party, called a hearing officer. The hearing officer, much like a judge, makes a decision and issues a binding order within 45 days from the date you formally requested due process (34 C.F.R. §300.511). If you or the school district disagree with the decision, you can appeal to a state or federal court.

Due process resolution is available for factual disputes—that is, when you and your child's school district cannot agree on eligibility or some part of the IEP plan. If the school district has ignored a legal rule—such as failed to hold an IEP meeting, do an assessment, meet a time limit or provide an agreed-to part of the IEP—you would file a complaint, not pursue due process. (Complaints are covered in Chapter 13.)

Don't Delay Filing for Due Process

In almost all kinds of legal disputes, states have something called a statute of limitations which establishes a time limit for taking legal action. Depending on the state and the kind of case, this may be anywhere from a few months to several years. If you fail to bring your legal action within your state's time limit, you will likely be barred from taking any legal action at all.

IDEA does not establish a time limit for filing for due process, submitting a complaint or appealing a due process decision to a court. Numerous courts have ruled, however, that state statutes of limitations apply to IDEA matters. To avoid losing your right to file for due process, it is therefore very important that you check with your state department of education or a local lawyer regarding your state's statute of limitations.

Alternatives to Informal Negotiations and Formal Due Process

Informal discussions with the school district and formal due process aren't the only ways to resolve disputes. Consider methods such as building parent coalitions and becoming involved in the local political process. These options are discussed in Chapter 15.

In addition, IDEA provides that a state or local school district can establish "alternative dispute resolution" (ADR) procedures for parents who choose not to use due process.

In ADR, you meet with a neutral third party who is under contract with a parent training center or community parent resource center, or who is from an appropriate alternative dispute resolution entity (20 U.S.C. §1415(e)(2)(B)). The intent of the meeting is for you to explore alternative ways to resolve your dispute and for the third party to explain to you the benefits of mediation. This ADR meeting is intended to be nonadversarial, while mediation is the first step to formal due process. Be aware that using ADR may delay resolution of the dispute.

If you're interested in ADR, call your school district or state department of education (see Appendix 2) to find out if ADR is available.

A. Before Due Process: Informal Negotiations

Before invoking due process, you may want to try to resolve your dispute through informal discussions or negotiations with the school. While resolving these problems might require formal action if not addressed immediately, many times these issues can be settled informally.

In addition, some disputes may not even qualify for due process. (See Section B.) For example, you and the school principal may disagree over when you can visit the classroom or why the assessor had to re-schedule your child's testing.

1. Pros and Cons of Informal Negotiation

Informal negotiation is useful for several reasons. Ultimately, it may save you stress, preparation time and money. It will also help you to maintain a more positive relationship with the school district, and will keep problems from escalating. Finally, informal negotiation is easier and may work.

Even if you eventually pursue your due process rights, informal negotiations might help. First, it will create a record of your efforts to resolve matters informally. This will show that you are reasonable and fair-minded, and don't immediately look to an adversarial method of settlement. Second, informal negotiations will help you understand the school district's position, which will be valuable if you end up in mediation or at a fair hearing.

In limited situations, however, there may be reasons to go immediately to due process:

- You need an immediate resolution because the issue affects your child's well-being, safety or health. An example would be if you felt your child needed psychological counseling for depression which affected his school work, but the district disagreed. You may not have time for informal meetings.
- The school administrator is so unpleasant or inflexible that you just don't want to deal with her.
- The IEP meeting made it clear that any time spent trying to informally resolve things will be a waste of time.

2. Basics of Informal Negotiation

To begin informal negotiations, call or write your child's teacher, school principal or special education administrator and ask to meet to discuss your concerns. You can raise the issues in your phone conversation or letter, but ideally you'll want an appointment to discuss the problem face-to-face.

Before the meeting, prepare a brief and clearly written description of the problem and a recommended solution. Also, find out if any school personnel support you. If so, ask them to attend the meeting or for permission for you to give their opinions.

During the meeting, emphasize problem solving, not winning. Try to structure the negotiation as a mutual attempt to solve a problem. Avoid personal attacks on school personnel. Respect the school's point of view even if you disagree. Acknowledge the school representatives' concerns. Even if you strongly disagree, you don't lose anything by saying, "I understand your concerns, but I think we can address those by doing …."

Finally, be respectful, but firm—for example, you can say "It is clear we disagreed at the IEP meeting. I am not adverse to trying to solve this informally, but I will not hesitate to pursue my due process rights if we cannot."

Good Books on Negotiation

Getting to Yes: Negotiating Agreement Without Giving In, by Roger Fisher and William Ury (Penguin Books). This classic book offers a strategy for coming to mutually acceptable agreements in all kinds of situations.

Getting Past No: Negotiating Your Way From Confrontation to Cooperation, by William Ury (Bantam Books). This sequel to *Getting to Yes* suggests techniques for negotiating with difficult people.

3. After Meeting Informally

If you do not resolve your dispute informally, send a letter, briefly stating the problem, the solution you think makes sense and what you are considering next, such as contacting an attorney, pursuing mediation or fair hearing, or filing a

complaint with your school board or with the state department of education.

If you resolve your problem informally, it is very important to follow-up the meeting with a confirming letter.

A sample letter confirming the results of your informal negotiation is shown below; a blank tear-out copy of this form is in Appendix 5.

Use the Law to Make Your Case

As you try to persuade your school district—in writing or in person—cite the legal authority for your case whenever possible. Referring to a section in IDEA or even a court decision may help your case. See Chapter 14, Section F, for tips on legal research.

If the meeting does not resolve the problem to your satisfaction, then you may proceed to due process (either mediation or a fair hearing) or file a complaint (if appropriate).

B. Typical Due Process Disputes

Remember, due process (mediation or fair hearing) is used to resolve factual disputes. The following is a list of common IEP disputes:

- eligibility for special education
- results of an assessment
- goals and objectives
- specific placement or program
- related services
- proposed changes to your child's current IEP program, and
- suspension or expulsion of your child.

Several kinds of disputes are *not* eligible for due process:

- requesting a specific teacher or service provider for your child

Sample Letter Confirming Informal Negotiation

Date: June 1, 199x

To: Michael Chan, Principal

Truman Elementary School

903 Dogwood Drive

Paterson, NJ 00000

Re: Tasha Kincaid, student in second grade class of Marlene Walker, Truman School

I appreciated the chance to meet on May 28 and discuss

Tasha's placement . I also appreciated your

point of view and the manner in which we solved the problem.

I want to confirm our agreement that Tasha will be placed in the regular third grade

class at Truman School for the upcoming school year. [If you have already requested

due process add: Once you have confirmed this in writing to me, I will formally withdraw

my due process request.] .

I greatly appreciate the manner in which you helped solve this problem. Please tell the

third grade teacher, Ms. Solarz, that I would be delighted to meet with her before

school starts to discuss effective ways to work with Tasha.

.

Thank you.

Sincerely,

André Kincaid

André Kincaid

4500 Fair Street

Paterson, NJ 00000

- hiring or firing school staff
- assigning a different school administrator to your case, or
- requesting a specific person to represent the school district in the IEP process.

These concerns may be addressed through non-IDEA activities, such as parent organizing (see Chapter 15) or informal negotiations with the school.

C. When to Pursue Due Process

Due process is hard; it takes time, energy and sometimes money. It is stressful. Deciding whether or not to pursue due process requires that you carefully and objectively consider five matters:

- **The precise nature of the problem.** You will have to pinpoint exactly what your dispute is, and make sure it is a factual dispute. For example, if you feel your child's education is generally not working (and you have not yet gone to an IEP meeting), or you object to the attitude of the school administrator, your concern is not yet ready for due process. If, however, your child has fallen behind in her regular class and you feel she should be in a special class, and the IEP team did not agree, you have a problem that qualifies for due process resolution.

Don't File for Due Process Until After the IEP Meeting

Many parents make the mistake of identifying a problem and requesting a fair hearing, before the issue is considered at an IEP meeting. Unless there are very unusual circumstances—for example, your child's health or well-being is threatened—you must go to an IEP meeting and reach an impasse there before you can request due process.

- **The importance of the issue to your child.** Placement or related service disputes are often central to your child's educational well-being. On the other hand, a dispute over goals and objectives or assessment conclusions may be important, but not significant enough to go to due process because it does not directly impact your child's placement and related services.
- **The strength of your case.** Can you win? What evidence do you have to support your position? What evidence exists against it? What are the qualifications of the people making supportive or contrary statements? Remember—the district is required to provide your child with an appropriate education, not the best possible one. After the IEP meeting, review and update your IEP Material Organizer form (discussed in Chapter 10) to determine what evidence exists for and against you. If you want other opinions on the strength of your case, consider these sources:
  - ▲ Nonschool employees, your independent assessor, an outside tutor or an attorney. Describe the disputed issue, your evidence and the evidence against you, and ask if they think you have a good chance of winning.
  - ▲ Other parents, particularly those who have been through due process with your school district. How does the school district react? Is the school likely to take a hard line position or might it offer a compromise after you show you are determined to go forward?
  - ▲ Local parent and disability organizations. (Chapter 15 discusses how to find and work with a parents' group.) If you need help finding a local group, start by contacting a national organization (see the list in Appendix 3).
- **The bottom line concerns for the school district.** For any disputed issue, the school district will have some bottom line concerns

—notably cost, and administrative difficulties providing what you want. For example, the school administrator may be willing to compromise on a dispute between two public school program options, rather than pay for costly private school placement. What you think the school's bottom line is may affect your bottom line and how far you'll go to get it.

- **The cost of going forward.** Due process witnesses (including independent assessors) and attorneys will charge for their time. If you prevail at a fair hearing, you are likely to be reimbursed for those costs, but not if you lose. (See Chapter 14 for information on using an attorney and attorney's fees.)

D. Your Child's Status During Due Process

While you are in dispute with the school district, your child is entitled to remain in her current placement until you reach an agreement with the school, settle the matter through mediation, have a fair hearing decision rendered without either you or the school district appealing or have a final court decision. This is called the "stay put" provision (34 C.F.R. §300.514; 20 U.S.C. §1415(j)). "Stay put" can be a complicated legal right. If you are concerned about whether your particular situation involves a "stay put" issue, see an attorney at once or contact a nonprofit disability rights organization.

Example:

Your child is in a regular sixth grade class with a one-to-one aide, two hours a day. At the IEP meeting, the school district offers a special day class, not a regular class, for seventh grade. You want your child to continue in a regular class. You are unable to reach an agreement at the IEP meeting. You initiate due process, during which time your child is entitled to remain in a regular classroom with the aide until the matter is resolved.

Exceptions to the Stay Put Rule

IDEA provides that your child is entitled to remain in her current placement pending due process except if your child carries a weapon to school or to a school function, or knowingly possesses, uses, sells or solicits illegal drugs while at school or a school function. In any of these situations involving weapons or drugs, the school district can change your child's placement to an appropriate interim alternative educational setting for up to 45 days, or suspend your child for ten or fewer school days (20 U.S.C. §1415 (k)). Because these exceptions to the stay put rule are complicated, we recommend you consult an attorney or one of the support groups listed in Appendix 3.

E. Using a Lawyer During Due Process

This section explains some specific concerns regarding using an attorney for due process. Chapter 14 discusses this topic in general terms.

The use of an attorney in due process certainly escalates the adversarial nature of the dispute, but by the time you've reached due process that is probably not a key concern. Using an attorney may also speed up the resolution and increase your chances of success.

In mediation, an attorney will present your case and counter school district arguments. In a fair hearing, an attorney should prepare witnesses, submit exhibits, make the opening statement and direct the proceeding. An attorney can also play a less active role, such as providing advice and helping you organize your case material, but not attending the proceeding. Your attorney will contact the district to indicate she's now involved.

Not surprisingly, legal costs can be considerable. To prepare for and attend a one-day mediation session, legal fees will likely range from $500 to $1,000—sometimes less, sometimes more. The cost for a two-three day fair hearing may range from $1,500 to $7,500 or more. It is not unusual for an attorney to use ten to 25 hours to prepare for a three-day hearing. If you use an attorney for advice only—for example, to help organize your case—naturally costs will be lower.

 See Chapter 14, Section D, for a thorough discussion of legal fees, how they're paid and how you may be reimbursed for them.

Check Out Free or Low-Cost Legal Services

The school district must provide you with a list of free or low-cost legal services available in your area. See Chapter 14, Section C, for advice on finding and working with an attorney.

---

1. Attorney Fees in Mediation

During mediation, your settlement position should include payment of your attorney fees by the school district. Since mediation is voluntary, the school district may or may not agree to pay attorney fees. Whether or not the school district agrees to pay will probably depend largely on how strong your case is and how motivated the school district is to settle.

The school district may try to avoid having to reimburse you by agreeing to provide the education you want, in exchange for your dropping the demand for payment of your attorney's fees. You will need to assess the strength of your case to determine if you are willing to forego your legal fees. Your attorney should advise you of the pros and cons in this situation.

2. Attorney Fees in Fair Hearing

If your case goes to fair hearing and you win, you will be entitled to reimbursement of your attorney's fees. If you lose the hearing, you're responsible for your own attorney's fees, but you will not have to pay the school district's attorney's fees.

3. Other Legal Advocates

There are non-attorney advocates who can be quite skilled in due process. Their fees are usually lower than a lawyers' fees, but you are not entitled to reimbursement of an advocate's fees if you settle in mediation or prevail in a fair hearing.

 See Chapter 14, Section D.2, for more details on reimbursement of attorney fees in due process.

Special education attorneys, nonprofit law centers and disability and parent support groups may know the names of special education advocates.

F. Requesting Due Process

You must formally request due process in order for a mediation or fair hearing to be scheduled. States vary as to what agency is responsible for due process, but it is usually within the state department of education. Your school district must provide you with the appropriate agency name, address and phone number. Call the agency and ask how you initiate due process. Usually, you will either complete a form provided by the agency or send a letter providing the following information:

- your name and address
- your child's name and grade
- the name of your child's school and the address of the school district
- a description of the disputed issues

- your desired resolution—state not only what you want for your child's education, but also that you want to be reimbursed for your due process costs, such as attorney's fees, witness fees and independent assessment costs, and
- whether you want mediation or to go directly to a fair hearing.

This information is required under IDEA.

Keep a copy of your completed form or letter for your records.

A sample letter requesting due process is shown below; a blank tear-out copy is in Appendix 5.

G. Preparing for Due Process

While a mediation session and a fair hearing are different, the preparation for the former will help as you get ready for the latter. In addition, the preparation you did for the IEP meeting will be of enormous help as you go through due process.

1. Organize Your Evidence

First, pull out your child's file, all reports, assessments and everything else in your IEP binder (Chapter 4), your blueprint (Chapter 5) and your IEP Material Organizer form (Chapter 10).

Make a list of the disputed issues. Using a blank IEP Material Organizer form, write next to each disputed issue who or what supports your point of view and who or what opposes it. You should make a separate list of your potential witnesses and think about making a list of who you think will be district witnesses (see Section I.4.d, below.)

Now find every piece of evidence you have to support your position. Review your binder, original Material Organizer forms and notes from the IEP meeting. Focus not only on reports and assessments, but also comments made at the meeting. Gather all your supportive evidence together or tab it in your binder and highlight key statements. Make photocopies of all written materials that support your point of view to have available during the mediation or hearing.

Now work on the school district's case—that is, find all evidence that contradicts your point of view. Look for any rebuttal comments.

2. Make a List of Expenses

Once you've gathered evidence, make a list of expenses you've incurred throughout the IEP process, such as the costs of:

- independent assessments
- tutors
- lost wages for attending IEPs
- private school or private related service costs
- personal transportation costs, such as those incurred driving your child to a private school
- attorney's fees
- costs for other professionals such as a private speech therapist or counselor, and
- photocopying.

Note the date a payment was made or cost incurred, the name of the payee and purpose of the expense. Attach all receipts.

Letter Requesting Due Process

Date: _March 1, 19xx_

To: _Philip Jones_   **Sent Certified Mail**

Due Process Unit

Wisconsin Department of Education

8987 Franklin Ave. 00000

Re: _Steven Howard_

Our son, Steven Howard, is a fourth grader at Clinton School in La Crosse. His school district is the Central La Crosse Elementary School District, 562 5th Ave., La Crosse, WI.

We are formally requesting due process, beginning with mediation. We believe _Steven requires a full-time one-on-one aide in order to be fully mainstreamed in next year's regular fifth grade class at Clinton School. The school district has refused to provide that aide._

We believe an appropriate solution would include, but should not be limited to, the following:

- _a qualified full-time academic aide, to work one-on-one with Steven in the regular fifth grade class at Clinton School for the 1999-2000 school year._
- _reimbursement for all attorney's fees, witnesses, independent assessments, and other such costs as accrued by us for the February 14, 19xx, IEP meeting and the subsequent due process._

We understand IDEA (34 C.F.R. §300.511) requires that a fair hearing decision be rendered within 45 days of receipt of this request. We would appreciate it if you would contact us at once regarding scheduling the mediation.

Sincerely,

William Howard   Kate Howard

William and Kate Howard

1983 Smiley Lane

La Crosse, WI 00000

Phones: 555-5569 (home); 555-2000 (work)

There are no IDEA rules for how you prepare or present these expenses. At mediation or the fair hearing, you will want to present the expenses; if the district agrees to pay some or all of them, or if the hearing officer rules in your favor, the receipts will be necessary proof of your expenses.

3. Prepare an Opening Statement

Finally, write an opening statement. At the beginning of a mediation session or fair hearing, you will need to state why you're there and what you want. Some people are comfortable making notes and then talking extemporaneously; others write out a complete statement and read it. Do what's easiest for you. The opening statement will include the following:

Description of your child. Briefly describe your child, including her age, current educational program, general areas of educational concern and disabling conditions. Give a short explanation of your child's educational history.

Description of items in dispute. Briefly describe the specific items in dispute—for example, the amount of a related service or the placement.

Description of what you want and why. Summarize what your child needs in detail—for example, speech therapy three times a week, in a one-to-one setting with a therapist qualified to work with students with language delays, or placement in the Smith School, or the use of the Lindamood-Bell program or the Orton-Gillingham method.

Description of your evidence. You'll want to end with a strong statement briefly summarizing evidence you have for your position. In most mediations, you'll want to wait until you meet the mediator to reveal all of your evidence. But neither of these are hard and fast rules. You may say nothing in your opening statement at the hearing or say all in your mediation opening. You will

have to judge the best approach considering the situation, the personalities involved, and even your intuition. See "How Much Evidence Do You Reveal in Mediation," below.

H. Mediation Specifics

Mediation is the first official step in due process. It is less confrontational than a fair hearing, and is specifically intended to explore possible compromise and settlement of your dispute. The IDEA requires that all states offer mediation (20 U.S.C. §1415(e); 34 C.F.R. §300.506).

The mediator is a neutral third party, usually hired by the state department of education, knowledgeable about IDEA and special education matters. The mediator has no authority to force a settlement on you. If you reach settlement, however, your agreement will be put into writing and will be made binding on you and the district— meaning you both must abide by and follow the written settlement which ends your IEP dispute.

Mediation is fairly simple, although sessions vary depending on the style of the mediator and rules established by your state.

Contact your state department of education to find out the details of your state's laws on mediation. See Appendix 2.

Mediation must be made available to you at no cost, and is completely voluntary. If you prefer, you can go straight to a fair hearing and skip mediation.

If mediation is not successful, any settlement offers and other comments made during the mediation cannot be used as evidence at the fair hearing or any subsequent legal proceedings. This is important because it allows you to discuss matters in a frank manner without fear that such discussion will later be used against you (or the school district).

1. Pros and Cons of Mediation

You may be asking yourself why you would try mediation, particularly because it involves compromise, whereas a fair hearing officer will rule for or against the parties. There are some compelling reasons to go to mediation:

- **Know thy enemy.** Mediation gives you a chance to understand more fully the school district's arguments. Of course, the school district gets the same opportunity about your case, but it is invaluable in assessing the school's case.
- **The school district may be motivated to compromise.** Mediation takes the school district one step closer to a fair hearing and the possibility of a ruling against the school, with all the attendant costs, including possible attorney's fees. The school administrator may be far more flexible in mediation than she was at the IEP meeting, feeling that the formality of due process gives her the justification to change the district's position.
- **Mediation is constructive.** Mediation involves the working out of disagreements, thus you may retain a positive relationship with your school district by mediating the dispute. You also keep control over the outcome—you agree or disagree. When you go to fair hearing, the decisionmaking power is out of your hands.
- **Mediation is cheap.** As a general rule, you will have few or even no costs at mediation; fair hearings can be expensive, particularly if you use an attorney.
- **Mediation can provide a reality check.** Even if you don't settle the case, mediation, gives you a chance to have a neutral party assess your case and point out its strengths and weaknesses.
- **You get two bites of the apple.** By going to mediation, you give yourself two chances at success. If you go straight to the fair hearing, you relinquish all authority to resolve the matter to the fair hearing officer.

There are downsides to mediation:

- **A half of a loaf can be disappointing.** Ideally, you can settle in mediation and get everything your child needs. In reality, however, mediation usually involves compromise, meaning you will probably settle for less than what you'd get if you won at fair hearing.
- **Mediation may delay resolution of your dispute.** The IDEA requirement that a fair hearing decision be issued within 45 days from the date you request due process is the same whether you go through mediation or go straight to fair hearing. In reality, however, extensions of that 45 day rule can be granted as a result of time spent in mediation. Unless you have a real time problem—your child must be placed in a specific program by a certain date or he will suffer dire consequences—most cases can stand the delay.
- **You do things twice.** If you go to mediation and then a fair hearing, you will have been involved in two procedures, doubling the time, inconvenience, stress and some costs.

The bottom line about mediation. Do it. While the facts and personalities in each case can vary much, mediation is very frequently worth the effort.

2. Mediators

The mediator's job is to help you and the school district reach a settlement. The mediator will not decide who is right and who is wrong.

A good mediator will:

- put you and school representatives at ease
- try to establish an atmosphere in which compromise is possible
- be objective
- give you and the school district a frank assessment of the strengths and weaknesses of your positions, and

- go beyond your stated positions and explore possible settlements that may not be initially apparent.

Some mediators play a more limited role—that is, they simply present everyone's positions without expressing any opinion, and hope that the weight of the evidence and formality of the process will lead to a settlement.

3. Who, Where and When of Mediation

Mediation sessions must be held at a time and place convenient for you. They are often at the school district's main office, but they can be elsewhere. Some people are concerned that having the mediation at a school office gives the district an advantage. You may want to suggest another place, but frankly, it rarely matters, unless you are affected by the location.

The amount of time for the mediation can vary, but sessions generally take many hours and often a full day. Expect the mediation session to take more time than you would think.

While districts vary, most will have the special education administrator and perhaps another person who has direct knowledge of your child at the mediation. While you can bring outside assessors, aides, tutors and any other individuals you want, including a lawyer, you normally save them for the fair hearing.

While bringing in experts might mean expense to you and difficulty in finding a convenient time for all participants, including (or excluding) experts will depend on:

- how forceful the experts can be
- whether there is any chance to change the district's mind, and
- what you may lose in revealing some of your evidence prior to the fair hearing.

If you expect a fair hearing and don't want to put all your cards on the table at mediation, don't bring the experts. On the other hand, if you want to settle quickly and your experts can aid in that process, have them come.

4. The Mediation Session Itself

You, the mediator and the school representatives will gather usually in a conference or meeting room. After brief introductions, the mediator will explain how the mediation process works, stressing that mediation is a voluntary attempt to resolve your disagreement.

a. Your Opening Statement

You begin by briefly explaining your side of the dispute. (Section G, above, shows how to prepare an opening statement.) Do not hesitate to express your feelings, to bring in the human element. Your child has important needs and his well-being is at stake. Say that. Say how worried you are. Say why you feel the school district has harmed your child—by failing to provide an appropriate education. It's important to show the mediator how imperative the matter is to you and your child. This does not mean tirades, irrational, off-the-wall, unfocused monologues or berating the school district. Give your opinion, but acknowledge that the school representatives have a point of view; don't question their honesty, professionalism or decency.

Your opening statement should not go on and on or discuss every possible problem. It should be clear and succinct and run about five to 20 minutes.

If the school has committed any legal violations (normally not the subject of due process disputes), you can raise these in your opening statement. While legal violations are subject to the complaint procedure (see Chapter 13), the evidence of a legal violation may be a powerful addition to your case, showing the school district's disregard or lack of understanding of the law, and possibly the district's lack of reliability. Nothing in IDEA prevents you from raising legal issues in the mediation. While the mediator cannot look to remedy legal violations, the mediator can use the information and say to district personnel, "You are in trouble because you clearly violated the law; you might want to think about settling this case now."

How Much Evidence Do You Reveal in Mediation?

In Section G, we suggest that you describe your evidence as a part of your opening statement. But you may not want to reveal all your supporting evidence at mediation. By telling all, you may help the school prepare for the fair hearing. On the other hand if your evidence is very strong, revealing it may lead to a settlement in your favor. If you're not sure what to do, ask the mediator's opinion in your private meeting. If the mediator feels the school realizes its case is weak or for some reason is close to settling, then of course it may be wise to share everything. On the other hand, if the mediator feels the school is rigid and unlikely to settle, then it may be better not to reveal all of your evidence.

In either case, you'll want to provide at least a synopsis of your evidence, noting where a professional (teacher, related service provider, administrator, doctor, outside assessor or private tutor) has made a clear statement about the disputed item. Furthermore, note the credentials of the person, particularly if he is well-known, loaded with degrees and has a lot of experience. Highlight all supporting materials (written or stated) by someone from the school district.

---

b. School District's Opening Statement

After you make your opening statement, the school district's representative will present the district's point of view, perhaps responding to what you have said. Don't interrupt or respond, even though the school's version of the dispute may be very different from yours. Take notes of their main points.

After the school representative finishes, the mediator may turn to you, and invite you to add anything you forgot or respond to the school's statement. If you respond, make it brief, succinct and to the point, focusing on why you disagree with the school's position.

c. Private Sessions With the Mediator

After you and the school representatives make your opening statements, the mediator will meet privately with you, then with the school representatives, then back with you, then back with the school representatives, continuing back and forth as necessary. When you meet privately with the

mediator, speak frankly. The mediator cannot disclose anything you say to the school representatives, unless you give the mediator permission. Be sure of this by clearly telling the mediator what you want conveyed to school district and what you want to be kept between you and the mediator.

In your first meeting, the mediator may want to clarify issues and begin exploring whether you're willing to compromise.

As the mediator shuttles back and forth, specific evidence may come up, related to a disputed issue. For example, you and the school district may have very different views on the validity of the district's assessment versus your independent assessment. You can say to the mediator something like, "Please convey to Mr. Roberts that my assessor is a recognized expert and is clear in her recommendations; the district's expert has limited knowledge of my child's disability."

Ultimately, during the first or second or fifth meeting, the mediator should be able to say how far the school will go, at which point, you will have to think about your bottom line. Hopefully, you thought about this before the meeting. Think about what is essential, what you can give up, how strong your case is and how strong the school line is. Make use of the mediator, by asking direct questions, such as:

- What do you think the school will do on the placement issue?
- Do they understand that Dr. Parnell said Victor needs placement in the private school?
- What is their bottom line?
- Do you think we have a case if we go to a fair hearing?

The strength of the evidence and the work of the mediator will convince the district to settle or not. If the district has moved from the position it held at the IEP meeting, but not far enough, you'll have to weigh the importance of the outstanding, non-resolved issues against the evidence you have for those issues and your willingness to go to a fair hearing.

Tips on Bargaining in Mediation

Bargaining is part of mediation. When presenting what you want, make your list as strong and inclusive as possible; put in everything you could possibly want including your expenses and even minor items. But know your priorities, and what you can live without and can use as bargaining chips.

Example

You feel your child should be in a private school, which costs $15,000 per year. You also want the school district to pay for your private assessment, which was $1,000. You also have some reimbursement costs, including a tutor, totaling several hundred dollars. Your case is strong enough to go after all of these items. But to compromise, you may have to forego the assessment and other costs.

The upside of making a strong and fully detailed list is that you present yourself to the school district as a determined parent with a potentially long list of items for a fair hearing and therefore a good deal of potential cost for the school.

The downside is that you may appear to be greatly over-reaching, leaving the school representatives feeling like there is no point in mediating, because you are simply too far away. And if you include items not supported by evidence, your credibility may be hurt.

Ultimately, though, it is best to start with the kitchen sink and go from there as your evidence takes you.

d. Wrapping Up the Mediation Session

After various private meetings with the mediator, there will be four possible outcomes:

- full settlement of all issues
- partial settlement—you agree on some issues and disagree on others
- no settlement, but you agree to try again with the mediator at a later date, or
- no settlement and no further mediation sessions scheduled.

A mediation settlement can contain anything you and the school district agree to—including a provision for all or part of what you want for your child and, if you have an attorney at mediation, reimbursement of your attorney fees.

Whatever the outcome, you will all return to the meeting room and the mediator will complete a mediation form. The mediator will write on a mediation form what the parties agreed to (if anything), what is outstanding (if anything) and what the next steps will be if full agreement was not reached.

If you don't reach a settlement on all or some issues, you have three options:

- go to a fair hearing
- drop the matter—this may make sense if you've settled most issues and only minor issues remain, or
- go directly to court—this highly unusual approach requires you to prove that the problem is so serious you can't spend time at a fair hearing and need a judge to look at the matter immediately; you will need a lawyer's help (see Chapter 14).

Once you and the school district sign the mediation, both of you are bound by whatever agreement you reached.

I. Fair Hearing

A fair hearing is like a court trial, although it won't be held in a courtroom. You and the school district submit evidence in the form of written documents and sworn testimony from witnesses. A neutral third party, called a hearing officer, reviews the evidence and makes a decision as to who is right and who is wrong. That decision is binding on you and the district. The hearing officer has the authority to act independently of you and the school district. The hearing office is in essence a judge. The hearing officer cannot be an employee of the school district or the state educational agency.

Although IDEA establishes specific rules for fair hearings (34 C.F.R. §§300.507-512), states can vary some of the procedural details. For example, Ohio provides that attorneys will act as hearing officers; other states specify qualifications, rather than require particular professions. In most states, the department of education provides a list of hearing officers or contracts with a qualified agency to do so. For instance, in California, the state department of education has contracted with a law school which in turn hires the hearing officers.

Contact your state department of education to find out the details of your state's laws on fair hearings. See Appendix 2.

A fair hearing is used to resolve factual disputes between you and your child's school district, including disagreements about placement, a related service (such as the amount of speech therapy), curricula or methodology. Section B, above, lists typical IEP due process disputes.

Often, a factual dispute contains a legal dispute within it. For example you want your child in a private school and the school district offers a special day class in the public school. The factual dispute involves which placement is appropriate for your child. The legal issue is whether IDEA allows a private school placement (it does) when supported by the facts.

Or, the school district wants to place your child in a special school 15 miles from your home; you want your child placed in a regular class at the local school. Again, the factual dispute involves finding the appropriate placement. The legal issue concerns IDEA's requirement that your child be placed in the least restrictive environment.

You may be asking at this point: "I thought legal problems were only subject to the complaint process?" Here's the difference: In a fair hearing, there may be legal issues, as exemplified above, which will impact on the factual analysis and outcome. In a complaint, you are only claiming that the school district broke the law—there is no factual dispute regarding an IEP issue (as there is in a fair hearing).

In some cases, you may simultaneously file a complaint and due process as discussed at the end of Chapter 13.

While a witness may testify about a legal issue, or you or the school district may raise a legal issue in your opening statements, in most cases legal issues are addressed in a post-hearing brief. (See Section 6, below.) The possibility of discussing legal issues at the hearing or in a brief may be quite daunting. If you anticipate major legal disputes, see Chapter 14 on lawyers and legal research, or contact an attorney for help on just this part of the process.

Fear of Fair Hearings

It's natural to be afraid of a fair hearing—after all, it's like a trial, and can be difficult and complicated. But many parents conduct fair hearings. So how do you get through one with your nerves intact?

- Be organized.
- Take time to think through the issues and your evidence.
- Know that everybody else is nervous, too.

In short, you can do it. In preparing for the IEP meeting (and perhaps mediation), you already did a good deal of the hard work.

---

1. Your Fair Hearing Rights and Responsibilities

IDEA sets out several rights and responsibilities you *and* the school district have during the fair hearing process (20 U.S.C. §1415(h)(i); 34 C.F.R. §§508-512). These include the following:

- During the entire proceeding, you have the right to be advised and accompanied by an attorney or another person with special knowledge or training.
- At least five days before the hearing, you and the school district must provide each other with a list of your witnesses and copies of all written evidence you will submit at the hearing, including any assessments. The hearing officer can exclude the testimony of anyone not on the witness list or any document not exchanged before the hearing.
- Before the hearing, you can subpoena witnesses to insure that they will attend. (Most state educational agencies have subpoena forms.) At the hearing, you can ask witnesses questions.
- Before the hearing, you have the right to declare the fair hearing closed or open to the public. An open hearing gives access to the public, including the press, which you may want. But, an open meeting may also increase the stress and invite district employees to come and go.
- At the hearing, you can present written evidence in the form of exhibits.
- After the hearing, you are entitled to a verbatim record of the hearing (either in writing or in electronic format). This means that the hearing officer will tape the proceedings.
- After the hearing, you're entitled to a written decision, including findings of fact, within 45 days of when you first requested due process.
- You have the right to appeal a fair hearing decision to a state or federal court.

2. Pros and Cons of a Fair Hearing

There are several reasons for going to a fair hearing.

- If you win, your child will receive the education he needs.
- If you win, you establish the correctness of your position and your clear determination. It's unlikely you will have to fight the battle again.
- If you win, your attorney's fees and other costs will be reimbursed. (If your case involves more than one disputed issue, reimbursement for attorney's fees may be limited if you prevail on only some of the disputed issues.)
- Whether or not you win, you buy time. If your child is currently in a placement you want to maintain, your child is entitled to remain there until the issue is finally resolved—either through the fair hearing decision or a final court decision, if you appeal. (Section D, above, discusses this "stay put" provision.)

There are also disadvantages to going to a fair hearing.

- Fair hearings are difficult, time-consuming, emotionally draining and contentious.
- You might lose.
- Your relationship with your school district will likely be strained and formal. Future IEPs may be hard. If you lose, the school district may feel invincible.
- If you lose, you won't be entitled to reimbursement for your costs and attorney's fees (you won't have to pay the school district's attorney's fees).

3. Who, What and Where of Fair Hearings

A fair hearing must be at a time and place convenient to you. Normally, fair hearings are held at the school district office, and last anywhere from one to several days.

Once you request a fair hearing, you will be sent a notice of the date and place of the hearing, as well as the name of the hearing officer or the due process hearing office if you need to contact the hearing officer before the hearing. You will also be given the name, address and phone number of the school district representative. This information is important, since you need to know who to send exhibits and witness lists.

4. Preparing for a Fair Hearing

If you go to mediation first, much of your preparation will be done by the time you go to fair hearing. But some very important and time-consuming work will still need to be done. Give yourself several weeks to prepare, more if you skip mediation and go straight to fair hearing.

a. Know Your Case

Review your child's file (Chapter 3), your binder (Chapter 4) and your IEP blueprint (Chapter 5). Be clear on the disputed issues—what you want, what the school district is offering and how you disagree. Don't confuse personality conflicts with your child's needs.

b. Determine Your Strategy

At the hearing, you must clearly state the issue and offer evidence to support your position. Evidence will be in the form of witnesses and written evidence.

Example

You want your child mainstreamed with a one-to-one aide, but your school district offers a special class. At the hearing, you will have to show that:

- the school district failed to offer mainstreaming placement

- an aide will help your child function in the classroom
- your child will do well socially because her friends are in the class, and
- a special class will be detrimental to your child because it will not address your child's unique needs and is contrary to IDEA's least restrictive environment requirement.

 Reimbursement for private school may be limited. You may not be reimbursed for your child's placement in a private school if you did not provide proper notice to the school district. As described at the end of Chapter 11, you must notify the district—either at the most recent IEP meeting, or at least ten business days before the actual removal—of your intent to place your child in a private program (20 U.S.C. §1412 (a) (10) (C)).

c. Prepare Exhibits of Written Material

Exhibits or written documents are anything in writing that contains supportive evidence or provides information that the hearing officer will need to make a decision. But be careful—you don't necessarily want to turn over your entire IEP binder. Again, be clear on the issues in dispute. Review all of your documents looking for every-thing that supports your position, such as an assessment or teacher's report. Note the specific place in each document where the supportive statement is made—that is, page number and paragraph. You have probably done much of this work with the Material Organizer form you developed for the IEP meeting.

Do not submit material that damages your case or may reveal private information you don't want known. As you review all material, note the negative and missing items. Your Material Organizer and blueprint can help you point to these items. The school district may submit negative items; obviously, you must not.

Example of exhibits typically presented at fair hearings include:

- IEP documents
- assessments and evaluations
- letters or reports from your child's teacher or physician
- articles about your child's disability, appro-priate teaching methods or any other issues in your case
- résumés of witnesses, articles they've written that relate to the issues in dispute, and
- your child's classroom work or artwork.

If in doubt, include the item. You never know when you might want to refer to something during the hearing. If you don't include the item when you prepare your exhibit exchange (at least five days before the hearing), you will probably be barred from including it at the hearing.

Arrange your exhibits in some order, such as the order in which you think you'll introduce them or alphabetical order. Place them in a folder or binder with numbered or lettered tabs and a table of contents. Be sure to page number each individual exhibit, too, so you can find specific statements easily.

You'll refer to these exhibits in your own testimony and when you question witnesses. At this stage, it is unlikely that you will have to develop new evidence. But if you do not yet have support for a disputed item, you may need new material—for example, a supportive letter or even an independent evaluation.

d. Choose and Prepare Witnesses

Witnesses are crucial to the outcome of a fair hearing. Choose and prepare your witnesses with care.

i. Choosing Witnesses

Double-check your list of *all* potential witnesses, both people who support you and people who might testify for the school district, including the IEP participants you prepared for the IEP meeting (see Chapter 10). Try to anticipate what each witness can testify about. One witness may be able to testify about several issues, while others may focus on only one disputed matter. In choosing your witnesses, look for the following:

- The strength of the witness's testimony and persuasiveness.
- The witness's experience, training, education and direct knowledge of your child.
- The witness's willingness to testify under oath. You must make sure a person is willing to testify at the hearing before you put her on your witness list. A witness's favorable or supportive report won't help if she equivocates in her testimony at the hearing. In that case, submit the person's written material if strong and have other witnesses refer to that report.

In some cases you may need to subpoena a reluctant witness to insure that they testify at the hearing.

ii. Preparing Witness Questions

For each witness you should write out a list of your questions. The following is a general outline:

- Ask the witness to identify herself—for example, "Please state your name, occupation and place of employment."
- Ask about the witness's experience, education, training and specific expertise in the area of dispute—you can refer the witness to his résumé or written articles which you included in your exhibits.
- Establish the witness's knowledge of your child—for example:
  - ▲ *"Have you met my son, Philip Jones?"*
  - ▲ *"Please tell us when, for how long and for what purpose."*
  - ▲ *"Did you also observe him in school?"*
  - ▲ *"Please tell us when that was and for how long."*
- Ask questions to elicit your witness's opinion about the issues in dispute, for example:
  - ▲ *"You stated that you tested Philip. What tests did you administer?"*

- ▲ *"What were the results?"*
- ▲ *"What do those results mean?"*
- ▲ *"What conclusions did you draw regarding Philip's reading difficulties?"*
- ▲ *"How severe are his difficulties?"*
- ▲ *"In your professional opinion, what is the appropriate way to help Philip improve his reading?"*
- ▲ *"Do you have any specific recommendations regarding Philip's reading needs?"*
- ▲ *"What is your professional opinion regarding Philip's prognosis as a successful reader if he is not provided the help you recommend?"*

iii. Preparing Your Witnesses

Before the hearing, meet with your witnesses and go over your questions in advance. Their answers may lead to new questions you'll want to ask, may trigger a new strategy or approach and will help you and your witnesses prepare for the hearing. Explain that after you're done asking questions, the school district representative will cross examine the witness by asking additional questions.

Some witnesses, particularly any school employees who agree to testify for your child, may be unwilling to meet during school hours. You may have to arrange to meet them at their home. Others may not want to meet at all. What should you do about witnesses who can help your case but won't talk to you ahead of time? If you can't discuss the case before the hearing, you won't know exactly how the witness will testify. Taking this kind of risk may backfire. One strategy is to leave the person off your witness list, and hope the district calls her so you can cross examine her. Of course, if the witness is the only person who can testify about a certain element of your case, then you'll probably need to take a chance and use the witness, even though you didn't talk in advance of the hearing.

Another strategy is to include the person on your witness list, not have him testify during your presentation, then either cross examine him if he is called as a witness by the school or use him as a rebuttal witness to counter something said by a different school district witness.

Just before the hearing date, get back in touch with your witnesses to tell them:

- the date, time and location of the hearing
- what time you need them to arrive to be ready to testify—be sure to let them know that they might not be called on time, as would be the case if an earlier witness took longer than expected or the hearing officer breaks early, and
- how long you expect their testimony will take.

iv. Preparing Yourself as a Witness

You will most likely be a witness. You have valuable information about your child, her history, her previous programs, her needs, your worries, your frustrations and what teachers have said to you about your child.

Your testimony must cover matters for which you have firsthand knowledge. At the same time, your testimony doesn't have to cover all aspects of the case. For example, you can testify about the assessment done on your child and what the assessor told you. On the other hand, the assessor is in a better position to give this testimony. In general, then, your testimony should cover the areas in which you are the expert and no one else will testify on the issue.

You can present your testimony in one of two ways: You can respond to questions (just like you will be asking questions of your witnesses) asked by your spouse, a relative or close friend, or you can make a statement covering all issues of importance. You can either read your statement or give it from notes. After you're done answering questions or making your statement, the school district representative will cross examine you.

You want your testimony to be clear, specific and objective. Break down your points into the following areas, using your mediation statement as a possible basis:

- a general description of your child, including his age, strengths and weaknesses (your child profile, discussed in Chapter 10, Section D, can help here)
- your child's disability and the effect of that disability—for example, your child has a learning disability and as a result, he has difficulty with simple computations, reading comprehension and visual memory
- any secondary difficulties due to the disability —such as emotional problems
- your child's educational history—that is, the classes he's been in, including his current program
- the particular issues in dispute and your desired resolution
- your observations at class visits, meetings with teachers and other professionals and the IEP meeting (for example, "On February 12, 19xx, I visited the second grade class at Tower School and I observed ….")
- oral statements others have made to you that support your point of view, including your reaction to those oral statements—for instance, "On November 3, 19xx, Mr. Mastin of the school district told me there was no room for my child in the second grade class at Tower School; I confirmed this conversation in a letter which is my Exhibit F and for which Mr. Mastin did not respond."
- your child's specific educational needs and the consequences if he is not provided them—for example, "Given the assessment by Dr. Pollack, I believe a placement in a program other than the second grade class at Tower School will have serious emotional and cognitive consequences for my child."

e. Prepare Questions for School Witnesses

Preparing questions for school witnesses is more difficult than preparing for your own witnesses because you don't know their exact testimony.

Still, you can develop questions. You probably know what many witnesses will say because you heard their opinions at the IEP meeting.

Start by reviewing your files, the transcript or your notes of the IEP meeting and the school district's exhibits (when you get them five days before the hearing). Then make a list of questions to strengthen your case or at least undermine what the school district's witnesses might say.

Example

Your child's teacher said something very important to you when you visited your child's class. You sent a letter confirming what was said ("Thanks for talking to me today. I was glad to hear that you agreed Jake should remain in a regular class with the help of an aide"). The teacher never objected to your confirming letter, but you now believe she will say the opposite at the hearing. Be ready to point out the discrepancy—for instance, "Ms. Jenkins, you testified this morning that you feel Jake should be placed in a special education class. Do you recall when we met on October 15th and you told me that Jake was doing well in the regular class but needed an aide to keep up? You don't recall that meeting? Please look at Exhibit B, my November 1st letter to you."

Rules of Evidence

You may have heard of something called the "rules of evidence." These formal rules, which are very specific and sometimes quite arcane, are used in courts to guide judges in deciding what evidence can be included and what must be excluded. These rules are not required to be followed at fair hearings, but the hearing officer can use them as appropriate.

For example, some rules relate to hearsay evidence—information that a witness did not hear or receive directly. "I saw Jack hit Frank" is not hearsay; "Jack told me that Frank hit Bill" is. Hearsay evidence can be excluded at a fair hearing.

In general, however, don't worry about formal rules of evidence. If the other side raises the rules of evidence or "objects" to a question you ask because it violates a rule of evidence, ask the hearing officer to explain the rule and then re-phrase your question or move on.

f. Exchange Witness Lists and Evidence

Remember, you must submit a list of your witnesses and copies of written exhibits at least five days before the hearing begins. Once you have your exhibits organized in binders and your list of witnesses, make two copies. Keep the originals for yourself and send one copy to the fair hearing officer and one copy to the school district representative. To be safe and to have proof that the others received the items list at least five days before the hearing, send them certified mail, return receipt requested.

5. The Fair Hearing Itself

The fair hearing normally proceeds as follows:

1. The hearing officer opens the hearing and explains the process, including the order of the hearing. The hearing office will usually identify and confirm the written testimony or exhibits you and the school district submitted. Finally, the officer will set up the tape recorder and determine if the parties are ready.

2. The parties introduce themselves.

3. The hearing officer turns the tape recorder on and the formal hearing begins.

4. You make your opening statement.

5. The school district makes its opening statement.

6. You question (direct examine) your witnesses.

7. The school representative questions (cross examines) your witnesses.

8. You ask more questions of your witnesses (re-direct) if you want, the school representative cross examines again (called re-cross), and so on.

9. The school district calls its witnesses with the same pattern of direct examination, cross-examination, re-direct and re-cross.

10. You call back any witnesses after the school finishes, if you want. They are called rebuttal witnesses and are used to clarify or contradict some testimony raised by the other side. The school district has the same right.

11. You give a closing statement, if you want.

12. The school district gives a closing statement, if it wants.

13. You and the school district submit written briefs discussing the facts presented at the hearing and any applicable law. (See Section 6, below.)

14. The hearing officer issues a decision within 45 days of when you requested due process.

Keeping Track During the Fair Hearing

You want to have an ongoing record of the testimony during the hearing because you may need to refer back to previously given testimony. For example, the district calls a witness and he testifies for 45 minutes on various issues. When you cross examine this witness, you want to refer back to a specific statement he made that contradicted other testimony, or you may want clarification on an issue or want to explore earlier testimony. You need to be able to refer to earlier statements.

Taking notes is the logical way to keep track; however, for you to do it while also conducting the hearing can be difficult. Instead, have someone else take copious notes for you, recording statements of all witnesses, while you also take notes on key statements. (You can do this on paper or a laptop computer.) If you had a notetaker at the IEP meeting, consider using the same person, who is now very familiar with the issues. You can tape the hearing, but you won't have time to review testimony other than during breaks, and it would probably be more difficult to try to find an exact statement on a tape than simply refer to written notes.

How do you use the notes? During your cross-examination you'd say something like, "Mr. Adams you testified, let me see [look at your notes], that and I quote, 'I don't think James needs an aide in class.' Is that correct?" If he concurs, then point out the other evidence which contradicts him, such as "In her testimony yesterday, Dr. Markham stated that you told her on April 29, 19xx, that James needed an aide. Which statement should we believe?"

a. Make an Opening Statement

The opening statement you prepared in Section G, above, can be used, but will need slight modification for a fair hearing. At mediation, you can say anything. Your aim is to reach a compromise, not prove your case. At a fair hearing, however, your aim is to prove your case. Your opening statement, therefore, should emphasize what you want for your child and how that is supported by evidence. This doesn't mean you shouldn't include items for which your evidence is weak, but it does mean you should still carefully think about what you're asking for and how viable is it. The hearing officer will consider not only your evidence, but your credibility. If you ask for a reasonable program, a reasonable curriculum and a related service unsupported by any evidence, your credibility may be affected.

Specifically, include the following in your opening statement:

- basic facts about your child, including her age, disability and current educational program
- a clear statement of your child's needs and the dispute that brought you to the hearing, and
- a brief statement that what you want is supported by evidence, such as "Cheryl needs a full-time aide, as we will clearly show with evidence, including the testimony of several different professionals and exhibits B, D and M."

Opening statements can be any length, but five to 15 minutes is typical. If you can, don't read a verbatim statement—instead, use notes to guide you in making your points. If you're very nervous, however, it's okay to read the statement. It is important to express your feelings and bring the human element into the hearing. Be careful not to go off on an unfocused monologue or make your argument personal regarding the school district.

b. Question Your Witnesses

After opening statements, you'll be invited to have your witnesses testify. Think carefully about the order. You are essentially telling a story—put some logic into your presentation. It's often best to begin with someone (possibly you) who can give general information about your child. Next might be a presentation on assessment data.

After that, you want to go to the core of the dispute and make your case. For example, you and the school district disagree on placement and a related service. During the past year, your child was in a regular class, with no assistance. You want your child to stay in that class with an aide; the school district has offered placement in a special day class. Your first witness can give the details of the regular class. The second can testify as to as to why your child needs that class. The third can describe the services offered by the aide. The fourth can explain why your child needs that aide.

Of course, you may have to modify the presentation and go out of order if a witness is available only on a certain day or at a certain time. Or, you may choose a different order to maximize impact. In some instances, the witness who will give the most dramatic and effective testimony should go last, so the hearing officer is left with that impression. Or that person might go first, so set a tone for the rest of the hearing. Only you can decide this strategy.

c. Question Reluctant Witnesses

Questioning reluctant witnesses takes care. You first want to ask the hearing officer to note that the witness is not cooperative. To insure the person's attendance at the hearing, you should have issued a subpoena. At the hearing, ask something like, "Mr. Jones are you testifying voluntarily?" The response will be something like, "No. As you know I was subpoenaed by you."

Another possibility is to begin your questioning with a statement such as, "This witness, Mr. Hobson the fourth grade teacher, would not talk to me prior to the hearing. I am calling him as a hostile witness."

Further Suggestions on Questioning Witnesses

No matter how much you do to prepare, you cannot plan out exactly how the questioning will go. Be ready to alter the order of questioning. For example, a witness might answer in a way slightly different from how you expected, requiring you to ask follow up questions. Or the witness may say the opposite of what you expect.

Here's how to deal with surprises when questioning witnesses:

- Ask for a brief break if you need to gather yourself or consider new questions.
- Keep track of your questions. If you veer off on a line of questioning you had not planned, mark where you are on your list of questions so you can come back to it later.
- Don't ask a question for which you don't know the answer, particularly of a school witness.
- Don't overwhelm the hearing officer with a ton of facts. There is a tendency for parents to try to get everything into the record at the hearing. Know the difference between important facts and minutiae.
- Know when to stop. Stop asking questions when something powerful has been stated. Further questioning will only dilute the impact.
- Don't badger a witness. Ask questions in a firm way and repeat them if necessary. But don't become hostile, belligerent or belittling.
- Don't play lawyer. You'll do fine with your own style and language.

---

d. How to Use Your Exhibits

Have your exhibits available when you question witnesses—for example, "Tell me Dr. Whitland, you said Monroe does not need psychotherapy. Would you please look at Exhibit B, page 4. You reported last year that Monroe had severe emotional difficulties that were interfering with his education. Now tell me why you don't think he needs therapy."

e. Closing Statements or Briefs

After all the evidence has been presented, and all witnesses have testified, the hearing officer will likely ask if you want to make closing arguments or submit a written brief. If your case is good, it is wise to go for the brief (see Section 6, below). Otherwise, make a closing statement.

f. Closing Statements

A closing statement is a summary of each party's key evidence as it relates to the disputed issues. For example, you might say, "Every witness called by us agreed that Michele needs four sessions of speech therapy; not one of the school district's witnesses contradicted that. This is fully consistent with Dr. Hanover's written report, Exhibit L." Your closing statement might also note that the recommended education is consistent with IDEA.

6. Post-Hearing Briefs

If you agree to submit briefs, the parties, with the help of the hearing officer, will set a short time-frame (usually no more than one week) to submit the briefs. The purposes of the briefs are to high-light the evidence that supports your case and expand on any legal issues pertinent to your dispute.

To develop your brief, first review your notes, your memory and the evidence. The written brief should precisely point out the evidence that supports your case and the evidence that contradicts the school district's point of view. If there are legal issues, you should review IDEA and any court cases that support your analysis of the law. See Chapter 14 for advice on legal research. You may also want to contact a lawyer or support organization for help.

J. Fair Hearing Decision

After the hearing, you're entitled to a written decision, including findings of fact, within 45 days of when you first requested due process.

Both you and the school district can appeal the hearing decision.

K. Appeals

Once the hearing officer issues a written decision, you or the district have the right to appeal the decision to state or federal court, theoretically all the way to the U.S. Supreme Court. If you lost, several factors will help you decide whether or not to appeal.

- **Strength of your case.** You should already have considered this as part of your decision to pursue due process. On an appeal, also keep in mind the following:

  - while you will start from scratch with the evidence (called a trial de novo), there is often a tendency on the part of the court to defer to the administrative decision, and
  - an ostensibly neutral third party has ruled against you, suggesting some problems with your case.

- **Costs of an appeal.** There are various costs in appealing a fair hearing decision to court, including filing fees, fees for serving papers on the school district, witness fees and other trial costs (such as copying exhibits). There's one more cost: potential attorney's fees. While non-attorneys can represent themselves in court, we strongly recommend against appealing without hiring an attorney. At the very least, have an attorney who specializes in IDEA review your case and advise you of your chances on appeal.

- **Time.** States vary as to when you must file your appeal (depending on their statute of limitations), and court loads may affect how soon your appeal is heard in court. Anticipate a lengthy process, taking many months. Remember, too, that as long as the case is active, your child must stay where she is. If you want to maintain the status quo, appealing will preserve it longer. Deciding to go to court, however, is a very serious step and should not be based merely on a desire to maintain status quo, particularly if your case is not strong. ■

13

Filing a Complaint for a Legal Violation

As mentioned in Chapter 12, informal negotiation or due process is typically used to resolve factual disputes between you and the school district. But what if your concern isn't over a program, service or other factual matter—that is, who is right and who is wrong—but rather, that the school district has violated a legal requirement under IDEA? You would then file a complaint.

A. When to File a Complaint

IDEA statutes and regulations set out legal obligations on the part of your child's school district. Excerpts of key sections of IDEA are contained in Appendix 1. The following list represents common omissions by school districts that constitute a violation of IDEA:

- failing to provide a child's records
- failing to do assessments
- failing to meet assessment and IEP timelines
- failing to hold an IEP meeting
- failing to allow a parent to effectively represent her child in the IEP meeting—for example, by limiting who can attend or by intimidating the parent
- failing to follow certain procedures before suspending or expelling a special education student. As mentioned previously, suspension and expulsion issues are not covered in this book. Check with support organizations, lawyers and other parents about this important issue
- failing to discuss all elements in an IEP meeting—goals and objectives, placement, related services, transition plans
- failing to implement an agreed-to IEP—for example, if your child's IEP calls for three sessions of speech therapy and the school district provides only one session, and
- failing to give notice before changing, or refusing to change, a child's IEP. Your district cannot change your child's IEP without giving you notice of that change and holding an IEP meeting, or refuse you the right to have an IEP meeting because you want a change.

B. Where to File a Complaint

Section A lists common violations of IDEA, but it is not an exhaustive list. If you believe your school district has violated IDEA or any state special education law, contact your state department of education (or a locally designated agency), or the U.S. Department of Education, Office for Civil Rights (OCR). Contact information for both is in Appendix 2.

You can file a complaint with either the state or federal education agency. Both handle violations of IDEA, state law or Section 504 of the Rehabilitation Act of 1973.

See Chapter 7, Section F, for a brief description of Section 504, which is primarily an anti-discrimination law that prohibits schools from denying access to children with disabilities.

State departments of education are primarily geared toward investigating IDEA violations, but will also look into complaints regarding Section 504. In contrast, the federal OCR is primarily concerned with Section 504 or discrimination violations, but will also investigate IDEA complaints.

Before deciding where to file a complaint, contact your state department of education and the regional office of the OCR and ask the following questions:

- What kinds of complaints do they investigate?
- What is the deadline for filing a complaint? Section 504 complaints must be filed within 180 days of the last alleged act of discrimination against your child. IDEA complaints must be filed within the time established in

your state statute of limitations (discussed in Chapter 12, Section A).

- How do they handle complaints? In some states, an IDEA or Section 504 complaint is initially investigated by the school district. If you have a choice, opt for something other than the district which is investigating itself.

- What are their timelines for investigating complaints?

- What remedies are available, such as reimbursement for attorney's fees or related services you paid for?

Notifying the U.S. Department of Education, Office of Special Education and Rehabilitation Services

In addition to filing a complaint, you can notify the U.S. Department of Education, Office of Special Education and Rehabilitation Services, Office of Special Education Programs (OSEP). OSEP will neither investigate the problem nor issue a decision. But OSEP has overall responsibility for monitoring how states implement IDEA and might consider your comments when conducting the annual review of the programs in your state. Contact information is in Appendix 2.

C. What to Include in a Complaint

Your state department of education may have a complaint form for you to use. OCR has one; its use is optional, not mandatory. Whether you use a form or simply write a letter, include the following information:

- Your name and address (a telephone number where you may be reached during business hours is helpful, but not required).

- Your child's name and school district.

- As precise a description as possible of the violation, providing the date, time and location. If you cite more than one violation or you have very broad concerns, be as specific as possible, describing each violation separately.

- The applicable section of IDEA or any state law, if you know it. We've cited the key sections of IDEA throughout this book and Appendix 1 includes excerpts of IDEA and its regulations. Contact your state department of education (Appendix 2) for state special education laws and regulations.

- What remedy you want, including reimbursement for costs incurred due to the district's violations.

A sample complaint letter is shown below.

Sample Complaint Letter

February 5, 20xx

John Harrington, Director
Compliance Unit
Special Education Division
Department of Education
721 Capitol Mall
Sacramento, CA 95814

Dear Mr. Harrington:

I am formally requesting that you investigate legal violations by the Valley Unified School District, 458-4th Street, Visalia, California. I am making this request pursuant to 34 C.F.R. §300.660.

The facts in this matter are as follows:

My request for an IEP meeting was made on October 14, 20xx, just after my child was determined eligible for special education. The school district did not contact us to schedule an IEP meeting until February 2, 20xx, at which time I was told that the meeting would be March 5, 20xx. This violates 34 C.F.R. §300.343, which provides that an IEP will be held within 30 days of a determination that a child needs special education and related services. I request that an IEP meeting be held within 15 days of the conclusion of your investigation. I also request reimbursement for the cost we incurred hiring a private physical therapist because of the school district's failure to address my child's needs.

Please contact me to confirm receipt of this request and to set up times for me to meet with your investigator and to establish timelines for completing the investigation.

Sincerely,

Becky Masteron

Becky Masteron
6004 Green St.
Visalia, CA 00000

D. What Happens When You File a Complaint

After you file your complaint, the investigating agency will most likely meet with you to review the case, review evidence and records, meet with the school district and then issue a decision. IDEA requires that the state issue a decision within 60 days after the complaint is filed. If the district is found to have violated IDEA, the agency will make recommendations that the school district must undertake to comply with the law. The decision can be appealed to the U.S. Secretary of Education (contact information in Appendix 2).

Due Process and Complaints

You can simultaneously go through due process and file a complaint if there is a legal violation. If the district is found out of compliance with the law, you would certainly want the fair hearing officer to know. Indeed you may want, if timing permits, to file your complaint first so you can submit the decision in an exhibit at the due process hearing.

14

Lawyers and Legal Research

Lawyers can play a role in the special education process. While the purpose of this book is to provide you sufficient information so you won't need an attorney, there may be times when you will find it necessary to hire or at least consult a lawyer.

This chapter covers:

- how a lawyer can help with the IEP and other IDEA processes
- what to consider when using an attorney in special education
- finding an effective attorney
- how lawyers are paid
- resolving problems with your lawyer, and
- doing your own legal research.

A. How a Lawyer Can Help With the IEP and Other IDEA Processes

Generally speaking, an attorney can help you in one of two ways. A lawyer can provide advice and assistance as needed throughout the IEP process, while you would do most of the work and then consult with an attorney to be sure you are proceeding effectively. Or, a lawyer can be directly involved, formally representing you.

Here are some of the specific tasks a lawyer can help you with:

- securing your child's school files
- requesting an assessment or an IEP meeting
- preparing for the IEP eligibility meeting
- preparing for the IEP program meeting—including drafting goals and objectives, your child's profile and program and service descriptions; reviewing supportive evidence and materials; suggesting what professionals should attend and what material will be most effective and providing pointers about the IEP meeting

- attending an IEP meeting (remember to notify your school district before the meeting if your lawyer will attend)
- reviewing assessments and IEPs before you sign the IEP
- researching a specific legal issue that is central to your case or the IEP itself
- helping you informally resolve a dispute with the school district
- assessing the strength of your case, if you're considering filing a complaint or pursuing due process
- preparing for and attending mediation and the due process hearing
- writing a post-hearing brief
- preparing a complaint for you to file with the appropriate educational agency, and
- representing you in court.

You may choose to have a lawyer do everything from beginning to end in the IEP process or only come in at certain points. Perhaps you'll do the IEP meeting yourself, but have an attorney review the IEP document before you sign it.

B. Factors in Hiring an Attorney

Consider these factors to determine whether or not you need an attorney.

- **Complexity of the case.** A dispute involving complicated placement and service issues, for example, might require the special knowledge and experience of an attorney.
- **Strength of your case.** An honest attorney should tell you how strong he thinks the case is and therefore whether or not your situation justifies hiring him.
- **Your time and energy.** If you work full-time, are a single parent or have a difficult schedule, you may want someone else to take charge. On the other hand, if you have the time and energy to represent yourself and your child, hiring an attorney may not be necessary.

- **Your budget.** Attorneys aren't cheap. Can you afford the help? Are you entitled to reimbursement for your legal costs? (See Section D, below.)
- **Your self-confidence.** The purpose of this book is not only to help you advocate for your child, but also to give you the confidence to be an effective advocate. Still, you may not want to be at the center of a fight and would prefer to hire a lawyer.
- **Who represents the school district.** If the school district has involved an attorney, you may want the same protection.
- **Your relationship with the district.** Hiring a lawyer may change your relationship with the school district. When you involve attorneys, the atmosphere becomes more formal and potentially combative. School personnel will likely be more on guard and view you as the troublemaker or squeaky wheel. Of course, if you are at the point where you may need an attorney, your relationship with the school district has already changed. Your child's welfare is more important than a cordial relationship with the school district.

C. Finding an Attorney

Special education attorneys are not as numerous as personal injury or business lawyers. It is also unlikely that attorneys working in more standard areas of law—such as wills and estates, criminal law, family matters or corporation law—will know anything about special education law.

It is understandable that you may want to hire the attorney who did your will, your sister-in-law who just graduated from law school or the attorney whose ad in the phone book promises the lowest rates. But special education law is highly specialized, and an attorney who does not know the law or have experience in special education will significantly increase your chance of failure, and

ultimately cost you more rather than less. When you pay an attorney, you are paying for all the time she spends on your case, including the time she does research. You don't want to pay an attorney for on-the-job training.

1. Compile a List of Potential Attorneys

Before finding the "right" lawyer, compile a list of potential candidates. Here's how:

- Ask other parents in the school district.
- Ask your pediatrician or other health care professionals.
- Ask school district personnel—the district is required to maintain a list of attorneys and other advocacy resources for parents.
- Contact your state special education advisory commission and ask for referrals. IDEA requires each state to have a special education commission, composed of educators and parents, which advises the state about special education.
- Contact your state department of education and ask for referrals (see Appendix 2).
- Contact a nearby Parent Training and Information Center (PTI) (see Appendix 3).
- Contact a local disability rights advocacy organization (see Appendix 3).
- Contact a low-cost or free legal clinic, such as legal aid—while most offices focus on common civil issues (such as domestic disputes or evictions), some offices do special education work for low-income people.
- Use your personal network—friends, colleagues, neighbors or co-workers who know special education lawyers or who know lawyers who can recommend good special education lawyers.

Nonprofit Legal Clinics

There are nonprofit organizations which provide legal assistance in special education, disability rights or in what is generally called "public interest law." Your school district should have a list of disability-specific or special education nonprofit legal clinics in your area. Also see the organizations listed in Appendix 3.

There are advantages and disadvantages to using a nonprofit legal clinic as opposed to using a private attorney. Advantages to using a nonprofit include:

- the attorneys have likely worked in special education and have handled many cases
- nonprofits often do not charge for their services or have significantly reduced rates, and
- nonprofits, particularly disability-focused offices, have special knowledge and often a strong passion about the issues.

But there are disadvantages to using a nonprofit:

- demand is often greater than supply; you may have to wait some time to for an appointment, even to have someone assess your case, and
- nonprofit organizations often have limited resources—some focus on either precedent-setting cases (unusual disputes) or cases that will have an impact on a large number of children—and don't handle individual cases.

How Not to Find a Special Education Lawyer

There are several bad choices for finding a special education lawyer.

- **Heavily advertised legal clinics.** While they may offer low flat rates for routine services such as drafting a will, most make their money on personal injury cases. Few legal clinics offer good, affordable representation to parents of special education children. This is because resolving IEP problems requires solutions that cannot be mass-produced.
- **Referral panels set up by local bar associations.** While bar association panels usually do minimal screening before qualifying lawyers as experts in certain areas, the emphasis is on the word "minimal." While you might get a good referral from these panels, usually these lists are full of inexperienced practitioners and those who have not been able to attract enough clients on their own. Experienced lawyers with plenty of business rarely put their names on these panels. Because there are relatively few special education lawyers, it is not likely you'll find one through a bar referral process.
- **Private referral services.** When it comes to services that advertise on TV and billboards, forget it. These groups typically make little effort to evaluate a lawyer's skill and experience. They simply supply names of lawyers who have paid to list with the service or have agreed to give the referral service a kickback based on the fees the lawyer collects.

2. Call the Attorneys on Your List

Once you have a list of recommended attorneys, you can either narrow it down to one or two individuals who were enthusiastically recommended, or you can make initial contact with everyone on your list.

Try to have a brief phone conversation or ask for a short meeting. Some attorneys will briefly chat with you over the phone to determine the nature of your case and whether or not you need an attorney. Other attorneys may have you speak with an assistant, complete a form describing your case or have you make an appointment to come in and talk about the case. Before making an appointment, find out the following information:

- attorney's fee
- how the attorney reviews the case and decides whether or not you should proceed, and
- how much the initial review costs.

3. Meet With the Best Candidates

Make an appointment with those candidates who seem like the best prospects. Naturally, if there is a fee for the initial intake, you may only want to see a few attorneys. Be sure to ask the attorney what records she needs to evaluate your case.

When you meet with an attorney, you want to ask about your specific case of course, but you also want to get the following information:

- years of experience
- specific special education experience
- experience with your particular legal issue (such as a due process hearing)
- knowledge of special education law and the IEP process
- experience with your school district
- general style—is the attorney confrontational, cooperative (for example, does he like mediation or think it's a waste of time and normally goes directly to a fair hearing?)
- references, and
- fees.

Pay attention to the answers. Does the attorney clearly answer your questions about fees, experience and your specific legal issues? Does the attorney try to assess your chances in due process? If the lawyer makes you uncomfortable, think carefully about whether his expertise and success rate is worth putting up with a difficult style.

Will the attorney provide the type of help you want? Is the attorney willing to advise you now, but hold off on full participation unless and until you need it? If the attorney wants to take over the case but you only want a consultant, you have the wrong attorney.

Will the attorney be accessible? This is important—the most common complaint about lawyers is that they don't return phone calls, respond to faxes or e-mail, and are generally unavailable when a client calls. Discuss the attorney's response time. While no attorney should be expected to respond instantly, you shouldn't have to wait more than one day.

SO MUCH FOR THE SMALL TALK! HOW MUCH DO YOU CHARGE?

Client's Responsibility in Working With an Attorney

Your attorney should be responsive and courteous, and keep you informed. But it's a two-part relationship. You can also affect the client-attorney relationship. Keep the following in mind:

- Vague questions are likely to receive vague responses; be clear and specific when you discuss matters or ask questions.
- No matter how good an attorney is, the quality of the case—that is, the strength of the evidence—is key to success. Your attorney cannot transform a bad case into a good one.
- You have some of the responsibility for controlling your legal bill; be aware of time.
- You cannot call up an attorney, chat for five minutes and have your problem resolved. I frequently receive phone calls that go something like this:

    "Hello. I have a question about special education. Do you know special education law?"

    "Yes."

    "My daughter has an IEP on Thursday. She is learning disabled and I want her placed in a private school. The school district has offered a special day class. What do you recommend?"

    Any attorney who tries to answer that question is doing a disservice to himself and the caller. And the caller is being unfair. Many lawyers will try to answer simple questions over the phone from first-time callers—such as, "Can you tell me if a school has to do an assessment of a child before the child enters special education?"—but most questions are more complicated than that. It is unfair to assume that an attorney can either provide a simple answer to a complex question or provide free advice.

4. Ask for a Case Evaluation

It is important that the attorney evaluates the evidence before advising you what to do and whether she should be involved. A good special education attorney will review your case materials and should be able to:

- tell you the strength of your case
- explain the process involved
- evaluate your documents and potential witnesses
- tell you if additional supportive material is needed
- estimate the cost of hiring an attorney for due process or beyond
- estimate the length of time your case may take
- provide insights into school district personnel, particularly if the attorney has worked with the district before, and
- provide a cost-benefit analysis of hiring the attorney to represent you versus using the attorney as an advisor only.

5. A Word on an Attorney's Style

Some attorneys are pleasant, patient and good listeners. Others are unpleasant, impatient and bad listeners. You may want the former but you may get the latter. Whatever the style of your attorney, make it clear that you know the attorney is busy, but you expect her to treat you courteously, explain matters, keep you fully posted about what is happening and include you as an active partner in the process. An effective professional relationship must be based on mutual respect.

Furthermore, the attorney should contact you regarding any decision to be made, whether scheduling a meeting, deciding on tactics, reviewing a key issue or considering a possible resolution of the dispute.

If at any time you don't understand what your attorney has said, requested or planned, ask for clarification. If the answer isn't clear, ask again.

Although you hired the attorney because of his professional expertise and knowledge—and therefore have relinquished a certain amount of control—it does not mean you should be kept in the dark.

D. How Attorneys Are Paid

How you pay your lawyer depends on the type of legal services you need and the amount of legal work involved. Once you choose a lawyer, ask for a written fee agreement explaining how fees and costs will be billed and paid. In some states, a written agreement is required by law; even if it isn't, always ask for one. A good attorney will provide you with a written contract (whether you ask or not). Be sure to discuss a cap or limit on legal fees, which should also be in your fee agreement.

As your case progresses, you'll want to make sure you receive a bill or statement at least once a month. Lawyer's time adds up quickly. If your lawyer will be delegating some of the work to a less experienced associate, paralegal or secretary, the delegated work should be billed at a lower hourly rate. Be sure this is stated in your written fee agreement.

1. Lawyers' Billing Methods

Lawyers use three basic ways to charge for their services.

Hourly rate. Most special education attorneys charge by the hour. In most parts of the U.S., you can secure competent representation for $100-$250 an hour. Many clients prefer an hourly rate to a flat fee (discussed next) because you pay for the attorney's actual time spent on your case. Comparison shopping among lawyers can help you avoid overpaying, but only if you compare lawyers with similar expertise. A highly experienced special education attorney (who has a higher hourly rate) may be cheaper in the long run than a general practitioner (at a lower rate). The special education attorney won't have to research routine questions and may be able to quickly evaluate your case.

Legal Time

How much time your attorney will spend on your case will depend on the nature of your dispute. The following can serve as a general guideline for the amount of time required for common legal tasks:

- initial review of your records and interview with you .... 2-5 hours
- help you with the IEP process— developing a blueprint, contacting assessors and school personnel; drafting goals and objectives .... 2-5 hours
- attend the IEP meeting .... 2-4 hours (per meeting)
- prepare for and attend mediation session .... 3-8 hours
- prepare for and attend fair hearing .... 10-35 hours

---

Flat rate. A flat rate is a single fee that will cover all agreed-to work—for example, the amount the attorney will charge you to prepare for and attend the IEP meeting or prepare for and do the fair hearing. You are obligated to pay the flat fee no matter how many hours the lawyer spends on your case, assuming the lawyer does the work. A flat fee can be quite economical if the fee is reasonable and you anticipate a lot of work. On the other hand, if the case is resolved early in the process, you may end up paying much more than you would have, had you paid the lawyer by the hour. Most special education attorneys charge by the hour and may be unwilling to work on a flat fee.

Contingency fee. Contingency fee arrangements are rarely used in special education cases because a contingency fee is a percentage of whatever money the party wins. Because almost all successful special education cases involve providing a program or service rather than an award of money, contingency fees are simply not applicable.

Legal Costs

In addition to the fees they charge for their time, lawyers bill for a variety of items. These costs can add up quickly and can include charges for:

- photocopies
- faxes
- postage
- overnight mail
- messenger services
- expert witness fees
- court filing fees
- long distance phone calls
- process servers
- work by investigators
- work by legal assistants or paralegals
- deposition transcripts
- online legal research, and
- travel.

Some lawyers absorb the cost of photocopies, faxes and local phone calls as normal office overhead, but that's not always the case. When working out the fee arrangement, ask for a list of costs you'll be expected to pay. If the lawyer seems intent on nickel-and-diming you or hitting you with $3 per page fax charge, you should talk to him. While this may not reflect the attorney's skills or ability to win a case, it may raise red flags about how he does business.

---

2. Reimbursement for Legal Fees and Costs

If you hire an attorney and pay for his services, *and* you prevail at mediation or the fair hearing, you are entitled to be reimbursed by your school district for your attorney's fees and other due process costs (20 U.S.C. §1415(i)(3)). See Chapter 12, Section E, for a discussion of attorney fees in mediation and fair hearings.

But your right to reimbursement can be limited. First, you are not entitled to reimbursement if you hire an attorney to attend the IEP meeting, unless the meeting was required as part of due process. This might happen if the fair hearing officer orders a second IEP meeting to discuss matters never covered in the first meeting.

Second, you are not entitled to reimbursement if the school district makes a settlement offer ten days before the due process hearing, you reject the offer *and* the hearing officer finds that what you win in due process is not more favorable than the school district's settlement offer. If the hearing officer finds that you were substantially justified in rejecting the settlement offer, however, the fees cannot be reduced. What constitutes "substantially justified" is not defined in IDEA.

Third, the hearing officer can reduce the amount of attorney's fees to which you are entitled if the officer finds that any of the following are true:

- you unreasonably protracted or extended the final resolution of the controversy
- the attorney's fees unreasonably exceed hourly rates in the community for similar services
- the time and services provided by the attorney were excessive, or
- the attorney failed to provide certain information required by law.

You should carefully discuss these reimbursement issues with your attorney before you evaluate any settlement offers.

3. Reducing Legal Fees

There are several ways to control legal fees.

Be organized. Especially when you are paying by the hour, it's important to gather important documents, write a short chronology of events and concisely explain a problem to your lawyer. Keep a copy of everything you give to the lawyer.

Be prepared before you meet your lawyer. Whenever possible, put your questions in writing and mail, fax or deliver them to your lawyer before all meetings or phone conversations. Early preparation also helps focus the meeting so there is less chance of digressing (at your expense) into unrelated topics.

Carefully review lawyer bills. Like everyone else, lawyers make mistakes. For example, .1 of an hour (six minutes) may be transposed into a 1. (one hour) when the data is entered into the billing system. That's $200 instead of $20 if your lawyer charges $200 per hour. Don't hesitate to question your bill. You have the right to a clear explanation of costs.

Ask your lawyer what work you can do. There are some things you can do that can save time. For example, you could go through the school's record and highlight key statements. Or you could talk with important witnesses to find out their attitudes about key issues in the case. Some attorneys may be comfortable with you doing anything substantial, others will not be. Be sure to discuss this ahead of time.

E. Resolving Problems With a Lawyer

If you see a problem emerging with your lawyer, don't just sit back and fume. Call or write your lawyer. Whatever it is that rankles—a too high bill, a missed deadline or a strategic move you don't understand—have an honest discussion about your feelings.

If you can't frankly discuss these matters with your lawyer or you are unsatisfied with the outcome of any discussion, it's time to consider finding another attorney. If you don't, you may in fact waste money on unnecessary legal fees and risk having matters turn out badly.

If you decide to change lawyers, be sure to end the first professional relationship before you hire a new attorney. If you don't, you could find yourself being billed by two lawyers at the same time. Also, be sure all important legal documents are returned to you. Tell your new lawyer what your old one has done to date and pass on the file.

Here are some tips on resolving specific problems:

- If you have a dispute over fees, the local bar association may be able to mediate it for you.
- If a lawyer has violated legal ethics—for example, had a conflict of interest, over-billed you or didn't represent you zealously —the state agency that licenses lawyers may discipline the lawyer.
- Where a major mistake has been made—for example, a lawyer missed the fair hearing deadline for submitting the witness list and exhibits—you can sue for malpractice.

Many lawyers carry malpractice insurance.

Remember, while there will be times when you question your attorney's tactics, you have hired someone because of his expertise and experience. Before confronting the attorney, ask yourself whether the attorney misfired or you are overreacting.

Mad at Your Lawyer, by Tanya Starnes (Nolo Press), shows you how to handle almost every imaginable problem with your lawyer.

Your Rights as a Client

As a client, you have the right to expect the following:

- courteous treatment by your lawyer and staff members
- an itemized statement of services rendered and a full advance explanation of billing practices
- charges for agreed-upon fees and no more
- prompt responses to phone calls and letters
- confidential legal conferences, free from unwarranted interruptions
- up-to-date information on the status of your case
- diligent and competent legal representation, and
- clear answers to all questions.

A final word on attorneys: We live in a time when public attitudes about attorneys are negative, to some degree rightfully so. There are, of course, many conscientious attorneys, particularly in special education, where you will actually find a high percentage of compassionate, able and decent professionals.

F. Doing Your Own Legal Research

Using this book is a good way to educate yourself about the laws that affect your rights as a parent of a special education child. Chapter 2 has already provided you with much of the key legal language of IDEA. But given the fact that the laws and court decisions of 50 states are involved, no one book can give you all the information you need.

There's a lot you can do on your own, once you understand a few basics about law libraries, statute books, court opinions and the general reference books that lawyers use to learn about issues. Some basic legal research skills can help you determine how strong your case is and the best and most effective way to go forward. Whether the issue is private school placement, the type or amount of a related service, an assessment question or an eligibility issue, IDEA and judicial decisions can provide the context for judging the strength of your case.

Examples

- You want your child in a private school that has an identical program to the one available in your school district. Legal research should lead you to the conclusion that your position isn't a winning one. The law is clear—there is no right to a private school in this situation.
- Your child is deaf and you want her to have an American Sign Language (ASL) interpreter in her mainstreamed class. You do some research and find that IDEA does not require a specific language or methodology in the class. You realize that you will have to prove that without ASL your child cannot benefit from her education.
- You want your child who has some autistic behaviors to be mainstreamed with an aide. You visit a law library and discover that in the case of *Board of Education v. Holland*, 4F.3d 1398 (9th Circuit, 1994) the U.S. Supreme Court established guidelines for determining when a child is entitled to be mainstreamed, including an analysis of:
  - ▲ the academic and non-academic benefits to the child
  - ▲ the effect of the placement on the teacher and other students, and
  - ▲ the cost of the aids and services needed to mainstream.

The materials you can research include the following:

- IDEA statutes and regulations (excerpts are in Appendix 1)
- state statutes

- court cases interpreting IDEA and other relevant statutes
- explanatory documents, such as the U.S. Department of Education policy guidelines and correspondence—these documents do not have the authority of law and therefore do not have to be followed, but can be useful in reflecting the Department's analysis of what the law means
- fair hearing decisions (available through your state department of education and the *Individuals with Disabilities Education Law Reporter*, discussed below)—these are not binding on anybody but the parties to that specific hearing—however, they may be of value to you in showing how hearing officers make decisions in your state, and
- law review and other articles about IDEA and special education issues.

1. Individuals With Disabilities Education Act (IDEA): Where to Find It

As you no doubt know by now, IDEA is the federal law which governs special education in this country. Like all federal laws, IDEA is found in a multi-volume series of books called the United States Code (U.S.C.) which are available in most libraries. The U.S.C. consists of separate numbered titles, each title covering a specific subject matter. IDEA is found in Title 20, beginning with Section 1400. Appendix 1 includes a copy of key sections of the IDEA statute and regulations.

You can find annotated versions of the U.S.C., which include not only IDEA, but also summaries of cases that interpret IDEA and a reference to where each case can be found. Annotated codes also list articles that discuss IDEA. Annotated codes have comprehensive indexes by topic, and are kept up-to-date with paperback supplements (called pocket parts) found inside the back cover of each volume or in a separate paperback volume. Supplements include changes to IDEA and recent cases.

Your school district is required to provide you with copies of federal law—that is, the statutes and regulations of IDEA. Your school district, however, is not required to inform you of any changes to IDEA made by Congress (infrequent as they are) or of any legal decisions on IDEA. One source of up-to-date information, including policy guidelines on the IDEA, is the U.S. Department of Education (see Appendix 2). But that's not the only source.

In most fields of law, special newsletters provide extensive detail about that particular field of law. Special education has one such publication called the *Individuals with Disabilities Education Law Reporter* (IDELR). It is published by LRP Publications (contact information is in Appendix 3). IDELR issues a bi-monthly highlights newsletter, along with the written decisions of IDEA court rulings, fair hearing decisions and Department of Education policy and other publications. IDELR has a subject index, making it easy to locate the specific cases you want to review. At a current cost of $890 per year, IDELR is aimed at special education lawyers and school districts.

Some law libraries subscribe to IDELR—call the nearest law libraries and ask. Some school districts also subscribe. If this fails, contact a local nonprofit special education or disability organization in your area and ask if they receive IDELR.

2. State Statutes

As noted in Chapter 2, each state has passed a law which parallels IDEA. States are allowed to develop laws which provide students with greater rights than provided in IDEA. You can take a look at your state's special education laws, which are available in many public libraries and all law libraries.

Many states also make their statutes available online. (See Section G, below.) In some states, statutes are organized by subject matter, with each title or chapter or code covering a particular legal area—for example, the vehicle code or the corporations code. Most states have some kind of education code. In some states, statutes are simply numbered sequentially, without regard to subject matter, meaning you'll have to use the index to find what you need. State codes are like the federal U.S.C. with annotated volumes, indexes and pocket parts.

Some states have their own regulations implementing special education laws; check your state department of education for information about these regulations.

 Appendix 2 includes addresses, phone numbers and Web sites of state departments of education.

3. Court Decisions

It is common for Congress to pass a law which cannot address all potential uncertainties, or clarify what each section of the law precisely means. It is the job of a court—federal or state—to assess facts and interpret the applicable laws. In so doing, they will often explain, clarify and even expand or limit what actually appears in a statute. This is often referred to as "case law," which means that courts have explained the law and how far it goes. Once a court decision is published, it becomes the law as much as the statute is the law.

Court decisions are published in state or federal reporters. Each decision has a name and a citation, indicating the volume, name and page of the reporter in which it appears, the court that issued the decision and the year of the decision. With the citation, you can locate the printed decision.

Example:

The first special education case to reach the U.S. Supreme Court was *Rowley v. Board of Education*. It concerned a deaf child who wanted a sign language interpreter in her regular classroom. The U.S. Supreme Court said she didn't need one.

The case was first decided by a federal trial court: the case citation is 483 F. Supp. 536 (S.D.N.Y. 1980). This means that the case can be found in volume 483 of a reporter called the Federal Supplement, starting at page 536. The court that issued the decision was the federal court for the Southern District of New York. The case was decided in 1980.

That decision was appealed, and the case citation is 623 F.2d 945 (2d Cir. 1980). This means that the decision can be found in volume 623 of the Federal Report (2d Series), starting at page 945. The court that ruled on the appeal was the Second Circuit Court of Appeals. The appeal was decided in 1980.

The U.S. Supreme Court decision is found at 102 S.Ct 3034 (1982). The decision can be found in volume 102 of the Supreme Court Reports, starting at page 3034. The court decided the case in 1982.

Most cases involving a federal law such as IDEA proceed through the federal courts. IDEA gives you or the school district the option of appealing the due process decision to a state court. Each state has a unique reporting system, but decisions are usually found in regional reporters. For example, in the case of *State of Connecticut v. Bruno*, 673 A.2d 1117 (Conn. 1996), the decision was published in volume 673 of the regional law reporter called the Atlantic Second Series and begins on page 1117. The case comes from the state of Connecticut (not surprising given the name of the case) and was decided in 1996.

4. Doing Research in a Law Library

Law libraries contain state and federal statutes. Law librarians, who increasingly have experience working with nonlawyers, can help you find the appropriate resources.

Look for a law library that's open to the public—there may be one in your main county courthouse or at your state capitol. Publicly funded law schools generally permit the public to use their libraries, and some private law schools grant access to the public, sometimes for a modest fee.

If you can't find an accessible law library, don't overlook the public library. Many large public libraries have sizable legal reference collections, including state and federal statutes. Also, if you work with a lawyer, ask about using the research materials in the lawyer's office.

Further Reading on Legal Research. *Legal Research: How to Find and Understand the Law*, by Stephen Elias and Susan Levinkind (Nolo Press), gives easy-to-use, step-by-step instructions on how to find legal information. *Legal Research Made Easy: A Roadmap Through the Law Library Maze*, by Robert C. Berring, (Nolo Press), is a videotape presentation on the subject.

When you do case research, be sure the case you find has not been overturned or replaced by a more recent court decision. You can do this with a set of books known as Shepard's. A friendly law librarian might have the time and patience to guide you, but Nolo's book *Legal Research* has an easy-to-follow explanation of how to use the Shepard's system to expand and update your research.

When you find a court decision, there will be a short synopsis of the decision at the beginning.

This synopsis will not only help you determine whether the case is relevant for you, but also will tell you what the court decided. In a law reporter, after the case synopsis there will be a list of numbered items, each item followed by a short summary. The numbers (1, 2, 3, etc.) refer to the location in the written decision where that legal issue is discussed.

Keep in mind that your situation may or may not relate exactly to a court decision. It will depend on the similarity of the facts and whether your situation and the legal decision involve the same sections of IDEA. The more alike the facts and pertinent parts of IDEA, the more you can use the decision to your advantage. But understand that the existence of a case that supports your position does not mean that the school district has to apply or even abide by that decision. It is certainly a very persuasive precedent, but it is just an example of how one court has ruled in a similar situation. If the decision was reached by the U.S. Supreme Court, the federal court of appeals covering your state, your federal district court or your state supreme court, the case represents the law in your area. The degree to which the facts and applicable parts of IDEA in that decision are different from your case will dictate how binding the decision is on your school district.

If you find a case that is close to yours and the decision is a good one, think about writing to your school district indicating why the school district would be foolish to go to due process.

Do legal research with care. Analyzing case law and the meaning and reach of legal statutes can be complicated. Make sure you know what you're talking about before you cite the law. While you can learn a good deal, becoming expert at legal research requires care, time and training. Proceed carefully and use what you learn with real caution.

Letter Encouraging School Board Settlement

Date: April 20, 19xx

To: Howard Yankolon, Superintendent
Eugene School District
l5578 South Main
Eugene, OR 00000

Re: Clara Centler, student in Westside School,
5th Grade

I appreciated your efforts at the April 14, 19xx, IEP meeting; as you know we are in disagreement about Clara's need for a one-to-one aide so she can be mainstreamed.

I have requested a fair hearing. I have also done some research on this matter and determined that the facts and the law in the U.S. Supreme Court's decision in *Board of Education v. Holland* is almost identical to our dispute. I strongly believe that with the Supreme Court's direction in that case, it would be a real waste of time and district money to go to due process.

I am therefore requesting that you consider this and we meet to discuss a possible settlement of our differences.

Sincerely,

Stuart Centler

Stuart Centler
78 Pine Ave.
Eugene, OR 00000
Phones: 555-5543 (home); 555-0933 (work)

G. Online Legal Research

Every day, a growing number of basic legal resources are available online through the Internet. There are a number of different ways to use the Internet to search for material, but by far the most important and common tool for doing research on the Internet is the World Wide Web, or the Web. The Web provides links among documents and makes it easy to jump from one resource to another. Each resource is organized graphically like a book, allowing you to skip from topic to topic.

In addition, a wide variety of secondary sources intended for both lawyers and the general public have been posted on the Internet by law schools and firms. If you are on the Web, for example, a good way to find these sources is to visit any of the following Web sites, each of which provides links to legal information by specific subject.

- http://www.courttv.com. This is the site to Court TV's Law Center. You can find links to many federal and state laws.
- http://www.law.cornell.edu/lii.table.html. This site is maintained by Cornell Law School. You can find the text of the U.S. Code, federal court decisions and some state court decisions. You can also search for material by topic.
- http://www.law.indiana.edu/law/v-lib/ lawindex.html. This site is maintained by Indiana University's School of Law at Bloomington. You can search by organization, including the U.S. government, state governments and law journals, or by topic.
- http://www.access.gpo.gov/nara/cfr/. This site provides the entire Federal Code of Regulations.
- State statutes online: Many states have posted their statutes online.

In addition, Appendix 3 includes a section entitled "Legal Resources for Parents of a Special Education Child." These resources include Web sites and most sites have key provisions of IDEA and other legal materials on special education. ∎

15

Parent Organizations and Special Education

The first word in IDEA is "Individuals." Special education law, philosophy and approach is based on the individual child, making it generally difficult to approach special education from a collective or group perspective. Each IEP is different. Although this book has focused on strategies and procedures for parents who are acting alone, in many cases a group of parents working together can have a tremendous impact on a school district.

A. Join a Parent Organization

There may be existing parent groups you can contact, including the PTA. In addition, most school districts have a parent advisory committee specifically formed for special education matters. If you haven't already done so, contact your school district to find out about that committee. It is likely composed of special education professionals and other parents. If you can't find information on a local group, try the state level. Appendix 3 contains a state-by-state list of Parent Training and Information Centers (PTIs). PTIs are organized parent-to-parent organizations that can provide advice, training and even advocacy help.

A parent organization can help you in several ways:

- There is strength in numbers. School districts often pay more attention to two parents than one, four parents than two, ten parents than five.
- A parent group can provide you with access to all kinds of important information about the school administrator, staff (including teachers who are not afraid to be frank), existing classes, the local IEP process and outside support professionals, such as independent assessors, private service providers, private schools and attorneys.
- A parent group can suggest successful educational strategies, methodologies geared for your child and even sophisti-

cated knowledge about IDEA and its legal mandates.

- A parent group can provide the emotional support and advice that is crucial to help you navigate the special education process and reinforce the important feeling that you are not alone.

One warning about community advisory committees: School personnel regularly attend meetings; thus, it may be difficult to speak frankly. If this is the only organization in your area, consider forming an independent parent organization.

B. Form a Parent Organization

If your community doesn't have a parent organization, the existing group is too tied to or influenced by the school district or the existing group doesn't meet your needs, you can organize a new group. How do you begin?

First, consider how wide or narrow you want your focus to be. If your numbers can support such a group, you may want to form an organization of parents whose children have similar disabling conditions. You don't need a lot of people. Three or four parents can be quite effective. There is certainly nothing wrong with forming a cross-disability group, and the parents in your area may prefer it. The strength that comes from a large group can often offset the challenges that come with a diversity of concerns.

Sometimes a few simple phone calls will lead to very useful recommendations. Here's how to get started and prepare for your first meeting:

- Invite all possible parents who fit within your narrow or broad scope.
- Ask them for agenda ideas, focusing on common issues and concerns.
- Ask them for the names of other parents to invite.
- Ask your child's teacher or pediatrician for names of other parents to invite.

- Ask the PTA and your school district to announce the meeting or to include information on it in any mailings.
- Place an announcement in your local newspaper.
- Contact local disability organizations. They may be able to connect you with other parent support groups in your state. They may also be able to advise you if you encounter problems.

At your first meeting, you can decide how formal you want to be and what issues you want to focus on. If you take the formal route, you'll need to select a name, elect officers, decide if you'll charge dues, and if so, how much, collect those dues and establish regular meetings.

No matter how formal or informal you are, you need to spend time discussing your purpose and what you hope to accomplish. Do you simply want to establish better ties with the school administration? Do you want to address specific concerns, such as the quality of a specific class, the intimidation used by school personnel during the IEP process or the unfairness of certain procedures? Decide how to formally contact the district and raise your concerns.

At later meetings, consider inviting guests, such as representatives of the school district to talk about resolving difficulties, or a local special education attorney. The attorney will probably charge for his time. Your dues or an additional contribution from each family can cover the cost. Also, consider developing a newsletter (online is easiest) to maintain communication with other parents in your area.

Get Involved With the School District

Regardless of whether you work alone or with a group, there are many ways to improve your child's educational program through direct involvement with the school district: Volunteer at school or in the administrative office, run for school board or assist in school fundraisers. Generally, this kind of activity gets you involved, opens doors and allows you to meet the people in charge. This often can foster a good relationship with school personnel, making it easier for you to pick up the phone and call about—and resolve—a problem.

Appendix 1

Special Education Law and Regulations

Individuals with Disabilities Education Act (Key Sections)

Sec. 1401. Definitions

Except as otherwise provided, as used in this chapter:

(1) Assistive technology device. The term "assistive technology device" means any item, piece of equipment, or product system, whether acquired commercially off the shelf, modified, or customized, that is used to increase, maintain, or improve functional capabilities of a child with a disability.

(2) Assistive technology service. The term "assistive technology service" means any service that directly assists a child with a disability in the selection, acquisition, or use of an assistive technology device. Such term includes:

(A) the evaluation of the needs of such child, including a functional evaluation of the child in the child's customary environment;

(B) purchasing, leasing, or otherwise providing for the acquisition of assistive technology devices by such child;

(C) selecting, designing, fitting, customizing, adapting, applying, maintaining, repairing, or replacing of assistive technology devices;

(D) coordinating and using other therapies, interventions, or services with assistive technology devices, such as those associated with existing education and rehabilitation plans and programs;

(E) training or technical assistance for such child, or, where appropriate, the family of such child; and

(F) training or technical assistance for professionals (including individuals providing education and rehabilitation services), employers, or other individuals who provide services to, employ, or are otherwise substantially involved in the major life functions of such child.

(3) Child with a disability

(A) *In general.* The term "child with a disability" means a child:

(i) with mental retardation, hearing impairments (including deafness), speech or language impairments, visual impairments (including blindness), serious emotional disturbance (hereinafter referred to as "emotional disturbance"), orthopedic impairments, autism, traumatic brain injury, other health impairments, or specific learning disabilities; and

(ii) who, by reason thereof, needs special education and related services.

(B) *Child aged 3 through 9.* The term "child with a disability" for a child aged 3 through 9 may, at the discretion of the State and the local educational agency, include a child:

(i) experiencing developmental delays, as defined by the State and as measured by appropriate diagnostic instruments and procedures, in one or more of the following areas: physical development, cognitive development, communication development, social or emotional development, or adaptive development; and

(ii) who, by reason thereof, needs special education and related services.

(4) Educational service agency. The term "educational service agency":

(A) means a regional public multiservice agency:

(i) authorized by State law to develop, manage, and provide services or programs to local educational agencies; and

(ii) recognized as an administrative agency for purposes of the provision of special education and related services provided within public elementary and secondary schools of the State; and

(B) includes any other public institution or agency having administrative control and direction over a public elementary or secondary school.

(5) Elementary school. The term "elementary school" means a nonprofit institutional day or residential school that provides elementary education, as determined under State law.

(6) Equipment. The term "equipment" includes:

(A) machinery, utilities, and built-in equipment and any necessary enclosures or structures to house such machinery, utilities, or equipment; and

(B) all other items necessary for the functioning of a particular facility as a facility for the provision of educational services, including items such as instructional equipment and necessary furniture; printed, published, and audio-visual instructional materials; telecommunications, sensory, and other technological aids and devices; and books, periodicals, documents, and other related materials.

(7) Excess costs. The term "excess costs" means those costs that are in excess of the average annual per-student expenditure in a local educational agency during the preceding school year for an elementary or secondary school student, as may be appropriate, and which shall be computed after deducting:

(A) amounts received:

(i) under subchapter II of this chapter;

(ii) under part A of title I of the Elementary and Secondary Education Act of 1965 (20 U.S.C. 6311 et seq.); or

(iii) under part A of title VII of that Act (20 U.S.C. 7401 et seq.); and

(B) any State or local funds expended for programs that would qualify for assistance under any of those parts.

(8) Free appropriate public education. The term "free appropriate public education" means special education and related services that:

(A) have been provided at public expense, under public supervision and direction, and without charge;

(B) meet the standards of the State educational agency;

(C) include an appropriate preschool, elementary, or secondary school education in the State involved; and

(D) are provided in conformity with the individualized education program required under section 1414(d) of this title.

(9) Indian. The term "Indian" means an individual who is a member of an Indian tribe.

(10) Indian tribe. The term "Indian tribe" means any Federal or State Indian tribe, band, rancheria, pueblo, colony, or community, including any Alaska Native village or regional village corporation (as defined in or established under the Alaska Native Claims Settlement Act (43 U.S.C. 1601 et seq.)).

(11) Individualized education program. The term "individualized education program" or "IEP" means a written statement for each child with a disability that is developed, reviewed, and revised in accordance with section 1414(d) of this title.

(12) Individualized family service plan. The term "individualized family service plan" has the meaning given such term in section 1436 of this title.

(13) Infant or toddler with a disability. The term "infant or toddler with a disability" has the meaning given such term in section 1432 of this title.

(14) Institution of higher education. The term "institution of higher education":

(A) has the meaning given that term in section 1141(a) of this title; and

(B) also includes any community college receiving funding from the Secretary of the Interior under the Tribally Controlled Community College Assistance Act of 1978 (25 U.S.C. 1801 et seq.).

(15) Local educational agency

(A) The term "local educational agency" means a public board of education or other public authority legally constituted within a State for either administrative control or direction of, or to perform a service function for, public elementary or secondary schools in a city, county, township, school district, or other political subdivision of a State, or for such combination of school districts or counties as are recognized in a State as an administrative agency for its public elementary or secondary schools.

(B) The term includes:

(i) an educational service agency, as defined in paragraph (4); and

(ii) any other public institution or agency having administrative control and direction of a public elementary or secondary school.

(C) The term includes an elementary or secondary school funded by the Bureau of Indian Affairs, but only to the extent that such inclusion makes the school eligible for programs for which specific eligibility is not provided to the school in another provision of law and the school does not have a student population that is smaller than the student population of the local educational agency receiving assistance under this chapter with the smallest student population, except that the school shall not be subject to the jurisdiction of any State educational agency other than the Bureau of Indian Affairs.

(16) Native language. The term "native language", when used with reference to an individual of limited English proficiency, means the language normally used by the individual, or in the case of a child, the language normally used by the parents of the child.

(17) Nonprofit. The term "nonprofit", as applied to a school, agency, organization, or institution, means a school, agency, organization, or institution owned and operated by one or more nonprofit corporations or associations no part of the net earnings of which inures, or may lawfully inure, to the benefit of any private shareholder or individual.

(18) Outlying area. The term "outlying area" means the United States Virgin Islands, Guam, American Samoa, and the Commonwealth of the Northern Mariana Islands.

(19) Parent. The term "parent":

(A) includes a legal guardian; and

(B) except as used in sections 1415(b)(2) and 1439(a)(5) of this title, includes an individual assigned under either of those sections to be a surrogate parent.

(20) Parent organization. The term "parent organization" has the meaning given that term in section 1482(g) of this title.

(21) Parent training and information center. The term "parent training and information center" means a center assisted under section 1482 or 1483 of this title.

(22) Related services. The term "related services" means transportation, and such developmental, corrective, and other supportive services (including speech-language pathology and audiology services, psychological services, physical and occupational therapy, recreation, including therapeutic recreation, social work services, counseling services, including rehabilitation counseling, orientation and mobility services, and medical services, except that such medical services shall be for diagnostic and evaluation purposes only) as may be required to assist a child with a disability to benefit from special education, and includes the early identification and assessment of disabling conditions in children.

(23) Secondary school. The term "secondary school" means a nonprofit institutional day or residential school that provides secondary education, as determined under State law, except that it does not include any education beyond grade 12.

(24) Secretary. The term "Secretary" means the Secretary of Education.

(25) Special education. The term "special education" means specially designed instruction, at no cost to parents, to meet the unique needs of a child with a disability, including:

(A) instruction conducted in the classroom, in the home, in hospitals and institutions, and in other settings; and

(B) instruction in physical education.

(26) Specific learning disability

(A) *In general.* The term "specific learning disability" means a disorder in one or more of the basic psychological processes involved in understanding or in using language, spoken or written, which disorder may manifest itself in imperfect ability to listen, think, speak, read, write, spell, or do mathematical calculations.

(B) *Disorders included.* Such term includes such conditions as perceptual disabilities, brain injury, minimal brain dysfunction, dyslexia, and developmental aphasia.

(C) *Disorders not included.* Such term does not include a learning problem that is primarily the result of visual, hearing, or motor disabilities, of mental retardation, of emotional disturbance, or of environmental, cultural, or economic disadvantage.

(27) State. The term "State" means each of the 50 States, the District of Columbia, the Commonwealth of Puerto Rico, and each of the outlying areas.

(28) State educational agency. The term "State educational agency" means the State board of education or other agency or officer primarily responsible for the State supervision of public elementary and secondary schools, or, if there is no such officer or agency, an officer or agency designated by the Governor or by State law.

(29) Supplementary aids and services. The term "supplementary aids and services" means aids, services, and other supports that are provided in regular education classes or other education-related settings to enable children with disabilities to be educated with nondisabled children to the maximum extent appropriate in accordance with section 1412(a)(5) of this title.

(30) Transition services. The term "transition services" means a coordinated set of activities for a student with a disability that:

(A) is designed within an outcome-oriented process, which promotes movement from school to post-school activities, including post-secondary education, vocational training, integrated employment (including supported employment), continuing and adult education, adult services, independent living, or community participation;

(B) is based upon the individual student's needs, taking into account the student's preferences and interests; and includes instruction, related services, community experiences, the development of employment and other post-school adult living objectives, and, when appropriate, acquisition of daily living skills and functional vocational evaluation.

Sec. 1412. State eligibility

(a) In general. A State is eligible for assistance under this subchapter for a fiscal year if the State demonstrates to the satisfaction of the Secretary that the State has in effect policies and procedures to ensure that it meets each of the following conditions:

(1) *Free appropriate public education*

(A) *In general.* A free appropriate public education is available to all children with disabilities residing in the State between the ages of 3 and 21, inclusive, including children with disabilities who have been suspended or expelled from school.

(B) *Limitation.* The obligation to make a free appropriate public education available to all children with disabilities does not apply with respect to children:

(i) aged 3 through 5 and 18 through 21 in a State to the extent that its application to those children would be inconsistent with State law or practice, or the order of any court, respecting the provision of public education to children in those age ranges; and

(ii) aged 18 through 21 to the extent that State law does not require that special education and related services under this subchapter be provided to children with disabilities who, in the educational placement prior to their incarceration in an adult correctional facility:

(I) were not actually identified as being a child with a disability under section 1401(3) of this title; or

(II) did not have an individualized education program under this subchapter.

(2) *Full educational opportunity goal.* The State has established a goal of providing full educational opportunity to all children with disabilities and a detailed timetable for accomplishing that goal.

(3) *Child find*

(A) I*n general.* All children with disabilities residing in the State, including children with disabilities attending private schools, regardless of the severity of their disabilities, and who are in need of special education and related services, are identified, located, and evaluated and a practical method is developed and implemented to determine which children with disabilities are currently receiving needed special education and related services.

(B) *Construction.* Nothing in this chapter requires that children be classified by their disability so long as each child who has a disability listed in section 1401 of this title and who, by reason of that disability, needs special education and related services is regarded as a child with a disability under this subchapter.

(4) *Individualized education program.* An individualized education program, or an individualized family service plan that meets the requirements of section 1436(d) of this title, is developed, reviewed, and revised for each child with a disability in accordance with section 1414(d) of this title.

(5) *Least restrictive environment*

(A) *In general.* To the maximum extent appropriate, children with disabilities, including children in public or private institutions or other care facilities, are educated with children who are not disabled, and special classes, separate schooling, or other removal of children with disabilities from the regular educational environment occurs only when the nature or severity of the disability of a child is such that education in regular classes with the use of supplementary aids and services cannot be achieved satisfactorily.

(B) *Additional requirement*

(i) In general. If the State uses a funding mechanism by which the State distributes State funds on the basis of the type of setting in which a child is served, the funding mechanism does not result in placements that violate the requirements of subparagraph (A).

(ii) Assurance. If the State does not have policies and procedures to ensure compliance with clause (i), the State shall provide the Secretary an assurance that it will revise the funding mechanism as soon as feasible to ensure that such mechanism does not result in such placements.

(6) *Procedural safeguards*

(A) *In general.* Children with disabilities and their parents are afforded the procedural safeguards required by section 1415 of this title.

(B) *Additional procedural safeguards.* Procedures to ensure that testing and evaluation materials and procedures utilized for the purposes of evaluation and placement of children with disabilities will be selected and administered so as not to be racially or culturally discriminatory. Such materials or procedures shall be provided and administered in the child's native language or mode of communication, unless it clearly is not feasible to do so, and no single procedure shall be the sole criterion for determining an appropriate educational program for a child.

(7) *Evaluation.* Children with disabilities are evaluated in accordance with subsections (a) through (c) of section 1414 of this title.

(8) *Confidentiality.* Agencies in the State comply with section 1417(c) of this title (relating to the confidentiality of records and information).

(9) *Transition from subchapter III to preschool programs.* Children participating in early-intervention programs assisted under subchapter III of this chapter, and who will participate in preschool programs assisted under this subchapter, experience a smooth and effective transition to those preschool programs in a manner consistent with section 1437(a)(8) of this title. By the third birthday of such a child, an individualized education program or, if consistent with sections 1414(d)(2)(B) and 1436(d) of this title, an individualized family service plan, has been developed and is being implemented for the child. The local educational agency will participate in transition planning conferences arranged by the designated lead agency under section 1437(a)(8) of this title.

(10) *Children in private schools*

(A) Children enrolled in private schools by their parents

(i) In general. To the extent consistent with the number and location of children with disabilities in the State who are enrolled by their parents in private elementary and secondary schools, provision is made for the participation of those children in the program assisted or carried out under this subchapter by providing for such children special education and related services in accordance with the following requirements, unless the Secretary has arranged for services to those children under subsection (f) of this section:

(I) Amounts expended for the provision of those services by a local educational agency shall be equal to a proportionate amount of Federal funds made available under this subchapter.

(II) Such services may be provided to children with disabilities on the premises of private, including parochial, schools, to the extent consistent with law.

(ii) Child-find requirement. The requirements of paragraph (3) of this subsection (relating to child find) shall apply with respect to children with disabilities in the State who are enrolled in private, including parochial, elementary and secondary schools.

(B) Children placed in, or referred to, private schools by public agencies

(i) In general. Children with disabilities in private schools and facilities are provided special education and related services, in accordance with an individualized education program, at no cost to their parents, if such children are placed in, or referred to, such schools or facilities by the State or appropriate local educational agency as the means of carrying out the requirements of this subchapter or any other applicable law requiring the provision of special education and related services to all children with disabilities within such State.

(ii) Standards. In all cases described in clause (i), the State educational agency shall determine whether such schools and facilities meet standards that apply to State and local educational agencies and that children so served have all the rights they would have if served by such agencies.

(C) Payment for education of children enrolled in private schools without consent of or referral by the public agency

(i) In general. Subject to subparagraph (A), this subchapter does not require a local educational agency to pay for the cost of education, including special education and related services, of a child with a disability at a private school or facility if that agency made a free appropriate public education available to the child and the parents elected to place the child in such private school or facility.

(ii) Reimbursement for private school placement. If the parents of a child with a disability, who previously received special education and related services under the authority of a public agency, enroll the child in a private elementary or secondary school without the consent of or referral by the public agency, a court or a hearing officer may require the agency to reimburse the parents for the cost of that enrollment if the court or hearing officer finds that the agency had not made a free appropriate public education available to the child in a timely manner prior to that enrollment.

(iii) Limitation on reimbursement. The cost of reimbursement described in clause (ii) may be reduced or denied:

(I) if:

(aa) at the most recent IEP meeting that the parents attended prior to removal of the child from the public school, the parents did not inform the IEP Team that they were rejecting the placement proposed by the public agency to provide a free appropriate public education to their child, including stating their concerns and their intent to enroll their child in a private school at public expense; or

(bb) 10 business days (including any holidays that occur on a business day) prior to the removal of the child from the public school, the parents did not give written notice to the public agency of the information described in division (aa);

(II) if, prior to the parents' removal of the child from the public school, the public agency informed the parents, through the notice requirements described in section 1415(b)(7) of this title, of its intent to evaluate the child (including a statement of the purpose of the evaluation that was appropriate and reasonable), but the parents did not make the child available for such evaluation; or

(III) upon a judicial finding of unreasonableness with respect to actions taken by the parents.

(iv) Exception. Notwithstanding the notice requirement in clause (iii)(I), the cost of reimbursement may not be reduced or denied for failure to provide such notice if:

(I) the parent is illiterate and cannot write in English;

(II) compliance with clause (iii)(I) would likely result in physical or serious emotional harm to the child;

(III) the school prevented the parent from providing such notice; or

(IV) the parents had not received notice, pursuant to section 1415 of this title, of the notice requirement in clause (iii)(I).

(11) *State educational agency responsible for general supervision*

(A) *In general.* The State educational agency is responsible for ensuring that:

(i) the requirements of this subchapter are met; and

(ii) all educational programs for children with disabilities in the State, including all such programs administered by any other State or local agency:

(I) are under the general supervision of individuals in the State who are responsible for educational programs for children with disabilities; and

(II) meet the educational standards of the State educational agency.

(B) Limitation Subparagraph (A) shall not limit the responsibility of agencies in the State other than the State educational agency to provide, or pay for some or all of the costs of, a free appropriate public education for any child with a disability in the State.

(C) *Exception.* Notwithstanding subparagraphs (A) and (B), the Governor (or another individual pursuant to State law), consistent with State law, may assign to any public agency in the State the responsibility of ensuring that the requirements of this subchapter are met with respect to children with disabilities who are convicted as adults under State law and incarcerated in adult prisons.

(12) *Obligations related to and methods of ensuring services*

(A) *Establishing responsibility for services.* The Chief Executive Officer or designee of the officer shall ensure that an interagency agreement or other mechanism for interagency coordination is in effect between each public agency described in subparagraph (B) and the State educational agency, in order to ensure that all services described in subparagraph (B)(i) that are needed to ensure a free appropriate public education are provided, including the provision of such services during the pendency of any dispute under clause (iii). Such agreement or mechanism shall include the following:

(i) Agency financial responsibility. An identification of, or a method for defining, the financial responsibility of each agency for providing services described in subparagraph (B)(i) to ensure a free appropriate public education to children with disabilities, provided that the financial responsibility of each public agency described in subparagraph (B), including the State Medicaid agency and other public insurers of children with disabilities, shall precede the financial responsibility of the local educational agency (or the State agency responsible for developing the child's IEP).

(ii) Conditions and terms of reimbursement. The conditions, terms, and procedures under which a local educational agency shall be reimbursed by other agencies.

(iii) Interagency disputes. Procedures for resolving interagency disputes (including procedures under which local educational agencies may initiate proceedings) under the agreement or other mechanism to secure reimbursement from other agencies or otherwise implement the provisions of the agreement or mechanism.

(iv) Coordination of services procedures. Policies and procedures for agencies to determine and identify the interagency coordination responsibilities of each agency to promote the coordination and timely and appropriate delivery of services described in subparagraph (B)(i).

(B) *Obligation of public agency*

(i) In general. If any public agency other than an educational agency is otherwise obligated under Federal or State law, or assigned responsibility under State policy or pursuant to subparagraph (A), to provide or pay for any services that are also considered special education or related services (such as,

but not limited to, services described in sections 1401(1) relating to assistive technology devices, 1401(2) relating to assistive technology services, 1401(22) relating to related services, 1401(29) relating to supplementary aids and services, and 1401(30) of this title relating to transition services) that are necessary for ensuring a free appropriate public education to children with disabilities within the State, such public agency shall fulfill that obligation or responsibility, either directly or through contract or other arrangement.

(ii) Reimbursement for services by public agency. If a public agency other than an educational agency fails to provide or pay for the special education and related services described in clause (i), the local educational agency (or State agency responsible for developing the child's IEP) shall provide or pay for such services to the child. Such local educational agency or State agency may then claim reimbursement for the services from the public agency that failed to provide or pay for such services and such public agency shall reimburse the local educational agency or State agency pursuant to the terms of the interagency agreement or other mechanism described in subparagraph (A)(i) according to the procedures established in such agreement pursuant to subparagraph (A)(ii).

(C) *Special rule.* The requirements of subparagraph (A) may be met through:

(i) state statute or regulation;

(ii) signed agreements between respective agency officials that clearly identify the responsibilities of each agency relating to the provision of services; or

(iii) other appropriate written methods as determined by the Chief Executive Officer of the State or designee of the officer.

(13) *Procedural requirements relating to local educational agency eligibility.* The State educational agency will not make a final determination that a local educational agency is not eligible for assistance under this subchapter without first affording that agency reasonable notice and an opportunity for a hearing.

(14) *Comprehensive system of personnel development.* The State has in effect, consistent with the purposes of this chapter and with section 1435(a)(8) of this title, a comprehensive system of personnel development that is designed to ensure an adequate supply of qualified special education, regular education, and related services personnel that meets the requirements for a State improvement plan relating to personnel development in subsections (b)(2)(B) and (c)(3)(D) of section 1453 of this title.

(15) *Personnel standards*

(A) *In general.* The State educational agency has established and maintains standards to ensure that personnel necessary to carry out this subchapter are appropriately and adequately prepared and trained.

(B) *Standards described.* Such standards shall:

(i) be consistent with any State-approved or State-recognized certification, licensing, registration, or other comparable requirements that apply to the professional discipline in which those personnel are providing special education or related services;

(ii) to the extent the standards described in subparagraph (A) are not based on the highest requirements in the State applicable to a specific profession or discipline, the State is taking steps to require retraining or hiring of personnel that meet appropriate professional requirements in the State; and

(iii) allow paraprofessionals and assistants who are appropriately trained and supervised, in accordance with State law, regulations, or written policy, in meeting the requirements of this subchapter to be used to assist in the provision of special education and related services to children with disabilities under this subchapter.

(C) *Policy.* In implementing this paragraph, a State may adopt a policy that includes a requirement that local educational agencies in the State make an ongoing good-faith effort to recruit and hire appropriately and adequately trained personnel to provide special education and related services to children with disabilities, including, in a geographic area of the State where there is a shortage of such personnel, the most qualified individuals available who are making satisfactory progress toward completing applicable course work necessary to meet the standards described in subparagraph (B)(i), consistent with State law, and the steps described in subparagraph (B)(ii) within three years.

(16) *Performance goals and indicators.* The State:

(A) has established goals for the performance of children with disabilities in the State that:

(i) will promote the purposes of this chapter, as stated in section 1400(d) of this title; and

(ii) are consistent, to the maximum extent appropriate, with other goals and standards for children established by the State;

(B) has established performance indicators the State will use to assess progress toward achieving those goals that, at a minimum, address the performance of children with disabilities on assessments, drop-out rates, and graduation rates;

(C) will, every two years, report to the Secretary and the public on the progress of the State, and of children with disabilities in the State, toward meeting the goals established under subparagraph (A); and

(D) based on its assessment of that progress, will revise its State improvement plan under part A of subchapter IV of this chapter as may be needed to improve its performance, if the State receives assistance under that part.

(17) *Participation in assessments*

(A) *In general.* Children with disabilities are included in general State and district-wide assessment programs, with appropriate accommodations, where necessary. As appropriate, the State or local educational agency:

(i) develops guidelines for the participation of children with disabilities in alternate assessments for those children who cannot participate in State and district-wide assessment programs; and

(ii) develops and, beginning not later than July 1, 2000, conducts those alternate assessments.

(B) *Reports.* The State educational agency makes available to the public, and reports to the public with the same frequency and in the same detail as it reports on the assessment of non-disabled children, the following:

(i) The number of children with disabilities participating in regular assessments.

(ii) The number of those children participating in alternate assessments.

(iii)

(I) The performance of those children on regular assessments (beginning not later than July 1, 1998) and on alternate assessments (not later than July 1, 2000), if doing so would be statistically sound and would not result in the disclosure of performance results identifiable to individual children.

(II) Data relating to the performance of children described under subclause (I) shall be disaggregated:

(aa) for assessments conducted after July 1, 1998; and

(bb) for assessments conducted before July 1, 1998, if the State is required to disaggregate such data prior to July 1, 1998.

(18) *Supplementation of State, local, and other Federal funds*

(A) *Expenditures.* Funds paid to a State under this subchapter will be expended in accordance with all the provisions of this subchapter.

(B) *Prohibition against commingling.* Funds paid to a State under this subchapter will not be commingled with State funds.

(C) *Prohibition against supplantation and conditions for waiver by Secretary.* Except as provided in section 1413 of this title, funds paid to a State under this subchapter will be used to supplement the level of Federal, State, and local funds (including funds that are not under the direct control of State or local educational agencies) expended for special education and related services provided to children with disabilities under this subchapter and in no case to supplant such Federal, State, and local funds, except that, where the State provides clear and convincing evidence that all children with disabilities have available to them a free appropriate public education, the Secretary may waive, in whole or in part, the requirements of this subparagraph if the Secretary concurs with the evidence provided by the State.

(19) *Maintenance of State financial support*

(A) *In general.* The State does not reduce the amount of State financial support for special education and related services for children with disabilities, or otherwise made available because of the excess costs of educating those children, below the amount of that support for the preceding fiscal year.

(B) *Reduction of funds for failure to maintain support.* The Secretary shall reduce the allocation of funds under section 1411 of this title for any fiscal year following the fiscal year in which the State fails to comply with the requirement of subparagraph (A) by the same amount by which the State fails to meet the requirement.

(C) *Waivers for exceptional or uncontrollable circumstances.* The Secretary may waive the requirement of subparagraph (A) for a State, for one fiscal year at a time, if the Secretary determines that:

(i) granting a waiver would be equitable due to exceptional or uncontrollable circumstances such as a natural disaster or a precipitous and unforeseen decline in the financial resources of the State; or

(ii) the State meets the standard in paragraph (18)(C) of this section for a waiver of the requirement to supplement, and not to supplant, funds received under this subchapter.

(D) *Subsequent years.* If, for any year, a State fails to meet the requirement of subparagraph (A), including any year for which the State is granted a waiver under subparagraph (C), the financial support required of the State in future years under subparagraph (A) shall be the amount that would have been required in the absence of that failure and not the reduced level of the State's support.

(E) *Regulations*

(i) The Secretary shall, by regulation, establish procedures (including objective criteria and consideration of the results of compliance reviews of the State conducted by the Secretary) for determining whether to grant a waiver under subparagraph (C)(ii).

(ii) The Secretary shall publish proposed regulations under clause (i) not later than 6 months after June 4, 1997, and shall issue final regulations under clause (i) not later than 1 year after June 4, 1997.

(20) *Public participation.* Prior to the adoption of any policies and procedures needed to comply with this section (including any amendments to such policies and procedures), the State ensures that there are public hearings, adequate notice of the hearings, and an opportunity for comment available to the general public, including individuals with disabilities and parents of children with disabilities.

(21) *State advisory panel*

(A) *In general.* The State has established and maintains an advisory panel for the purpose of providing policy guidance with respect to special education and related services for children with disabilities in the State.

(B) *Membership.* Such advisory panel shall consist of members appointed by the Governor, or any other official authorized under State law to make such appointments, that is representative of the State population and that is composed of individuals involved in, or concerned with, the education of children with disabilities, including:

(i) parents of children with disabilities;

(ii) individuals with disabilities;

(iii) teachers;

(iv) representatives of institutions of higher education that prepare special education and related services personnel;

(v) State and local education officials;

(vi) administrators of programs for children with disabilities;

(vii) representatives of other State agencies involved in the financing or delivery of related services to children with disabilities;

(viii) representatives of private schools and public charter schools;

(ix) at least one representative of a vocational, community, or business organization concerned with the provision of transition services to children with disabilities; and

(x) representatives from the State juvenile and adult corrections agencies.

(C) *Special rule.* A majority of the members of the panel shall be individuals with disabilities or parents of children with disabilities.

(D) *Duties.* The advisory panel shall:

(i) advise the State educational agency of unmet needs within the State in the education of children with disabilities;

(ii) comment publicly on any rules or regulations proposed by the State regarding the education of children with disabilities;

(iii) advise the State educational agency in developing evaluations and reporting on data to the Secretary under section 1418 of this title;

(iv) advise the State educational agency in developing corrective action plans to address findings identified in Federal monitoring reports under this subchapter; and

(v) advise the State educational agency in developing and implementing policies relating to the coordination of services for children with disabilities.

(22) *Suspension and expulsion rates*

(A) *In general.* The State educational agency examines data to determine if significant discrepancies are occurring in the rate of long-term suspensions and expulsions of children with disabilities:

(i) among local educational agencies in the State; or

(ii) compared to such rates for nondisabled children within such agencies.

(B) *Review and revision of policies.* If such discrepancies are occurring, the State educational agency reviews and, if appropriate, revises (or requires the affected State or local educational agency to revise) its policies, procedures, and practices relating to the development and implementation of IEPs, the use of behavioral interventions, and procedural safeguards, to ensure that such policies, procedures, and practices comply with this chapter.

(b) State educational agency as provider of free appropriate public education or direct services. If the State educational agency provides free appropriate public education to children with disabilities, or provides direct services to such children, such agency:

(1) shall comply with any additional requirements of section 1413(a) of this title, as if such agency were a local educational agency; and

(2) may use amounts that are otherwise available to such agency under this subchapter to serve those children without regard to section 1413(a)(2)(A)(i) of this title (relating to excess costs).

(c) Exception for prior State plans

(1) *In general.* If a State has on file with the Secretary policies and procedures that demonstrate that such State meets any requirement of subsection (a) of this section, including any policies and procedures filed under this subchapter as in effect before the effective date of the Individuals with Disabilities Education Act Amendments of 1997, the Secretary shall consider such State to have met such requirement for purposes of receiving a grant under this subchapter.

(2) *Modifications made by State.* Subject to paragraph (3), an application submitted by a State in accordance with this section shall remain in effect until the State submits to the Secretary such modifications as the State deems necessary. This section shall apply to a modification to an application to

the same extent and in the same manner as this section applies to the original plan.

(3) *Modifications required by Secretary.* If, after the effective date of the Individuals with Disabilities Education Act Amendments of 1997, the provisions of this chapter are amended (or the regulations developed to carry out this chapter are amended), or there is a new interpretation of this chapter by a Federal court or a State's highest court, or there is an official finding of noncompliance with Federal law or regulations, the Secretary may require a State to modify its application only to the extent necessary to ensure the State's compliance with this subchapter.

(d) Approval by Secretary

(1) *In general.* If the Secretary determines that a State is eligible to receive a grant under this subchapter, the Secretary shall notify the State of that determination.

(2) *Notice and hearing.* The Secretary shall not make a final determination that a State is not eligible to receive a grant under this subchapter until after providing the State:

(A) with reasonable notice; and

(B) with an opportunity for a hearing.

(e) Assistance under other Federal programs. Nothing in this chapter permits a State to reduce medical and other assistance available, or to alter eligibility, under titles V and XIX of the Social Security Act (42 U.S.C. 701 et seq., 1396 et seq.) with respect to the provision of a free appropriate public education for children with disabilities in the State.

(f) By-pass for children in private schools

(1) *In general.* If, on December 2, 1983, a State educational agency is prohibited by law from providing for the participation in special programs of children with disabilities enrolled in private elementary and secondary schools as required by subsection (a)(10)(A) of this section, the Secretary shall, notwithstanding such provision of law, arrange for the provision of services to such children through arrangements which shall be subject to the requirements of such subsection.

(2) *Payments*

(A) Determination of amounts. If the Secretary arranges for services pursuant to this subsection, the Secretary, after consultation with the appropriate public and private school officials, shall pay to the provider of such services for a fiscal year an amount per child that does not exceed the amount determined by dividing:

(i) the total amount received by the State under this subchapter for such fiscal year; by

(ii) the number of children with disabilities served in the prior year, as reported to the Secretary by the State under section 1418 of this title.

(B) Withholding of certain amounts. Pending final resolution of any investigation or complaint that could result in a determination under this subsection, the Secretary may withhold from the allocation of the affected State educational agency the amount the Secretary estimates would be necessary to pay the cost of services described in subparagraph (A).

(C) Period of payments. The period under which payments are made under subparagraph (A) shall continue until the Secretary determines that there will no longer be any failure or

inability on the part of the State educational agency to meet the requirements of subsection (a)(10)(A) of this section.

(3) *Notice and hearing*

(A) *In general.* The Secretary shall not take any final action under this subsection until the State educational agency affected by such action has had an opportunity, for at least 45 days after receiving written notice thereof, to submit written objections and to appear before the Secretary or the Secretary's designee to show cause why such action should not be taken.

(B) *Review of action.* If a State educational agency is dissatisfied with the Secretary's final action after a proceeding under subparagraph (A), such agency may, not later than 60 days after notice of such action, file with the United States court of appeals for the circuit in which such State is located a petition for review of that action. A copy of the petition shall be forthwith transmitted by the clerk of the court to the Secretary. The Secretary thereupon shall file in the court the record of the proceedings on which the Secretary based the Secretary's action, as provided in section 2112 of title 28.

(C) *Review of findings of fact.* The findings of fact by the Secretary, if supported by substantial evidence, shall be conclusive, but the court, for good cause shown, may remand the case to the Secretary to take further evidence, and the Secretary may thereupon make new or modified findings of fact and may modify the Secretary's previous action, and shall file in the court the record of the further proceedings. Such new or modified findings of fact shall likewise be conclusive if supported by substantial evidence.

(D) *Jurisdiction of court of appeals; review by United States Supreme Court.* Upon the filing of a petition under subparagraph (B), the United States court of appeals shall have jurisdiction to affirm the action of the Secretary or to set it aside, in whole or in part. The judgment of the court shall be subject to review by the Supreme Court of the United States upon certiorari or certification as provided in section 1254 of title 28.

Sec. 1414. Evaluations, eligibility determinations, individualized education programs, and educational placements

(a) Evaluations and reevaluations

(1) *Initial evaluations*

(A) *In general.* A State educational agency, other State agency, or local educational agency shall conduct a full and individual initial evaluation, in accordance with this paragraph and subsection (b) of this section, before the initial provision of special education and related services to a child with a disability under this subchapter.

(B) *Procedures.* Such initial evaluation shall consist of procedures:

(i) to determine whether a child is a child with a disability (as defined in section 1401(3) of this title); and

(ii) to determine the educational needs of such child.

(C) *Parental consent*

(i) In general. The agency proposing to conduct an initial evaluation to determine if the child qualifies as a child with a disability as defined in section 1401(3)(A) or 1401(3)(B) of this title shall obtain an informed consent from the parent of such child before the evaluation is conducted. Parental consent for evaluation shall not be construed as consent for placement for receipt of special education and related services.

(ii) Refusal. If the parents of such child refuse consent for the evaluation, the agency may continue to pursue an evaluation by utilizing the mediation and due process procedures under section 1415 of this title, except to the extent inconsistent with State law relating to parental consent.

(2) *Reevaluations.* A local educational agency shall ensure that a reevaluation of each child with a disability is conducted:

(A) if conditions warrant a reevaluation or if the child's parent or teacher requests a reevaluation, but at least once every 3 years; and

(B) in accordance with subsections (b) and (c) of this section.

(b) Evaluation procedures

(1) *Notice.* The local educational agency shall provide notice to the parents of a child with a disability, in accordance with subsections (b)(3), (b)(4), and (c) of section 1415 of this title, that describes any evaluation procedures such agency proposes to conduct.

(2) *Conduct of evaluation.* In conducting the evaluation, the local educational agency shall:

(A) use a variety of assessment tools and strategies to gather relevant functional and developmental information, including information provided by the parent, that may assist in determining whether the child is a child with a disability and the content of the child's individualized education program, including information related to enabling the child to be involved in and progress in the general curriculum or, for preschool children, to participate in appropriate activities;

(B) not use any single procedure as the sole criterion for determining whether a child is a child with a disability or determining an appropriate educational program for the child; and

(C) use technically sound instruments that may assess the relative contribution of cognitive and behavioral factors, in addition to physical or developmental factors.

(3) *Additional requirements.* Each local educational agency shall ensure that:

(A) tests and other evaluation materials used to assess a child under this section:

(i) are selected and administered so as not to be discriminatory on a racial or cultural basis; and

(ii) are provided and administered in the child's native language or other mode of communication, unless it is clearly not feasible to do so; and

(B) any standardized tests that are given to the child:

(i) have been validated for the specific purpose for which they are used;

(ii) are administered by trained and knowledgeable personnel; and

(iii) are administered in accordance with any instructions provided by the producer of such tests;

(C) the child is assessed in all areas of suspected disability; and

(D) assessment tools and strategies that provide relevant information that directly assists persons in determining the educational needs of the child are provided.

(4) *Determination of eligibility.* Upon completion of administration of tests and other evaluation materials:

(A) the determination of whether the child is a child with a disability as defined in section 1401(3) of this title shall be made by a team of qualified professionals and the parent of the child in accordance with paragraph (5); and

(B) a copy of the evaluation report and the documentation of determination of eligibility will be given to the parent.

(5) *Special rule for eligibility determination.* In making a determination of eligibility under paragraph (4)(A), a child shall not be determined to be a child with a disability if the determinant factor for such determination is lack of instruction in reading or math or limited English proficiency.

(c) Additional requirements for evaluation and reevaluations

(1) *Review of existing evaluation data.* As part of an initial evaluation (if appropriate) and as part of any reevaluation under this section, the IEP Team described in subsection (d)(1)(B) of this section and other qualified professionals, as appropriate, shall:

(A) review existing evaluation data on the child, including evaluations and information provided by the parents of the child, current classroom-based assessments and observations, and teacher and related services providers observation; and

(B) on the basis of that review, and input from the child's parents, identify what additional data, if any, are needed to determine:

(i) whether the child has a particular category of disability, as described in section 1401 (3) of this title, or, in case of a reevaluation of a child, whether the child continues to have such a disability;

(ii) the present levels of performance and educational needs of the child;

(iii) whether the child needs special education and related services, or in the case of a reevaluation of a child, whether the child continues to need special education and related services; and

(iv) whether any additions or modifications to the special education and related services are needed to enable the child to meet the measurable annual goals set out in the individualized education program of the child and to participate, as appropriate, in the general curriculum.

(2) *Source of data.* The local educational agency shall administer such tests and other evaluation materials as may be needed to produce the data identified by the IEP Team under paragraph (1)(B).

(3) *Parental consent.* Each local educational agency shall obtain informed parental consent, in accordance with subsection (a)(1)(C) of this section, prior to conducting any reevaluation of a child with a disability, except that such informed parent consent need not be obtained if the local educational agency can demonstrate that it had taken reasonable measures to obtain such consent and the child's parent has failed to respond.

(4) *Requirements if additional data are not needed.* If the IEP Team and other qualified professionals, as appropriate, determine that no additional data are needed to determine whether the child continues to be a child with a disability, the local educational agency:

(A) shall notify the child's parents of:

(i) that determination and the reasons for it; and

(ii) the right of such parents to request an assessment to determine whether the child continues to be a child with a disability; and

(B) shall not be required to conduct such an assessment unless requested to by the child's parents.

(5) *Evaluations before change in eligibility.* A local educational agency shall evaluate a child with a disability in accordance with this section before determining that the child is no longer a child with a disability.

(d) Individualized education programs.

(1) *Definitions*

As used in this chapter:

(A) *Individualized education program.* The term "individualized education program" or "IEP" means a written statement for each child with a disability that is developed, reviewed, and revised in accordance with this section and that includes:

(i) a statement of the child's present levels of educational performance, including:

(I) how the child's disability affects the child's involvement and progress in the general curriculum; or

(II) for preschool children, as appropriate, how the disability affects the child's participation in appropriate activities;

(ii) a statement of measurable annual goals, including benchmarks or short-term objectives, related to:

(I) meeting the child's needs that result from the child's disability to enable the child to be involved in and progress in the general curriculum; and

(II) meeting each of the child's other educational needs that result from the child's disability;

(iii) a statement of the special education and related services and supplementary aids and services to be provided to the child, or on behalf of the child, and a statement of the program modifications or supports for school personnel that will be provided for the child:

(I) to advance appropriately toward attaining the annual goals;

(II) to be involved and progress in the general curriculum in accordance with clause (i) and to participate in extracurricular and other nonacademic activities; and

(III) to be educated and participate with other children with disabilities and nondisabled children in the activities described in this paragraph;

(iv) an explanation of the extent, if any, to which the child will not participate with nondisabled children in the regular class and in the activities described in clause

(iii);

(v)

(I) a statement of any individual modifications in the administration of State or districtwide assessments of student achievement that are needed in order for the child to participate in such assessment; and

(II) if the IEP Team determines that the child will not participate in a particular State or districtwide assessment of student achievement (or part of such an assessment), a statement of:

(aa) why that assessment is not appropriate for the child; and

(bb) how the child will be assessed;

(vi) the projected date for the beginning of the services and modifications described in clause (iii), and the anticipated frequency, location, and duration of those services and modifications;

(vii) a statement of:

(I) beginning at age 14, and updated annually, a statement of the transition service needs of the child under the applicable components of the child's IEP that focuses on the child's courses of study (such as participation in advanced-placement courses or a vocational education program);

(II) beginning at age 16 (or younger, if determined appropriate by the IEP Team), a statement of needed transition services for the child, including, when appropriate, a statement of the interagency responsibilities or any needed linkages; and

(III) beginning at least one year before the child reaches the age of majority under State law, a statement that the child has been informed of his or her rights under this chapter, if any, that will transfer to the child on reaching the age of majority under section 1415(m) of this title; and

(viii) a statement of:

(I) how the child's progress toward the annual goals described in clause (ii) will be measured; and

(II) how the child's parents will be regularly informed (by such means as periodic report cards), at least as often as parents are informed of their nondisabled children's progress, of:

(aa) their child's progress toward the annual goals described in clause (ii); and

(bb) the extent to which that progress is sufficient to enable the child to achieve the goals by the end of the year.

(B) *Individualized education program team.* The term "individualized education program team" or "IEP Team" means a group of individuals composed of:

(i) the parents of a child with a disability;

(ii) at least one regular education teacher of such child (if the child is, or may be, participating in the regular education environment);

(iii) at least one special education teacher, or where appropriate, at least one special education provider of such child;

(iv) a representative of the local educational agency who:

(I) is qualified to provide, or supervise the provision of, specially designed instruction to meet the unique needs of children with disabilities;

(II) is knowledgeable about the general curriculum; and

(III) is knowledgeable about the availability of resources of the local educational agency;

(v) an individual who can interpret the instructional implications of evaluation results, who may be a member of the team described in clauses (ii) through (vi);

(vi) at the discretion of the parent or the agency, other individuals who have knowledge or special expertise regarding the child, including related services personnel as appropriate; and

(vii) whenever appropriate, the child with a disability.

(2) *Requirement that program be in effect*

(A) *In general.* At the beginning of each school year, each local educational agency, State educational agency, or other State agency, as the case may be, shall have in effect, for each child with a disability in its jurisdiction, an individualized education program, as defined in paragraph (1)(A).

(B) *Program for child aged 3 through 5.* In the case of a child with a disability aged 3 through 5 (or, at the discretion of the State educational agency, a 2-year-old child with a disability who will turn age 3 during the school year), an individualized family service plan that contains the material described in section 1436 of this title, and that is developed in accordance with this section, may serve as the IEP of the child if using that plan as the IEP is:

(i) consistent with State policy; and

(ii) agreed to by the agency and the child's parents.

(3) *Development of IEP*

(A) *In general.* In developing each child's IEP, the IEP Team, subject to subparagraph (C), shall consider:

(i) the strengths of the child and the concerns of the parents for enhancing the education of their child; and

(ii) the results of the initial evaluation or most recent evaluation of the child.

(B) *Consideration of special factors.* The IEP Team shall:

(i) in the case of a child whose behavior impedes his or her learning or that of others, consider, when appropriate, strategies, including positive behavioral interventions, strategies, and supports to address that behavior;

(ii) in the case of a child with limited English proficiency, consider the language needs of the child as such needs relate to the child's IEP;

(iii) in the case of a child who is blind or visually impaired, provide for instruction in Braille and the use of Braille unless the IEP Team determines, after an evaluation of the child's reading and writing skills, needs, and appropriate reading and writing media (including an evaluation of the child's future needs for instruction in Braille or the use of Braille), that instruction in Braille or the use of Braille is not appropriate for the child;

(iv) consider the communication needs of the child, and in the case of a child who is deaf or hard of hearing, consider the child's language and communication needs, opportunities for direct communications with peers and professional personnel in the child's language and communication mode, academic level, and full range of needs, including opportunities for direct instruction in the child's language and communication mode; and

(v) consider whether the child requires assistive technology devices and services.

(C) *Requirement with respect to regular education teacher.* The regular education teacher of the child, as a member of the IEP Team, shall, to the extent appropriate, participate in the development of the IEP of the child, including the determination of appropriate positive behavioral interventions and strategies and the determination of supplementary aids and services, program modifications, and support for school personnel consistent with paragraph (1)(A)(iii).

(4) *Review and revision of IEP*

(A) *In general.* The local educational agency shall ensure that, subject to subparagraph (B), the IEP Team:

(i) reviews the child's IEP periodically, but not less than annually to determine whether the annual goals for the child are being achieved; and

(ii) revises the IEP as appropriate to address:

(I) any lack of expected progress toward the annual goals and in the general curriculum, where appropriate;

(II) the results of any reevaluation conducted under this section;

(III) information about the child provided to, or by, the parents, as described in subsection (c)(1)(B) of this section;

(IV) the child's anticipated needs; or

(V) other matters.

(B) *Requirement with respect to regular education teacher.* The regular education teacher of the child, as a member of the IEP Team, shall, to the extent appropriate, participate in the review and revision of the IEP of the child.

(5) *Failure to meet transition objectives.* If a participating agency, other than the local educational agency, fails to provide the transition services described in the IEP in accordance with paragraph (1)(A)(vii), the local educational agency shall reconvene the IEP Team to identify alternative strategies to meet the transition objectives for the child set out in that program.

(6) *Children with disabilities in adult prisons*

(A) *In general.* The following requirements do not apply to children with disabilities who are convicted as adults under State law and incarcerated in adult prisons:

(i) The requirements contained in section 1412(a)(17) of this title and paragraph (1)(A)(v) of this subsection (relating to participation of children with disabilities in general assessments).

(ii) The requirements of subclauses (I) and (II) of paragraph (1)(A)(vii) of this subsection (relating to transition planning and transition services), do not apply with respect to such children whose eligibility under this subchapter will end, because of their age, before they will be released from prison.

(B) *Additional requirement.* If a child with a disability is convicted as an adult under State law and incarcerated in an adult prison, the child's IEP Team may modify the child's IEP or placement notwithstanding the requirements of section 1412 (a)(5)(A) of this title and subsection (d)(1)(A) of this section if the State has demonstrated a bona fide security or compelling penological interest that cannot otherwise be accommodated.

(e) **Construction.** Team to include information under one component of a child's IEP that is already contained under another component of such IEP.

(f) **Educational placements.** Each local educational agency or State educational agency shall ensure that the parents of each child with a disability are members of any group that makes decisions on the educational placement of their child.

Sec. 1415. Procedural safeguards

(a) **Establishment of procedures.** Any State educational agency, State agency, or local educational agency that receives assistance under this subchapter shall establish and maintain procedures in accordance with this section to ensure that children with disabilities and their parents are guaranteed procedural safeguards with respect to the provision of free appropriate public education by such agencies.

(b) Types of procedures. The procedures required by this section shall include:

(1) an opportunity for the parents of a child with a disability to examine all records relating to such child and to participate in meetings with respect to the identification, evaluation, and educational placement of the child, and the provision of a free appropriate public education to such child, and to obtain an independent educational evaluation of the child;

(2) procedures to protect the rights of the child whenever the parents of the child are not known, the agency cannot, after reasonable efforts, locate the parents, or the child is a ward of the State, including the assignment of an individual (who shall not be an employee of the State educational agency, the local educational agency, or any other agency that is involved in the education or care of the child) to act as a surrogate for the parents;

(3) written prior notice to the parents of the child whenever such agency:

(A) proposes to initiate or change; or

(B) refuses to initiate or change; the identification, evaluation, or educational placement of the child, in accordance with subsection (c) of this section, or the provision of a free appropriate public education to the child;

(4) procedures designed to ensure that the notice required by paragraph (3) is in the native language of the parents, unless it clearly is not feasible to do so;

(5) an opportunity for mediation in accordance with subsection (e) of this section;

(6) an opportunity to present complaints with respect to any matter relating to the identification, evaluation, or educational placement of the child, or the provision of a free appropriate public education to such child;

(7) procedures that require the parent of a child with a disability, or the attorney representing the child, to provide notice (which shall remain confidential):

(A) to the State educational agency or local educational agency, as the case may be, in the complaint filed under paragraph (6); and

(B) that shall include:

(i) the name of the child, the address of the residence of the child, and the name of the school the child is attending;

(ii) a description of the nature of the problem of the child relating to such proposed initiation or change, including facts relating to such problem; and

(iii) a proposed resolution of the problem to the extent known and available to the parents at the time; and

(8) procedures that require the State educational agency to develop a model form to assist parents in filing a complaint in accordance with paragraph (7).

(c) Content of prior written notice. The notice required by subsection (b)(3) of this section shall include:

(1) a description of the action proposed or refused by the agency;

(2) an explanation of why the agency proposes or refuses to take the action;

(3) a description of any other options that the agency considered and the reasons why those options were rejected;

(4) a description of each evaluation procedure, test, record, or report the agency used as a basis for the proposed or refused action;

(5) a description of any other factors that are relevant to the agency's proposal or refusal;

(6) a statement that the parents of a child with a disability have protection under the procedural safeguards of this subchapter and, if this notice is not an initial referral for evaluation, the means by which a copy of a description of the procedural safeguards can be obtained; and

(7) sources for parents to contact to obtain assistance in understanding the provisions of this subchapter.

(d) Procedural safeguards notice

(1) *In general.* A copy of the procedural safeguards available to the parents of a child with a disability shall be given to the parents, at a minimum:

(A) upon initial referral for evaluation;

(B) upon each notification of an individualized education program meeting and upon reevaluation of the child; and

(C) upon registration of a complaint under subsection (b)(6) of this section.

(2) *Contents.* The procedural safeguards notice shall include a full explanation of the procedural safeguards, written in the native language of the parents, unless it clearly is not feasible to do so, and written in an easily understandable manner, available under this section and under regulations promulgated by the Secretary relating to:

(A) independent educational evaluation;

(B) prior written notice;

(C) parental consent;

(D) access to educational records;

(E) opportunity to present complaints;

(F) the child's placement during pendency of due process proceedings;

(G) procedures for students who are subject to placement in an interim alternative educational setting;

(H) requirements for unilateral placement by parents of children in private schools at public expense;

(I) mediation;

(J) due process hearings, including requirements for disclosure of evaluation results and recommendations;

(K) State-level appeals (if applicable in that State);

(L) civil actions; and

(M) attorneys' fees.

(e) Mediation

(1) *In general.* Any State educational agency or local educational agency that receives assistance under this subchapter shall ensure that procedures are established and implemented to allow parties to disputes involving any matter described in subsection (b)(6) of this section to resolve such disputes through a mediation process which, at a minimum, shall be available whenever a hearing is requested under subsection (f) or (k) of this section.

(2) *Requirements.* Such procedures shall meet the following requirements:

(A) The procedures shall ensure that the mediation process:

(i) is voluntary on the part of the parties;

(ii) is not used to deny or delay a parent's right to a due process hearing under subsection (f) of this section, or to deny any other rights afforded under this subchapter; and

(iii) is conducted by a qualified and impartial mediator who is trained in effective mediation techniques.

(B) A local educational agency or a State agency may establish procedures to require parents who choose not to use the mediation process to meet, at a time and location convenient to the parents, with a disinterested party who is under contract with:

(i) a parent training and information center or community parent resource center in the State established under section 1482 or 1483 of this title; or

(ii) an appropriate alternative dispute resolution entity; to encourage the use, and explain the benefits, of the mediation process to the parents.

(C) The State shall maintain a list of individuals who are qualified mediators and knowledgeable in laws and regulations relating to the provision of special education and related services.

(D) The State shall bear the cost of the mediation process, including the costs of meetings described in subparagraph (B).

(E) Each session in the mediation process shall be scheduled in a timely manner and shall be held in a location that is convenient to the parties to the dispute.

(F) An agreement reached by the parties to the dispute in the mediation process shall be set forth in a written mediation agreement.

(G) Discussions that occur during the mediation process shall be confidential and may not be used as evidence in any subsequent due process hearings or civil proceedings and the parties to the mediation process may be required to sign a confidentiality pledge prior to the commencement of such process.

(f) Impartial due process hearing

(1) *In general.* Whenever a complaint has been received under subsection (b)(6) or (k) of this section, the parents involved in such complaint shall have an opportunity for an impartial due process hearing, which shall be conducted by the State educational agency or by the local educational agency, as determined by State law or by the State educational agency.

(2) *Disclosure of evaluations and recommendations*

(A) *In general.* At least 5 business days prior to a hearing conducted pursuant to paragraph (1), each party shall disclose to all other parties all evaluations completed by that date and recommendations based on the offering party's evaluations that the party intends to use at the hearing.

(B) *Failure to disclose.* A hearing officer may bar any party that fails to comply with subparagraph (A) from introducing the relevant evaluation or recommendation at the hearing without the consent of the other party.

(3) *Limitation on conduct of hearing.* A hearing conducted pursuant to paragraph (1) may not be conducted by an employee of the State educational agency or the local educational agency involved in the education or care of the child.

(g) Appeal. If the hearing required by subsection (f) of this section is conducted by a local educational agency, any party aggrieved by the findings and decision rendered in such a hearing may appeal such findings and decision to the State educational agency. Such agency shall conduct an impartial review of such decision. The officer conducting such review shall make an independent decision upon completion of such review.

(h) Safeguards. Any party to a hearing conducted pursuant to subsection (f) or (k) of this section, or an appeal conducted pursuant to subsection (g) of this section, shall be accorded:

(1) the right to be accompanied and advised by counsel and by individuals with special knowledge or training with respect to the problems of children with disabilities;

(2) the right to present evidence and confront, cross-examine, and compel the attendance of witnesses;

(3) the right to a written, or, at the option of the parents, electronic verbatim record of such hearing; and

(4) the right to written, or, at the option of the parents, electronic findings of fact and decisions (which findings and decisions shall be made available to the public consistent with the requirements of section 1417(c) of this title (relating to the confidentiality of data, information, and records) and shall also be transmitted to the advisory panel established pursuant to section 141 (a)(21) of this title).

(i) Administrative procedures

(1) *In general*

(A) *Decision made in hearing.* A decision made in a hearing conducted pursuant to subsection (f) or (k) of this section shall be final, except that any party involved in such hearing may appeal such decision under the provisions of subsection (g) of this section and paragraph (2) of this subsection.

(B) *Decision made at appeal.* A decision made under subsection (g) of this section shall be final, except that any party may bring an action under paragraph (2) of this subsection.

(2) *Right to bring civil action*

(A) *In general.* Any party aggrieved by the findings and decision made under subsection (f) or (k) of this section who does not have the right to an appeal under subsection (g) of this section, and any party aggrieved by the findings and decision under this subsection, shall have the right to bring a civil action with respect to the complaint presented pursuant to this section, which action may be brought in any State court of competent jurisdiction or in a district court of the United States without regard to the amount in controversy.

(B) *Additional requirements.* In any action brought under this paragraph, the court:

(i) shall receive the records of the administrative proceedings;

(ii) shall hear additional evidence at the request of a party; and

(iii) basing its decision on the preponderance of the evidence, shall grant such relief as the court determines is appropriate.

(3) *Jurisdiction of district courts; attorneys' fees*

(A) *In general.* The district courts of the United States shall have jurisdiction of actions brought under this section without regard to the amount in controversy.

(B) *Award of attorneys' fees.* In any action or proceeding brought under this section, the court, in its discretion, may award reasonable attorneys' fees as part of the costs to the parents of a child with a disability who is the prevailing party.

(C) *Determination of amount of attorneys' fees.* Fees awarded under this paragraph shall be based on rates prevailing in the community in which the action or proceeding arose for the kind and quality of services furnished. No bonus or multiplier may be used in calculating the fees awarded under this subsection.

(D) *Prohibition of attorneys' fees and related costs for certain services*

(i) Attorneys' fees may not be awarded and related costs may not be reimbursed in any action or proceeding under this section for services performed subsequent to the time of a written offer of settlement to a parent if:

(I) the offer is made within the time prescribed by Rule 68 of the Federal Rules of Civil Procedure or, in the case of an administrative proceeding, at any time more than 10 days before the proceeding begins;

(II) the offer is not accepted within 10 days; and

(III) the court or administrative hearing officer finds that the relief finally obtained by the parents is not more favorable to the parents than the offer of settlement.

(ii) Attorneys' fees may not be awarded relating to any meeting of the IEP Team unless such meeting is convened as a result of an administrative proceeding or judicial action, or, at the discretion of the State, for a mediation described in subsection (e) of this section that is conducted prior to the filing of a complaint under subsection (b)(6) or (k) of this section.

(E) *Exception to prohibition on attorneys' fees and related costs.* Notwithstanding subparagraph (D), an award of attorneys' fees and related costs may be made to a parent who is the prevailing party and who was substantially justified in rejecting the settlement offer.

(F) *Reduction in amount of attorneys' fees.* Except as provided in subparagraph (G), whenever the court finds that:

(i) the parent, during the course of the action or proceeding, unreasonably protracted the final resolution of the controversy;

(ii) the amount of the attorneys' fees otherwise authorized to be awarded unreasonably exceeds the hourly rate prevailing in the community for similar services by attorneys of reasonably comparable skill, reputation, and experience;

(iii) the time spent and legal services furnished were excessive considering the nature of the action or proceeding; or

(iv) the attorney representing the parent did not provide to the school district the appropriate information in the due process complaint in accordance with subsection (b)(7) of this section; the court shall reduce, accordingly, the amount of the attorneys' fees awarded under this section.

(G) *Exception to reduction in amount of attorneys' fees.* The provisions of subparagraph (F) shall not apply in any action or proceeding if the court finds that the State or local educational agency unreasonably protracted the final resolution of the action or proceeding or there was a violation of this section.

(j) Maintenance of current educational placement. Except as provided in subsection (k)(7) of this section, during the pendency of any proceedings conducted pursuant to this section, unless the State or local educational agency and the parents otherwise agree, the child shall remain in the then-current educational placement of such child, or, if applying for initial admission to a public school, shall, with the consent of the parents, be placed in the public school program until all such proceedings have been completed.

(k) Placement in alternative educational setting

(1) *Authority of school personnel*

(A) School personnel under this section may order a change in the placement of a child with a disability:

(i) to an appropriate interim alternative educational setting, another setting, or suspension, for not more than 10 school days (to the extent such alternatives would be applied to children without disabilities); and

(ii) to an appropriate interim alternative educational setting for the same amount of time that a child without a disability would be subject to discipline, but for not more than 45 days if:

(I) the child carries a weapon to school or to a school function under the jurisdiction of a State or a local educational agency; or

(II) the child knowingly possesses or uses illegal drugs or sells or solicits the sale of a controlled substance while at school or a school function under the jurisdiction of a State or local educational agency.

(B) Either before or not later than 10 days after taking a disciplinary action described in subparagraph (A):

(i) if the local educational agency did not conduct a functional behavioral assessment and implement a behavioral intervention plan for such child before the behavior that resulted in the suspension described in subparagraph (A), the agency shall convene an IEP meeting to develop an assessment plan to address that behavior; or

(ii) if the child already has a behavioral intervention plan, the IEP Team shall review the plan and modify it, as necessary, to address the behavior.

(2) *Authority of hearing officer.* A hearing officer under this section may order a change in the placement of a child with a disability to an appropriate interim alternative educational setting for not more than 45 days if the hearing officer:

(A) determines that the public agency has demonstrated by substantial evidence that maintaining the current placement of such child is substantially likely to result in injury to the child or to others;

(B) considers the appropriateness of the child's current placement;

(C) considers whether the public agency has made reasonable efforts to minimize the risk of harm in the child's current placement, including the use of supplementary aids and services; and

(D) determines that the interim alternative educational setting meets the requirements of paragraph (3)(B).

(3) *Determination of setting*

(A) *In general.* The alternative educational setting described in paragraph (1)(A)(ii) shall be determined by the IEP Team.

(B) *Additional requirements.* Any interim alternative educational setting in which a child is placed under paragraph (1) or (2) shall:

(i) be selected so as to enable the child to continue to participate in the general curriculum, although in another setting, and to continue to receive those services and modifications, including those described in the child's current IEP, that will enable the child to meet the goals set out in that IEP; and

(ii) include services and modifications designed to address the behavior described in paragraph (1) or paragraph (2) so that it does not recur.

(4) *Manifestation determination review*

(A) *In general.* If a disciplinary action is contemplated as described in paragraph (1) or paragraph (2) for a behavior of a child with a disability described in either of those paragraphs, or if a disciplinary action involving a change of placement for more than 10 days is contemplated for a child with a disability who has engaged in other behavior that violated any rule or code of conduct of the local educational agency that applies to all children:

(i) not later than the date on which the decision to take that action is made, the parents shall be notified of that decision and of all procedural safeguards accorded under this section; and

(ii) immediately, if possible, but in no case later than 10 school days after the date on which the decision to take that action is made, a review shall be conducted of the relationship between the child's disability and the behavior subject to the disciplinary action.

(B) *Individuals to carry out review.* A review described in subparagraph (A) shall be conducted by the IEP Team and other qualified personnel.

(C) *Conduct of review.* In carrying out a review described in subparagraph (A), the IEP Team may determine that the behavior of the child was not a manifestation of such child's disability only if the IEP Team:

(i) first considers, in terms of the behavior subject to disciplinary action, all relevant information, including:

(I) evaluation and diagnostic results, including such results or other relevant information supplied by the parents of the child;

(II) observations of the child; and

(III) the child's IEP and placement; and

(ii) then determines that:

(I) in relationship to the behavior subject to disciplinary action, the child's IEP and placement were appropriate and the special education services, supplementary aids and services, and behavior intervention strategies were provided consistent with the child's IEP and placement;

(II) the child's disability did not impair the ability of the child to understand the impact and consequences of the behavior subject to disciplinary action; and

(III) the child's disability did not impair the ability of the child to control the behavior subject to disciplinary action.

(5) *Determination that behavior was not manifestation of disability*

(A) *In general.* If the result of the review described in paragraph (4) is a determination, consistent with paragraph (4)(C), that the behavior of the child with a disability was not a manifestation of the child's disability, the relevant disciplinary procedures applicable to children without disabilities may be applied to the child in the same manner in which they would be applied to children without disabilities, except as provided in section 1412(a)(1) of this title.

(B) *Additional requirement.* If the public agency initiates disciplinary procedures applicable to all children, the agency shall ensure that the special education and disciplinary records of the child with a disability are transmitted for consideration by the person or persons making the final determination regarding the disciplinary action.

(6) *Parent appeal*

(A) *In general*

(i) If the child's parent disagrees with a determination that the child's behavior was not a manifestation of the child's disability or with any decision regarding placement, the parent may request a hearing.

(ii) The State or local educational agency shall arrange for an expedited hearing in any case described in this subsection when requested by a parent.

(B) *Review of decision*

(i) In reviewing a decision with respect to the manifestation determination, the hearing officer shall determine whether the public agency has demonstrated that the child's behavior was not a manifestation of such child's disability consistent with the requirements of paragraph (4)(C).

(ii) In reviewing a decision under paragraph (1)(A)(ii) to place the child in an interim alternative educational setting, the hearing officer shall apply the standards set out in paragraph (2).

(7) *Placement during appeals*

(A) *In general.* When a parent requests a hearing regarding a disciplinary action described in paragraph (1)(A)(ii) or paragraph (2) to challenge the interim alternative educational setting or the manifestation determination, the child shall remain in the interim alternative educational setting pending the decision of the hearing officer or until the expiration of the time period provided for in paragraph (1)(A)(ii) or paragraph (2), whichever occurs first, unless the parent and the State or local educational agency agree otherwise.

(B) *Current placement.* If a child is placed in an interim alternative educational setting pursuant to paragraph (1)(A)(ii) or paragraph (2) and school personnel propose to change the child's placement after expiration of the interim alternative placement, during the pendency of any proceeding to challenge the proposed change in placement, the child shall remain in the current placement (the child's placement prior to the interim alternative educational setting), except as provided in subparagraph (C).

(C) *Expedited hearing*

(i) If school personnel maintain that it is dangerous for the child to be in the current placement (placement prior to removal to the interim alternative education setting) during the pendency of the due process proceedings, the local educational agency may request an expedited hearing.

(ii) In determining whether the child may be placed in the alternative educational setting or in another appropriate placement ordered by the hearing officer, the hearing officer shall apply the standards set out in paragraph (2).

(8) *Protections for children not yet eligible for special education and related services*

(A) *In general.* A child who has not been determined to be eligible for special education and related services under this subchapter and who has engaged in behavior that violated any rule or code of conduct of the local educational agency, including any behavior described in paragraph (1), may assert any of the protections provided for in this subchapter if the local educational agency had knowledge (as determined in accordance with this paragraph) that the child was a child with a disability before the behavior that precipitated the disciplinary action occurred.

(B) *Basis of knowledge.* A local educational agency shall be deemed to have knowledge that a child is a child with a disability if:

(i) the parent of the child has expressed concern in writing (unless the parent is illiterate or has a disability that prevents compliance with the requirements contained in this clause) to personnel of the appropriate educational agency that the child is in need of special education and related services;

(ii) the behavior or performance of the child demonstrates the need for such services;

(iii) the parent of the child has requested an evaluation of the child pursuant to section 1414 of this title; or

(iv) the teacher of the child, or other personnel of the local educational agency, has expressed concern about the behavior or performance of the child to the director of special education of such agency or to other personnel of the agency.

(C) *Conditions that apply if no basis of knowledge*

(i) In general. If a local educational agency does not have knowledge that a child is a child with a disability (in accordance with subparagraph (B)) prior to taking disciplinary measures against the child, the child may be subjected to the same disciplinary measures as measures applied to children without disabilities who engaged in comparable behaviors consistent with clause (ii).

(ii) Limitations. If a request is made for an evaluation of a child during the time period in which the child is subjected to disciplinary measures under paragraph (1) or (2), the evaluation shall be conducted in an expedited manner. If the child is determined to be a child with a disability, taking into consideration information from the evaluation conducted by the agency and information provided by the parents, the agency shall provide special education and related services in accordance with the provisions of this subchapter, except that, pending the results of the evaluation, the child shall remain in the educational placement determined by school authorities.

(9) *Referral to and action by law enforcement and judicial authorities*

(A) Nothing in this subchapter shall be construed to prohibit an agency from reporting a crime committed by a child with a disability to appropriate authorities or to prevent State law enforcement and judicial authorities from exercising their responsibilities with regard to the application of Federal and State law to crimes committed by a child with a disability.

(B) An agency reporting a crime committed by a child with a disability shall ensure that copies of the special education and disciplinary records of the child are transmitted for consideration by the appropriate authorities to whom it reports the crime.

(10) *Definitions.* For purposes of this subsection, the following definitions apply:

(A) *Controlled substance.* The term "controlled substance" means a drug or other substance identified under schedules I, II, III, IV, or V in section 20 (c) of the Controlled Substances Act (21 U.S.C. 81 (c)).

(B) *Illegal drug.* The term "illegal drug":

(i) means a controlled substance; but

(ii) does not include such a substance that is legally possessed or used under the supervision of a licensed health-care professional or that is legally possessed or used under any other authority under that Act (21 U.S.C. 801 et seq.) or under any other provision of Federal law.

(C) *Substantial evidence.* The term "substantial evidence" means beyond a preponderance of the evidence.

(D) *Weapon.* The term "weapon" has the meaning given the term "dangerous weapon" under paragraph (2) of the first subsection (g) of section 930 of title 18.

(l) Rule of construction. Nothing in this chapter shall be construed to restrict or limit the rights, procedures, and remedies available under the Constitution, the Americans with Disabilities Act of 1990 (42 U.S.C. 12101 et seq.), title V of the Rehabilitation Act of 1973 (29 U.S.C. 790 et seq.), or other Federal laws protecting the rights of children with disabilities, except that before the filing of a civil action under such laws seeking relief that is also available under this subchapter, the procedures under subsections (f) and (g) of this section shall be exhausted to the same extent as would be required had the action been brought under this subchapter.

(m) Transfer of parental rights at age of majority

(1) *In general.* A State that receives amounts from a grant under this subchapter may provide that, when a child with a disability reaches the age of majority under State law (except for a child with a disability who has been determined to be incompetent under State law):

(A) the public agency shall provide any notice required by this section to both the individual and the parents;

(B) all other rights accorded to parents under this subchapter transfer to the child;

(C) the agency shall notify the individual and the parents of the transfer of rights; and

(D) all rights accorded to parents under this subchapter transfer to children who are incarcerated in an adult or juvenile Federal, State, or local correctional institution.

(2) *Special rule.* If, under State law, a child with a disability who has reached the age of majority under State law, who has not been determined to be incompetent, but who is determined not to have the ability to provide informed consent with respect to the educational program of the child, the State shall establish procedures for appointing the parent of the child, or if the parent is not available, another appropriate individual, to represent the educational interests of the child throughout the period of eligibility of the child under this subchapter.

IDEA Regulations (Key Sections)

Note on IDEA Regulations: The U.S. Department of Education issued new IDEA regulations which became effective in May, 1999, several months after publication of this book. Almost all of the old regulations have been retained and are included in this Appendix. The new regulations are based on IDEA statutes, included in the first part of this Appendix. (The IDEA statute is explained in Chapter 2 of this book.)

The key changes in the IDEA regulatory language involve the following areas:
- charter schools
- additions to the list of eligible "disabilities," including ADD/ADHD
- participation of special education children in statewide assessments
- related services, such as orientation and mobility services
- special education students who are incarcerated
- requirements regarding migrant and homeless children
- procedures for children who are removed from school because of inappropriate behavior
- assistive technology devices
- the use of mediation to resolve disputes
- special education children's access to the general curriculum, and
- special factors that the IEP team must consider for children who have limited English proficiency, who are deaf, hard of hearing or visually impaired, or whose behavior impedes learning.

We recommend that you see the new IDEA regulations for a full description of the changes that became effective in May, 1999. You can find the most current regulations online at www.access.gpo.gov/nara/cfr. Look at Title 34 of the Code of Federal Regulations, Part 300. You can also get a copy of current IDEA regulations from the U.S. Department of Education, Office of Special Education, or your state department of education. See Appendix 2 for addresses and phone numbers of federal and state departments of education. Also, be sure to contact your local school district if you have questions as to how the new regulations will affect your child. Finally, check "Legal Resources for Parents of a Special Education Child" listed in Appendix 3 for information on the latest IDEA regulations.

The key changes in regulatory language will cover how children are to be involved in the general curriculum; the procedures for determining when and how a special education child can be removed from his placement because of inappropriate behavior; details about transition plans; the "special factors" that IEP teams must consider for children with "limited English proficiency," whose behavior impedes learning, who are visually impaired and who are deaf or hard of hearing, and what assistive technology devices are needed; and how special education children will be involved in statewide assessments. Check "Legal Resources for Parents of a Special Education Child" listed in Appendix 3, or contact the U.S. Department of Education, (see Appendix 2) to get a copy of the latest regulations when they are available some-

time in 1999. The Code of Federal Regulations is also available online at www.access.gpo.gov/nara/cfr. Also, be sure to contact your local school district or your state department of education (listed in Appendix 2) if you have questions as to how the new regulations will affect your child.

Assistance to States For The Education of Children With Disabilities

34 C.F.R. Part 300

Subpart A: General Purpose, Applicability, and Regulations That Apply to This Program

Sec. 300.7. Children with disabilities

(a)(1) As used in this part, the term "children with disabilities" means those children evaluated in accordance with Secs. 300.530-300.534 as having mental retardation, hearing impairments including deafness, speech or language impairments, visual impairments including blindness, serious emotional disturbance, orthopedic impairments, autism, traumatic brain injury, other health impairments, specific learning disabilities, deaf-blindness, or multiple disabilities, and who because of those impairments need special education and related services.

(2) The term "children with disabilities" for children aged 3 through 5 may, at a State's discretion, include children:

(i) Who are experiencing developmental delays, as defined by the State and as measured by appropriate diagnostic instruments and procedures, in one or more of the following areas: physical development, cognitive development, communication development, social or emotional development, or adaptive development; and

(ii) Who, for that reason, need special education and related services.

(b) The terms used in this definition are defined as follows:

(1) "Autism" means a developmental disability significantly affecting verbal and nonverbal communication and social interaction, generally evident before age 3, that adversely affects a child's educational performance. Other characteristics often associated with autism are engagement in repetitive activities and stereotyped movements, resistance to environmental change or change in daily routines, and unusual responses to sensory experiences. The term does not apply if a child's educational performance is adversely affected primarily because the child has a serious emotional disturbance, as defined in paragraph (b)(9) of this section.

(2) "Deaf-blindness" means concomitant hearing and visual impairments, the combination of which causes such severe communication and other developmental and educational problems that they cannot be accommodated in special education programs solely for children with deafness or children with blindness.

(3) "Deafness" means a hearing impairment that is so severe that the child is impaired in processing linguistic information through hearing, with or without amplification, that adversely affects a child's educational performance.

(4) "Hearing impairment" means an impairment in hearing, whether permanent or fluctuating, that adversely affects a child's educational performance but that is not included under the definition of deafness in this section.

(5) "Mental retardation" means significantly subaverage general intellectual functioning existing concurrently with deficits in adaptive behavior and manifested during the developmental period that adversely affects a child's educational performance.

(6) "Multiple disabilities" means concomitant impairments (such as mental retardation-blindness, mental retardation-orthopedic impairment, etc.), the combination of which causes such severe educational problems that they cannot be accommodated in special education programs solely for one of the impairments. The term does not include deaf-blindness.

(7) "Orthopedic impairment" means a severe orthopedic impairment that adversely affects a child's educational performance. The term includes impairments caused by congenital anomaly (e.g., clubfoot, absence of some member, etc.), impairments caused by disease (e.g., poliomyelitis, bone tuberculosis, etc.), and impairments from other causes (e.g., cerebral palsy, amputations, and fractures or burns that cause contractures).

(8) "Other health impairment" means having limited strength, vitality or alertness, due to chronic or acute health problems such as a heart condition, tuberculosis, rheumatic fever, nephritis, asthma, sickle cell anemia, hemophilia, epilepsy, lead poisoning, leukemia, or diabetes that adversely affects a child's educational performance.

(9) "Serious emotional disturbance" is defined as follows:

(i) The term means a condition exhibiting one or more of the following characteristics over a long period of time and to a marked degree that adversely affects a child's educational performance:

(A) An inability to learn that cannot be explained by intellectual, sensory, or health factors;

(B) An inability to build or maintain satisfactory interpersonal relationships with peers and teachers;

(C) Inappropriate types of behavior or feelings under normal circumstances;

(D) A general pervasive mood of unhappiness or depression; or

(E) A tendency to develop physical symptoms or fears associated with personal or school problems.

(ii) The term includes schizophrenia. The term does not apply to children who are socially maladjusted, unless it is determined that they have a serious emotional disturbance.

(10) "Specific learning disability" means a disorder in one or more of the basic psychological processes involved in understanding or in using language, spoken or written, that may manifest itself in an imperfect ability to listen, think, speak, read, write, spell, or to do mathematical calculations. The term includes such conditions as perceptual disabilities, brain injury, minimal brain dysfunction, dyslexia, and developmental aphasia. The term does not apply to children who have learning problems that are primarily the result of visual, hearing, or motor disabilities, of mental retardation, of

emotional disturbance, or of environmental, cultural, or economic disadvantage.

(11) "Speech or language impairment" means a communication disorder such as stuttering, impaired articulation, a language impairment, or a voice impairment that adversely affects a child's educational performance.

(12) "Traumatic brain injury" means an acquired injury to the brain caused by an external physical force, resulting in total or partial functional disability or psychosocial impairment, or both, that adversely affects a child's educational performance. The term applies to open or closed head injuries resulting in impairments in one or more areas, such as cognition; language; memory; attention; reasoning; abstract thinking; judgment; problem-solving; sensory, perceptual and motor abilities; psychosocial behavior; physical functions; information processing; and speech. The term does not apply to brain injuries that are congenital or degenerative, or brain injuries induced by birth trauma.

(13) "Visual impairment including blindness" means an impairment in vision that, even with correction, adversely affects a child's educational performance. The term includes both partial sight and blindness.

(Authority: 20 U.S.C. 1401(a)(1))

Note: If a child manifests characteristics of the disability category "autism" after age 3, that child still could be diagnosed as having "autism" if the criteria in paragraph (b)(1) of this section are satisfied.

Sec. 300.8. Free appropriate public education

As used in this part, the term "free appropriate public education" means special education and related services that—

(a) Are provided at public expense, under public supervision and direction, and without charge;

(b) Meet the standards of the SEA, including the requirements of this part;

(c) Include preschool, elementary school, or secondary school education in the State involved; and

(d) Are provided in conformity with an IEP that meets the requirements of Secs. 300.340-300.350.

(Authority: 20 U.S.C. 1401(a)(18))

Sec. 300.12 Native language

As used in this part, the term "native language" has the meaning given that term by section 703(a)(2) of the Bilingual Education Act, which provides as follows:

The term "native language," when used with reference to an individual of limited English proficiency, means the language normally used by that individual, or in the case of a child, the language normally used by the parents of the child.

(Authority: 20 U.S.C. 3283(a)(2); 1401(a)(22))

Note: Section 602(a)(22) of the Act states that the term "native language" has the same meaning as the definition from section 703(a)(2) of the Bilingual Education Act. (The term is used in the prior notice and evaluation sections under Sec. 300.505(b)(2) and Sec. 300.532(a)(1).) In using the term, the Act does not prevent the following means of communication:

(1) In all direct contact with a child (including evaluation of the child), communication would be in the language normally used by the child and not that of the parents, if there is a difference between the two.

(2) For individuals with deafness or blindness, or for individuals with no written language, the mode of communication would be that normally used by the individual (such as sign language, braille, or oral communication).

Sec. 300.16 Related services

(a) As used in this part, the term "related services" means transportation and such developmental, corrective, and other supportive services as are required to assist a child with a disability to benefit from special education, and includes speech pathology and audiology, psychological services, physical and occupational therapy, recreation, including therapeutic recreation, early identification and assessment of disabilities in children, counseling services, including rehabilitation counseling, and medical services for diagnostic or evaluation purposes. The term also includes school health services, social work services in schools, and parent counseling and training.

(b) The terms used in this definition are defined as follows:

(1) "Audiology" includes—

(i) Identification of children with hearing loss;

(ii) Determination of the range, nature, and degree of hearing loss, including referral for medical or other professional attention for the habilitation of hearing;

(iii) Provision of habilitative activities, such as language habilitation, auditory training, speech reading (lip-reading), hearing evaluation, and speech conservation;

(iv) Creation and administration of programs for prevention of hearing loss;

(v) Counseling and guidance of pupils, parents, and teachers regarding hearing loss; and

(vi) Determination of the child's need for group and individual amplification, selecting and fitting an appropriate aid, and evaluating the effectiveness of amplification.

(2) "Counseling services" means services provided by qualified social workers, psychologists, guidance counselors, or other qualified personnel.

(3) "Early identification and assessment of disabilities in children" means the implementation of a formal plan for identifying a disability as early as possible in a child's life.

(4) "Medical services" means services provided by a licensed physician to determine a child's medically related disability that results in the child's need for special education and related services.

(5) "Occupational therapy" includes—

(i) Improving, developing or restoring functions impaired or lost through illness, injury, or deprivation;

(ii) Improving ability to perform tasks for independent functioning when functions are impaired or lost; and

(iii) Preventing, through early intervention, initial or further impairment or loss of function.

(6) "Parent counseling and training" means assisting parents in understanding the special needs of their child and providing parents with information about child development.

(7) "Physical therapy" means services provided by a qualified physical therapist.

(8) "Psychological services" includes—

(i) Administering psychological and educational tests, and other assessment procedures;

(ii) Interpreting assessment results;

(iii) Obtaining, integrating, and interpreting information about child behavior and conditions relating to learning.

(iv) Consulting with other staff members in planning school programs to meet the special needs of children as indicated by psychological tests, interviews, and behavioral evaluations; and

(v) Planning and managing a program of psychological services, including psychological counseling for children and parents.

(9) "Recreation" includes—

(i) Assessment of leisure function;

(ii) Therapeutic recreation services;

(iii) Recreation programs in schools and community agencies; and

(iv) Leisure education.

(10) "Rehabilitation counseling services" means services provided by qualified personnel in individual or group sessions that focus specifically on career development, employment preparation, achieving independence, and integration in the workplace and community of a student with a disability. The term also includes vocational rehabilitation services provided to students with disabilities by vocational rehabilitation programs funded under the Rehabilitation Act of 1973, as amended.

(11) "School health services" means services provided by a qualified school nurse or other qualified person.

(12) "Social work services in schools" includes—

(i) Preparing a social or developmental history on a child with a disability;

(ii) Group and individual counseling with the child and family;

(iii) Working with those problems in a child's living situation (home, school, and community) that affect the child's adjustment in school; and

(iv) Mobilizing school and community resources to enable the child to learn as effectively as possible in his or her educational program.

(13) "Speech pathology" includes—

(i) Identification of children with speech or language impairments;

(ii) Diagnosis and appraisal of specific speech or language impairments;

(iii) Referral for medical or other professional attention necessary for the habilitation of speech or language impairments;

(iv) Provision of speech and language services for the habilitation or prevention of communicative impairments; and

(v) Counseling and guidance of parents, children, and teachers regarding speech and language impairments.

(14) "Transportation" includes—

(i) Travel to and from school and between schools;

(ii) Travel in and around school buildings; and

(iii) Specialized equipment (such as special or adapted buses, lifts, and ramps), if required to provide special transportation for a child with a disability.

(Authority: 20 U.S.C. 1401(a)(17))

Note: With respect to related services, the Senate Report states:

The Committee bill provides a definition of related services, making clear that all such related services may not be required for each individual child and that such term includes early identification and assessment of handicapping conditions and the provision of services to minimize the effects of such conditions. (S. Rep. No. 94-168, p. 12 (1975))

The list of related services is not exhaustive and may include other developmental, corrective, or supportive services (such as artistic and cultural programs, and art, music, and dance therapy), if they are required to assist a child with a disability to benefit from special education.

There are certain kinds of services that might be provided by persons from varying professional backgrounds and with a variety of operational titles, depending upon requirements in individual States. For example, counseling services might be provided by social workers, psychologists, or guidance counselors, and psychological testing might be done by qualified psychological examiners, psychometrists, or psychologists, depending upon State standards.

Each related service defined under this part may include appropriate administrative and supervisory activities that are necessary for program planning, management, and evaluation.

Sec. 300.17 Special education

(a)(1) As used in this part, the term "special education" means specially designed instruction, at no cost to the parents, to meet the unique needs of a child with a disability, including—

(i) Instruction conducted in the classroom, in the home, in hospitals and institutions, and in other settings; and

(ii) Instruction in physical education.

(2) The term includes speech pathology, or any other related service, if the service consists of specially designed instruction, at no cost to the parents, to meet the unique needs of a child with a disability, and is considered special education rather than a related service under State standards.

(3) The term also includes vocational education if it consists of specially designed instruction, at no cost to the parents, to meet the unique needs of a child with a disability.

(b) The terms in this definition are defined as follows:

(1) "At no cost" means that all specially designed instruction is provided without charge, but does not preclude incidental fees that are normally charged to nondisabled students or their parents as a part of the regular education program.

(2) "Physical education" is defined as follows:

(i) The term means the development of—

(A) Physical and motor fitness;

(B) Fundamental motor skills and patterns; and

(C) Skills in aquatics, dance, and individual and group games and sports (including intramural and lifetime sports).

(ii) The term includes special physical education, adaptive physical education, movement education, and motor development.

(Authority: 20 U.S.C. 1401(a)(16))

(3) Vocational education means organized educational programs that are directly related to the preparation of individuals for paid or unpaid employment, or for additional preparation for a career requiring other than a baccalaureate or advanced degree.

(Authority: 20 U.S.C. 1401(16))

Note 1: The definition of special education is a particularly important one under these regulations, since a child does not have a disability under this part unless he or she needs special education. (See the definition of children with disabilities in Sec. 300.7.) The definition of related services (Sec. 300.16) also depends on this definition, since a related service must be necessary for a child to benefit from special education. Therefore, if a child does not need special education, there can be no related services, and the child is not a child with a disability and is therefore not covered under the Act.

Note 2: The above definition of vocational education is taken from the Vocational Education Act of 1963, as amended by Public Law 94-482. Under that Act, "vocational education" includes industrial arts and consumer and homemaking education programs. [57 FR 44798, Sept. 29, 1992; 57 FR 48694, Oct. 27, 1992]

Individualized Education Programs

Sec. 300.340 Definitions

(a) As used in this part, the term individualized education program means a written statement for a child with a disability that is developed and implemented in accordance with Secs. 300.341-300.350.

(b) As used in Secs. 300.346 and 300.347, participating agency means a State or local agency, other than the public agency responsible for a student's education, that is financially and legally responsible for providing transition services to the student.

(Authority: 20 U.S.C. 1401(a)(20))

Subpart C—Services

Sec. 300.342 When individualized education programs must be in effect

(a) At the beginning of each school year, each public agency shall have in effect an IEP for every child with a disability who is receiving special education from that agency.

(b) An IEP must—

(1) Be in effect before special education and related services are provided to a child; and

(2) Be implemented as soon as possible following the meetings under Sec. 300.343.

(Authority: 20 U.S.C. 1412(2)(B), (4), (6); 1414(a)(5); Pub. L. 94-142, Sec. 8(c) (1975))

Note: Under paragraph (b)(2) of this section, it is expected that the IEP of a child with a disability will be implemented immediately following the meetings under Sec. 300.343. An exception to this would be (1) when the meetings occur during the summer or a vacation period, or (2) where there are circumstances that require a short delay (e.g., working out transportation arrangements). However, there can be no undue delay in providing special education and related services to the child.

Sec. 300.343 Meetings

(a) **General.** Each public agency is responsible for initiating and conducting meetings for the purpose of developing, reviewing, and revising the IEP of a child with a disability (or, if consistent with State policy and at the discretion of the LEA, and with the concurrence of the parents, an individualized family service plan described in section 677(d) of the Act for each child with a disability, aged 3 through 5).

(b) **[Reserved]**

(c) **Timeline.** A meeting to develop an IEP for a child must be held within 30 calendar days of a determination that the child needs special education and related services.

(d) **Review.** Each public agency shall initiate and conduct meetings to review each child's IEP periodically and, if appropriate, revise its provisions. A meeting must be held for this purpose at least once a year.

(Authority: 20 U.S.C. 1412(2)(B), (4), (6); 1414(a)(5))

Note: The date on which agencies must have IEPs in effect is specified in Sec. 300.342 (the beginning of each school year). However, except for new children with disabilities (i.e., those evaluated and determined to need special education and related services for the first time), the timing of meetings to develop, review, and revise IEPs is left to the discretion of each agency.

In order to have IEPs in effect at the beginning of the school year, agencies could hold meetings either at the end of the preceding school year or during the summer prior to the next school year. Meetings may be held any time throughout the year, as long as IEPs are in effect at the beginning of each school year.

The statute requires agencies to hold a meeting at least once each year in order to review and, if appropriate, revise each child's IEP. The timing of those meetings could be on the anniversary date of the child's last IEP meeting, but this is left to the discretion of the agency. (Approved by the Office of Management and Budget under control number 1820-0030) [57 FR 44798, Sept. 29, 1992, as amended at 58 FR 13528, Mar. 11, 1993]

Sec. 300.344 Participants in meetings

(a) **General.** The public agency shall ensure that each meeting includes the following participants:

(1) A representative of the public agency, other than the child's teacher, who is qualified to provide, or supervise the provision of, special education.

(2) The child's teacher.

(3) One or both of the child's parents, subject to Sec. 300.345.

(4) The child, if appropriate.

(5) Other individuals at the discretion of the parent or agency.

(b) **Evaluation personnel.** For a child with a disability who has been evaluated for the first time, the public agency shall ensure—

(1) That a member of the evaluation team participates in the meeting; or

(2) That the representative of the public agency, the child's teacher, or some other person is present at the meeting, who is knowledgeable about the evaluation procedures used with the child and is familiar with the results of the evaluation.

(c) **Transition services participants.**

(1) If a purpose of the meeting is the consideration of transition services for a student, the public agency shall invite—

(i) The student; and

(ii) A representative of any other agency that is likely to be responsible for providing or paying for transition services.

(2) If the student does not attend, the public agency shall take other steps to ensure that the student's preferences and interests are considered; and

(3) If an agency invited to send a representative to a meeting does not do so, the public agency shall take other steps to obtain the participation of the other agency in the planning of any transition services.

(Authority: 20 U.S.C. 1401(a)(19), (a)(20); 1412(2)(B), (4), (6); 1414(a)(5))

Note 1: In deciding which teacher will participate in meetings on a child's IEP, the agency may wish to consider the following possibilities:

(a) For a child with a disability who is receiving special education, the teacher could be the child's special education teacher. If the child's disability is a speech impairment, the teacher could be the speech-language pathologist.

(b) For a child with a disability who is being considered for placement in special education, the teacher could be the child's regular teacher, or a teacher qualified to provide education in the type of program in which the child may be placed, or both.

(c) If the child is not in school or has more than one teacher, the agency may designate which teacher will participate in the meeting.

Either the teacher or the agency representative should be qualified in the area of the child's suspected disability.

For a child whose primary disability is a speech or language impairment, the evaluation personnel participating under paragraph (b)(1) of this section would normally be the speech-language pathologist.

Note 2: Under paragraph (c) of this section, the public agency is required to invite each student to participate in his or her IEP meeting, if a purpose of the meeting is the consideration of transition services for the student. For all students who are 16 years of age or older, one of the purposes of the annual meeting will always be the planning of transition services, since transition services are a required component of the IEP for these students.

For a student younger than age 16, if transition services are initially discussed at a meeting that does not include the student, the public agency is responsible for ensuring that, before a decision about transition services for the student is made, a subsequent IEP meeting is conducted for that purpose, and the student is invited to the meeting.

Sec. 300.345 Parent participation

(a) Each public agency shall take steps to ensure that one or both of the parents of the child with a disability are present at each meeting or are afforded the opportunity to participate, including—

(1) Notifying parents of the meeting early enough to ensure that they will have an opportunity to attend; and

(2) Scheduling the meeting at a mutually agreed on time and place.

(b)(1) The notice under paragraph (a)(1) of this section must indicate the purpose, time, and location of the meeting and who will be in attendance;

(2) If a purpose of the meeting is the consideration of transition services for a student, the notice must also—

(i) Indicate this purpose;

(ii) Indicate that the agency will invite the student; and

(iii) Identify any other agency that will be invited to send a representative.

(c) If neither parent can attend, the public agency shall use other methods to ensure parent participation, including individual or conference telephone calls.

(d) A meeting may be conducted without a parent in attendance if the public agency is unable to convince the parents that they should attend. In this case the public agency must have a record of its attempts to arrange a mutually agreed on time and place such as—

(1) Detailed records of telephone calls made or attempted and the results of those calls;

(2) Copies of correspondence sent to the parents and any responses received; and

(3) Detailed records of visits made to the parent's home or place of employment and the results of those visits.

(e) The public agency shall take whatever action is necessary to ensure that the parent understands the proceedings at a meeting, including arranging for an interpreter for parents with deafness or whose native language is other than English.

(f) The public agency shall give the parent, on request, a copy of the IEP.

(Authority: 20 U.S.C. 1401(a)(20); 1412 (2)(B), (4), (6); 1414(a)(5))

Note: The notice in paragraph (a) of this section could also inform parents that they may bring other people to the meeting.

As indicated in paragraph (c) of this section, the procedure used to notify parents (whether oral or written or both) is left to the discretion of the agency, but the agency must keep a record of its efforts to contact parents. (Approved by the Office of Management and Budget under control number 1820-0030) [57 FR 44798, Sept. 29, 1992, as amended at 58 FR 13528, Mar. 11, 1993]

Sec. 300.346 Content of individualized education program

(a) General. The IEP for each child must include—

(1) A statement of the child's present levels of educational performance;

(2) A statement of annual goals, including short-term instructional objectives;

(3) A statement of the specific special education and related services to be provided to the child and the extent that the child will be able to participate in regular educational programs;

(4) The projected dates for initiation of services and the anticipated duration of the services; and

(5) Appropriate objective criteria and evaluation procedures and schedules for determining, on at least an annual basis, whether the short term instructional objectives are being achieved.

(b) Transition services

(1) The IEP for each student, beginning no later than age 16 (and at a younger age, if determined appropriate), must include a statement of the needed transition services as defined in Sec. 300.18, including, if appropriate, a statement of each public agency's and each participating agency's responsibilities or linkages, or both, before the student leaves the school setting.

(2) If the IEP team determines that services are not needed in one or more of the areas specified in Sec. 300.18 (b)(2)(i) through (b)(2)(iii), the IEP must include a statement to that effect and the basis upon which the determination was made.

(Authority: 20 U.S.C. 1401 (a)(19), (a)(20); 1412 (2)(B), (4), (6); 1414(a)(5))

Note 1: The legislative history of the transition services provisions of the Act suggests that the statement of needed transition services referred to in paragraph (b) of this section should include a commitment by any participating agency to meet any financial responsibility it may have in the provision of transition services. See House Report No. 101-544, p. 11 (1990).

Note 2: With respect to the provisions of paragraph (b) of this section, it is generally expected that the statement of needed transition services will include the areas listed in Sec. 300.18 (b)(2)(i) through (b)(2)(iii). If the IEP team determines that services are not needed in one of those areas, the public agency must implement the requirements in paragraph (b)(2) of this section. Since it is a part of the IEP, the IEP team must reconsider its determination at least annually.

Note 3: Section 602(a)(20) of the Act provides that IEPs must include a statement of needed transition services for students beginning no later than age 16, but permits transition services to students below age 16 (i.e., "* * * and, when determined appropriate for the individual, beginning at age 14 or younger."). Although the statute does not mandate transition services for all students beginning at age 14 or younger, the provision of these services could have a significantly positive effect on the employment and independent living outcomes for many of these students in the future, especially for students who are likely to drop out before age 16. With respect to the provision of transition services to students below age 16, the Report of the House Committee on Education and Labor on Public Law 101-476 includes the following statement:

Although this language leaves the final determination of when to initiate transition services for students under age 16 to the IEP process, it nevertheless makes clear that Congress expects consideration to be given to the need for transition services for some students by age 14 or younger. The Committee encourages that approach because of their concern that age 16 may be too late for many students, particularly those at risk of dropping out of school and those with the most severe disabilities. Even for those students who stay in school until age 18, many will need more than two years of transitional services. Students with disabilities are now dropping out of school before age 16, feeling that the education system has little to offer them. Initiating services at a younger age will be critical. (House Report No. 101-544, 10 (1990).) (Approved by the Office of Management and Budget under control number 1820-0030) [57 FR 44798, Sept. 29, 1992, as amended at 58 FR 13528, Mar. 11, 1993]

Sec. 300.348 Private school placements by public agencies

(a) Developing individualized education programs

(1) Before a public agency places a child with a disability in, or refers a child to, a private school or facility, the agency shall initiate and conduct a meeting to develop an IEP for the child in accordance with Sec. 300.343.

(2) The agency shall ensure that a representative of the private school or facility attends the meeting. If the representative cannot attend, the agency shall use other methods to ensure participation by the private school or facility, including individual or conference telephone calls.

(3) [Reserved]

(b) Reviewing and revising individualized education programs

(1) After a child with a disability enters a private school or facility, any meetings to review and revise the child's IEP may be initiated and conducted by the private school or facility at the discretion of the public agency.

(2) If the private school or facility initiates and conducts these meetings, the public agency shall ensure that the parents and an agency representative:

(i) Are involved in any decision about the child's IEP; and

(ii) Agree to any proposed changes in the program before those changes are implemented.

(c) Responsibility. Even if a private school or facility implements a child's IEP, responsibility for compliance with this part remains with the public agency and the SEA.

(Authority: 20 U.S.C. 1413(a)(4)(B))

Sec. 300.349 Children with disabilities in parochial or other private schools

If a child with a disability is enrolled in a parochial or other private school and receives special education or related services from a public agency, the public agency shall—

(a) Initiate and conduct meetings to develop, review, and revise an IEP for the child, in accordance with Sec. 300.343; and

(b) Ensure that a representative of the parochial or other private school attends each meeting. If the representative cannot attend, the agency shall use other methods to ensure participation by the private school, including individual or conference telephone calls.

(Authority: 20 U.S.C. 1413(a)(4)(A)) (Approved by the Office of Management and Budget under control number 1820-0030) [57 FR 44798, Sept. 29, 1992, as amended at 58 FR 13528, Mar. 11, 1993]

Subpart D—Private Schools

Children With Disabilities in Private Schools Placed or Referred by Public Agencies

Sec. 300.400 Applicability of Secs. 300.400-300.402

Sections 300.401-300.402 apply only to children with disabilities who are or have been placed in or referred to a private school or facility by a public agency as a means of providing special education and related services.

(Authority: 20 U.S.C. 1413(a)(4)(B))

Sec. 300.403 Placement of children by parents

(a) If a child with a disability has FAPE available and the parents choose to place the child in a private school or facility, the public agency is not required by this part to pay for the child's education at the private school or facility. However, the public agency shall make services available to the child as provided under Secs. 300.450-300.452.

(b) Disagreements between a parent and a public agency regarding the availability of a program appropriate for the child, and the question of financial responsibility, are subject to the due process procedures of Secs. 300.500-300.515.

(Authority: 20 U.S.C. 1412(2)(B); 1415)

Children With Disabilities Enrolled by Their Parents in Private Schools

Sec. 300.452 Local educational agency responsibility

Each LEA shall provide special education and related services designed to meet the needs of private school children with disabilities residing in the jurisdiction of the agency.

(Authority: 20 U.S.C. 1413(a)(4)(A); 1414(a)(6))

Subpart E—Procedural Safeguards

Due Process Procedures for Parents and Children

Sec. 300.502 Opportunity to examine records

The parents of a child with a disability shall be afforded, in accordance with the procedures of Secs. 300.562-300.569, an opportunity to inspect and review all education records with respect to—

(a) The identification, evaluation, and educational placement of the child; and

(b) The provision of FAPE to the child.

(Authority: 20 U.S.C. 1415(b)(1)(A))

Sec. 300.503 Independent educational evaluation

(a) General

(1) The parents of a child with a disability have the right under this part to obtain an independent educational evaluation of the child, subject to paragraphs (b) through (e) of this section.

(2) Each public agency shall provide to parents, on request, information about where an independent educational evaluation may be obtained.

(3) For the purposes of this part:

(i) Independent educational evaluation means an evaluation conducted by a qualified examiner who is not employed by the public agency responsible for the education of the child in question.

(ii) Public expense means that the public agency either pays for the full cost of the evaluation or ensures that the evaluation is otherwise provided at no cost to the parent, consistent with Sec. 300.301.

(b) Parent right to evaluation at public expense. A parent has the right to an independent educational evaluation at public expense if the parent disagrees with an evaluation obtained by the public agency. However, the public agency may initiate a hearing under Sec. 300.506 to show that its evaluation is appropriate. If the final decision is that the evaluation is appropriate, the parent still has the right to an independent educational evaluation, but not at public expense.

(c) Parent initiated evaluations. If the parent obtains an independent educational evaluation at private expense, the results of the evaluation—

(1) Must be considered by the public agency in any decision made with respect to the provision of FAPE to the child; and

(2) May be presented as evidence at a hearing under this subpart regarding that child.

(d) Requests for evaluations by hearing officers. If a hearing officer requests an independent educational evaluation as part of a hearing, the cost of the evaluation must be at public expense.

(e) Agency criteria. Whenever an independent evaluation is at public expense, the criteria under which the evaluation is obtained, including the location of the evaluation and the qualifications of the examiner, must be the same as the criteria which the public agency uses when it initiates an evaluation.

(Authority: 20 U.S.C. 1415(b)(1)(A))

Sec. 300.504 Prior notice; parent consent

(a) Notice. Written notice that meets the requirements of Sec. 300.505 must be given to the parents of a child with a disability a reasonable time before the public agency—

(1) Proposes to initiate or change the identification, evaluation, or educational placement of the child or the provision of FAPE to the child; or

(2) Refuses to initiate or change the identification, evaluation, or educational placement of the child or the provision of FAPE to the child.

(b) Consent; procedures if a parent refuses consent

(1) Parental consent must be obtained before—

(i) Conducting a preplacement evaluation; and

(ii) Initial placement of a child with a disability in a program providing special education and related services.

(2) If State law requires parental consent before a child with a disability is evaluated or initially provided special education and related services, State procedures govern the public agency in overriding a parent's refusal to consent.

(3) If there is no State law requiring consent before a child with a disability is evaluated or initially provided special education and related services, the public agency may use the hearing procedures in Secs. 300.506-300.508 to determine if the child may be evaluated or initially provided special education and related services without parental consent. If it does so and the hearing officer upholds the agency, the agency may evaluate or initially provide special education and related services to the child without the parent's consent, subject to the parent's rights under Secs. 300.510-300.513.

(c) Additional State consent requirements. In addition to the parental consent requirements described in paragraph (b) of this section, a State may require parental consent for other services and activities under this part if it ensures that each public agency in the State establishes and implements effective procedures to ensure that a parent's refusal to consent does not result in a failure to provide the child with FAPE.

(d) Limitation. A public agency may not require parental consent as a condition of any benefit to the parent or the child except for the service or activity for which consent is required under paragraphs (b) or (c) of this section.

(Authority: 20 U.S.C. 1415(b)(1)(C), (D); 1412(2), (6))

Note 1: Any changes in a child's special education program after the initial placement are not subject to the parental consent requirements in paragraph (b)(1) of this section, but are subject to the prior notice requirement in paragraph (a) of this section and the IEP requirements of Secs. 300.340-300.350.

Note 2: Paragraph (b)(2) of this section means that if State law requires parental consent before evaluation or before special education and related services are initially provided, and the parent refuses (or otherwise withholds) consent, State procedures, such as obtaining a court order authorizing the public agency to conduct the evaluation or provide the education and related services, must be followed.

If, however, there is no legal requirement for consent outside of these regulations, the public agency may use the due process procedures of Secs. 300.506-300.508 to obtain a decision to allow the evaluation or services without parental consent. The agency must notify the parent of its actions, and the parent has appeal rights as well as rights at the hearing itself.

Note 3: If a State adopts a consent requirement in addition to those described in paragraph (b) of this section and consent is refused, paragraph (d) of this section requires that the public agency must nevertheless provide the services and activities that are not in dispute. For example, if a State requires parental consent to the provision of all services identified in an IEP and the parent refuses to consent to physical therapy services included in the IEP, the agency is not relieved of its obligation to implement those portions of the IEP to which the parent consents.

If the parent refuses to consent and the public agency determines that the service or activity in dispute is necessary to provide FAPE to the child, paragraph (c) of this section requires that the agency must implement its procedures to override the refusal. This section does not preclude the agency from reconsidering its proposal if it believes that circumstances warrant.

Sec. 300.505 Content of notice

(a) The notice under Sec. 300.504 must include—

(1) A full explanation of all of the procedural safeguards available to the parents under Sec. 300.500, Secs. 300.502-300.515, and Secs. 300.562-300.569;

(2) A description of the action proposed or refused by the agency, an explanation of why the agency proposes or refuses to take the action, and a description of any options the agency considered and the reasons why those options were rejected;

(3) A description of each evaluation procedure, test, record, or report the agency uses as a basis for the proposal or refusal; and

(4) A description of any other factors that are relevant to the agency's proposal or refusal.

(b) The notice must be—

(1) Written in language understandable to the general public; and

(2) Provided in the native language of the parent or other mode of communication used by the parent, unless it is clearly not feasible to do so.

(c) If the native language or other mode of communication of the parent is not a written language, the SEA or LEA shall take steps to ensure—

(1) That the notice is translated orally or by other means to the parent in his or her native language or other mode of communication;

(2) That the parent understands the content of the notice; and

(3) That there is written evidence that the requirements in paragraphs (c)(1) and (2) of this section have been met.

(Authority: 20 U.S.C. 1415(b)(1)(D)) (Approved by the Office of Management and Budget under control number 1820-0030) [57 FR 44798, Sept. 29, 1992, as amended at 58 FR 13528, Mar. 11, 1993]

Sec. 300.506 Impartial due process hearing

(a) A parent or a public educational agency may initiate a hearing on any of the matters described in Sec. 300.504(a)(1) and (2).

(b) The hearing must be conducted by the SEA or the public agency directly responsible for the education of the child, as determined under State statute, State regulation, or a written policy of the SEA.

(c) The public agency shall inform the parent of any free or low-cost legal and other relevant services available in the area if—

(1) The parent requests the information; or

(2) The parent or the agency initiates a hearing under this section.

(Authority: 20 U.S.C. 1415(b)(2))

Note: Many States have pointed to the success of using mediation as an intervening step prior to conducting a formal due process hearing. Although the process of mediation is not required by the statute or these regulations, an agency may wish to suggest mediation in disputes concerning the identification, evaluation, and educational placement of children with disabilities, and the provision of FAPE to those children. Mediations have been conducted by members of SEAs or LEA personnel who were not previously involved in the particular case. In many cases, mediation leads to resolution of differences between parents and agencies without the development of an adversarial relationship and with minimal emotional stress. However, mediation may not be used to deny or delay a parent's rights under Secs. 300.500-300.515.

Sec. 300.507 Impartial hearing officer

(a) A hearing may not be conducted—

(1) By a person who is an employee of a public agency that is involved in the education or care of the child; or

(2) By any person having a personal or professional interest that would conflict with his or her objectivity in the hearing.

(b) A person who otherwise qualifies to conduct a hearing under paragraph (a) of this section is not an employee of the agency solely because he or she is paid by the agency to serve as a hearing officer.

(c) Each public agency shall keep a list of the persons who serve as hearing officers. The list must include a statement of the qualifications of each of those persons.

(Authority: 20 U.S.C. 1414(b)(2))

Sec. 300.508 Hearing rights

(a) Any party to a hearing has the right to:

(1) Be accompanied and advised by counsel and by individuals with special knowledge or training with respect to the problems of children with disabilities.

(2) Present evidence and confront, cross-examine, and compel the attendance of witnesses.

(3) Prohibit the introduction of any evidence at the hearing that has not been disclosed to that party at least five days before the hearing.

(4) Obtain a written or electronic verbatim record of the hearing.

(5) Obtain written findings of fact and decisions. The public agency, after deleting any personally identifiable information, shall—

(i) Transmit those findings and decisions to the State advisory panel established under Sec. 300.650; and

(ii) Make those findings and decisions available to the public.

(b) Parents involved in hearings must be given the right to—

(1) Have the child who is the subject of the hearing present; and

(2) Open the hearing to the public.

(Authority: 20 U.S.C. 1415(d))

Sec. 300.509 Hearing decision; appeal

A decision made in a hearing conducted under Sec. 300.506 is final, unless a party to the hearing appeals the decision under Sec. 300.510 or Sec. 300.511.

(Authority: 20 U.S.C. 1415(c))

Sec. 300.510 Administrative appeal; impartial review

(a) If the hearing is conducted by a public agency other than the SEA, any party aggrieved by the findings and decision in the hearing may appeal to the SEA.

(b) If there is an appeal, the SEA shall conduct an impartial review of the hearing. The official conducting the review shall:

(1) Examine the entire hearing record.

(2) Ensure that the procedures at the hearing were consistent with the requirements of due process.

(3) Seek additional evidence if necessary. If a hearing is held to receive additional evidence, the rights in 300.508 apply.

(4) Afford the parties an opportunity for oral or written argument, or both, at the discretion of the reviewing official.

(5) Make an independent decision on completion of the review.

(6) Give a copy of written findings and the decision to the parties.

(c) The SEA, after deleting any personally identifiable information, shall—

(1) Transmit the findings and decisions referred to in paragraph (b)(6) of this section to the State advisory panel established under Sec. 300.650; and

(2) Make those findings and decisions available to the public.

(d) The decision made by the reviewing official is final unless a party brings a civil action under Sec. 300.511.

(Authority: 20 U.S.C. 1415(c), (d); H. R. Rep. No. 94-664, at p. 49 (1975))

Note 1: The SEA may conduct its review either directly or through another State agency acting on its behalf. However, the SEA remains responsible for the final decision on review.

Note 2: All parties have the right to continue to be represented by counsel at the State administrative review level, whether or not the reviewing official determines that a further hearing is necessary. If the reviewing official decides to hold a hearing to receive additional evidence, the other rights in Sec. 300.508 relating to hearings also apply. (Approved by the Office of Management and Budget under control number 1820-0030) [57 FR 44798, Sept. 29, 1992, as amended at 58 FR 13528, Mar. 11, 1993]

Sec. 300.511 Civil action

Any party aggrieved by the findings and decision made in a hearing who does not have the right to appeal under Sec. 300.510, and any party aggrieved by the decision of a reviewing officer under Sec. 300.510, has the right to bring a civil action under section 615(e)(2) of the Act.

(Authority: 20 U.S.C. 1415)

Sec. 300.512 Timelines and convenience of hearings and reviews

(a) The public agency shall ensure that not later than 45 days after the receipt of a request for a hearing—

(1) A final decision is reached in the hearing; and

(2) A copy of the decision is mailed to each of the parties.

(b) The SEA shall ensure that not later than 30 days after the receipt of a request for a review—

(1) A final decision is reached in the review; and

(2) A copy of the decision is mailed to each of the parties.

(c) A hearing or reviewing officer may grant specific extensions of time beyond the periods set out in paragraphs (a) and (b) of this section at the request of either party.

(d) Each hearing and each review involving oral arguments must be conducted at a time and place that is reasonably convenient to the parents and child involved.

(Authority: 20 U.S.C. 1415) (Approved by the Office of Management and Budget under control number 1820-0030) [57 FR 44798, Sept. 29, 1992, as amended at 58 FR 13528, Mar. 11, 1993]

Sec. 300.513 Child's status during proceedings

(a) During the pendency of any administrative or judicial proceeding regarding a complaint, unless the public agency and the parents of the child agree otherwise, the child involved in the complaint must remain in his or her present educational placement.

(b) If the complaint involves an application for initial admission to public school, the child, with the consent of the parents, must be placed in the public school program until the completion of all the proceedings.

(Authority: 20 U.S.C. 1415(e)(3))

Note: Section 300.513 does not permit a child's placement to be changed during a complaint proceeding, unless the parents and agency agree otherwise. While the placement may not be changed, this does not preclude the agency from using its normal procedures for dealing with children who are endangering themselves or others.

Sec. 300.515 Attorneys' fees

Each public agency shall inform parents that in any action or proceeding under section 615 of the Act, courts may award parents reasonable attorneys' fees under the circumstances described in section 615(e)(4) of the Act.

(Authority: 20 U.S.C. 1415(b)(1)(D); 1415(e)(4))

Protection in Evaluation Procedures

Sec. 300.531 Preplacement evaluation

Before any action is taken with respect to the initial placement of a child with a disability in a program providing special education and related services, a full and individual evaluation of the child's educational needs must be conducted in accordance with the requirements of Sec. 300.532.

(Authority: 20 U.S.C. 1412(5)(C))

Sec. 300.532 Evaluation procedures

State educational agencies and LEAs shall ensure, at a minimum, that:

(a) Tests and other evaluation materials—

(1) Are provided and administered in the child's native language or other mode of communication, unless it is clearly not feasible to do so;

(2) Have been validated for the specific purpose for which they are used; and

(3) Are administered by trained personnel in conformance with the instructions provided by their producer.

(b) Tests and other evaluation materials include those tailored to assess specific areas of educational need and not merely those that are designed to provide a single general intelligence quotient.

(c) Tests are selected and administered so as best to ensure that when a test is administered to a child with impaired sensory, manual, or speaking skills, the test results accurately reflect the child's aptitude or achievement level or whatever other factors the test purports to measure, rather than reflecting the child's impaired sensory, manual, or speaking skills (except where those skills are the factors that the test purports to measure).

(d) No single procedure is used as the sole criterion for determining an appropriate educational program for a child.

(e) The evaluation is made by a multidisciplinary team or group of persons, including at least one teacher or other specialist with knowledge in the area of suspected disability.

(f) The child is assessed in all areas related to the suspected disability, including, if appropriate, health, vision, hearing, social and emotional status, general intelligence, academic performance, communicative status, and motor abilities.

(Authority: 20 U.S.C. 1412(5)(C))

Note: Children who have a speech or language impairment as their primary disability may not need a complete battery of assessments (e.g., psychological, physical, or adaptive behavior). However, a qualified speech-language pathologist would: (1)

Evaluate each child with a speech or language impairment using procedures that are appropriate for the diagnosis and appraisal of speech and language impairments, and (2) if necessary, make referrals for additional assessments needed to make an appropriate placement decision. (Approved by the Office of Management and Budget under control number 1820-0030) [57 FR 44798, Sept. 29, 1992, as amended at 58 FR 13528, Mar. 11, 1993]

Sec. 300.533 Placement procedures

(a) In interpreting evaluation data and in making placement decisions, each public agency shall—

(1) Draw upon information from a variety of sources, including aptitude and achievement tests, teacher recommendations, physical condition, social or cultural background, and adaptive behavior;

(2) Ensure that information obtained from all of these sources is documented and carefully considered;

(3) Ensure that the placement decision is made by a group of persons, including persons knowledgeable about the child, the meaning of the evaluation data, and the placement options; and

(4) Ensure that the placement decision is made in conformity with the LRE rules in Secs. 300.550-300.554.

(b) If a determination is made that a child has a disability and needs special education and related services, an IEP must be developed for the child in accordance with Secs. 300.340-300.350.

(Authority: 20 U.S.C. 1412(5)(C); 1414(a)(5))

Note: Paragraph (a)(1) of this section includes a list of examples of sources that may be used by a public agency in making placement decisions. The agency would not have to use all the sources in every instance. The point of the requirement is to ensure that more than one source is used in interpreting evaluation data and in making placement decisions. For example, while all of the named sources would have to be used for a child whose suspected disability is mental retardation, they would not be necessary for certain other children with disabilities, such as a child who has a severe articulation impairment as his primary disability. For such a child, the speech-language pathologist, in complying with the multiple source requirement, might use: (1) A standardized test of articulation, and (2) observation of the child's articulation behavior in conversational speech. (Approved by the Office of Management and Budget under control number 1820-0030) [57 FR 44798, Sept. 29, 1992, as amended at 58 FR 13528, Mar. 11, 1993]

Sec. 300.534 Reevaluation

Each SEA and LEA shall ensure—

(a) That the IEP of each child with a disability is reviewed in accordance with Secs. 300.340-300.350; and

(b) That an evaluation of the child, based on procedures that meet the requirements of Sec. 300.532, is conducted every three years, or more frequently if conditions warrant, or if the child's parent or teacher requests an evaluation.

(Authority: 20 U.S.C. 1412(5)(c))

Additional Procedures for Evaluating Children With Specific Learning Disabilities

Sec. 300.540 Additional team members

In evaluating a child suspected of having a specific learning disability, in addition to the requirements of Sec. 300.532, each public agency shall include on the multidisciplinary evaluation team—

(a)(1) The child's regular teacher; or

(2) If the child does not have a regular teacher, a regular classroom teacher qualified to teach a child of his or her age; or

(3) For a child of less than school age, an individual qualified by the SEA to teach a child of his or her age; and

(b) At least one person qualified to conduct individual diagnostic examinations of children, such as a school psychologist, speech-language pathologist, or remedial reading teacher.

(Authority: 20 U.S.C. 1411 note)

Sec. 300.541 Criteria for determining the existence of a specific learning disability

(a) A team may determine that a child has a specific learning disability if—

(1) The child does not achieve commensurate with his or her age and ability levels in one or more of the areas listed in paragraph (a)(2) of this section, when provided with learning experiences appropriate for the child's age and ability levels; and

(2) The team finds that a child has a severe discrepancy between achievement and intellectual ability in one or more of the following areas—

(i) Oral expression;

(ii) Listening comprehension;

(iii) Written expression;

(iv) Basic reading skill;

(v) Reading comprehension;

(vi) Mathematics calculation; or

(vii) Mathematics reasoning.

(b) The team may not identify a child as having a specific learning disability if the severe discrepancy between ability and achievement is primarily the result of—

(1) A visual, hearing, or motor impairment;

(2) Mental retardation;

(3) Emotional disturbance; or

(4) Environmental, cultural or economic disadvantage.

(Authority: 20 U.S.C. 1411 note)

Sec. 300.542 Observation

(a) At least one team member other than the child's regular teacher shall observe the child's academic performance in the regular classroom setting.

(b) In the case of a child of less than school age or out of school, a team member shall observe the child in an environment appropriate for a child of that age.

(Authority: 20 U.S.C. 1411 note)

Sec. 300.543 Written report

(a) The team shall prepare a written report of the results of the evaluation.

(b) The report must include a statement of—

(1) Whether the child has a specific learning disability;

(2) The basis for making the determination;

(3) The relevant behavior noted during the observation of the child;

(4) The relationship of that behavior to the child's academic functioning;

(5) The educationally relevant medical findings, if any;

(6) Whether there is a severe discrepancy between achievement and ability that is not correctable without special education and related services; and

(7) The determination of the team concerning the effects of environmental, cultural, or economic disadvantage.

(c) Each team member shall certify in writing whether the report reflects his or her conclusion. If it does not reflect his or her conclusion, the team member must submit a separate statement presenting his or her conclusions.

(Authority: 20 U.S.C. 1411 note) (Approved by the Office of Management and Budget under control number 1820-0030) [57 FR 44798, Sept. 29, 1992, as amended at 58 FR 13528, Mar. 11, 1993]

Least Restrictive Environment

Sec. 300.550 General

(a) Each SEA shall ensure that each public agency establishes and implements procedures that meet the requirements of Secs. 300.550-300.556.

(b) Each public agency shall ensure—

(1) That to the maximum extent appropriate, children with disabilities, including children in public or private institutions or other care facilities, are educated with children who are nondisabled; and

(2) That special classes, separate schooling or other removal of children with disabilities from the regular educational environment occurs only when the nature or severity of the disability is such that education in regular classes with the use of supplementary aids and services cannot be achieved satisfactorily.

(Authority: 20 U.S.C. 1412(5)(B); 1414(a)(1)(C)(iv))

Sec. 300.551 Continuum of alternative placements

(a) Each public agency shall ensure that a continuum of alternative placements is available to meet the needs of children with disabilities for special education and related services.

(b) The continuum required in paragraph (a) of this section must—

(1) Include the alternative placements listed in the definition of special education under Sec. 300.17 (instruction in regular

classes, special classes, special schools, home instruction, and instruction in hospitals and institutions); and

(2) Make provision for supplementary services (such as resource room or itinerant instruction) to be provided in conjunction with regular class placement.

(Authority: 20 U.S.C. 1412(5)(B))

Sec. 300.552 Placements

Each public agency shall ensure that:

(a) The educational placement of each child with a disability—

(1) Is determined at least annually;

(2) Is based on his or her IEP; and

(3) Is as close as possible to the child's home.

(b) The various alternative placements included at Sec. 300.551 are available to the extent necessary to implement the IEP for each child with a disability.

(c) Unless the IEP of a child with a disability requires some other arrangement, the child is educated in the school that he or she would attend if nondisabled.

(d) In selecting the LRE, consideration is given to any potential harmful effect on the child or on the quality of services that he or she needs.

(Authority: 20 U.S.C. 1412(5)(B))

Note: Section 300.552 includes some of the main factors that must be considered in determining the extent to which a child with a disability can be educated with children who are non-disabled. The overriding rule in this section is that placement decisions must be made on an individual basis. The section also requires each agency to have various alternative placements available in order to ensure that each child with a disability receives an education that is appropriate to his or her individual needs.

The requirements of Sec. 300.552, as well as the other requirements of Secs. 300.550-300.556, apply to all preschool children with disabilities who are entitled to receive FAPE. Public agencies that provide preschool programs for non-disabled preschool children must ensure that the requirements of Sec. 300.552(c) are met. Public agencies that do not operate programs for nondisabled preschool children are not required to initiate such programs solely to satisfy the requirements regarding placement in the LRE embodied in Secs. 300.550-300.556. For these public agencies, some alternative methods for meeting the requirements of Secs. 300.550-300.556 include—

(1) Providing opportunities for the participation (even part-time) of preschool children with disabilities in other preschool programs operated by public agencies (such as Head Start);

(2) Placing children with disabilities in private school programs for nondisabled preschool children or private school preschool programs that integrate children with disabilities and nondisabled children; and

(3) Locating classes for preschool children with disabilities in regular elementary schools.

In each case the public agency must ensure that each child's placement is in the LRE in which the unique needs of that child

can be met, based upon the child's IEP, and meets all of the other requirements of Secs. 300.340-300.350 and Secs. 300.550-300.556.

The analysis of the regulations for section 504 of the Rehabilitation Act of 1973 (34 CFR part 104—Appendix, Paragraph 24) includes several points regarding educational placements of children with disabilities that are pertinent to this section:

1. With respect to determining proper placements, the analysis states: "* * * it should be stressed that, where a handicapped child is so disruptive in a regular classroom that the education of other students is significantly impaired, the needs of the handicapped child cannot be met in that environment. Therefore regular placement would not be appropriate to his or her needs * * *."

2. With respect to placing a child with a disability in an alternate setting, the analysis states that among the factors to be considered in placing a child is the need to place the child as close to home as possible. Recipients are required to take this factor into account in making placement decisions. The parents' right to challenge the placement of their child extends not only to placement in special classes or separate schools, but also to placement in a distant school, particularly in a residential program. An equally appropriate education program may exist closer to home; and this issue may be raised by the parent under the due process provisions of this subpart.

Section 504 of the Rehabilitation Act of 1973 (Key Regulations)

Part 104—Nondiscrimination On the Basis of Handicap In Programs and Activities Receiving Federal Financial Assistance

Sec. 104.1 Purpose

The purpose of this part is to effectuate section 504 of the Rehabilitation Act of 1973, which is designed to eliminate discrimination on the basis of handicap in any program or activity receiving Federal financial assistance.

Sec. 104.2 Application

This part applies to each recipient of Federal financial assistance from the Department of Education and to each program or activity that receives or benefits from such assistance.

Sec. 104.3 Definitions

As used in this part, the term:

(a) The Act means the Rehabilitation Act of 1973, Pub. L. 93-112, as amended by the Rehabilitation Act Amendments of 1974, Pub. L. 93-516, 29 U.S.C. 794.

(b) Section 504 means section 504 of the Act.

(c) Education of the Handicapped Act means that statute as amended by the Education for all Handicapped Children Act of 1975, Pub. L. 94-142, 20 U.S.C. 1401 et seq.

(d) Department means the Department of Education.

(e) Assistant Secretary means the Assistant Secretary for Civil Rights of the Department of Education.

(f) Recipient means any state or its political subdivision, any instrumentality of a state or its political subdivision, any public or private agency, institution, organization, or other entity, or any person to which Federal financial assistance is extended directly or through another recipient, including any successor, assignee, or transferee of a recipient, but excluding the ultimate beneficiary of the assistance.

(g) Applicant for assistance means one who submits an application, request, or plan required to be approved by a Department official or by a recipient as a condition to becoming a recipient.

(h) Federal financial assistance means any grant, loan, contract (other than a procurement contract or a contract of insurance or guaranty), or any other arrangement by which the Department provides or otherwise makes available assistance in the form of:

(1) Funds;

(2) Services of Federal personnel; or

(3) Real and personal property or any interest in or use of such property, including:

(i) Transfers or leases of such property for less than fair market value or for reduced consideration; and

(ii) Proceeds from a subsequent transfer or lease of such property if the Federal share of its fair market value is not returned to the Federal Government.

(i) Facility means all or any portion of buildings, structures, equipment, roads, walks, parking lots, or other real or personal property or interest in such property.

(j) Handicapped person—

(1) Handicapped persons means any person who (i) has a physical or mental impairment which substantially limits one or more major life activities, (ii) has a record of such an impairment, or (iii) is regarded as having such an impairment.

(2) As used in paragraph (j)(1) of this section, the phrase:

(i) Physical or mental impairment means (A) any physiological disorder or condition, cosmetic disfigurement, or anatomical loss affecting one or more of the following body systems: neurological; musculoskeletal; special sense organs; respiratory, including speech organs; cardiovascular; reproductive, digestive, genito-urinary; hemic and lymphatic; skin; and endocrine; or (B) any mental or psychological disorder, such as mental retardation, organic brain syndrome, emotional or mental illness, and specific learning disabilities.

(ii) Major life activities means functions such as caring for one's self, performing manual tasks, walking, seeing, hearing, speaking, breathing, learning, and working.

(iii) Has a record of such an impairment means has a history of, or has been misclassified as having, a mental or physical impairment that substantially limits one or more major life activities.

(iv) Is regarded as having an impairment means (A) has a physical or mental impairment that does not substantially limit major life activities but that is treated by a recipient as constituting such a limitation; (B) has a physical or mental impairment that substantially limits major life activities only as a result of the attitudes of others toward such impairment; or (C) has none of the impairments defined in paragraph

(j)(2)(i) of this section but is treated by a recipient as having such an impairment.

(k) Qualified handicapped person means:

(1) With respect to employment, a handicapped person who, with reasonable accommodation, can perform the essential functions of the job in question;

(2) With respect to public preschool elementary, secondary, or adult educational services, a handicappped person (i) of an age during which nonhandicapped persons are provided such services, (ii) of any age during which it is mandatory under state law to provide such services to handicapped persons, or (iii) to whom a state is required to provide a free appropriate public education under section 612 of the Education of the Handicapped Act; and

(3) With respect to postsecondary and vocational education services, a handicapped person who meets the academic and technical standards requisite to admission or participation in the recipient's education program or activity;

(4) With respect to other services, a handicapped person who meets the essential eligibility requirements for the receipt of such services.

(l) Handicap means any condition or characteristic that renders a person a handicapped person as defined in paragraph (j) of this section.

Sec. 104.4 Discrimination prohibited

(a) General. No qualified handicapped person shall, on the basis of handicap, be excluded from participation in, be denied the benefits of, or otherwise be subjected to discrimination under any program or activitiy which receives or benefits from Federal financial assistance.

(b) Discriminatory actions prohibited. (1) A recipient, in providing any aid, benefit, or service, may not, directly or through contractual, licensing, or other arrangements, on the basis of handicap:

(i) Deny a qualified handicapped person the opportunity to participate in or benefit from the aid, benefit, or service;

(ii) Afford a qualified handicapped person an opportunity to participate in or benefit from the aid, benefit, or service that is not equal to that afforded others;

(iii) Provide a qualified handicapped person with an aid, benefit, or service that is not as effective as that provided to others;

(iv) Provide different or separate aid, benefits, or services to handicapped persons or to any class of handicapped persons unless such action is necessary to provide qualified handicapped persons with aid, benefits, or services that are as effective as those provided to others;

(v) Aid or perpetuate discrimination against a qualified handicapped person by providing significant assistance to an agency, organization, or person that discriminates on the basis of handicap in providing any aid, benefit, or service to beneficiaries of the recipients program;

(vi) Deny a qualified handicapped person the opportunity to participate as a member of planning or advisory boards; or

(vii) Otherwise limit a qualified handicapped person in the enjoyment of any right, privilege, advantage, or opportunity enjoyed by others receiving an aid, benefit, or service.

(2) For purposes of this part, aids, benefits, and services, to be equally effective, are not required to produce the identical result or level of achievement for handicapped and nonhandicapped persons, but must afford handicapped persons equal opportunity to obtain the same result, to gain the same benefit, or to reach the same level of achievement, in the most integrated setting appropriate to the person's needs.

(3) Despite the existence of separate or different programs or activities provided in accordance with this part, a recipient may not deny a qualified handicapped person the opportunity to participate in such programs or activities that are not separate or different.

(4) A recipient may not, directly or through contractual or other arrangements, utilize criteria or methods of administration (i) that have the effect of subjecting qualified handicapped persons to discrimination on the basis of handicap, (ii) that have the purpose or effect of defeating or substantially impairing accomplishment of the objectives of the recipient's program with respect to handicapped persons, or (iii) that perpetuate the discrimination of another recipient if both recipients are subject to common administrative control or are agencies of the same State.

(5) In determining the site or location of a facility, an applicant for assistance or a recipient may not make selections (i) that have the effect of excluding handicapped persons from, denying them the benefits of, or otherwise subjecting them to discrimination under any program or activity that receives or benefits from Federal financial assistance or (ii) that have the purpose or effect of defeating or substantially impairing the accomplishment of the objectives of the program or activity with respect to handicapped persons.

(6) As used in this section, the aid, benefit, or service provided under a program or activity receiving or benefiting from Federal financial assistance includes any aid, benefit, or service provided in or through a facility that has been constructed, expanded, altered, leased or rented, or otherwise acquired, in whole or in part, with Federal financial assistance.

(c) Programs limited by Federal law. The exclusion of nonhandicapped persons from the benefits of a program limited by Federal statute or executive order to handicapped persons or the exclusion of a specific class of handicapped persons from a program limited by Federal statute or executive order to a different class of handicapped persons is not prohibited by this part.

Sec.104.5 Assurances required

(a) Assurances. An applicant for Federal financial assistance for a program or activity to which this part applies shall submit an assurance, on a form specified by the Assistant Secretary, that the program will be operated in compliance with this part. An applicant may incorporate these assurances by reference in subsequent applications to the Department.

(b) Duration of obligation

(1) In the case of Federal financial assistance extended in the form of real property or to provide real property or structures on the property, the assurance will obligate the recipient or, in the case of a subsequent transfer, the transferee, for the period during which the real property or structures are used for the purpose for which Federal financial assistance is extended or for another purpose involving the provision of similar services or benefits.

(2) In the case of Federal financial assistance extended to provide personal property, the assurance will obligate the recipient for the period during which it retains ownership or possession of the property.

(3) In all other cases the assurance will obligate the recipient for the period during which Federal financial assistance is extended.

(c) Covenants

(1) Where Federal financial assistance is provided in the form of real property or interest in the property from the Department, the instrument effecting or recording this transfer shall contain a covenant running with the land to assure nondiscrimination for the period during which the real property is used for a purpose for which the Federal financial assistance is extended or for another purpose involving the provision of similar services or benefits.

(2) Where no transfer of property is involved but property is purchased or improved with Federal financial assistance, the recipient shall agree to include the covenant described in paragraph (b)(2) of this section in the instrument effecting or recording any subsequent transfer of the property.

(3) Where Federal financial assistance is provided in the form of real property or interest in the property from the Department, the covenant shall also include a condition coupled with a right to be reserved by the Department to revert title to the property in the event of a breach of the covenant. If a transferee of real property proposes to mortgage or otherwise encumber the real property as security for financing construction of new, or improvement of existing, facilities on the property for the purposes for which the property was transferred, the Assistant Secretary may, upon request of the transferee and if necessary to accomplish such financing and upon such conditions as he or she deems appropriate, agree to forbear the exercise of such right to revert title for so long as the lien of such mortgage or other encumbrance remains effective.

Sec.104.21 Discrimination prohibited

No qualified handicapped person shall, because a recipient's facilities are inaccessible to or unusable by handicapped persons, be denied the benefits of, be excluded from participation in, or otherwise be subjected to discrimination under any program or activity to which this part applies.

Sec.104.22 Existing facilities

(a) Program accessibility. A recipient shall operate each program or activity to which this part applies so that the program or activity, when viewed in its entirety, is readily accessible to handicapped persons. This paragraph does not require a recipient to make each of its existing facilities or every part of a facility accessible to and usable by handicapped persons.

(b) Methods. A recipient may comply with the requirements of paragraph (a) of this section through such means as redesign of equipment, reassignment of classes or other services to accessible buildings, assignment of aides to beneficiaries, home visits, delivery of health, welfare, or other social services at alternate accessible sites, alteration of existing facilities and construction of new facilities in conformance with the requirements of Sec. 104.23, or any other methods that result in making its program or activity accessible to handicapped persons. A recipient is not required to make structural changes in existing facilities where other methods are effective in achieving compliance with paragraph (a) of this section. In choosing among available methods for meeting the requirement of paragraph (a) of this section, a recipient shall give priority to those methods that offer programs and activities to handicapped persons in the most integrated setting appropriate.

(c) Small health, welfare, or other social service providers. If a recipient with fewer than fifteen employees that provides health, welfare, or other social services finds, after consultation with a handicapped person seeking its services, that there is no method of complying with paragraph (a) of this section other than making a significant alteration in its existing facilities, the recipient may, as an alternative, refer the handicapped person to other providers of those services that are accessible.

(d) Time period. A recipient shall comply with the requirement of paragraph (a) of this section within sixty days of the effective date of this part except that where structural changes in facilities are necessary, such changes shall be made within three years of the effective date of this part, but in any event as expeditiously as possible.

(e) Transition plan. In the event that structural changes to facilities are necessary to meet the requirement of paragraph (a) of this section, a recipient shall develop, within six months of the effective date of this part, a transition plan setting forth the steps necessary to complete such changes. The plan shall be developed with the assistance of interested persons, including handicapped persons or organizations representing handicapped persons. A copy of the transition plan shall be made available for public inspection. The plan shall, at a minimum:

(1) Identify physical obstacles in the recipient's facilities that limit the accessibility of its program or activity to handicappped persons;

(2) Describe in detail the methods that will be used to make the facilities accessible;

(3) Specify the schedule for taking the steps necessary to achieve full program accessibility and, if the time period of the transition plan is longer than one year, identify the steps of that will be taken during each year of the transition period; and

(4) Indicate the person responsible for implementation of the plan.

(f) Notice. The recipient shall adopt and implement procedures to ensure that interested persons, including persons with impaired vision or hearing, can obtain information as to the existence and location of services, activities, and facilities that are accessible to and usuable by handicapped persons.

Sec.104.23 New construction

(a) Design and construction. Each facility or part of a facility constructed by, on behalf of, or for the use of a recipient shall be designed and constructed in such manner that the facility or part of the facility is readily accessible to and usable by handicapped persons, if the construction was commenced after the effective date of this part.

(b) Alteration. Each facility or part of a facility which is altered by, on behalf of, or for the use of a recipient after the effective date of this part in a manner that affects or could affect the usability of the facility or part of the facility shall, to the maximum extent feasible, be altered in such manner that the altered portion of the facility is readily accessible to and usable by handicapped persons.

(c) Conformance with Uniform Federal Accessibility Standards

(1) Effective as of January 18, 1991, design, construction, or alteration of buildings in conformance with sections 3-8 of the Uniform Federal Accessibility Standards (UFAS) (Appendix A to 41 CFR subpart 101-19.6) shall be deemed to comply with the requirements of this section with respect to those buildings. Departures from particular technical and scoping requirements of UFAS by the use of other methods are permitted where substantially equivalent or greater access to and usability of the building is provided.

(2) For purposes of this section, section 4.1.6(1)(g) of UFAS shall be interpreted to exempt from the requirements of UFAS only mechanical rooms and other spaces that, because of their intended use, will not require accessibility to the public or beneficiaries or result in the employment or residence therein of persons with physical handicaps.

(3) This section does not require recipients to make building alterations that have little likelihood of being accomplished without removing or altering a load-bearing structural member. [45 FR 30936, May 9, 1980; 45 FR 37426, June 3, 1980, as amended at 55 FR 52138, 52141, Dec. 19, 1990]

Subpart D—Preschool, Elementary, and Secondary Education

Sec.104.31 Application of this subpart
Subpart D applies to preschool, elementary, secondary, and adult education programs and activities that receive or benefit from Federal financial assistance and to recipients that operate, or that receive or benefit from Federal financial assistance for the operation of, such programs or activities.

Sec.104.32 Location and notification
A recipient that operates a public elementary or secondary education program shall annually:

(a) Undertake to identify and locate every qualified handicapped person residing in the recipient's jurisdiction who is not receiving a public education; and

(b) Take appropriate steps to notify handicapped persons and their parents or guardians of the recipient's duty under this subpart.

Sec.104.33 Free appropriate public education
(a) General. A recipient that operates a public elementary or secondary education program shall provide a free appropriate public education to each qualified handicapped person

who is in the recipient's jurisdiction, regardless of the nature or severity of the person's handicap.

(b) Appropriate education

(1) For the purpose of this subpart, the provision of an appropriate education is the provision of regular or special education and related aids and services that (i) are designed to meet individual educational needs of handicapped persons as adequately as the needs of nonhandicapped persons are met and (ii) are based upon adherence to procedures that satisfy the requirements of Secs. 104.34, 104.35, and 104.36.

(2) Implementation of an individualized education program developed in accordance with the Education of the Handicapped Act is one means of meeting the standard established in paragraph (b)(1)(i) of this section.

(3) A recipient may place a handicapped person in or refer such person to a program other than the one that it operates as its means of carrying out the requirements of this subpart. If so, the recipient remains responsible for ensuring that the requirements of this subpart are met with respect to any handicapped person so placed or referred.

(c) Free education—

(1) *General.* For the purpose of this section, the provision of a free education is the provision of educational and related services without cost to the handicapped person or to his or her parents or guardian, except for those fees that are imposed on non-handicapped persons or their parents or guardian. It may consist either of the provision of free services or, if a recipient places a handicapped person in or refers such person to a program not operated by the recipient as its means of carrying out the requirements of this subpart, of payment for the costs of the program. Funds available from any public or private agency may be used to meet the requirements of this subpart. Nothing in this section shall be construed to relieve an insurer or similar third party from an otherwise valid obligation to provide or pay for services provided to a handicapped person.

(2) *Transportation.* If a recipient places a handicapped person in or refers such person to a program not operated by the recipient as its means of carrying out the requirements of this subpart, the recipient shall ensure that adequate transportation to and from the program is provided at no greater cost than would be incurred by the person or his or her parents or guardian if the person were placed in the program operated by the recipient.

(3) *Residential placement.* If placement in a public or private residential program is necessary to provide a free appropriate public education to a handicapped person because of his or her handicap, the program, including non-medical care and room and board, shall be provided at no cost to the person or his or her parents or guardian.

(4) *Placement of handicapped persons by parents.* If a recipient has made available, in conformance with the requirements of this section and Sec. 104.34, a free appropriate public education to a handicapped person and the person's parents or guardian choose to place the person in a private school, the recipient is not required to pay for the person's education in the private school. Disagreements between a parent or guardian and a

recipient regarding whether the recipient has made such a program available or otherwise regarding the question of financial responsibility are subject to the due process procedures of Sec. 104.36

(d) Compliance. A recipient may not exclude any qualified handicapped person from a public elementary or secondary education after the effective date of this part. A recipient that is not, on the effective date of this regulation, in full compliance with the other requirements of the preceding paragraphs of this section shall meet such requirements at the earliest practicable time and in no event later than September 1, 1978.

Sec. 104.34　Educational setting

(a) Academic setting. A recipient to which this subpart applies shall educate, or shall provide for the education of, each qualified handicapped person in its jurisdiction with persons who are not handicapped to the maximum extent appropriate to the needs of the handicapped person. A recipient shall place a handicapped person in the regular educational environment operated by the recipient unless it is demonstrated by the recipient that the education of the person in the regular environment with the use of supplementary aids and services cannot be achieved satisfactorily. Whenever a recipient places a person in a setting other than the regular educational environment pursuant to this paragraph, it shall take into account the proximity of the alternate setting to the person's home.

(b) Nonacademic settings. In providing or arranging for the provision of nonacademic and extracurricular services and activities, including meals, recess periods, and the services and activities set forth in Sec. 104.37(a)(2), a recipient shall ensure that handicapped persons participate with nonhandicapped persons in such activities and services to the maximum extent appropriate to the needs of the handicapped person in question.

(c) Comparable facilities. If a recipient, in compliance with paragraph (a) of this section, operates a facility that is identifiable as being for handicapped persons, the recipient shall ensure that the facility and the services and activities provided therein are comparable to the other facilities, services, and activities of the recipient.

Sec. 104.35　Evaluation and placement

(a) Preplacement evaluation. A recipient that operates a public elementary or secondary education program shall conduct an evaluation in accordance with the requirements of paragraph (b) of this section of any person who, because of handicap, needs or is believed to need special education or related services before taking any action with respect to the initial placement of the person in a regular or special education program and any subsequent significant change in placement.

(b) Evaluation procedures. A recipient to which this subpart applies shall establish standards and procedures for the evaluation and placement of persons who, because of handicap, need or are believed to need special education or related services which ensure that:

(1) Tests and other evaluation materials have been validated for the specific purpose for which they are used and are administered by trained personnel in conformance with the instructions provided by their producer;

(2) Tests and other evaluation materials include those tailored to assess specific areas of educational need and not merely those which are designed to provide a single general intelligence quotient; and

(3) Tests are selected and administered so as best to ensure that, when a test is administered to a student with impaired sensory, manual, or speaking skills, the test results accurately reflect the student's aptitude or achievement level or whatever other factor the test purports to measure, rather than reflecting the student's impaired sensory, manual, or speaking skills (except where those skills are the factors that the test purports to measure).

(c) Placement procedures. In interpreting evaluation data and in making placement decisions, a recipient shall (1) draw upon information from a variety of sources, including aptitude and achievement tests, teacher recommendations, physical condition, social or cultural background, and adaptive behavior, (2) establish procedures to ensure that information obtained from all such sources is documented and carefully considered, (3) ensure that the placement decision is made by a group of persons, including persons knowledgeable about the child, the meaning of the evaluation data, and the placement options, and (4) ensure that the placement decision is made in conformity with Sec. 104.34.

(d) Reevaluation. A recipient to which this section applies shall establish procedures, in accordance with paragraph (b) of this section, for periodic reevaluation of students who have been provided special education and related services. A reevaluation procedure consistent with the Education for the Handicapped Act is one means of meeting this requirement.

Sec. 104.36 Procedural safeguards

A recipient that operates a public elementary or secondary education program shall establish and implement, with respect to actions regarding the identification, evaluation, or educational placement of persons who, because of handicap, need or are believed to need special instruction or related services, a system of procedural safeguards that includes notice, an opportunity for the parents or guardian of the person to examine relevant records, an impartial hearing with opportunity for participation by the person's parents or guardian and representation by counsel, and a review procedure. Compliance with the procedural safeguards of section 615 of the Education of the Handicapped Act is one means of meeting this requirement.

Sec. 104.37 Nonacademic services

(a) General

(1) A recipient to which this subpart applies shall provide nonacademic and extracurricular services and activities in such manner as is necessary to afford handicapped students an equal opportunity for participation in such services and activities.

(2) Nonacademic and extracurricular services and activities may include counseling services, physical recreational athletics, transportation, health services, recreational activities, special interest groups or clubs sponsored by the recipients, referrals to agencies which provide assistance to handicapped persons, and employment of students, including both employment by the recipient and assistance in making available outside employment.

(b) Counseling services. A recipient to which this subpart applies that provides personal, academic, or vocational counseling, guidance, or placement services to its students shall provide these services without discrimination on the basis of handicap. The recipient shall ensure that qualified handicapped students are not counseled toward more restrictive career objectives than are nonhandicapped students with similar interests and abilities.

(c) Physical education and athletics. (1) In providing physical education courses and athletics and similar programs and activities to any of its students, a recipient to which this subpart applies may not discriminate on the basis of handicap. A recipient that offers physical education courses or that operates or sponsors interscholastic, club, or intramural athletics shall provide to qualified handicapped students an equal opportunity for participation in these activities.

(2) A recipient may offer to handicapped students physical education and athletic activities that are separate or different from those offered to nonhandicapped students only if separation or differentiation is consistent with the requirements of Sec. 104.34 and only if no qualified handicapped student is denied the opportunity to compete for teams or to participate in courses that are not separate or different.

Sec. 104.38 Preschool and adult education programs

A recipient to which this subpart applies that operates a preschool education or day care program or activity or an adult education program or activity may not, on the basis of handicap, exclude qualified handicapped persons from the program or activity and shall take into account the needs of such persons in determining the aid, benefits, or services to be provided under the program or activity.

Sec.104.39 Private education programs

(a) A recipient that operates a private elementary or secondary education program may not, on the basis of handicap, exclude a qualified handicapped person from such program if the person can, with minor adjustments, be provided an appropriate education, as defined in Sec. 104.33(b)(1), within the recipient's program

(b) A recipient to which this section applies may not charge more for the provision of an appropriate education to handicapped persons than to nonhandicapped persons except to the extent that any additional charge is justified by a substantial increase in cost to the recipient.

(c) A recipient to which this section applies that operates special education programs shall operate such programs in accordance with the provisions of Secs. 104.35 and 104.36. Each recipient to which this section applies is subject to the provisions of Secs. 104.34, 104.37, and 104.38. ■

Appendix 2

Federal and State Departments of Education

Federal Department of Education Offices

The federal Department of Education, Office of Special Education, has the responsibility to ensure that all states meet the requirments of IDEA. For information on IDEA, contact the DOE at:

> U.S. Department of Education
> Office of Special Education and Rehabilitation
>   Services
> 330 C Street, SW
> Washington, DC 20202
> 202-205-5507 (voice)
> 202-205-9252 (fax)
> http://www.ed.gov/offices/OSERS (Website)

The federal Department of Education, Office for Civil Rights, is one place to file a complaint for IDEA violations. You can contact any of the following OCR offices:

Main Office

> U.S. Department of Education
> Office for Civil Rights
> 330 C Street, SW
> Washington, DC 20202
> 202-205-5413 (voice)
> 800-421-3481 (voice)
> 202-205-5166 (TDD)
> 202-205-9862 (fax)
> ocr@ed.gov (e-mail)
> http://www.ed.gov/offices/OCR (Website)

Connecticut, Maine, Massachusetts, New Hampshire, Rhode Island, Vermont

> U.S. Department of Education
> Office for Civil Rights
> J. W. McCormack Post Office and Courthouse
> Room 222, 01-0061
> Boston, MA 02109-4557
> 617-223-9662 (voice)
> 617-223-9695 (TDD)
> 617-223-9669 (fax)
> ocr_boston@ed.gov (e-mail)

New Jersey, New York

> U.S. Department of Education
> Office for Civil Rights
> 75 Park Place, 14th Floor
> New York, NY 10007-2146
> 212-637-6466 (voice)
> 212-637-0478 (TDD)
> 212-264-3803 (fax)
> ocr_newyork@ed.gov (e-mail)

Delaware, Kentucky, Maryland, Pennsylvania, West Virginia

> U.S. Department of Education
> Office for Civil Rights
> Wanamaker Building, Suite 515
> 100 Penn Square East
> Philadelphia, PA 19107
> 215-656-8541 (voice)
> 215-656-8604 (TDD)
> 215-656-8605 (fax)
> ocr_philadelphia@ed.gov (e-mail)

Alabama, Florida, Georgia, South Carolina, Tennessee

> Office for Civil Rights, Atlanta Office
> U.S. Department of Education
> 61 Forsyth St. SW, Suite 19T70
> Atlanta, GA 30303-3104
> 404-562-6350 (voice)
> 404-331-7236 (TDD)
> 404-562-6455 (fax)
> ocr_atlanta@ed.gov (e-mail)

Arkansas, Louisiana, Mississippi, Oklahoma, Texas

> U.S. Department of Education
> Office for Civil Rights
> 1999 Bryan Street, Suite 2600
> Dallas, TX 75201
> 214-880-2459 (voice)
> 214-880-2456 (TDD)
> 214-880-3082 (fax)
> ocr_dallas@ed.gov (e-mail)

District of Columbia, North Carolina, Virginia

U.S. Department of Education
Office for Civil Rights
1100 Pennsylvania Ave, NW, Rm. 316
P.O. Box 14620
Washington, DC 20044-4620
202-208-2545 (voice)
202-208-7741 (TDD)
202-208-7797 (fax)
ocr@ed.gov (e-mail)

Illinois, Indiana, Minnesota, Wisconsin

U.S. Department of Education
Office for Civil Rights
111 N. Canal Street, Suite 1053
Chicago, IL 60606-7204
312-886-8434 (voice)
312-353-2540 (TDD)
312-353-4888 (fax)
ocr_chicago@ed.gov (e-mail)

Michigan, Ohio

U.S. Department of Education
Office for Civil Rights
600 Superior Avenue East
Bank One Center, Room 750
Cleveland, OH 44114-2611
216-522-4970 (voice)
216-522-4944 (TDD)
216-522-2573 (fax)
ocr_cleveland@ed.gov (e-mail)

Iowa, Kansas, Missouri, Nebraska, North Dakota, South Dakota

U.S. Department of Education
Office for Civil Rights
10220 North Executive Hills Boulevard
8th Floor, 07-6010
Kansas City, MO 64153-1367
816-880-4200 (voice)
816-891-0582 (TDD)
816-891-0644 (fax)
ocr_kansascity@ed.gov (e-mail)

Arizona, Colorado, Montana, New Mexico, Utah, Wyoming

U.S. Department of Education
Office for Civil Rights
Federal Building, Suite 310, 08-7010
1244 Speer Boulevard
Denver, CO 80204-3582
303-844-5695 (voice)
303-844-3417 (TDD)
303-844-4303 (fax)
ocr_denver@ed.gov (e-mail)

California

U.S. Department of Education
Office for Civil Rights
Old Federal Building, 09-8010
50 United Nations Plaza, Room 239
San Francisco, CA 94102-4102
415-437-7700 (voice)
415-437-7786 (TDD)
415-437-7783 (fax)
ocr_sanfrancisco@ed.gov (e-mail)

Alaska, Hawaii, Idaho, Nevada, Oregon, Washington

U.S. Department of Education
Office for Civil Rights
915 Second Avenue
Room 3310, 10-9010
Seattle, WA 98174-1099
206-220-7900 (voice)
206-220-7907 (TDD)
206-220-7887 (fax)
ocr_seattle@ed.gov (e-mail)

State Department of Education Offices

Your state department of education is the place to go to find legislation, curriculum material or information on state special education programs as well as information about the IDEA and its requirements.

Alabama

Alabama Department of Education
Division of Special Education Services
(Gordon Persons Building)
P.O. Box 302101
Montgomery, AL 36130-2101
334-242-8114 (voice)
334-242-9708 (fax)
http://www.alsde.edu (Website)

Alaska

Alaska Department of Education
Office of Special and Supplemental Services
801 W. 10th Street, Suite 200
Juneau, AK 99801-1894
907-465-2971 (voice)
907-465-3396 (fax)
http://www.educ.state.ak.us (Website)

Arizona

Arizona Department of Education
Office of Special Education
1535 W. Jefferson
Phoenix, AZ 85007-3280
602-542-3084 (voice)
602-542-3073 (fax)
http://www.ade.state.az.us (Website)

Arkansas

Arkansas Department of Education
Office of Special Education
Education Building, Room 105-C
#4 Capitol Mall
Little Rock, AR 72201-1071
501-682-4221 (voice)
501-682-4313 (fax)
http://arkedu.state.ar.us (Website)

California

California Department of Education
Office of Special Education
721 Capitol Mall
Sacramento, CA 95814
916-445-4613 (voice)
916-657-4975 (fax)
http://goldmine.cde.ca.gov (Website)

Colorado

Colorado Department of Education
Special Education Services Unit
201 E. Colfax
Denver, CO 80203
303-866-6697 (voice)
303-830-0793 (fax)
http://www.cde.state.co.us (Website)

Connecticut

Connecticut Department of Education
Bureau of Special Education and Pupil
  Personnel Services
25 Industrial Park Road
Middletown, CT 06457
860-638-4265 (voice)
860-632-1854 (fax)
http://www.state.ct.us/sde (Website)

Delaware

Delaware Department of Public Instruction
Exceptional Children Team
Townsend Building
P.O. Box 1402
Dover, DE 19903
302-739-4371 (voice)
302-739-4654 (fax)
http://www.dpi.state.de.us (Website)

District of Columbia

District of Columbia
Office of Special Education, Groding School
10th & F Street, NE
Washington, DC 20002
202-724-4800 (voice)
202-724-5116 (fax)

Florida

Florida Education Center
Bureau of Education for Exceptional Students
325 W. Gaines Street, Suite 614
Tallahassee, FL 32399-0400
904-488-1570 (voice)
904-413-0378 (fax)
http://www.firn.edu/doe (Website)

Georgia

Georgia Department of Education
Division for Exceptional Children
1952 Twin Towers East
205 Butler Street
Atlanta, GA 30334-5040
404-656-3963 (voice)
404-651-8737 (fax)
http://www.doe.k12.ga.us (Website)

Hawaii

Hawaii Department of Education
Special Education Section
3430 Leahi Avenue
Honolulu, HI 96815
808-733-4990 (voice)
808-586-3234 (fax)
http://www.k12.hi.us (Website)

Idaho

Idaho Department of Education
Special Education Section
P.O. Box 83720
Boise, ID 83720-0027
208-332-6910 (voice)
208-334-2228 (fax)
http://www.sde.state.id.us (Website)

Illinois

Illinois State Board of Education
Department of Special Education
Mail Code E-216, 100 North First Street
Springfield, IL 62777-0001
217-524-0713 (voice)
217-524-8585 (fax)
http://www.isbe.state.il.us (Website)

Indiana

Indiana Department of Education
Division of Special Education
Room 229, State House
Indianapolis, IN 46204-2798
317-232-0570 (voice)
317-233-6502 (fax)
http://ideanet.doe.state.in.us (Website)

Iowa

Iowa Department of Public Instruction
Bureau of Special Education
200 East Grand Avenue
Des Moines, IA 50309
515-281-5735 (voice)
515-242-5988 (fax)
http://www.state.ia.us/educate/depteduc/
    index.html (Website)

Kansas

Kansas State Board of Education
Special Education Outcomes Team
120 SE Tenth Street
Topeka, KS 66612-1182
913-296-4946 (voice)
913-296-7933 (fax)
http://www.ksbe.state.ks.us (Website)

Kentucky

Kentucky Department of Education
Division of Exceptional Children's Services
500 Mero Street, Room 805
Frankfort, KY 40601
502-564-3301 (voice)
502-564-5680 (fax)
http://www.kde.state.ky.us (Website)

Louisiana

Louisiana Department of Education
Office of Special Education Services
P.O. Box 94064
626 N. Fourth Street, 9th Floor
Baton Rouge, LA 70804-9064
504-342-3631 (voice)
504-342-7316 (fax)
http://www.doe.state.la.us (Website)

Maine

Maine Department of Education
Division of Special Education
Station #23
Augusta, ME 04333
207-287-5310 (voice)
207-287-5900 (fax)
http://www.state.me.us/education (Website)

Maryland

Maryland State Department of Education
Division of Special Education
200 W. Baltimore Street, 4th Floor
Baltimore, MD 21201-2595
410-767-0238 (voice)
410-333-6033 (fax)
http://www.msde.state.md.us (Website)

Massachusetts

Massachusetts Department of Education
Program Quality Assurance
350 Main Street
Malden, MA 02148-5023
617-388-3300 (voice)
617-388-3394 (fax)
http://doe.mass.edu (Website)

Michigan

Michigan Department of Education
Special Education Services
P.O. Box 30008
Lansing, MI 48909-7508
517-373-9433 (voice)
517-335-4565 (fax)
http://www.mde.stae.mi.us (Website)

Minnesota

Minnesota Department of Education
Special Education Section
811 Capitol Square Building
550 Cedar Street
St. Paul, MN 55101-2233
612-296-1793 (voice)
612-297-7368 (fax)
http://children.state.mn.us (Website)

Mississippi

Mississippi Department of Education
Office of Special Services
P.O. Box 771
Jackson, MS 39205-0771
601-359-3498 (voice)
601-359-2326 (fax)
http://mdek12.state.ms.us (Website)

Missouri

Missouri Department of Elementary and Secondary
  Education
Special Education Programs
P.O. Box 480
205 Jefferson Street
Jefferson City, MO 65102-0480
573-751-2965 (voice)
573-526-4404 (fax)
http://services.dese.state.mo.us (Website)

Montana

Montana Office of Public Instruction
Division of Special Education
P.O. Box 202510
State Capitol, Room 106
Helena, MT 59620-2501
406-444-4429 (voice)
406-444-2893 (fax)
http://161.7.114.15/OPI/opi.htm (Website)

Nebraska

Nebraska Department of Education
Office of Special Education
Box 94987
301 Centennial Mall South
Lincoln, NE 68509-4987
402-471-2471 (voice)
402-471-0117 (fax)
http://www.nde.state.ne.us (Website)

Nevada

Nevada Department of Education
Special Education Branch
Capitol Complex
440 W. King Street
Carson City, NV 89701-5096
702-687-9142 (voice)
702-687-9101 (fax)
http://www.nsn.k12.nv.us/nvdoe (Website)

New Hampshire

New Hampshire Department of Education
Bureau for Special Education Services
101 Pleasant Street
Concord, NH 03301-3860
603-271-6693 (voice)
603-271-3454 (fax)
http://www.state.nh.us.doe/education.html
  (Website)

New Jersey

New Jersey Department of Education
Division of Special Education
CN 500
Trenton, NJ 08625-0500
609-292-8066 (voice)
609-777-4099 (fax)
http://www.state.nj.us.education/ (Website)

New Mexico

New Mexico Department of Education
Office of Special Education
300 Don Gasper Avenue
Sante Fe, NM 87501-2786
505-827-6696 (voice)
505-827-6791 (fax)
http://sde.state.nm.us (Website)

New York

New York State Education Department
Office for Special Education Services
1624 One Commerce Plaza
Albany, NY 12234-0001
518-474-5548 (voice)
518-474-8802 (fax)
http://www.nysed.gov (Website)

North Carolina

North Carolina Department of Public Instruction
Division of Exceptional Children's Services
301 N. Wilmington Street
Raleigh, NC 27601-2825
919-715-1506 (voice)
919-715-2237 (fax)
http://www.dpi.state.nc.us (Website)

North Dakota

North Dakota Department of Public Instruction
Office of Special Education
600 E. Boulevard
Bismarck, ND 58505-0440
701-328-2277 (voice)
701-328-2461 (fax)
http://www.dpi.state.nd.us (Website)

Ohio

Ohio Department of Education
Division of Special Education
933 High Street
Worthington, OH 43085-4087
614-466-2650 (voice)
614-728-1097 (fax)
http://www.ode.ohio.gov (Website)

Oklahoma

Oklahoma Department of Education
Special Education Section
2500 N. Lincoln Blvd., Suite 411
Oklahoma City, OK 73105-4599
405-521-3351 (voice)
405-521-3502 (fax)
http://www.sde.state.ok.us (Website)

Oregon

Oregon Department of Education
Special Education and Student Services Division
Public Service Building
255 Capitol NE
Salem, OR 97310-0290
503-378-3598 (voice)
503-373-7968 (fax)
http://www.ode.state.or.us (Website)

Pennsylvania

Pennsylvania Department of Education
Bureau of Special Education
333 Market Street, 7th Floor
Harrisburg, PA 17126-6802
717-783-6913 (voice)
717-783-6802 (fax)
http://www.pde.psu.edu/ (Website)

Rhode Island

Rhode Island Department of Education
Office of Special Needs
Shepard Building
255 Westminster Street
Providence, RI 02903
401-277-6030 (voice)
401-277-6178 (fax)
http://instruct.ride.ri.net (Website)

South Carolina

South Carolina Department of Education
Office of Programs for Exceptional Children
Rutledge Building
1429 Senate Street, Room 808
Columbia, SC 29201
803-734-8806 (voice)
803-734-6142 (fax)
http://www.state.sc.us/sde (Website)

South Dakota

South Dakota Department of Education & Cultural
  Affairs
Office of Special Education
700 Governors Drive
Pierre, SD 57501-2291
605-773-3678 (voice)
605-773-6139 (fax)
http://www.state.sd.us/state/executive/deca (Website)

Tennessee

Tennessee Department of Education
Special Education Programs
Gateway Plaza
710 James Robertson Parkway, 8th Floor
Nashville, TN 37243-0380
615-741-2851 (voice)
615-532-8536 (fax)
http://www.state.tn.us/education (Website)

Texas

Texas Education Agency
Special Education Unit
1701 N. Congress
Austin, TX 78701-2486
512-463-9414 (voice)
512-463-9008 (fax)
http://www.tea.state.tx.us (Website)

Utah

Utah State Office of Education
At-Risk and Special Education Services Unit
250 E. 500 South
Salt Lake City, UT 84111-3204
801-538-7706 (voice)
801-538-7521 (fax)
http://www.usoe.k12.ut.us (Website)

Vermont

Vermont Department of Education
Division of Special Education
State Office Building
120 State Street
Montpelier, VT 05620-2501
802-828-3141 (voice)
802-828-3140 (fax)
http://www.state.vt.us/educ (Website)

Virginia

Virginia Department of Education
Division of Pre & Early Adolescent Education
Special Education Unit
P.O. Box 2120
Richmond, VA 23216-2120
804-225-2402 (voice)
804-371-0154 (fax)
http://www.pen.k12.va.us (Website)

Washington

Washington Department of Public Instruction
Special Education Section
P.O. Box 47200
Olympia, WA 98504-7200
360-753-6733 (voice)
360-586-6172 (fax)
http://www.ospi.wednet.edu (Website)

West Virginia

West Virginia Department of Education
Office of Special Education
Building #6
1900 Kanawha Boulevard, Room B-304
Charleston, WV 25305
304-558-2696 (voice)
304-558-0048 (fax)

Wisconsin

Wisconsin Department of Public Instruction
Division of Handicapped Children and Pupil Services
P.O. Box 7841
125 S. Webster
Madison, WI 53707-7841
608-266-1649 (voice)
608-267-1052 (fax)
http://www.dpi.state.wi.us (Website)

Wyoming

Wyoming Department of Education
Special Education Unit
Hathaway Building
2300 Capitol Avenue, 2nd Floor
Cheyenne, WY 82002-0052
307-777-7417 (voice)
307-777-6234 (fax)
http://www.k12.wy.us (Website)

Appendix 3

Support Groups, Advocacy Organizations and Other Resources

General Resources for Parents of a Special Education Child

Adapted Physical Education National Standards

Curry School of Education
University of Virginia
Charlottesville, VA 22903
804-924-3334 (voice)
804-924-0888 (fax)
lek@virginia.edu (e-mail)
http://teach.virginia.edu/go/apens/home.html
   (Website)

Ensures that physical education instruction for students with disabilities is provided by qualified physical education instructors. The project has developed national standards for the profession and a national certification examination to measure knowledge of these standards.

American Council on Rural Special Education

Kansas State University
2323 Anderson Avenue, Suite 226
Manhattan, KS 66502
785-532-2737 (voice)
785-532-7732 (fax)
acres@ksu.edu (e-mail)
http://www. ksu.ksu.edu/acres (Website)

Provides support and information to families of special education children living in rural America. ACRES publishes a national journal called the Rural Special Education Quarterly, and maintains an archive of article abstracts on its Website. ACRES also publishes a bimonthly newsletter called RuraLink.

Child and Family Studies Program

Allegheny University of the Health Sciences
One Allegheny Center, Suite 510
Pittsburgh, PA 15212
412-359-1600 (voice)
412-359-1601 (fax)
salisbur@pgh.auhs.edu (e-mail)
http://www.asri.edu/cfsp (Website)

Has a mission to enhance the overall quality of life for children who are at-risk for, or who experience, developmental disabilities, and

their families. The Website includes information on CFSP projects, including:

- Action Research Network Listserv (ARNet) —to promote communication among practitioners, administrators, researchers and consumers about action research and other participatory approaches to improving teaching, learning and educational supports for all children.
- Consortium on Inclusive Schooling Practices (CISP)—to build the capacity of state and local education agencies to serve children and youth with and without disabilities in school and community settings. The focus of the project is on systemic reform, not just changes in special education systems.
- Disability/Exceptionality Web Resource Library
- Principals' Project—to describe, enhance and replicate effective strategies for ensuring that students with disabilities are integrally included as part of building-wide school improvement and reform initiatives and are accommodated accordingly.

Education Development Center, Inc.

55 Chapel Street
Newton, MA 02458-1060
617-969-7100 (voice)
617-969-5979 (fax)
617-964-5448 (TTY)
http://www.edc.org/FSC/NCIP (Website)

Promotes the effective use of technology to enhance educational outcomes for students with sensory, cognitive, physical and social/ emotional disabilities. The Website includes:

- NCIPnet—facilitated discussions about technology use for students with disabilities
- Various "Spotlights"—such as exploring the ins and outs of using voice recognition technology to address writing difficulties
- NCIP Library—resources about technology and special education, and
- Video Profiles—videos of students using assistive and instructional technologies.

ERIC Clearinghouse on Disabilities and Gifted Education

The Council for Exceptional Children
1920 Association Drive
Reston, VA 20191-1598
703-264-9474 (voice)
800-328-0272 (voice)
703-620-2521 (fax)
703-264-9449 (TTY)
ericec@cec.sped.org (e-mail)
http://www.cec.sped.org/ericec.htm (Website)

Provides a variety of services and products on a broad range of education-related issues. The AskERIC forum is a personalized Internet-based service providing education information to teachers, librarians, counselors, administrators, parents and others. You can search ERIC's extensive database. A search of "IEP," for example, returned 250 documents.

Family.com

http://family.disney.com/ (Website)

Is an Internet site with information on nearly 100 articles, including:

- Mainstreaming Special Needs Kids
- How Can I Help My Child in School?
- Extra-Special Education
- How Kids' Learning Styles Differ
- Librarians: How They Help Your Kids
- When Should a Struggling Child Repeat a Grade?
- Inclusion in the Schools: A Team Effort
- ADD in the Classroom
- Educating a Learning Disabled Child
- Gifted but Learning Disabled: A Puzzling Paradox
- What's So Special About Special Education?
- Obtaining a Free Appropriate Public Education (FAPE)
- Constructing a Culturally Sensitive Education for Gifted Deaf Students

Family Education Network

Visitor Support
Family Education Company
20 Park Plaza, Suite 1215
Boston, MA 02116
617-542-6500, ext. 127 (voice)
617-542-6564 (fax)
support@familyeducation.com (e-mail)
http://familyeducation.com (Website)

Includes information on learning disabilities and children with special needs. Website features include a monthly column by a special education lawyer, "Ask the Expert"—what their expert has to say about learning issues, resources and special education news.

Federal Resource Center for Special Education

1875 Connecticut Avenue, NW, Suite 900
Washington, DC 20009
202-884-8215 (voice)
202-884-8443 (fax)
800-695-0285 (TDD)
frc@aed.org (e-mail)
http://www.dssc.org/frc (Website)

Supports a nationwide special education technical assistance network (funded by the U.S. Department of Education's Office of Special Education and Rehabilitative Services), plans national meetings of education professionals, provides a national perspective for establishing technical assistance activities across regions by identifying emerging issues and trends in special education, and assists in linking Regional Resource Centers with each other and with other technical assistance providers.

The Website includes the text of certain federal regulations, a list of links to disabled organizations, publications including the RRFC Links Online Newsletter and proceedings of certain government conferences.

Federation for Children With Special Needs Parent Training and Information Centers (PTI)

The U.S. Department of Education, Office of Special Education Programs, works with the Federation for Children With Special Needs to fund organized parent-to-parent programs. The work is done locally through programs known as Parent Training and Information (PTI) Centers. PTI Centers enable parents to participate more effectively with professionals in meeting the educational needs of children with disabilities. You can contact the Federation or a local PTI for information; PTI online information is available through the Federation's Website.

Federation for Children with Special Needs

95 Berkeley Street, Suite 104
Boston, MA 02116
617-482-2915 (voice/TDD)
800-331-0688 (voice—Massachusetts only)
617-695-2939 (fax)
fcsninfo@fcsn.org (e-mail)
http://www.fcsn.org (Website)

PTI Center—Alabama

Special Education Action Committee, Inc.
600 Bel Air Blvd., #210
Mobile, AL 36606-3501
334-478-1208 (voice)
800-222-7322 (voice)
334-473-7877 (fax)
seacmob1@juno.com (e-mail)

PTI Center—Alaska

Alaska PARENTS Resource Center
4743 E. Northern Lights Blvd.
Anchorage, AK 99508
907-337-7678 (voice)
800-478-7678 (voice—Alaska only)
907-337-7671 (fax)
parents@alaska.net (e-mail)

PTI Center—Arizona

Pilot Parent Partnerships
4750 N. Black Canyon Hwy., Suite 101
Phoenix, AZ 85017
602-242-4366 (voice)
800-237-3007 (voice)
602-242-4306 (fax)

PTI Center—Arkansas

FOCUS, Inc.
305 W. Jefferson Avenue
Jonesboro, AR 72401
501-935-2750 (voice)
501-221-1330 (voice/TDD)
501-931-3755 (fax)
focusinc@ipa.net (e-mail)

PTI Center—Arkansas

Arkansas Disability Coalition
2801 Lee Avenue, Suite B
Little Rock, AR 72205
501-614-7020 (voice/TDD)
501-614-9082 (fax)
adc@cei.net (e-mail)

PTI Center—California

Teams of Advocates for Special Kids, Inc. (TASK)
100 West Cerritos Avenue
Anaheim, CA 92805-6546
714-533-8275 (voice)
714-533-2533 (fax)
taskca@aol.com (e-mail)

PTI Center—California

Disability Rights Education and Defense Fund, Inc.
2212 Sixth Street
Berkeley, CA 94710
510-644-2555 (voice and TTD)
510-841-8645 (fax)
dredf@dredf.org (e-mail)

PTI Center—California

Exceptional Parents Unlimited
4120 North First Street
Fresno, CA 93726
209-229-2000 (voice)
209-229-2956 (fax)
epu@cybergate.com (e-mail)

PTI Center—California

Loving Your Disabled Child
4715 Crenshaw Blvd.
Los Angeles, CA 90043
213-299-2925 (voice)
213-299-4373 (fax)
lydc@pacbell.net (e-mail)

PTI Center—California

Support for Families of Children With Disabilities
2601 Mission Street, Suite 710
San Francisco, CA 94110-3111
415-282-7494 (voice)
415-282-1226 (fax)
sfcdmission@aol.com (e-mail)

PTI Center—California

Matrix, A Parent Network and Resource Center
94 Galli Drive, Suite C
Novato, CA 94949
415-884-3535 (voice)
415-884-3555 (fax)
matrix@matrixparents.org (e-mail)

PTI Center—California

Parents Helping Parents
3041 Olcott Street
Santa Clara, CA 95054-3222
408-727-5775 (voice)
408-727-7655 (voice)
408-727-7227 (Lincs)
408-727-0182 (fax)
info@php.com (e-mail)

PTI Center—Colorado

PEAK Parent Center, Inc.
6055 Lehman Drive, Suite 101
Colorado Springs, CO 80918
719-531-9400 (voice)
800-284-0251 (voice)
719-531-9403 (TTD)
719-531-9452 (fax)
pkparent@aol.com (e-mail)

PTI Center—Connecticut

Connecticut Parent Advocacy Center, Inc.
338 Main Street
Niantic, CT 06357
860-739-3089 (voice)
800-445-2722 (voice—Connecticut only)
860-739-7460 (fax)
cpacinc@aol.com (e-mail)

PTI Center—Delaware

Parent Information Center
700 Barksdale Road, Suite 3
Newark, DE 19711
302-366-0152 (voice)
302-366-0178 (TTD)
302-366-0276 (fax)
pep700@aol.com (e-mail)

PTI Center—District of Columbia

COPE Experimental Parent Center
300 I Street, NE, Suite 112
Washington, DC 20002
202-543-6482 (voice)
800-515-2673 (voice)
202-855-1234 (TTY)
202-543-6682 (fax)
cope@erols.com (e-mail)

PTI Center—Florida

Family Network on Disabilities
2735 Whitney Road
Clearwater, FL 33760
813-523-1130 (voice/TDD)
800-825-5736 (voice—Florida only)
813-523-8687 (fax)
fnd@gate.net (e-mail)

PTI Center—Georgia

Parent Educating Parents and Professionals for All
   Children
8313 Durelee Lane, Suite 101
Douglasville, GA 30134
770-577-7771 (voice/TDD)
770-577-7774 (fax)
peppac@bellsouth.net (e-mail)

PTI Center—Hawaii

AWARE
200 North Vineyard Blvd., Suite 310
Honolulu, HI 96817
808-536-9864 (voice/TDD)
808-536-2280 (voice)
808-537-6780 (fax)
ldah@gte.net (e-mail)

PTI Center—Idaho

Idaho Parents Unlimited, Inc.
Parent Education Resource Center
4696 Overland Road, Suite 478
Boise, ID 83705
208-342-5884 (voice/TDD)
800-242-4785 (voice)
208-342-1408 (fax)
ipul@rmci.net (e-mail)

PTI Center—Illinois

Family Resource Center on Disabilities
20 East Jackson Blvd., Suite 900
Chicago, IL 60604
312-939-3513 (voice)
312-939-3519 (TDD/TTY)
312-939-7297 (fax)

PTI Center—Indiana

Indiana Resource Center for Families With Special
   Needs
809 N. Michigan Street
South Bend, IN 46601
219-234-7107 (voice)
800-322-4433 (voice—Indiana only)
219-234-7279 (fax)
insour@speced.doe.state.in.us (e-mail)

PTI Center—Iowa

SEEK Parent Center
406 SW School Street, Suite 207
Ankeny, IA 50021
515-965-0155 (voice)
888-431-4332 (voice—Iowa only)
515-276-8470 (fax)

PTI Center—Kansas

Families Together, Inc.
3340 W. Douglas, Suite 102
Wichita, KS 67203
316-945-7747 (voice)
888-815-6364 (voice—Iowa only)
316-945-1195 (fax)
fmin@feist.com (e-mail)

PTI Center—Kentucky

Family Training and Information Center
2210 Goldsmith Lane, Suite 118
Louisville, KY 40218
502-456-0923 (voice)
800-525-7746 (voice)
502-456-0893 (fax)
familytrng@aol.com (e-mail)

PTI Center—Louisiana

Program of Families Helping Families of Greater
  New Orleans: Project PROMPT
4323 Division Street, Suite 110
Metairie, LA 70002-3179
504-888-9111 (voice)
800-766-7736 (voice)
504-888-0246 (fax)
lafhforg@iamerica.net (e-mail)

PTI Center—Maine

Special Needs Parents Information Network (SPIN)
P.O. Box 2067
Augusta, ME 04330-2067
207-582-2540 (voice)
800-870-7746 (voice—Maine only)
207-582-3638 (fax)
info@mpf.org (e-mail)

PTI Center—Maryland

Parents Place of Maryland, Inc.
7257 Parkway Drive, Suite 210
Hanover, MD 21076
410-712-0900 (voice/TDD)
410-712-0902 (fax)
parplace@aol.com (e-mail)

PTI Center—Massachusetts

95 Berkeley Street, Suite 104
Boston, MA 02116
617-482-2915 (voice/TDD)
800-331-0688 (voice—Massachusetts only)
617-695-2939 (fax)
fcsninfo@fcsn.org (e-mail)

PTI Center—Michigan

Citizens Alliance to Uphold Special Education
  (CAUSE)
3303 W. Saginaw Street, Suite F1
Lansing, MI 48917-2303
517-886-9167 (voice/TDD)
800-221-9105 (voice—Michigan only)
517-886-9775 (fax)

PTI Center—Michigan

Parents Are Experts: Parents Training Parents Project
23077 Greenfield Road, Suite 205
Southfield, MI 48075-3744
248-557-5070 (voice/TDD)
248-557-4456 (fax)
ucpdetroit@aol.com (e-mail)

PTI Center—Minnesota

PACER Center, Inc.
4826 Chicago Avenue South
Minneapolis, MN 55417
612-827-2966 (voice)
612-827-7770 (TTY)
888-248-0822 (voice—nationwide)
612-827-3065 (fax)
pacer@pacer.org (e-mail)

PTI Center—Mississippi

Parent Partners
3111 N. State Street
Jackson, MS 39216
601-366-5707 (voice)
601-362-7361 (fax)
ptiofms@misnet.com (e-mail)

PTI Center—Missouri

Missouri Parents Act (MPACT)
208 East High Street, Suite I
Jefferson City, MO 65101
573-635-1189 (voice/TDD)
800-743-7634 (voice—Missouri only)
573-635-7802 (fax)

PTI Center—Missouri

Parent Education and Advocacy Resource Support
  Project (PEARS)
MPACT—Kansas City
1 West Armour, Suite 301
Kansas City, MO 64111
816-531-7070 (voice)
816-531-4777 (fax)
mpactcs@coop.crn.org (e-mail)

PTI Center—Montana

Parents Let's Unite for Kids (PLUK)
1500 North 30th Street, Suite 267
Billings, MT 59101-0298
406-657-2055 (voice)
800-222-7585 (voice—Montana only)
406-657-2061 (fax)
plukmt@wtp.org (e-mail)

PTI Center—Nebraska

Nebraska Parents' Center
1941 South 42nd Street, Suite 122
Omaha, NE 68105-2942
402-346-0525 (voice/TDD)
800-284-8520 (voice)
402-346-5253 (fax)
npc@uswest.ne.net (e-mail)

PTI Center—Nevada

Nevada PEP
601 S. Rancho Drive, Suite C25
Las Vegas, NV 89106
702-388-8899 (voice/TDD)
800-216-5188 (voice)
702-388-2966 (fax)
nvpep@vegas.infi.net (e-mail)

PTI Center—New Hampshire

Parent Information Center
151A Manchester Street
P.O. Box 2405
Concord, NH 03302-1422
603-224-7005 (voice/TDD)
800-232-0986 (voice—New Hampshire only)
603-224-4365 (fax)
picnh@aol.com (e-mail)

PTI Center—New Jersey

Statewide Parent Advocacy Network, Inc. (SPAN)
35 Halsey Street, 4th Floor
Newark, NJ 07102

973-642-8100 (voice)
800-654-7726 (voice)
973-642-7880 (fax)
autind@aol.com (e-mail)

PTI Center—New Mexico

EPIC Project
S.W. Communication Resources, Inc.
P.O. Box 788
412 Don Tomas
Bernalillo, NM 87004
505-867-3396 (voice/TDD)
800-765-7320 (voice/TDD)
505-867-3398 (fax)
epics@highfiver.com (e-mail)

PTI Center—New Mexico

Parents Reaching Out (PRO)
Project ADOBE
1000A Main Street, NW
Los Lunas, NM 87031
505-865-3700 (voice/TDD)
800-524-5176 (voice—New Mexico only)
505-865-3737 (fax)
sallievc@aol.com (e-mail)

PTI Center—New York

Advocates for Children of New York, Inc.
105 Court Street
Brooklyn, NY 11201
718-624-8450 (voice)
718-624-1260 (fax)
advocat1@idt.com (e-mail)

PTI Center—New York

Parent Network Center
452 Delaware Avenue, Third Floor
Buffalo, NY 14202-1515
716-853-1570 (voice)
716-853-1573 (TDD)
800-724-7408 (voice—New York only)
716-853-1574 (fax)

PTI Center—New York

Resources for Children With Special Needs
200 Park Avenue South, Suite 816
New York, NY 10003
212-677-4650 (voice)
212-254-4070 (fax)
resourcesnyc@prodigy.net (e-mail)

PTI Center—New York

Upstate New York Training and Education Advocacy
  Center, Inc.
277 Alexander Street, Suite 500
Rochester, NY 14607
716-546-1700 (voice)
716-546-7069 (fax)
advocacy@frontiernet.net (e-mail)

PTI Center—North Carolina

Exceptional Children's Assistance Center
P.O. Box 16
Davidson, NC 28036
704-892-1321 (voice)
800-962-6817 (voice—North Carolina only)
704-892-5028 (fax)
ecac1@aol.com (e-mail)

PTI Center—North Dakota

Pathfinder Family Center
Arrowhead Shopping Center
1600 Second Avenue, SW
Minot, ND 58701
701-852-9426 (voice)
701-852-9436 (TDD)
701-838-9324 (fax)
ndpath01@minot.ndak.net (e-mail)

PTI Center—Ohio

Child Advocacy Center
1821 Summit Road, Suite 303
Cincinnati, OH 45237
513-821-2400 (voice/TDD)
513-821-2442 (fax)
cadcenter@aol.com (e-mail)

PTI Center—Ohio

Ohio Coalition for the Education of Children With
  Disabilities
Bank One Building
165 West Center Street, Suite 302
Marion, OH 43302-3741
740-382-5452 (voice/TDD)
800-374-2806 (voice—Ohio only)
740-383-6421 (fax)
ocecd@edu.gte.net (e-mail)

PTI Center—Oklahoma

Parents Reaching Out in Oklahoma
1817 South Harvard Avenue
Oklahoma City, OK 73128

405-681-9710 (voice/TDD)
800-759-4142 (voice)
405-685-4006 (fax)
prook1@aol.com (e-mail)

PTI Center—Oregon

Oregon COPE Project
999 Locust Street, NE
Box B
Salem, OR 97303
503-581-8156 (voice/TDD)
888-505-2673 (voice)
503-391-0429 (fax)
orcope@open.org (e-mail)

PTI Center—Pennsylvania

Parents Union for Public Schools
311 So. Juniper Street, Suite 602
Philadelphia, PA 19107
215-546-1166 (voice)
215-731-1688 (fax)
parentsu@aol.com (e-mail)

PTI Center—Pennsylvania

Parent Education Network
333 East Seventh Avenue
York, PA 17404
717-845-9722 (voice/TDD)
800-522-5827 (voice—Pennsylvania only)
800-441-5028 (Spanish voice—Pennsylvania only)
717-848-3654 (fax)
pen@parentednet.org (e-mail)

PTI Center—Rhode Island

Rhode Island Parent Information Center
500 Prospect Street
Pawtucket, RI 02860
401-727-4144 (voice)
401-727-4151 (TDD)
800-464-3399 (voice—Rhode Island only)
401-727-4040 (fax)

PTI Center—South Carolina

PRO Parents
2712 Middleburg Drive, Suite 102
Columbia, SC 29204
803-779-3859 (voice/TDD)
800-759-4776 (voice—South Carolina only)
803-252-4513 (fax)
proparents@aol.com (e-mail)

PTI Center—South Dakota

South Dakota Parent Connection
3701 W. 49th, Suite 299B
Sioux Falls, SD 57106
605-361-3171 (voice/TDD)
800-640-4553 (voice—South Dakota only)
605-361-2928 (fax)
jdieh@sdparentconnection.com (e-mail)

PTI Center—Tennessee

Support & Training for Exceptional Parents (STEP)
424 Bernard Avenue, Suite 3
Greenville, TN 37745
423-639-2464 (voice)
800-280-7837 (voice—Tennessee only)
423-636-8217 (fax)
tnstep@aol.com (e-mail)

PTI Center—Texas

Partners Resource Network, Inc./PATH
1090 Longfellow Drive, Suite B
Beaumont, TX 77706-4889
409-898-4684 (voice/TDD)
800-866-4726
409-898-4869 (fax)
Tdirector@pnx.com (e-mail)

PTI Center—Texas

Special Kids, Inc. (SKI)
6202 Belmark
P.O. Box 61628
Houston, TX 77208-1628
713-643-9576 (voice)
713-643-6291 (fax)

PTI Center—Texas

Project PODER
1017 Main Avenue, Suite 207
San Antonio, TX 78212
210-222-2637 (voice/TDD)
800-682-9747 (voice—Texas only)
210-222-2638 (fax)
poder@world-net.com (e-mail)

PTI Center—Utah

Utah Parent Center (UPC)
2290 East 4500 South, Suite 110
Salt Lake City, UT 84117
801-272-1051 (voice)
800-468-1160 (voice—Utah only)
801-272-1067-(Spanish voice)

801-272-8907 (fax)
upc@inconnect.com (e-mail)

PTI Center—Vermont

Vermont Parent Information Center (VPIC)
The Chace Mill
1 Mill Street, Suite A7
Burlington, VT 05401
802-658-5315 (voice/TDD)
800-639-7170 (voice—Vermont only)
802-658-5395 (fax)
vpic@together.net (e-mail)

PTI Center—Virginia

Parent Educational Advocacy Training Center
  (PEATC)
10340 Democracy Lane, Suite 206
Fairfax, VA 22030
703-691-7826 (voice)
800-869-6782 (voice—/TDD only)
703-691-8148 (fax)
peatcinc@aol.com (e-mail)

PTI Center—Washington

Washington PAVE
6316 South 12th Street
Tacoma, WA 98465-1900
253-565-2266 (voice/TTY)
800-572-7368 (voice—Washington only)
253-566-8052 (fax)
wapave9@washingtonpave.com (e-mail)

PTI Center—West Virginia

West Virginia PTI
371 Broaddus Avenue
Clarksburg, WV 26301
304-624-1436 (voice/TDD)
800-527-7368 (voice—West Virginia only)
304-624-1438 (fax)
wvpti@aol.com (e-mail)

PTI Center—Wisconsin

Parent Education Project of Wisconsin, Inc. (PEP WI)
2192 South 60th Street
West Allis, WI 53219-1568
414-328-5520 (voice)
414-328-5525 (TDD)
800-231-8382
414-328-5520 (fax)
pmcolletti@aol.com (e-mail)

PTI Center—Wyoming
Wyoming PIC
5 North Lobban
Buffalo, WY 82834
307-684-2277 (voice/TDD)
800-660-9742 (voice—Wyoming only)
307-684-5314 (fax)
tdawson@vcn.com (e-mail)

Internet Resources for Special Children
julioc@one.net (e-mail)
http://www.irsc.org (Website)

Is an Internet site that provides lists of links relating to the needs of children with disabilities for parents, family members, caregivers, friends, educators and medical professionals. Categories are extensive, including almost every possible disability affecting children.

National Early Childhood Technical Assistance System
137 East Franklin Street
Chapel Hill, NC 27514
919-962-2001 (voice)
919-966-4041 (TDD)
919-966-7463 (fax)
nectas@unc.edu (e-mail)
http://www.nectas.unc.edu (Website)

Is a program of the Child Development Center at the University of North Carolina at Chapel Hill. NEC*TAS has resources on childhood disabilities, the text of IDEA and descriptions of programs developed under IDEA.

National Information Center for Children and Youth With Disabilities
P.O. Box 1492
Washington, DC 20013
800-695-0285 (voice)
202-884-8441 (fax)
(800-695-0285 (TTY)
nichy@aed.org (e-mail)
http://www.nichcy.org (Website)

Provides information on disabilities and disability-related issues for families, educators and other professionals. The Website contains:
- contact information for local disability organizations
- lists of disability organizations and government agencies by state
- an in-depth look at current disability issues such as parent concerns, legal issues, assessment and inclusion
- information on preparing youth with disabilities to make the transition from high school to the adult world
- overviews of specific disabilities and lists of resources
- answers to questions and concerns that parents and people who work with parents or children with disabilities typically have, and
- publications on the federal education rights of children and youth with disabilities.

National Parent Network on Disabilities
1727 King Street, Suite 305
Alexandria, VA 22314
703-684-6763 (voice/TDD)
703-836-1232 (fax)
npnd@cs.com (e-mail)
http://www.npnd.org (Website)

Promotes and supports the power of parents to influence and effect policy issues at all levels. NPND serves to provide a national voice for the full diversity of families and parent organizations advocating for children and youth with special needs and disabilities. NPND works to increase the participation of parents of children with special needs in school reform.

Parent Soup
http://www.parentsoup.com (Website)

Is an Internet resource that includes an Education Central area. Topics include mainstreaming, ADD, ADHD, dyslexia and IEPs. The site sponsors an expert message board and chat rooms for parents.

School Psychology Resources Online
http://www.bcpl.net/~sandyste/school_psych.html (Website)

Is an Internet site with information on learning disabilities, ADHD, gifted, autism, adolescence, parenting, psychological assessment, classroom management, special education, K-12, mental health, reading, research and more. You can download handouts aimed at parents and teachers.

Schwab Foundation for Learning

1650 South Amphlett Blvd., Suite 300
San Mateo, CA 94402
800-230-0988 (voice)
650-655-2411 (fax)
infodesk@schwablearning.org (e-mail)
http://www.schwablearning.org (Website)

Seeks to raise awareness about learning differences and equips parents, teachers and other professionals with the resources they need to improve the lives of students with learning differences. The Schwab Foundation provides parents and educators in the San Francisco area quarterly educational programs, information and referrals and guidance counseling. The Website includes extensive resources in areas such as:

- attention deficit-hyperactivity disorder
- assessment
- dyslexia
- homework
- IEP
- learning disabilities
- legal issues, and
- special education.

Special Education Links for Teachers and Parents

Special Education Team
Middle School at Parkside
2400 West Fourth Street
Jackson, MI 49203
http://www.members.aol.com/lcantlin/middle.html
  (Website)

Is an Internet directory of special education links divided by category, including:

- federal, state and local governments
- universities and colleges
- business and industry
- national and regional organizations
- attention deficit disorder
- autism
- educable mentally impaired

- emotionally impaired
- hearing impaired
- inclusion
- learning disabilities
- medicine and health
- parent and family resources
- physically and otherwise health impaired
- special education legislation
- speech and language services
- teacher resources
- visually impaired, and
- suggested links posted by other visitors.

Special Education Resources on the Internet

http://www.hood.edu/seri/serihome.htm (Website)

Is a collection of Internet-accessible information in the field of special education. Information includes:

- attention deficit disorder
- autism
- behavior disorders
- general disabilities information
- gifted and talented
- hearing impairment
- learning disabilities
- legal and law resources
- mental retardation
- parents and educator's resources
- physical and health disorders
- special education discussion groups
- speech impairment, and
- vision impairment.

The Association for Persons With Severe Handicaps (TASH)

29 West Susquehanna Avenue, Suite 210
Baltimore, MD 21204
410-828-8274 (voice)
410-828-6706 (fax)
info@tash.org (e-mail)
http://web.syr.edu~thechp/subtash.htm (Website)

Provides information on current trends and issues in the field of disabilities, organizes conferences and workshops, advocates for legislative changes, distributes publications and videos and disseminates information through electronic media.

Technical Perspectives, Inc.

1400 East Campbell Road, Suite 1900
Richardson, TX 75081-1967
800-594-3779 (voice)
972-705-9420 (fax)
info@classplus.com (e-mail)
http://www.classplus.com/classplus (Website)

Publishes a software program called Classplus, which you can use to create an Individual Education Plan (IEP). Classplus allows you to develop:

- comprehensive set of curricula
- goals and objectives for every subject
- goals and objectives for all special populations
- criterion-referenced tests in every subject and area, and
- functional assessments.

On the Website, you can see sample reports containing:

- list of goals
- list of objectives
- standard IEP
- progress report
- student information
- objective/student analysis, and
- IEP analysis.

Legal Resources for Parents of a Special Education Child

American Bar Association Commission on Mental and Physical Disability Law

740 15th Street, NW
Washington, DC 20005
202-662-1570 (voice)
202-662-1012 (TDD)
202-662-1032 (fax)
cmpdl@cmpdl@abanet.org (e-mail)
http://www.abanet.org/disability/home (Website)

Puts out several books, reporters and other publications to assist lawyers who advocate for the rights of the disabled. The Commission also maintains a library of research materials and provides seminars and workshops.

Bazelon Center

1101 15th Street, NW, Suite 1212
Washington, DC 20005
202-467-5730 (voice)
202-467-4232 (TDD)
202-223-0409 (fax)
baxelon@nicom.com (e-mail)
http://www.bazelon.org (Website)

Is a public interest law firm that conducts test case litigation to defend the rights of people with mental disabilities. The Bazelon Center provides legal support to protection and advocacy agencies, legal services offices and private attorneys, and monitors legislation and regulations.

Center for Law and Education

1875 Connecticut Avenue, NW, Suite 510
Washington, DC 20009-5728
202-986-3000 (voice)
202-462-7688 (publications)
202-986-6648 (fax)
http://www.cleweb.org (Internet)

Assists local legal services programs and litigates certain cases in matters concerning education of low-income people. As a national support center, CLE has developed enormous expertise about the legal rights and responsibilities of students and school personnel as well as about key education programs and initiatives, including vocational education programs and special education for students with disabilities.

As one of the few national organizations that is firmly rooted in both disability rights and school reform, CLE has focused increasingly on bringing the two together—in order to help ensure, for example, that individualized education programs, assessment practices, etc., are aimed at ensuring that students with disabilities meet high standards, rather than being vehicles for lower expectations. In addition, CLE has pushed for federal policy to strengthen parent and community involvement.

CLE can help in a number of ways, including:

- training of parents, students, community members and educators
- assistance to attorneys and advocates representing students and parents

- policy analysis and policy drafting
- assistance in dealing with state and federal policy-makers
- assistance in using their publications on program implementation.

Publications include:

- IDEA Amendments Stress Quality, Education Reform for Students with Disabilities
- Inclusion of Students with Disabilities Who Are Labeled "Disruptive": Issues Papers for Legal Advocates
- Educational Rights of Children with Disabilities: A Primer for Advocates
- When Parents and Educators Do Not Agree: Using Mediation to Resolve Conflicts About Special Education.

Children's Defense Fund

25 E Street, NW
Washington, DC 20001
202-628-8787 (voice)
202-662-2510 (fax)
cdfinfo@childrensdefense.org (e-mail)
http://www.tmn.com/cdf/index.html (Website)

Assesses the adequacy of the screening, diagnosis and treatment programs for Medicaid-eligible children.

Disability Rights Education and Defense Fund, Inc.

2212 Sixth Street
Berkeley, CA 94710
510-644-2555 (voice/TDD)
510-841-8645 (fax)
dredf@dredf.org (e-mail)
http://www.dredf.org (Website)

Is dedicated to protecting and advancing the civil rights of people with disabilities through legislation, litigation, advocacy, technical assistance, and education and training of lawyers, people with disabilities and parents of children with disabilities.

EDLAW, Inc.

P.O. Box 81-7327
Hollywood, FL 33081
954-966-4489 (voice)
954-966-8561 (fax)
edlawinc@access.digex.net (e-mail)
http://www.edlaw.net (Website)

Develops and sponsors projects for systemic change related to special education. The Website includes information on newsletters, books and conferences, a list of attorneys who specialize in special education and full texts of special education statutes, regulations and administrative interpretations. EDLAW also maintains a database of attorneys and advocates through COPAA (the Council of Parent Attorneys and Advocates).

LRP Publications

747 Dresher Road
P.O. Box 980
Horsham, PA 19044-0980
800-341-7874 (voice)
215-658-0938 (TTY)
215-784-9639 (fax)
http://www.lrp.com (Website)

Has an extensive library of legal materials, including special education publications. The Website includes access to over 65 special education documents, including:

- Individuals with Disabilities Education Law Report
- Special Education Law on CD-ROM
- The Special Educator Newsletter
- Inclusive Education Programs Newsletter
- Special Education Law Monthly Newsletter
- Laws Affecting Children with Special Needs: Selected Federal Statutes and Regulations
- The Educational Rights of Children with Disabilities: Analysis, Decisions and Commentary
- Least Restrictive Environment: The Paradox of Inclusion
- What Do I Do When...The Answer Book on Special Education Law
- What Do I Do When...The Answer Book on Individualized Education Program
- Individuals with Disabilities Education Act (IDEA)
- The 1997 IDEA Amendments: A Guide for Educators, Parents and Attorneys

- The Face of Inclusion—A Parent's Perspective (Video).

Special Ed Advocate

P.O. Box 1008
Deltaville, VA 23043
804-257-0857 (voice)
webmaster@wrightslaw.com (e-mail)
http://www.wrightslaw.com (Website)

Is maintained by Pete and Pam Wright. Pete is an attorney who has represented special education children for more than 20 years. Pam is a psychotherapist who has worked with children and families in mental health centers, psychiatric clinics, schools, juvenile detention facilities, hospitals and homes. Their Website includes articles about special education advocacy; statutes, regulations and cases; information on ordering their advocacy package; information about books, conferences and other projects; and links to other useful information on the Internet.

Resources Concerning Specific Disabilities

Alexander Graham Bell Association

3417 Volta Place, NW
Washington, DC 20007-2778
202-337-5220 (voice/TDD)
bellmembers@aol.com (e-mail)
http://www.agbell.org (Website)

Provides hearing-impaired children with information and special education programs and acts as a support group for parents of deaf children.

American Association of the Deaf-Blind

814 Thayer Avenue
Silver Spring, MD 20910
800-735-2258 (voice)
301-588-8705 (fax)
301-588-6545 (TDD)
110104.2207@compuserve.com (e-mail)
http://www.tr.wov.edu/dblink/aadb.htm (Website)

Advocates for people who have combined hearing and vision impairments, and provides technical assistance to families, educators and service providers of people who are deaf-blind.

American Council of the Blind

1155 15th Street, NW, Suite 720
Washington, DC 20005
202-467-5081 (voice)
800-424-8666 (voice)
202-467-5085 (fax)
http://www.acb.org (Website)

Advocates for legislative changes, particularly to improve educational and rehabilitation facilities.

American Foundation for the Blind

11 Penn Plaza, Suite 300
New York, NY 10001
212-502-7600 (voice)
212-502-7774 (fax)
212-502-7662 (TDD)
afbinfo@afb.org (e-mail)
http://www.afb.org (Website)

Provides information on specialized services in education for sight-impaired children and works to improve the quality of educational services for children and youths with visual impairments.

American Society for Deaf Children

1820 Tribute Road, Suite A
Sacramento, CA 95815
916-641-6084 (voice/TDD)
800-942-2732 (voice)
916-641-6085 (fax)
ASDC1@aol.com (e-mail)
http://www.deafchildren.org (Website)

Advocates for deaf or hard of hearing children's total quality participation in education, including use of signing for enhancing and broadening the social, personal and educational aspects of deaf and hard of hearing children's lives. ASDC supports flexible, innovative and effective strategies for facilitating deaf and hard of hearing children's education.

ARC

500 East Border Street, Suite 300
Arlington, TX 76010
817-261-6003 (voice)

817-277-3491 (fax)
817-277-0553 (TDD)
thearc@metronet.com (e-mail)
http://thearc.org (Website)

Advocates and provides support for families of
people with mental retardation and developmental disabilities.

A-T Children's Project

1 West Camino Real, Suite 212
Boca Raton, FL 33432-5966
800-543-5627 (voice)
561-395-2621 (voice)
561-395-2640 (fax)
rosa#atcp.org (e-mail)
http://www.med.jhu.edu/ataxia (Website)

Provides physicians, research scientists, families
and support providers with information about
an inherited childhood disease called Ataxia-
Telangiectasia.

Attention Deficit Information Network, Inc.

475 Hillside Avenue
Needham, MA 02194
781-455-9895 (voice)
781-444-5466 (fax)
adin@gis.net (e-mail)
http://www.addinfonetwork.com (Website)

Offers support and information to families of
children with ADD, provides training programs,
conferences and workshops for parents and
professionals who work with individuals with
ADD.

Autism Society of America

7910 Woodmont Avenue, Suite 650
Bethesda, MD 20814-3015
301-657-0881 (voice)
800-328-8476 (voice)
301-657-0869 (fax)
http://www.autism-society.org (Website)

Monitors legislation and regulations affecting
support, education, training, research and other
services for individuals with autism. ASA also
offers referral services. Its Website has several
articles, including:
- Getting Started (for the newly diagnosed)
- Educating Children With Autism

- Autism Society of America's National
  Conference, and
- Notice of Proposed Rulemaking for IDEA
  1997 Reauthorization.

Blind Childrens' Center

4120 Marathon Street
Los Angeles, CA 90029
213-664-2153 (voice)
800-222-3567 (voice—California only)
800-222-3566 (voice)
213-664-3828 (fax)
info@blindcntr.org (e-mail)
http://blindcntr.org (Website)

Is located in Los Angeles and has posted
information on their site about the Center and
general information aimed at parents of blind
children.

Children and Adults with Attention Deficit Disorder (CHADD)

8181 Professional Place, Suite 201
Landover, MD 20785
301-306-7070 (voice)
301-306-7090 (fax)
http://www.chadd.org (Website)

Provides a network for parents of children with
ADD, provides a forum of education for parents
of and professionals who work with people
with ADD and works to provide positive
educational experiences for children with ADD.
CHADD publishes a quarterly newsletter and
educators' manual. The online site contains fact
sheets on several different topics, including
Parenting a Child With Attention Deficit
Disorder, Treating a Child With Attention
Deficit Disorder, Attention Deficit Disorder in
the Classroom and Legal Rights and Services
For Children With ADD.

Council for Exceptional Children, Division for Learning Disabilities

1920 Association Drive
Reston, VA 20191-1598
888-232-7733 (voice)
703-264-9494 (fax)
703-264-9446 (TDD)
service@cec.sped.org (e-mail)
http://www.cec.sped.org (Website)

Works to improve the education and life success of individuals with learning disabilities. The Website includes information on the DLD's publications (Learning Disabilities Research and Practice Journal, Thinking About Inclusion & Learning Disabilities, Research on Classroom Ecologies and DLD Times Newsletter), information on upcoming conferences and links to other organizations and government agencies.

Council for Learning Disabilities

P.O. Box 40303
Overland Park, KS 66204
913-492-8755 (voice)
913-492-2546 (fax)
eversr@winthrop.edu (e-mail)
http://coe.winthrop.edu/CLD (Website)

Is an organization of and for professionals who represent diverse disciplines and who are committed to enhance the education and life-span development of individuals with learning disabilities. CLD establishes standards of excellence and promotes innovative strategies for research and practice through interdisciplinary collegiality, collaboration and advocacy.

Deaf World Web

403-444-5829 (TTY)
dww@deafworldweb.org (e-mail/UNIX)
http://dww.deafworldweb.org (Website)

Is the largest Internet site for deaf-related resources.

Epilepsy Foundation of America

4351 Garden City Drive
Landover, MD 20785-2267
301-459-3700 (voice)
800-332-1000 (voice)
301-577-2684 (fax)
800-332-2070 (TDD)
postmaster@efa.org (e-mail)
http://www.efa.org (Website)

Promotes research and treatment of epilepsy, disseminates information and educational materials, provides direct services for people with epilepsy and makes referrals, when necessary.

Families of Spinal Muscular Atrophy

P.O. Box 196
Libertyville, IL 60048-0196
708-367-7620 (voice)
800-886-1762 (voice)
708-367-7623 (fax)
sma@interaccess.com (e-mail)
http://www.familyvillage.wisc.edu/lib_spma.htm (Website)

Promotes and funds research, provides families with the use of an equipment pool to help alleviate the high cost of medical equipment, promotes public awareness and publishes a quarterly newsletter.

Federation of Families for Children's Mental Health

1021 Prince Street
Alexandria, VA 22314-2971
703-684-7710 (voice)
703-836-1040 (fax)
ffcmh@crosslink.net (e-mail)
http://www.ffcmh.org (Website)

Focuses on the needs of children with emotional, behavioral or mental disorders, specifically by providing information and advocating in several areas, including family support, education and transition services. The Website includes down-loadable publications, IDEA updates and links with local organizations.

The International Dyslexia Society

The Chester Building, Suite 382
8600 LaSalle Road
Baltimore, MD 21286-2044
410-296-0232 (voice)
800-222-3123 (messages)
410-321-5069 (fax)
info@interdys.org (e-mail)
www.interdys.org (Website)

Promotes effective teaching approaches and related clinical educational intervention strategies for people with dyslexia, supports research and disseminates research through conferences, publications and local and regional offices.

LD Online

http://www.ldonline.org (Website)

Is an Internet site devoted exclusively to learning disabilities. The Website contains extensive information on learning disabilities, including:

- highlights of new information in the field of learning disabilities—exclusive articles, research findings and political news
- Bulletin Boards for parents, teachers and students to share their experiences with learning disabilities
- opportunities to communicate directly with experts in the field of learning disabilities through a special bulletin board
- comprehensive listing of resources on learning disabilities—national and state organizations and agencies and online resources, and
- a calendar of learning disabilities events on the Internet.

Learning Disabilities Association

4156 Library Road
Pittsburgh, PA 15234-1349
412-341-1515 (voice)
412-344-0224 (fax)
ldanatl@usar.net (e-mail)
http://www.ldanatl.org (Website)

Works to enhance the quality of life for all individuals with learning disabilities and their families, to alleviate the restricting effects of learning disabilities and to support endeavors to determine the causes of learning disabilities. Members receive a national newsletter along with state and local chapter newsletters. Members receive information on advocating for their children, receive information on state and federal laws and have access to support groups. LDA's Website has information on:

- educational standards
- free and appropriate education (FAPE)
- GED tests
- home schooling
- IEPs
- parents' rights and responsibilities, and
- post-secondary entrance tests.

Learning Disabilities Network

72 Sharp Street, Suite A2
Hingham, MA 02043
781-340-5605 (voice)
781-340-5603 (fax)
ldntwk@aol.com (e-mail)

Provides educational and referral services for individuals with learning disabilities and their families, and professionals, primarily in the Northeast. LDN has printed material about learning disabilities, and offers conferences and seminars.

National Aphasia Association

156 Fifth Avenue, Suite 707
New York, NY 10010
800-922-4622 (voice)
http://www.aphasia.org (Website)

Promotes public education, research, rehabilitation and support services to assist people with aphasia and their families.

National Association of the Deaf

814 Thayer Avenue
Silver Spring, MD 20910-4500
301-587-1788 (voice)
301-587-1789 (TTY)
301-587-1791 (fax)
naalhge@juno.com (e-mail)
http://www.nad.org (Website)

Is a consumer advocacy group promoting equal access to communication, education and employment for people who are deaf or hard of hearing.

National Association of Psychiatric Treatment Centers for Children

1025 Connecticut Avenue, NW, Suite 1012
Washington, DC 20036
202-857-9735 (voice)
202-362-5145 (fax)
naptcc@aol.com (e-mail)
http://www.air-dc.org/teams/stratpart/naptcc.htm
  (Website)

Is a group whose mission is to promote the availability and delivery of appropriate and relevant services to children and youth with, or at risk of, serious emotional or behavioral disturbances and their families.

National Center for Learning Disabilities, Inc.

381 Park Avenue South, Suite 1401
New York, NY 10016
212-545-7510 (voice)
888-575-7373 (voice)
212-545-9665 (fax)
http://www.ncld.org (Website)

Provides information on learning disabilities
and resources available in communities nationwide to parents, professionals and adults with
learning disabilities. One of NCLD's areas of
primary concern is early identification and
intervention, and teacher preparation. The
Website includes links to other LD organizations and school testing organizations, and information on legal issues, gifted/learning disabilities, ADD/ADHD and home schooling.

National Down Syndrome Congress

1605 Chantilly Drive, Suite 250
Atlanta, GA 3032403269
404-633-1555 (voice)
800-232-6372 (voice)
404-633-2817 (fax)
ndsc@charitiesusa.com (e-mail)
http://www.carol.net/~ndsc/ (Website)

Offers support to parents of children with
Down syndrome through annual seminars, fact
sheets, pamphlets, booklets, newsletter, audio-
tapes and other educational materials. NDSC
maintains an advocate telephone helpline.

National Down Syndrome Society

666 Broadway, 8th Floor
New York, NY 10012-2317
800-221-4602 (voice)
212-460-9330 (voice)
212-979-2873 (fax)
http://www.ndss.org (Website)

Helps families whose special education needs
concern a child with Down syndrome.

National Federation of the Blind

1800 Johnson Street
Baltimore, MD 21230
410-659-9314 (voice)
410-685-5653 (fax)
epc@roudley.com (e-mail)
http://www.nfb.org (Website)

Provides referrals and information on adaptive
equipment, advocacy services, protection of
civil rights, development and evaluation of
technology and support for blind people and
their families. NFB has a special division called
the National Organization of Parents of Blind
Children.

National Fragile X Foundation

1441 York Street
Denver, CO 80206
303-333-6155 (voice)
800-688-8765 (voice)
303-333-4369 (fax)
natlfx@sprintmail.com (e-mail)
http://www.nfx.org (Website)

Has information for educators, on upcoming
conferences and on support groups for parents
and children, and maintains a family resource
center.

National Brain Injury Foundation

105 N. Alfred Street
Alexandria, VA 22314
703-236-6000 (voice)
800-444-6443 (voice)
703-236-6001 (fax)
http://biavsa.org (Website)

Provides information and support to families of
people with brain injuries.

National Spinal Cord Injury Association

8300 Colesville Road
Silver Spring, MD 20910
301-588-6959 (voice)
301-588-9414 (fax)
nscia@aol.com (e-mail)
http://www.spinalcord.org (Website)

Provides information and support to people
with spinal cord injuries and their families.

National Tourette Syndrome Association, Inc.

42-40 Bell Blvd.
Bayside, NY 11361-2820
718-224-2999 (voice)
718-279-9596 (fax)
tourette@ix.netcom.com (e-mail)
http://neuro-www2.mgh.harvard.edu/tsa/
   tsamain.nclk (Website)

Has information about TS, its treatment, scientific research and consumer services. NTSA publishes a quarterly newsletter, maintains a crisis hotline and produces literature for people with TS and their families, medical professionals, educators and legislators.

Signing Exact English Center for the Advancement of Deaf Children

P.O. Box 1181
Los Alamitos, CA 90720
562-430-1467 (voice/TDD)
562-795-6614 (fax)
seectr@aol.com (e-mail)

Promotes the understanding of signing exact English to improve English skills for deaf children. SEE Center services include a telephone information service about deafness, workshops, videotapes, and a parent information packet, questions for parents to ask, especially in the school setting.

Spina Bifida Association of America

4590 MacArthur Blvd., NW, Suite 250
Washington, DC 20007-4226
202-944-3285 (voice)
800-621-3141 (voice)
202-944-3295 (fax)
ir@sbaa.org (e-mail)
http://www.sbaa.org (Website)

Offers educational programs and support services for people with spina bifida, their families and concerned professionals; acts as a clearinghouse on information related to spina bifida; provides referral services; conducts seminars; and monitors legislation and regulations.

United Cerebral Palsy Association

1600 L Street, NW, Suite 700
Washington, DC 20036
800-872-5827 (voice/TDD)
800-776-0414 (fax)
ucpnatl@ucpa.org (e-mail)
http://www.ucpa.org (Website)

Assists individuals with cerebral palsy and other developmental disabilities and their families. UCPA provides parent education, early intervention information, family support, respite services and information on assistive technology.

Miscellaneous Organizations

Ability OnLine Support Network

919 Alness Street
North York, ONM 3J2J1
Canada
416-650-6207 (voice)
416-650-5073 (fax)
416-650-5411 (modem)
info@ablelink.org (e-mail)
bbs.ablelink.org (Telnet)
http://www.ablelink.org (Website)

Is an electronic mail system that connects young people with disabilities or chronic illness to disabled and nondisabled peers and mentors. This network removes the social barriers that can come with having a disability and illness, providing opportunities to form friendships, build self-confidence, exchange information and share hope and encouragement through e-mail messages.

Ability OnLine is also a valuable resource for families and friends anxious to know more about an illness and help manage it. The network provides disabled youngsters and their families with up-to-date information on medical treatments, educational strategies and employment opportunities through peer support.

Best Buddies

1325 G Street, NW, Suite 500
Washington, DC 20005
202-347-7265 (voice)
202-824-0200 (fax)
bbmegan@juno.com (e-mail)
http://bestbudies.org (Website)

Is a volunteer organization that pairs high school students, college students and working adults in one-to-one friendships with mentally retarded individuals.

Bibliography

If you can, pay a visit to a large public library or bookstore to see the array of materials geared toward parents and teacher of children with disabilities. Here are a few that cover specific issues or are presented in non-book format.

- Compton, Carolyn, *A Guide to 85 Tests for Special Education* (Simon and Schuster Education Group)
- Curran, Dolores, *Working With Parents: Dolores Curran's Guide to Successful Parent Groups* (AGS Press)
- Des Jardins, Charlotte, *How to Organize an Effective Parent/Advocacy Group and Move Bureaucracies* (Family Resource Center on Disabilities, 20 East Jackson Blvd., Suite 900, Chicago, IL 60604; 313-939-3513 (voice); 312-939-3519 (TDD))
- Goldstein, Dr. Sam, and Dr. Michael Goldstein, *Educating Inattentive Children—Videotape* (Neurology, Learning and Behavior, 230 South 500 East, Suite 100, Salt Lake City, UT 84102; 801-532-1484)
- Lavoie, Richard D., *Integrating Learning Disabled Students—Audiotape* (Lingui Systems, 3100 4th Avenue, East Moline, IL 61244; 800-776-4332)
- Levine, Dr. Mel, *Keeping A Head in School: A Student's Book About Learning Abilities and Learning Disorders—Audiotape* (Educators Publishing Service, Inc., 75 Moulton Street, Cambridge, MA 02138-1104)

- Mann, Philip, *A Guide for Educating Mainstreamed Students* (Allyn & Bacon)
- McMullough, Virginia E., *Testing and Your Child: What You Should Know About 150 of the Most Common Medical, Educational and Psychological Tests* (Plume Books)
- Michaels, Craig A., editor, *Transition Strategies for Persons With Learning Disabilities* (Singular Publishing Group)
- Shore, Milton F., Patrick J. Brice and Barbara G. Love, *When Your Child Needs Testing: What Parents, Teachers and Other Helpers Need to Know About Psychological Testing* (Crossroads Publishing, Inc.)
- Swanson, James M., *School-Based Assessments and Interventions for ADD Students* (K.C. Publishing)
- Taylor, John F., *The School Success Tool Kit—Videotape* (Sun Media, 1095 25th Street, SE, Suite 107, Salem, OR 97301; 800-847-1233)
- Trapani, Catherine, *Transition Goals for Adolescents With Learning Disabilities* (College-Hill Press)
- Wallace, Gerald, Stephen C. Larsen and Linda K. Elksnin, *Educational Assessment of Learning Problems* (Allyn & Bacon).

■

Appendix 4

Sample IEP Form

Every school district, in every state, has their own IEP form. While the forms vary, they must include the same information. We strongly recommend that you request a copy of your school's IEP form early in the process.

To get you familiar with IEP forms, we have included a sample here, reprinted with permission of the Marin County (California) Office of Education. This is not the complete Marin County IEP form, but includes the key sections discussed in this book. Marin County's IEP form reflects all the changes made as a result of the 1997 authorization of the IDEA (as discussed in Chapter 2, Section B). Although your school district's IEP form may be very similar or very different, it should also reflect IDEA's changes as follows:

- How your child will participate in any district or statewide assessment of student achievement as used for the general education population, and whether your child needs any modifications or accommodations in order to take the district or state-wide assessment.
- Details about transition services.
- For children who are blind or visually impaired, the need for instruction in Braille.
- For children who are deaf or hard of hearing, a consideration of the child's communication needs, including opportunities for direct communication with peers and staff, and direct instruction, in the child's language and communication mode.
- For children whose behavior impedes learning or that of others, strategies, including positive behavioral interventions, to address that behavior.
- For children who need assistive technology, what specific devices and services are needed.

Pupil Placement Summary
Individualized Education Program

MARIN
Special Education
Local Plan Area
IEP

Date _____

Shaded boxes are situational.
All other areas must be addressed.

IDENTIFYING INFORMATION

Student: _____ Birthdate _____ Grade _____ ❏ M ❏ F

❏ LCI
Parent/Guardian _____ ❏ Foster Home _____

Address _____ Home Language _____

Home Phone _____ _____ Work Phone(s) _____ _____

School/Program _____ District of Residence _____

Student's Language Profiency   ❏ English Only ❏ Fluent English Proficient ❏ Limited English Proficient ❏ Non English Proficient

Determined by _____ Date _____
Name of Test

English Level _____ Primary Language Level _____

Primary Language of Instruction:
❏ English Only   ❏ Student's Primary Language ❏ English with primary language assistance
Service Delivery Model _____

DATES OF ANTICIPATED MEETINGS

Anticipated Annual Review _____ Anticipated 3-yr. Reevaluation _____

IEP MEETING INFORMATION

Type of meeting:
❏ Initial   ❏ Annual Review   ❏ Review Based on 3-yr. Reevaluation
❏ Manifestation Determination   ❏ Transition   ❏ Parent Request   ❏ _____

❏ Parents have been advised of their rights.
❏ Parents have been provided with a written copy of the "Parents Rights and Responsibilities and Due Process."

The purpose of the meeting: (Check all that apply)
❏ review assessments   ❏ determine eligibility   ❏ develop goals and objectives   ❏ develop/review behavioral plan
❏ manifestation determination   ❏ recommend placement/service(s)   ❏ _____
❏ amend IEP dated _____

Present at the the meeting:

Distribution: White-Permanent File   Canary-Parent   Pink-CUM   Copies may be made for other team members

IEP

Student _____   Date of Meeting _____

The following assessment report(s) were reviewed. Report(s) include description(s) of the child's strengths.
(Please list name of report, examiner(s), and date of report)

ELIGIBILITY AS AN INDIVIDUAL WITH EXCEPTIONAL NEEDS

Based on these assessments, the IEP team determined that _____
1. Meets eligibility criteria as indicated:
❏ Mentally Retarded   ❏ Hard of Hearing   ❏ Multi-Handicapped   ❏ Visually Impaired
❏ Orthopedically Impaired   ❏ Other Health Impaired *Specific Impairment* _____
❏ Deaf/Blind   ❏ Autistic-Like Behaviors   ❏ Traumatic Brain Injury
❏ Specific Learning Disability ❏ Language or Speech Disorder   ❏ Emotionally Disturbed ❏ Deaf
Functional Description of Handicap
_____
_____
_____

2. Specific eligibility was unable to be determined. Recommend: _____
_____

3. Does not meet eligibility for handicaps considered:
❏ Mentally Retarded   ❏ Hard of Hearing   ❏ Multi-Handicapped   ❏ Visually Impaired
❏ Orthopedically Impaired   ❏ Other Health Impaired *Specific Impairment* _____
❏ Deaf/Blind   ❏ Autistic-Like Behaviors   ❏ Traumatic Brain Injury
❏ Specific Learning Disability ❏ Language or Speech Disorder   ❏ Emotionally Disturbed ❏ Deaf

---

Eligibility for Specific Learning Disability and Language or Speech Disorder must be documented on intial referral and three year reevaluation.

For Specific Learning Disability - **All Five of the Following Criteria Must Be Met.**

❏ 1. The severe discrepancy was demonstrated in the area of *(check the box(es) that apply)*:

Test and Discrepancy	Test and Discrepancy
❏ Oral expression _____	❏ Listening comprehension_____
❏ Written expression _____	❏ Basic reading skills _____
❏ Reading comprehension _____	❏ Mathematics calculation _____
❏ Mathematics reasoning_____	

A severe discrepancy is demonstrated by the following: **IQ - Achievement Test Score = Discrepancy**
The discrepancy is:
•**most probably significant** if it is 17 or greater •**not significant** if it is less than 17
Intellectual ability includes both acquired learning and learning potential. The level of achievement includes the pupil's level of competence in materials and subject matter explicitly taught in school.

❏ 2. There is a disorder in the following basic psychological process *(check the box(es) that apply)*:
     ❏ Attention   ❏ Visual processing   ❏ Auditory processing   ❏ Sensory motor skills   ❏ Cognitive: association,
     Test _____   conceptualization and expression
❏ 3. The discrepancy is not due to factors of environment, cultural difference or economic disadvantage.
❏ 4. The discrepancy is not the result of visual, hearing, or motor handicaps, mental retardation, limited school experience, or poor
     attendance.
❏ 5. The discrepancy cannot be accommodated through other regular, categorical services offered within regular instructional program.

IEP

Student _____ Date of Meeting _____

For Language or Speech Disorder - **Must Meet One or More of Criteria 1-5 and Criteria 6 and 7.**

❑ 1. **Articulation Disorder -** Such that the pupil's production of speech significantly interferes with communication and attracts adverse attention. Significant interference in communication occurs when the pupil's production of single or multiple speech sounds on a developmental scale of articulation competency is below that expected for his or her chronological age or developmental level.

	Test Name	Age Equivalent, Standard Score or %ile
Articulation Test	_____	_____

❑ 2. **Abnormal Voice -** A pupil has an abnormal voice which is characterized by persistent, defective voice quality, pitch or loudness. (Student must have medical clearance for voice therapy.)

❑ 3. **Fluency Disorders -** A pupil has a fluency disorder when the flow of verbal expression including rate and rhythm adversely affects communication between the pupil and listener.

❑ 4. **Language or Speech Disorder** - Which is the result of a hearing loss

❑ 5. **Language Disorder** - *The pupil has an expressive or receptive language disorder when he or she meets one of the following criteria:*

  ❑ The pupil scores at least 1.5 standard deviations below the mean or below the 7th percentile, for his or her chronological age or developmental level on *two or more* standardized tests in one or more of the following areas of language development:

	Test Name	Discrepancy	%ile
❑ Morphology	_____	_____	_____
❑ Syntax	_____	_____	_____
❑ Semantics	_____	_____	_____
❑ Pragmatics	_____	_____	_____

  ❑ The pupil scores at least 1.5 standard deviations below the mean or the score is below the 7%ile for his or her chronological age or developmental level on one or more standardized tests in one of the areas listed above *AND* displays inappropriate or inadequate usage of expressive or receptive language as measured by a representative spontaneous or elicited language sample of fifty utterances.

❑ 6. **Adversely affects educational performance**

❑ 7. **Cannot be corrected without special education and related services.**

Additional Eligibility for children birth to 4 years 9 months - Must Meet Criteria 1 and 2

❑ 1. **Meets eligibility criteria as indicated:**

❑ Mentally Retarded	❑ Hard of Hearing	❑ Multi-Handicapped	❑ Visually Impaired
❑ Orthopedically Impaired	❑ Other Health Impaired *Specific Impairment* _____		
❑ Deaf/Blind	❑ Autistic-Like Behaviors	❑ Traumatic Brain Injury	
❑ Specific Learning Disability	❑ Language or Speech Disorder	❑ Emotionally Disturbed ❑ Deaf	

❑ 2. **Requires intensive services by meeting one of the following :**

❑ A. Functions at or below 50% of his or her chronological age level in any one of the following skill areas:

OR

❑ B. Functions between 51% and 75% of his or her chronological age level in any two of the following skill areas:

❑ gross or fine motor development   ❑ receptive or expressive language development
❑ social or emotional development   ❑ cognitive development   ❑ visual development

OR

❑ C. The child has a disabling medical condition or congenital syndrome which the IEP team determines has a high predictability of requiring intensive special education and services. Specify:_____

PARENTAL CONCERNS FOR ENHANCING THE CHILD'S EDUCATION

Distribution: White-Permanent File   Canary-Parent   Pink-CUM   Copies may be made for other team members

IEP

Student _____ Date of Meeting _____

PRIMARY LEARNING NEEDS

❑ Draft IEP goals and objectives were reviewed, revised, and are recommended.
❑ IEP goals and objectives were recommended on _____ and are continued.
❑ In addition to IEP goals and objectives continued from the meeting on _____ additional goals and
   objectives were reviewed, reivised and are recommended.
   Must be within last 12 months.

PARTICIPATION IN DISTRICT OR STATEWIDE ASSESSMENTS OF STUDENT ACHIEVEMENT

❑ Student can participate in the district or statewide achievement testing program without individual accommodation.
❑ Student can participate in the district or statewide achievement testing program with the following accommodations:

	2nd-11th gr. Reading	2nd-11th gr. Writing	2nd-11th gr. Spelling	2nd-11th gr. Math	9th-11th gr. History/ S. Science	9th-11th gr. Science
Flexible Setting	❑	❑	❑	❑	❑	❑
Larger Print Text	❑	❑	❑	❑	❑	❑
Out of Level Testing (specify grade level)	❑ ___	❑ ___	❑ ___	❑ ___	❑ ___	❑ ___
Revised Test Directions	❑	❑	❑	❑	❑	❑
Braille Test	❑	❑	❑	❑	❑	❑
Flexible Scheduling	❑	❑	❑	❑	❑	❑
Revised Test Format	❑	❑	❑	❑	❑	❑
Use of Aids and/or Aides to Interpret Test Items	❑	❑	❑	❑	❑	❑

❑ Student will participate in an alternate achievement assessment program based on IEP specified goals and objectives,
   due to nature and intensity of student's disability for: ❑ all content areas   ❑ specific content areas (please list)
   _____

CULMINATION GOAL (FOR SECONDARY STUDENTS)

1. Working toward:
   ❑ certificate of completion-goal is acquisition of vocational training/independent living skills
   OR
   ❑ diploma
   a. The following proficiency tests have been passed: ❑ Math   ❑ Reading   ❑ Written Language
   b. The pupil is able to attain the district's regular proficiency standards without accommodations ❑ Yes ❑ No
   c. If the answer to "b" is "No", specify the accommodations: _____
   _____
   _____
   _____

   d. If accommodations are unsuccessful, specify differential standards: _____
   _____
   _____
   _____

PRE-VOCATIONAL EDUCATION (GRADES K-6) OR VOCATIONAL EDUCATION (GRADES 7-12)

❑ Regular Program   ❑ IEP Goal and Objective Page(s)_____

Distribution: White-Permanent File   Canary-Parent   Pink-CUM   Copies may be made for other team members

Statement of Needed Transition Services

For all students 14 years and older

MARIN
Special Education
Local Plan Area
IEP

Date of Meeting _____

IDENTIFYING INFORMATION

Student _____ Birthdate _____

Anticipated Graduation/
Transition Date _____

DESIRED POST-SCHOOL OUTCOME STATEMENT

Employment/Career
❏ 1.1 Full time/Part time employment as a _____

❏ 1.2 Supported Employment
❏ 1.3 Volunteer work as a _____
❏ 1.4 Sheltered Workshop
❏ 1.5 Activity Center
❏ _____

Education/Training
❏ 2.1 Full time/Part time college - Objective _____

❏ 2.2 Vocational Training - Course _____

❏ 2.3 None due to full time employment

❏ _____

Living Arrangements
❏ 3.1 Independent
❏ 3.2 Family/Relatives
❏ 3.3 Supervised Apartment
❏ 3.4 Group Home/Facility
❏ 3.5 Board and Care

Community Experiences
❏ 4.1 Recreation activities with family and friends
❏ 4.2 Activities through Parks and Recreation
❏ 4.3 Recreation activities at Community College
❏ 4.4 Recreation programs for individuals with disabilities
❏ _____

Transportation
❏ 5.1 Use of paratransit
❏ 5.2 Use of public transportation
❏ 5.3 Use of own vehicle
❏ _____

Income/Financial
❏ 6.1 Supplemental Security Income (SSI/SSDI)
❏ 6.2 Plan for achieving self-sufficiency
❏ 6.3 Impairment related work experience
❏ 6.4 Public assistance
❏ 6.5 Family support
❏ 6.6 Wages
❏ 6.7 Medi-Cal
❏ 6.8 Health Benefits
❏ 6.9 Conservatorship
❏ 6.10 Estate planning/Trust funds
❏ _____

COMPLETED CAREER PREPARATION ACTIVITIES DISCUSSED

❏ *ROP Classes*
❏ *Vocational Classes*
❏ *Programs (Work Experiences, Project WorkAbility, Marin Conservation Corps, JTPA)*
❏ *Work History/Volunteer Service*

Distribution: White-Permanent File   Canary-Parent   Pink-CUM   Copies may be made for other team members

IEP

Student: _____ Date of Meeting _____

WHAT DOES THE STUDENT NEED IN THE AREAS OF:

Statement of Needed Transition Services	Activities/Objectives If no activity needed in 1, 2, 3, or 4, explain why.	Agency/Person Responsible	Time Line	Date Completed
1. Instruction				
2. Community Experiences				
3. Employment				
4. Post School Living				
5. Daily Living Skills (Optional)				
6. Functional Vocational Evaluation (Optional)				
7. Summarize Interagency Responsibilities and/or Linkages				

Distribution: White-Permanent File   Canary-Parent   Pink-CUM   Copies may be made for other team members

Level 1 Behavior Assessment & Intervention Plan

MARIN
**Special Education
Local Plan Area
IEP**

Date of Meeting _____

IDENTIFYING INFORMATION

Student _____ Birthdate _____

LEVEL 1 BEHAVIOR ASSESSMENT

Date of the Incident _____

Description of Incident Preceding Suspension

At the time of the incident was the student placed in the appropriate educational program with adequate support services?
❑ Yes ❑ No
Describe Services

Method of behavioral analysis (i.e. interview, observation, etc.)

What factors contributed to the incident?

LEVEL 1 BEHAVIORAL INTERVENTION PLAN

Recommendations to Address Behavior in the Future

Rationale Why the Behavior Is Not Expected to Reoccur

Distribution: White-Permanent File   Canary-Parent   Pink-Cumulative File   Goldenrod-Temporary File

Level 2 Behavioral Intervention Plan

MARIN
**Special Education
Local Plan Area
IEP**

Date of Meeting _____

IDENTIFYING INFORMATION

Student _____ Birthdate _____

LEVEL 2 BEHAVIORAL INTERVENTION PLAN

Date of the Incident _____

Description of Incident Preceding Suspension

General Recommendations

Specific Strategies to Increase Appropriate Behaviors

Behavior	Strategies

Specific Strategies to Decrease Inappropriate Behaviors

Behavior	Strategies

Distribution: White-Permanent File   Canary-Parent   Pink-Cumulative File

Manifestation
Determination Findings
Individualized Education Program

MARIN
Special Education
Local Plan Area
IEP-MD

Student _____ Date of Present Meeting _____

Functional behavioral assessment conducted? ❑ Yes ❑ No   Date _____

Behavioral intervention plan in place? ❑ Yes ❑ No   Date implemented _____

Description of behavior/actions of student:

Disciplinary action taken or proposed by site administration:

Date on which decision to take disciplinary action was made _____

INFORMATION CONSIDERED

In determining whether the student's behavior was a manifestation of his/her disability, the IEP Team considered the following in relation to the behavior subject to discipline (check applicable items):

❑ Evaluation and diagnostic results. *List: report(s) and date prepared*
   ❑ Pre-Expulsion Pyschoeducational Evaluation Report   Date Prepared

❑ Observations of the student. *List*

_____

Distribution: White-Permanent File   Canary-Parent   Pink-Cumulative File   Copies may be made for other members of the IEP team

IEP-MD

Student:_____ Date of Meeting_____

INFORMATION CONSIDERED (CONTINUED)

❑ Student's IEP, services, and placement. *Describe*

❑ Other relevant information. *List*

DETERMINATION AND FINDINGS OF THE IEP TEAM

(Check the appropriate box)

❑ Yes ❑ No   In relationship to the behavior subject to disciplinary action, were the student's IEP and placement appropriate, and were the special education services, supplementary aids and services, and behavior intervention strategies provided consistent with the student's IEP and placement?

Comments:

❑ Yes ❑ No   Did the student's disability impair the ability of the student to understand the impact and consequences of the behavior subject to disciplinary action; **and**

Comments:

❑ Yes ❑ No   Did the student's disability impair the ability of the student to control the behavior subject to disciplinary action?

Comments:

The student's behavior ❑ was   ❑ was not a manifestation of his/her disability.

Parent(s) ❑ agrees ❑ disagrees with the determination of the IEP Team.

Comments of parent, if any:

Follow up action(s) of the IEP Team, if any:

Functional Behavioral Assessment Plan provided to parents? ❑ Yes ❑ No   Date _____

Distribution: White-Permanent File Canary-Parent Pink-Cumulative File   Copies may be made for other members of the IEP team

IEP

Student _____ Date of Meeting _____

PHYSICAL EDUCATION

❑ Regular Program   ❑ Teacher Designed   ❑ _____

PLACEMENT, SERVICES, AND EQUIPMENT CONSIDERED AND RECOMMENDED
(Put a ✓ on the line if the placement, service, or equipment was considered by the IEP team.
Put a ✓ in the box if the placement, service or equipment is recommended by the IEP team.
NOTE: Equipment and Service requests must be based upon recent evauations.)

Considered	IEP Team Recommends		**Dates** Unless otherwise specified, services will be for the regular school year.		**Location** Please check appropriate box(es) to describe location	
__	❑ Special Day Class	From_____ To _____	❑ Day ❑ Residential	❑ Public-Home School ❑ Pursuant to AB 2726 ❑ Public-Other Than Home School* ❑ Certified Non Public School* ❑ _____*	

Comments:_____
_____

*If not home school, rationale:
❑ Needs cannot be met at home school
❑ Student would benefit from program available at site other than home school

Considered	IEP Team Recommends		**Dates** Services checked below will be provided until the next annual review excluding holidays, non-student days, and all vacations unless otherwise specified. Such services will not be provided in the event of death, illness, labor walkouts or strikes, Acts of God, or other unforeseen reasons.	**Frequency**	**Location** C = Classroom; R = Room Other Than Reg. Ed. or Spec. Day Classroom (inc. RS Room or S/L Office); OC = Off-Site Clinic; ❑ = Other
__	❑ Resource Specialist	From_____ To _____ ❑ Direct ❑ Consult		_____	❑ C ❑ R ❑ OC ❑ _____
__	❑ Language/Speech	From_____ To _____ ❑ Direct ❑ Consult		_____	❑ C ❑ R ❑ OC ❑ _____
__	❑ Assistive Services	From_____ To _____ ❑ Direct ❑ Consult		_____	❑ C ❑ R ❑ OC ❑ _____
__	❑ Occupational Tx	From_____ To _____ ❑ Direct ❑ Consult		_____	❑ C ❑ R ❑ OC ❑ _____
__	❑ Physical Therapy	From_____ To _____ ❑ Direct ❑ Consult		_____	❑ C ❑ R ❑ OC ❑ _____
__	❑ CCS Services	From_____ To _____ ❑ Direct ❑ Consult		_____	❑ C ❑ R ❑ OC ❑ _____
	❑ Occupational Therapy ❑ Physical Therapy				
__	❑ Orientation & Mobility	From_____ To _____ ❑ Direct ❑ Consult		_____	❑ C ❑ R ❑ OC ❑ _____
__	❑ Vision Services	From_____ To _____ ❑ Direct ❑ Consult		_____	❑ C ❑ R ❑ OC ❑ _____
__	❑ Reader Services	From_____ To _____ ❑ Direct ❑ Consult		_____	❑ C ❑ R ❑ OC ❑ _____

Distribution: White-Permanent File   Canary-Parent   Pink-CUM   Copies may be made for other team members

IEP

Student _____ Date of Meeting _____

PLACEMENT, SERVICES, AND EQUIPMENT CONSIDERED AND OPTIONS RECOMMENDED-CONTINUED

___ ❏ Braille Transcription From_____ To _____ ❏ C ❏ R ❏ OC ❏ _____
                ❏ Direct   ❏ Consult

___ ❏ Braille Instruction From_____ To _____ ❏ C ❏ R ❏ OC ❏ _____
                ❏ Direct   ❏ Consult

___ ❏ Deaf and HH From_____ To _____ ❏ C ❏ R ❏ OC ❏ _____
                ❏ Direct   ❏ Consult

___ ❏ Interpreter Services From_____ To _____ ❏ C ❏ R ❏ OC ❏ _____
                ❏ Direct   ❏ Consult

___ ❏ Health/Nursing Serv. From_____ To _____ ❏ C ❏ R ❏ OC ❏ _____
                ❏ Direct   ❏ Consult

___ ❏ Behavior Mngmnt. From_____ To _____ ❏ C ❏ R ❏ OC ❏ _____
                ❏ Direct   ❏ Consult

___ ❏ Home/Hospital From_____ To _____ ❏ C ❏ R ❏ OC ❏ _____
                ❏ Direct   ❏ Consult

___ ❏ Add. Classroom From_____ To _____ ❏ C ❏ R ❏ OC ❏ _____
      Support   ❏ Direct   ❏ Consult

___ ❏ Community Mental From_____ To _____ ❏ C ❏ R ❏ OC ❏ _____
      Health   ❏ Direct   ❏ Consult

___ ❏ _____ From_____ To _____ ❏ C ❏ R ❏ OC ❏ _____
                ❏ Direct   ❏ Consult

___ ❏ Specialized Equipment _____
_____
_____

___ ❏ Low Incidence Services _____
_____
_____

___ ❏ Assistive Technology _____
_____
_____

___ ❏ Transportation _____

OTHER RECOMMENDATIONS AND/OR REFERRALS

IEP

Student _____ Date of Meeting _____

Regular Program Participation
❏ Physical Education   ❏ Lunch, Recess, Passing Periods   ❏ Enrichment
❏ Bilingual Program/ESL   ❏ Title 1   ❏ Community Experiences
❏ Academic Areas: ❏ Language Arts   ❏ Social Studies   ❏ Math   ❏ Science
❏ Electives   ❏ _____
Percent of time in Special Education _____

Justification: What are the reasons for service delivery outside the general education classroom?
❏ Specific skill training
❏ Alternative curriculum
❏ Requires structured classroom
❏ Requires specialized behavior management
❏ _____

EXTENDED SCHOOL YEAR

❏ Does not require special education and related services in excess of the regular academic year.

❏ Recommended based upon unique or severe needs.

Setting/DIS Service	Number of Weeks	Frequency	Location
			Please use appropriate code:
			P =Public School; N=Non-Public School; OC=Off-site Clinic; or Other
❏ Special Day Class	for _____ weeks		❏ P ❏ N ❏ OC ❏ _____
_____	for _____ weeks	_____	❏ P ❏ N ❏ OC ❏ _____
_____	for _____ weeks	_____	❏ P ❏ N ❏ OC ❏ _____
_____	for _____ weeks	_____	❏ P ❏ N ❏ OC ❏ _____
_____	for _____ weeks	_____	❏ P ❏ N ❏ OC ❏ _____

PLAN TO TRANSITION FROM NPS OR SDC TO REGULAR CLASS PROGRAM

Conference with regular ed. teacher/other personnel		Schedule of special education support
Conference with parent		Length of time:
Training for regular ed. teacher and/or other staff		Type of support:
Topic:		Person(s) responsible:
		Provide regular education assignments to student while still in special education class
Provided by:		
		Special education teacher and/or student visit the regular education class
Date		
Special conference to allow parents and all service		Regular education class routine reviewed with student
providers to talk about the special needs of student		Assignment of peer mentor from regular education class
Discussion with students in the regular class		
Topic:		Gradual transition into regular class beginning on
Conducted by:		_____
Behavior plan for use in regular class (see attached)		

IEP

Student _____ Date of Meeting _____

This IEP document contains the following pages:
1❑ 2❑ 3❑ 4❑ 5❑ 6❑ 7❑ 8❑ 9❑ 10❑ 11❑ 12❑ 13❑ 14❑ 15❑ 16❑ 17❑ 18❑ __ ❑ __ ❑ __ ❑ __ ❑ __ ❑

and Goals and Objectives pages _____ through _____

TEAM MEMBERS - The following persons affirm that they were in attendance at the IEP Meeeting

Administrator _____	Occupational Therapist _____
Administrator _____	Physical Therapist _____
Administrator _____	Teacher for the Visually Impaired _____
Psychologist _____	Hearing Impaired Specialist _____
Nurse _____	Orientation/Mobility Instructor _____
Resource Specialist _____	Speech/Language Specialist _____
SDC Teacher _____	Community Mental Health _____
Teacher _____	CCS _____
Teacher _____	Social Worker _____
Teacher _____	Agency Rep. _____
Student _____	_____

PARENT DECISION/SIGNATURE

❑ I was notified of the IEP meeting and was able to attend; I have reviewed the IEP and consent to it.
❑ I was notified of the IEP meeting and was able to attend. I choose not to make a decision at this time.
❑ I agree and give my consent for the above recommendations to be implemented with the exception of :
    ❑ assessment   ❑ eligibility   ❑ specific instruction/services   ❑ instructional setting

❑ I request a copy of the IEP to be provided in my primary language or alternative format (braille or tape recording).
❑ I acknowledge that my child is not an individual with exceptional needs and thus not eligible for Special Ed. services.
❑ I disagree and wish to schedule: ❑ an IEP meeting   ❑ prehearing mediation conference
                                 ❑ informal meeting   ❑ mediation conference   ❑ state due process hearing

❑ I have been informed of the rights that will transfer to me at the age of 18 _____

Student's Signature

_____   _____
Signature of Parent/Guardian Signature/Authorized Representative   Date

_____   _____
Signature of Parent/Guardian Signature/Authorized Representative   Date

Distribution: White-Permanent File   Canary-Parent   Pink-CUM   Copies may be made for other team members

IEP

Student: _____ Date of Meeting _____

ADDITIONAL COMMENTS

Distribution: White-Permanent File   Canary-Parent   Pink-CUM   Copies may be made for other team members

IEP Goals and Objectives

MARIN
Special Education
Local Plan Area
IEP Goals and Objectives
10/98

Student _____ Date of Meeting _____

Page _____ of _____

Implementor _____
_____

PRESENT LEVEL OF PERFORMANCE _____

ANNUAL GOAL _____

BENCHMARKS/SHORT TERM INSTRUCTIONAL OBJECTIVES	Criteria for Mastery	Method of Evaluation	REPORT OF PROGRESS Grading Periods				Extended School Year
			1st Date___	2nd Date___	3rd Date___	4th Date___	
	____% or ☐ other _____ _____						
	____% or ☐ other _____ _____						
	____% or ☐ other _____ _____						
	____% or ☐ other _____ _____						

Methods of Evaluation
TM = Teacher-made test   TO = Teacher observation   WS = Work Samples
DC = Data Collection   ST = Standardized tests   O = Other

Report of Progress
1 = Objective met, proceed to next
2 = Continue with objective–some progress made, more time needed
3 = Less than expected
4 = Excessive absences/tardiness affecting progress
5 = Not applicable during this grading period.

Copies may be made for other members of the IEP team.

Distribution: White-Permanent File   Canary-Parent   Pink-Cumulative File

Appendix 5

Tear-Out Forms

Request for Information on Special Education

Request to Begin Special Education Process and Assessment

Request for Child's School File

Request to Amend Child's School File

Special Education Contacts

IEP Journal

Monthly IEP Calendar

IEP Blueprint

Letter Requesting Assessment Report

Request for Joint IEP Eligibility/Program Meeting

Progress Chart

Program Visitation Request Letter

Class Visitation Checklist

Goals and Objectives Chart

IEP Material Organizer Form

IEP Meeting Participants

IEP Meeting Attendance Objection Letter

Letter Confirming Informal Negotiation

Letter Requesting Due Process

Request for Information on Special Education

Date: _____

To: _____

_____

_____

_____

Re: _____

I am writing to you because my child is experiencing difficulties in school. I understand there is a special process for evaluating a child and then determining eligibility for special education programs and services. Please send me all written information about that process. Would you also send me information about how I can contact other parents and local support groups involved in special education.

Thank you very much for your kind assistance. I look forward to talking with you further about special education.

Sincerely,

_____

_____

_____

_____

_____

Request to Begin Special Education Process and Assessment

Date: _____

To: _____

_____

_____

_____

Re: _____

I am writing you because my child is experiencing difficulties in school. _____

_____

_____

_____

_____

_____ .

I am formally requesting that the school's special education process begin at once, including initial assessment for eligibility. I understand that you will send me an assessment plan which explains what tests may be given to my child. Because I realize the assessment can take some time, I would appreciate receiving the assessment plan within ten days. Would you let me know when the assessment will be scheduled, once you receive my approval for the assessment?

I would also appreciate any other information regarding the assessment process, how eligibility is determined and the general IEP process.

Thank you very much for your kind assistance. I look forward to working with you and your staff.

Sincerely,

_____

_____

_____

_____

_____

Request for Child's School File

Date: _____

To: _____

_____

_____

_____

Re: _____

I would like a copy of my child's file, including all tests, reports, assessments, grades, notes by teachers or other staff members, memoranda, photographs—in short, *everything* in my child's school file. I understand I have a right to these files under _____

_____

_____

_____

_____.

I would greatly appreciate having these files within the next five days. I would be happy to pick them up. I will call you to confirm the details of getting copies.

Thank you for your kind assistance.

Sincerely,

_____

_____

_____

_____

_____

Request to Amend Child's School File

Date: _____

To: _____

_____

_____

_____

Re: _____

I recently reviewed a copy of my child's file and would like to have a portion of the file amended, specifically:

_____

_____

_____

_____

_____

_____ .

IDEA provides that I have the right to request that all information that is "inaccurate or misleading, or violates the privacy of [my] child" be amended (34 C.F.R. §300.567). I feel that this is just such a case and, therefore, request that you immediately rectify the situation.

Please notify me in writing as soon as possible of your decision regarding this matter. Thank you.

Sincerely,

_____

_____

_____

_____

_____

Special Education Contacts

Name, Address, Phone & Fax Numbers, and E-Mail Address

School Staff

_____

_____

_____

_____

_____

_____

_____

Outside Professionals

_____

_____

_____

_____

_____

_____

Other Parents

_____

_____

_____

_____

_____

Support Groups

_____

_____

State Department of Education

_____

_____

_____

Other

_____

_____

_____

_____

IEP Journal

Date: _____ **Time:** _____ a.m./p.m.

Action: ☐ Phone Call _____ ☐ Meeting _____

☐ Other: _____

Person(s) Contacted: _____

Notes: _____

_____

_____

_____

_____

_____

_____

_____

_____

_____

_____

_____

■■■

IEP Journal

Date: _____ **Time:** _____ a.m./p.m.

Action: ☐ Phone Call _____ ☐ Meeting _____

☐ Other: _____

Person(s) Contacted: _____

Notes: _____

_____

_____

_____

_____

_____

_____

_____

_____

_____

_____

Monthly IEP Calendar

Month and Year: _____

1	2	3	4	5	6	7
8	9	10	11	12	13	14
15	16	17	18	19	20	21
22	23	24	25	26	27	28
29	30	31				

IEP Blueprint

The IEP Blueprint represents the ideal IEP for your child. Use it as a guide to make and record the educational desires you have for your child.

Areas of the IEP	Preferred Situation for Your Child
1. Classroom Setting and Peer Needs— issues to consider:	
☐ regular versus special education class	_____
☐ partially or fully mainstreamed	_____
☐ type of special education class	_____
☐ number of children in the classroom	_____
☐ ages and cognitive ranges of children in class	_____ _____
☐ kinds of students and what behaviors might or might not be appropriate for your child, and	_____ _____ _____
☐ language similarities.	_____
2. Teacher and Staff Needs—issues to consider:	
☐ number of teachers and aides	_____
☐ teacher-pupil ratio	_____
☐ experience, training and expertise of the teacher, and	_____ _____
☐ training and expertise of aides.	_____ _____
3. Curricula and Teaching Methodology— be specific. If you don't know what you *do* want, specify what you *don't* want.	_____ _____ _____ _____ _____ _____ _____ _____

Areas of the IEP	Ideal Situation for Your Child

4. Related Services—issues to consider:

☐ specific needed services

☐ type of services

☐ frequency of services, and

☐ length of services.

5. Identified Programs—specify known programs in known schools you think would work for your child.

6. Goals and Objectives—goals are long range in nature, while objectives are more short term.

7. Classroom Environment and Other Features—issues to consider:

☐ distance from home

☐ transition plans for mainstreaming

☐ vocational needs

☐ extracurricular and social needs, and

☐ environmental needs.

Letter Requesting Assessment Report

Date: _____

To: _____

_____

_____

_____

Re: _____

I appreciate your involvement in my child's assessment and look forward to your report. Would you please:

1. Send me a copy of a draft of your report before you finalize it. As you can imagine, the process can be overwhelming for parents and it would be most helpful to me to see your report because the proposed tests are complicated and I need time to evaluate the results.

2. Send me your final report at least four weeks before the IEP meeting.

Again thank you for your kind assistance.

Sincerely,

_____

_____

_____

_____

_____

Request for Joint IEP Eligibility/Program Meeting

Date: _____

To: _____

_____

_____

_____

Re: _____

I believe there is sufficient information for us to discuss my child's eligibility for special education and then the specific IEP goals and objectives, services and program. I would appreciate it if you would plan enough time to discuss both those important items at the _____ IEP meeting. I would also like to see any and all reports and other written material that you will be introducing at the IEP meeting, at least two weeks before the meeting.

Thanks in advance for your help. I hope to hear from you soon.

Sincerely,

_____

_____

_____

_____

_____

Progress Chart

Student: _____

Class: _____

Date: _____

Key Goals and Objectives	Current Status	Comments
Math	Progressing appropriately? ☐ yes ☐ no	_____ _____ _____
Reading	Progressing appropriately? ☐ yes ☐ no	_____ _____ _____
Writing	Progressing appropriately? ☐ yes ☐ no	_____ _____ _____
Spelling	Progressing appropriately? ☐ yes ☐ no	_____ _____ _____
Social-Behavioral	Progressing appropriately? ☐ yes ☐ no	_____ _____ _____
Language development	Progressing appropriately? ☐ yes ☐ no	_____ _____ _____
Motor development	Progressing appropriately? ☐ yes ☐ no	_____ _____ _____
Other	Progressing appropriately? ☐ yes ☐ no	_____ _____ _____

Program Visitation Request Letter

Date: _____

To: _____

_____

_____

_____

Re: _____

I appreciate the concerns you have and realize you can't know what programs are appropriate for my child until after the IEP meeting. Nonetheless, I think it would be very helpful for me to see existing programs so I can be a more effective member of the IEP team. I do not feel I can make an informed IEP decision without seeing, firsthand, all possible options. I want to assure you that I understand that by giving me the names of existing programs, you are not stating an opinion as to their appropriateness for my child.

I assure you that I will abide by all rules and regulations for parental visits. If those rules and regulations are in writing, please send me a copy.

Thanks in advance for your help. I hope to hear from you soon.

Sincerely,

_____

_____

_____

_____

_____

Class Visitation Checklist

Date: _____ Time: _____ a.m./p.m.

School: _____

Class: _____

Student Description:

Total students:_____ Gender range:_____

Age range: _____

Cognitive range: _____

_____

_____

Language/communication range: _____

_____

_____

_____

Disability range: _____

_____

_____

_____

Behavioral range: _____

_____

_____

_____

Other observations: _____

_____

_____

_____

Staff Description:

Teachers: _____

_____

_____

_____

Aides: _____

_____

_____

_____

Other observations: _____

_____

_____

Curricula/Classroom Strategies:

Curricula: _____

_____

_____

_____

_____

Strategies: _____

_____

_____

_____

_____

_____

Classroom Environment:

Description: _____

_____

_____

_____

_____

_____

_____

Related Services:

_____

_____

_____

Other Comments:

_____

_____

_____

_____

_____

How This Program Relates to IEP Blueprint:

_____

_____

_____

_____

_____

_____

Goals and Objectives Chart

Skill Area	Annual Goal	Short-Term Objective (or Benchmark)	Present Performance Level	How Progress Measured	Date of Completion
Reading					
Math					
Emotional and psychological					

Skill Area	Annual Goal	Short-Term Objective (or Benchmark)	Present Performance Level	How Progress Measured	Date of Completion
Social-behavioral					
Linguistic and communication					
Self-help and independent living skills (transition services)					

IEP Material Organizer Form

Use this form to track documents and persons that provide support for or opposition to your goals.

Issue: _____

Document or Witness* Name(s):	Binder Location (if applicable)	Helps You	Hurts You	Key Supportive or Oppositional Information	Rebuttal Document or Witness Name(s) (If hurts) (If none, what will you say at meeting?)

* A "witness" is someone (teacher, doctor, assessor, tutor, psychologist) who gives their oral or written opinion regarding your child's needs at the IEP meeting.

IEP Meeting Participants

Name	Position/Employer	Purpose for Attending	Point of View

IEP Meeting Attendance Objection Letter

Date: _____

To: _____

           _____

           _____

           _____

Re: _____

I understand that _____,

will be at _____ IEP meeting. _____

knows nothing about _____and appears to have no knowledge that

might be of use to the IEP team. I am formally requesting that _____

not attend, unless there is some clear reason that makes _____

attendance appropriate and necessary for the development of _____

IEP plan. As you know, IEP meetings can be particularly difficult for parents. We are already anxious about ours and would prefer that you not take action that will heighten our stress level.

If you insist on _____attending without any reason, then we will file a complaint with the state and federal departments of education.

I will call you in a few days to find out your decision on this issue. Thank you for considering my request.

Sincerely,

_____

_____

_____

_____

_____

Letter Confirming Informal Negotiation

Date: _____

To: _____

     _____

     _____

     _____

Re: _____

I appreciated the chance to meet on _____ and discuss
_____. I also appreciated your
point of view and the manner in which we solved the problem.

I want to confirm our agreement that _____
_____
_____
_____.

I greatly appreciate the manner in which you helped solve this problem. _____
_____
_____
_____.

Thank you.

Sincerely,

_____

_____

_____

_____

_____

Letter Requesting Due Process

Date: _____

To: _____

         _____

         _____

         _____

Re: _____

_____

_____

We are formally requesting due process, beginning with mediation. We believe _____

_____

_____

_____ .

We believe an appropriate solution would include, but should not be limited to, the following:

_____

_____

_____

_____

_____ .

We understand IDEA (34 C.F.R. §300.511) requires that a fair hearing decision be rendered within 45 days of receipt of this request. We would appreciate it if you would contact us at once regarding scheduling the mediation.

Sincerely,

_____

_____

_____

_____

_____

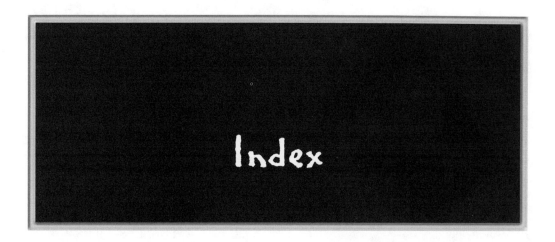

Index

CATALOG

▣ Book with disk   ⊙ Book with CD-ROM

CALL 800-992-6656 OR USE THE ORDER FORM IN THE BACK OF THE BOOK

	PRICE	CODE
How to Seal Your Juvenile & Criminal Records (California Edition)	$24.95	CRIM
How to Sue For Up to $25,000...and Win!	$29.95	MUNI
Mad at Your Lawyer	$21.95	MAD
Represent Yourself in Court: How to Prepare & Try a Winning Case	$29.95	RYC

HOMEOWNERS, LANDLORDS & TENANTS

		PRICE	CODE
	Contractors' and Homeowners' Guide to Mechanics' Liens (Book w/Disk—PC)	$39.95	MIEN
	The Deeds Book (California Edition)	$24.95	DEED
	Dog Law	$14.95	DOG
▣	Every Landlord's Legal Guide (National Edition, Book w/Disk—PC)	$34.95	ELLI
	Every Tenant's Legal Guide	$26.95	EVTEN
	For Sale by Owner in California	$24.95	FSBO
	How to Buy a House in California	$24.95	BHCA
	The Landlord's Law Book, Vol. 1: Rights & Responsibilities (California Edition)	$34.95	LBRT
	The Landlord's Law Book, Vol. 2: Evictions (California Edition)	$34.95	LBEV
	Leases & Rental Agreements (Quick & Legal Series)	$18.95	LEAR
	Neighbor Law: Fences, Trees, Boundaries & Noise	$17.95	NEI
	Renters' Rights (National Edition—Quick & Legal Series))	$15.95	RENT
	Stop Foreclosure Now in California	$29.95	CLOS
	Tenants' Rights (California Edition)	$21.95	CTEN

IMMIGRATION

	PRICE	CODE
How to Get a Green Card: Legal Ways to Stay in the U.S.A.	$24.95	GRN
U.S. Immigration Made Easy	$44.95	IMEZ

MONEY MATTERS

		PRICE	CODE
▣	101 Law Forms for Personal Use (Quick & Legal Series, Book w/disk—PC)	$24.95	SPOT
	Bankruptcy: Is It the Right Solution to Your Debt Problems? (Quick & Legal Series)	$15.95	BRS
	Chapter 13 Bankruptcy: Repay Your Debts	$29.95	CH13
	Credit Repair (Quick & Legal Series)	$15.95	CREP
▣	The Financial Power of Attorney Workbook (Book w/disk—PC)	$24.95	FINPOA
	How to File for Chapter 7 Bankruptcy	$26.95	HFB
	IRAs, 401(k)s & Other Retirement Plans: Taking Your Money Out	$21.95	RET
	Money Troubles: Legal Strategies to Cope With Your Debts	$19.95	MT
	Nolo's Law Form Kit: Personal Bankruptcy	$16.95	KBNK
	Stand Up to the IRS	$24.95	SIRS
	Take Control of Your Student Loans	$19.95	SLOAN

PATENTS AND COPYRIGHTS

		PRICE	CODE
▣	The Copyright Handbook: How to Protect and Use Written Works (Book w/disk—PC)	$29.95	COHA
	Copyright Your Software	$24.95	CYS
	How to Make Patent Drawings Yourself	$29.95	DRAW
	The Inventor's Notebook	$19.95	INOT
▣	License Your Invention (Book w/Disk—PC)	$39.95	LICE
	Patent, Copyright & Trademark	$24.95	PCTM
	Patent It Yourself	$46.95	PAT
	Patent Searching Made Easy	$24.95	PATSE
◉	Software Development: A Legal Guide (Book with CD-ROM)	$44.95	SFT

RESEARCH & REFERENCE

		PRICE	CODE
	Legal Research: How to Find & Understand the Law	$24.95	LRES
◉	Legal Research Online & in the Library (Book w/CD-ROM—Windows/Macintosh)	$39.95	LRO

SENIORS

	PRICE	CODE
Beat the Nursing Home Trap	$21.95	ELD
The Conservatorship Book (California Edition)	$44.95	CNSV
Social Security, Medicare & Pensions	$21.95	SOA

SOFTWARE

Call or check our website at www.nolo.com

for special discounts on Software!

		PRICE	CODE
◉	LeaseWriter CD—Windows/Macintosh	$99.95	LWD1
◉	Living Trust Maker CD—Windows/Macintosh	$79.95	LTD2
◉	Small Business Legal Pro 3 CD—Windows/Macintosh	$79.95	SBCD3
◉	Personal RecordKeeper 5.0 CD—Windows/Macintosh	$59.95	RKD5
◉	Patent It Yourself CD—Windows	$229.95	PPC12
◉	WillMaker 7.0 CD—Windows/Macintosh	$69.95	WMD7

SPECIAL UPGRADE OFFER—Get 35% off the latest edition of your Nolo book

It's important to have the most current legal information. Because laws and legal procedures change often, we update our books regularly. To help keep you up-to-date we are extending this special upgrade offer. Cut out and mail the title portion of the cover of your old Nolo book and we'll give you 35% off the retail price of the NEW EDITION of that book when you purchase directly from us. For more information call us at 1-800-992-6656. This offer is to individuals only.

▣ Book with disk ◉ Book with CD-ROM

ORDER FORM

Code	Quantity	Title	Unit price	Total
		Subtotal		
		California residents add Sales Tax		
		Basic Shipping ($3.95)		
		UPS RUSH delivery $8.00–any size order*		
		TOTAL		

Name

Address

(UPS to street address, Priority Mail to P.O. boxes)   * Delivered in 3 business days from receipt of order.
S.F. Bay Area use regular shipping.

FOR FASTER SERVICE, USE YOUR CREDIT CARD AND OUR TOLL-FREE NUMBERS

Order 24 hours a day	1-800-992-6656
Fax your order	1-800-645-0895
Online	www.nolo.com

METHOD OF PAYMENT

☐ Check enclosed
☐ VISA   ☐ MasterCard   ☐ Discover Card   ☐ American Express

Account #   Expiration Date

Authorizing Signature

Daytime Phone

PRICES SUBJECT TO CHANGE.

VISIT OUR OUTLET STORE!   VISIT US ONLINE!

You'll find our complete line of books and software, all at a discount.

BERKELEY
950 Parker Street
Berkeley, CA 94710
1-510-704-2248

on the Internet
www.nolo.com